the
SPIELBERG
complete

Ian Freer

Dedication

To Mum – SYTIJ

This edition first published in 2001 by
Virgin Publishing Ltd
Thames Wharf Studios
Rainville Road
London
W6 9HA

A catalogue record for this book is available from the British Library.

ISBN 0 7535 0556 8

Phototypeset by Intype London Ltd

Printed and bound in Great Britain by Mackays of Chatham PLC

Contents

Acknowledgements

First and foremost, my thanks are due to Joanne Brooks who gave me my shot, displayed unflagging patience, and whose e-encouragement got me over the finishing line; David Hughes for the sneak peaks at his Kubrick opus; the bods at the BFI and New York's Museum of Television and Radio; the E.T.s (Editorial Talents) at *Empire* movie magazine – Emma (for the last time, it *is* i before e!) Caz, Kelly, Mark, Katharine, Kev, Colin and Dave; Hannah Whitlow for the sympathetic air; Helen Blair for all the secret squirreling back in the day, even though she walked out of *Saving Private Ryan*; Simon Braund for his authoritative knowledge of the arts; Adam Smith for the totally unhelpful, unrelenting Spielberg-baiting ('He is the dreamer who dreams the dream . . .'); Ian Nathan for being Johnny on the Spot with counselling sessions, expert analysis ('Oskar *Scheeendler*') and the bass-line to In Trance As Mission; Grenache girl Liz Beardsworth for her unwavering faith and endless enthusiasm; Bruce Wishart, the Indiana Jones of telecommunications and Steven Topper, the Wild Bill Kelso of mobile phones, for sitting through *Raiders Of The Lost Ark* umpteen times (or was it *Victor/Victoria*?); Stephen Baker, the world's biggest Steven Spielberg fan, for the countless hours discussing the man, his work and '*Lassie*? The dog movie?'

But, most of all, I would like to thank Steven Spielberg whose cinematic daydreams changed this boy's life forever; my brother Paul for kick-starting it all by buying the *Close Encounters* diary and my mum Doreen Freer, who has suffered and supported this Spielberg obsession for nigh on 25 years. For that, she shares all the credit for this book.

The Greatest Showman on Earth

If any director has entered the public consciousness as the embodiment of a film-maker, it is Steven Spielberg. Although this pre-eminent position has much to do with being the world's most commercially successful film-maker – over one third of the most popular films of all time have been directed or produced by Spielberg – this alone does not contain the whole story. To the current crop of film-goers, Spielberg's adventures about sharks, UFOs, archaeologists and loveable aliens are the films that got us excited about movies in the first place and, as Spielberg's films have reached into the darker recesses of the Holocaust and D-Day, we too have matured with them. While other movie masters are from bygone eras (Capra, Hitchcock, Ford) or just too darn maverick (Scorsese, Tarantino, the Coens), the excitement of the latest Steven Spielberg film can be experienced in the here and now right at the heart of contemporary pop culture. As such, he is the only great director the multiplex generation have the right to claim for themselves.

While Spielberg has accrued his fair share of detractors over the years – at best they have labelled him an artful manipulator, at worst a cynical peddler of schmaltzy claptrap – few can deny the extent of his influence: both on the way movies are made – his predilection for storyboards, his skill at directing kids, his development of special effects – to the wider cinematic zeitgeist: practically inventing the notion of the summer blockbuster and redrawing the way films are released and marketed.

Outside the cinema, Spielberg is the subject of over 30 websites, one honorary knighthood (not to mention one over-zealous stalker), and has been the creative dynamo behind countless TV shows, computer games, CD-Roms, restaurants and theme park rides. No other fans of a film-maker are so easily identifiable. With a strict dress code (jeans, sneakers, glasses, baseball cap), the Spielberg acolyte is such a recognisable cultural figure that teen angst TV show *Dawson's Creek* is built around such a wannabe film-maker.

Yet behind the bank balance, the creative clout and the public persona lie the movies; precisely what *The Complete Spielberg* seeks to explore and celebrate. Surprisingly, there have been very few books that have looked solely at Spielberg's films. Biographies have charted his obsession with film as a teen outsider, the wunderkind years of the 70s and 80s and his current status as a modern mogul. Academic studies have discussed the phallic symbolism of a plastic-looking shark. And no end of trite psychoanalytical waffle has declared 'he speaks to the child in all of us'. But, over the years, the power and potency of the films themselves seem to have been marginalised, almost buried under the brand name. If this book has one aim, it is to instil within you a burning desire to discover or revisit some of the most exciting celluloid ever to run through a projector.

Continuing the format laid out in *The Complete Hitchcock* and *The Complete*

Kubrick, each entry begins with vital statistics such as year, running time, studio, key/selected cast and crew, certification and budget as well as mixing and matching the following sections as appropriate:

TITLE SEQUENCE: Spielberg is a director who really knows the value of the title sequence. This entry will provide a brief description of each movie's opening credits and how they prepare us for what is to follow.

PLOT SUMMARY: Does exactly what it says on the tin. Warning: major plot points revealed!

ORIGINS: Few film-makers have seen more films than Steven Spielberg so this section highlights the influences that permeate his movies. And it ain't just Disney!

BACKSTORY: A potted history of the genesis of each project.

CASTING: The yarns behind the creation of Spielberg's cast lists. Original choices revealed plus assessments of those who made the cut.

PRODUCTION: A brief history of the shoot.

TICS OF THE TRADE: Spielberg's directorial flourishes demystified.

CLASSIC LINES: The best cuts of Spielberg-derived dialogue.

COMIC RELIEF: Like Hitchcock, Spielberg is a master at injecting the perfectly-timed gag to succinctly diffuse the drama. This section pays tribute to these laugh-inducing abilities.

VISUAL EFFECTS: A vital weapon in Spielberg's arsenal laid bare.

SOUND EFFECTS: From rolling rocks to raptor roars, this section traces the creation of some of cinema's most famous sounds.

WHAT'S THE SCORE? The stories behind some of the world's best-loved film music.

CUT SCENES: A catalogue of scenes shot that never made the final grade such as a planned bath-time sequence for E.T. or Indy whipping himself to the periscope in *Raiders*.

UNSUNG HERO(ES): Giving credit to a backroom boy/girl who made an underrated contribution to the film's success.

GEDDIT! A guide to the in-jokes and recurring actors and images within Spielberg movies.

FACTOID FRENZY: Mountains of trivia – such as did you know that Spielberg's name in German means 'play mountain'?

THE CRITICAL FACULTY: Choice bouquets and brickbats from the world's press.

BOX OFFICE: The financial facts and figures with the stories behind them.

AWARDS: Spielberg's roller-coaster relationship with the Oscars and beyond.

THE SIZZLE! Plagiarism, creative differences, drugged-up actors, lawsuits, racism, death threats – the controversy surrounding Spielberg's flicks.

JOIN THE DOTS: A section that traces favourite themes and ideas across the Spielberg universe.

SEND IN THE CLONES! Spielberg's movies are among the most commercially successful in film history hence film-makers frequently steal his scenes, plots and, in certain cases, entire movies. This entry traces the 'influence' Spielberg's work has exerted on others.

SPIELBERG GOES POP: How Spielberg's films have entered pop culture; from the obvious (*The Simpsons*) to the not so obvious (Durex commercials).

FINAL ANALYSIS: A brief appreciation of the overall achievement and how it fits within Spielberg's filmography.

SPIELBERG ON SPIELBERG: Always a source of snappy soundbites, a final word from the man himself.

Amateur Films

Steven Spielberg began his film-making exploits taking over the production of family home movies. With the exception of *Amblin'*, the films on this list have never been made available for public consumption since the screenings mentioned here, although clips have appeared on various documentaries and at award ceremonies.

The Last Train Wreck (1957)

(Black and white, 3 mins)

PRODUCTION: Spielberg was eleven when he shot his first creative endeavour with an 8mm camera. Probably inspired by the first movie he ever saw, *The Greatest Show On Earth* (1952), Spielberg recorded a spectacular crash with his toy trains.

The Last Gun (1958)

(Black and white, 9 mins)

CAST: Jim Sollenberger, Barry Sollenberger

PRODUCTION: A nine-minute Western made for an Eagle Scout photography merit badge. The film was edited 'in camera' and starred neighbourhood friends (and film-makers) the Sollenbergers and fellow Scouts, and was filmed outside the Pinnacle Patio (a steak house in Arizona) which had a red stagecoach parked out front. In interviews over the years, Spielberg has variously referred to this film as *The Last Gunfight*, *The Last Shootout* and *Gunsmog*.

A Day In The Life Of Thunder (1958)

(Black and white)

PRODUCTION: An experimental documentary involving Thunder, the family cocker spaniel, who towed the camera around the neighbourhood. Spielberg's first 'creature feature'.

USSR Documentary (1959)

(Black and white)

PRODUCTION : A family travelogue to Russia given the Spielberg touch.

Untitled Western (1959)

(Black and white, 6 mins)

CAST: Terry Mechling, Steve Swift

PRODUCTION: A Western heist movie shot in Mechling's garden.

Films Of Ingleside Elementary School (1959)

(Black and white)

PRODUCTION: In the seventh grade, Spielberg shot footage of the school's flag football matches, a non-contact version of US gridiron, which involved grabbing flags from opponents instead of tackling.

Fighter Squadron (1960)

(Black and white, 15 mins)

PRODUCTION: A World War Two aircraft movie, *Fighter Squadron* represented Spielberg's most ambitious work to date. The movie integrated shots of actors in cockpits of vintage fighter planes at the local airport – Spielberg would even tilt the camera to imitate the planes banking – with documentary footage of actual dogfights. A precursor of *1941*'s and *Empire Of The Sun*'s (among others) interest in aviation.

Film Noir (1960)

(Black and white)

CAST: Jim Sollenberger

PRODUCTION: Spielberg moved on to another genre, experimenting with an anamorphic lens and using numerous low angles to create menacing effects.

Steve Spielberg Home Movies (1960)

(Black and white)

PRODUCTION: A series of sight gags – including extensive trick photography – and Keystone Kops-style chases, this is an early foray into the *1941* arena of slapstick comedy

3

Career Exploration Project (1961)

(Black and white)

PRODUCTION: In response to a school initiative to develop students' interest in their future careers, Spielberg made another Western, this time adding a primitive tape-recorded soundtrack involving screams and gallops.

Scary Hollow (1961)

(Black and white)

PRODUCTION: A filmed record of the school play – a mystery.

Escape To Nowhere (1962)

(Colour, 40 mins)

CAST: Haven Peters, Jim Sollenberger, Barry Sollenberger, George Mills, Leah Spielberg

PLOT SUMMARY: Having dealt with the conflict in the air in *Fighter Squadron*, Spielberg turned his attentions to land war with this ambitious combat picture. It is the story of a US platoon surrounded by German soldiers as they attempt to secure a strategic hill, which the young Spielberg set in East Africa although the Americans only ever fought in North Africa.

CASTING: Spielberg press-ganged 20 to 30 school friends into playing soldiers. To make the numbers look bigger, the cast played both American and German troops. As the squadron leader, Spielberg cast a high school bully, thus winning his tormentor over by appealing to his macho instincts. Both Spielberg's parents drove the jeep.

PRODUCTION: Shot in and around Camelback Mountain in Arizona, the movie was a step up from *Fighter Squadron* as it involved an elaborate use of props and physical effects. At one point, the shoot was interrupted by the police as the film-makers had been reported to have been trooping around in Nazi get-up with rifles. That anyone could have been confused is frankly ridiculous: Spielberg had attempted to dye white T-shirts grey to replicate German uniforms but the process went awry so the German army were actually sporting a light-blue costume. To suggest a larger number of troops, Spielberg made full use of the limited supply of army helmets by setting up a relay system where kids would run past the camera and hand the hat on to the next soldier, who would then also run in front of the camera. Such was the extent of the shoot that a local TV news crew reported from the set: even at an early age, the director displayed an unerring talent for self promotion.

Firelight (1964)

(Colour, 135 mins)

Producers Arnold Spielberg, Leah Spielberg for American Artists Production
Screenplay Steven Spielberg
Camera Steven Spielberg
Editor Steven Spielberg
Script Supervisor Anne Spielberg
Sound Technicians Bruce Palmer, Dennis LaFevre
Production Assistants Warner Marshall, Arnold Spielberg, Beth Weber, Jean Weber

CAST: Clark 'Lucky' Lohr (*Howard Richards*), Carolyn Owen (*Lisa's Mother*), Robert Robyn (*Tony Karcher*), Nancy Spielberg (*Lisa*), Beth Weber (*Debbie*), Margaret Peyou (*Helen Richards*), Warner Marshall (*National Guardsman*), Charles G. Case II, Dede Pisani (*Orange Grove Lovers*), Tina Lanser (*Maid*).

BUDGET: $400

PLOT SUMMARY: *Firelight* follows a group of scientists – particularly Tony Karcher and UFO freak Howard Richards – investigating a series of coloured lights in the sky and the subsequent disappearance of people, animals and objects from the (fictional) town of Freeport, Arizona. Among those kidnapped by the alien Altarians are a dog, a unit of National Guardsmen and a young girl Lisa, whose abduction induces a fatal attack in her mother. Spielberg, showing remarkable maturity for a teenager, has sub-plots involving marital discord between Karcher and his wife Debbie and the obsessive quest of Richards to convince the CIA that alien life does exist. The twist comes as the aliens, represented by three mysterious figures, reveal their purpose: to transport Freeport to their home planet Altaris and create a kind of human zoo.

BACKSTORY: Apart from Spielberg's teenage fascination with science-fiction movies and literature, the direct derivation behind *Firelight* seems to have come from a Boy Scout's camping trip that Spielberg did not go on. The whole troop reported to Spielberg that they had seen a red light rising in the sky – the fabricated yarn which subsequently set the youngster's imagination with narrative possibilities.

'I remember knocking out a script by staying up for twenty-four hours,' Spielberg told *Starlog*'s Steve Poster. 'The ideas were coming out of my brain in what you might call stream of consciousness as fast as I could type. A week later I began making *Firelight*.'

To raise money for the movie, Spielberg whitewashed citrus trees at 75c a tree, raising around $100 and his father threw in the rest. For winning the state amateur film contest with *Escape To Nowhere*, Spielberg's prize was a 16mm Kodak movie camera. Realising he would never be able to afford film stock for the semi-professional camera, Spielberg traded it in for a top of the line 8mm camera which allowed him to do relatively sophisticated effects – stop motion, double exposures – that were incorporated into the script.

CASTING: Many of the cast for *Firelight* were culled from the Arcadia High School productions of *Guys And Dolls* and *I Remember Mama*. A casting calamity struck when Carol Stromme and Andy Owen quit after the first two weeks of shooting. Spielberg coolly recast their parts with Beth Weber and Bob Robyn, refilming the opening scene at a later date.

PRODUCTION: Shot at weekends and in the evenings for about a year, the majority of *Firelight* was filmed in and around the Spielberg family home and garage. For a scene where Debbie's maid forgets to watch the pressure cooker while making dessert, which results in the kitchen being covered in exploding pie, Spielberg coerced his mother to put 30 cans of cherry pie filling into the pressure cooker and let it detonate. The scene alludes to an actual moment in the Spielberg household – the director incorporated similar kitchen-style mayhem in *Gremlins* (1984). Displaying a precocious gift of the gab, Spielberg also persuaded a local hospital to let him shoot in a room kitted out with a bed and oxygen mask and sweet-talked American Airlines into letting him borrow a jet for a ten-minute shoot at the local airport.

VISUAL EFFECTS: Created with the help of Spielberg's father, a computer technician, *Firelight* featured some sophisticated effects for a teen's 8mm effort. For the abduction of Lisa set piece, Spielberg had his sister Nancy crawl across the garden. He then rewound the film in camera, then double exposed it, adding an effect of a firelight spacecraft, created by shooting through two glass plates filled with jelly. When Spielberg was denied access to artillery by the National Guard, he created the scene in miniature with the battle between aliens and the army taking place via stop-motion photography in front of a papier mâché mountain. To create the death of Richards at the hands of E.T.s, Spielberg shot eight frames at a time, changing actor Clark Lohr's make-up in between takes to create an ever more horrific state. The final shot was of a plastic skull, very reminiscent of Nazi Toht's death in *Raiders of the Lost Ark*.

SOUND EFFECTS: Spielberg re-recorded all the dialogue in his living room, the mouth movements matched to the picture projected on the wall.

WHAT'S THE SCORE: Spielberg composed the music for *Firelight*, his first original score, on his clarinet. Spielberg's mother, a former concert pianist, transposed the score to the piano and subsequently created sheet music. The finished version was performed by the Arcadia High School band.

BOX OFFICE: *Firelight* had its world premiere on 24 March 1964 at Spielberg's local cinema, the Phoenix Little Theatre in Arizona. Spielberg sold 500 tickets at a dollar each, making roughly one hundred dollars profit on the night – his biggest box office success to date.

FINAL ANALYSIS: Hunting for film work in Los Angeles, Spielberg gave two reels of *Firelight* to a commercials producer as a showcase of the youngster's abilities. When he returned a week later, the company had gone bust and the producer had vanished with the biggest indication of Spielberg's talents at that time. From the surviving clips, the film boasted stilted, risible dialogue and wooden performances but also displayed flashes of visual audacity and bravura showmanship that would come to the fore in years to come. *Firelight* is also significant as a dry run for *Close Encounters* both in terms of broad themes – alien invasion of a suburban milieu, marital discord, military paranoia – and specific incidents and characters: a child kidnapped by a UFO represented by a blaze of red light, a couple on the run from cautious authorities, an obsessive scientist all have their roots in this

8mm incarnation. What at the time looked like an impressive effort from a resourceful teenager now looks like the rough sketch for a modern classic.

SPIELBERG ON SPIELBERG: 'One of the five worst movies ever made.'

American Football (1964)

(Black and white)

PRODUCTION: Spielberg captured matches with his camera from the touchlines.

Rocking Chair (1965)

(3 mins)

PRODUCTION: Following the death of John F. Kennedy, Spielberg, in collaboration with buddy Mike Augustine, made a film around a wooden Kennedy rocking chair that was made for the 1964 election and put out after his assassination. The film was captured at twilight as the musical chair played *Happy Days Are Here Again*.

Senior Sneak Day (1965)

(Black and white)

PRODUCTION: A record of the senior year school outing to a beach-front amusement park. Filled with numerous beach-based pratfalls, human pyramids and a pie-eating contest, the film also features a parody of *The Birds* (1963) involving marauding seagulls.

Encounter (1965)

(Black and white, 20 mins)

CAST: Roger Ernest, Peter Maffia

PRODUCTION: Spielberg's first foray into 16mm was a twenty-minute long noirish thriller. In it, a sailor is set upon by an unknown assailant, leading to a knife and gun fight atop a water tower. The twist in the tale comes as the murderer is revealed to have engineered the attack to kill off his identical twin brother. The title had obvious resonances toward a later Spielberg movie.

The Great Race (1966)

(Black and white)

CAST: Roger Ernest, Halina Junnysek

PRODUCTION: A further venture into broad comedy made in collaboration with Charles Hays, this slapstick effort centred around a young man who, falling out with his girlfriend, chases her all around the college campus. Incidentally, Roger Ernest went on to play small roles in both *The Sugarland Express* and *Close Encounters*.

Amblin' (1968)

(Colour, 26 mins)

Producer Dennis Hoffman
In Charge Of Production Ralph Burris
Screenplay Steven Spielberg
Editing Steven Spielberg
Director Of Photography Allen Daviau
Music Michael Lloyd
Performed by October Country
Continuity Supervisor Anne Spielberg

CAST: Richard Levin (*Guy*), Pamela McMyler (*Girl*)

BUDGET: $20,000

PLOT SUMMARY: A young guy, carrying a closely guarded guitar case, hooks up with a free-spirited girl when hitchhiking across the desert in Southern California en route to the Pacific coast. Along the way, the boy engages the girl in an olive-spitting contest and the girl initiates the boy into the joys of dope smoking and sex in a sleeping bag. As the pair reach the beach, the guy frolics in the surf and the girl checks out the contents of his guitar case: a suit and tie, toothpaste, mouth wash, a roll of toilet paper and a copy of Arthur C Clarke's *The City and the Stars*. The girl smiles in bemusement, perhaps sensing all along that her companion was a closet geek.

BACKSTORY: *Amblin'* became a reality after Spielberg was introduced to wannabe producer Dennis Hoffman. Refusing to provide the finance to complete *Slipstream* (see **Unseen Spielberg**), Hoffman asked the director to come up with story ideas that fitted the following criteria: no dialogue, part of it must be filmed at Hoffman's Cinefx studio and the story must facilitate the use of songs by October Country, a pop group managed by Hoffman. Spielberg's first story – a tale about spooky goings on in a drive-in movie theatre – was expensive on the page and failed to incorporate October Country's music. So Spielberg went back to the drawing board and cannily concocted a story that had youthful appeal – sex, drugs, the open road – yet bore a sceptical view towards hippiedom that would have been shared by the film's target audience – the studio executives who could give Spielberg a job.

CASTING: Spielberg found his lead actor Richard Levin working as a librarian in the Beverly Hills library. For the mysterious redhead, Spielberg discovered Pamela McMyler from the *Academy Players Directory*. She had previously been a member of the Pasadena Playhouse and had played an insignificant role in *The Boston Strangler*.

PRODUCTION: *Amblin'* started shooting on 6 July 1968 at Dennis Hoffman's Cinefx soundstage. The filming commenced with a complicated tracking shot following a trail of matches leading to a bonfire (reminiscent of *Jaws'* opening scene) which was shot in the studio in order that cinematographer Allen Daviau – who would later shoot *E.T. The Extra-Terrestrial*, *The Color Purple* and *Empire Of The Sun* – could control the lighting. After Cinefx and the filming of the film's final sequence outside Jack Palance's beach house in Malibu, the crew moved on to various desert locations around Pearblossom, North California, for the remaining eight days of filming. Under the tough terrain and punishing 105 degree sun, many of Spielberg's unpaid crew left before the shoot was completed. Spielberg confessed to one crew member that he had vomited every day before he went to the set.

SOUND EFFECTS: The only actual sound in the film is a giggle from Pamela McMyler during a pot-smoking sequence.

WHAT'S THE SCORE? With a likeable, upbeat, guitar-driven score, Michael Lloyd's music covers the whole running time of *Amblin'*.

GEDDIT! In July 1975, Spielberg formed a production company named after *Amblin'*. For some unexplained reason, Spielberg left off the apostrophe when he formed Amblin Entertainment in 1984.

THE CRITICAL FACULTY: 'A 24-minute [sic] short that packs the wallop of a rock'n'roll concert, the beauty of a Renoir painting, the excitement of a roller coaster ride, the subtle humour of O. Henry and the warmth of a summer evening.' (*Atlanta Film Festival Programme*)

BOX OFFICE: Opening on 18 December, 1968, Spielberg's twenty-second birthday, at Lowe's Crest Theater in Los Angeles, *Amblin'* shared a double bill with Otto Preminger's *Skidoo*, the following week-long run meaning the short film would be eligible for Academy Award consideration.

AWARDS: Won an award at the Atlanta Film Festival but too counter-culture to get nominated for an Oscar.

SEND IN THE CLONES! Directed by and starring Noah Butler, *Meanderin'* (1993) featured a hippie guy and a girl (played by a guy) hitting the open road – the secret inside the guitar case being revealed as a machine gun which the 'girl' uses to blast the guy while he romps in the sea.

FINAL ANALYSIS: Spielberg landed a seven-year contract at Universal and an agent (Mike Medavoy) primarily on the strength of *Amblin'*. Although somewhat dated now – it serves as an entertaining lexicon of 60s counter-culture concerns – the film remains a mightily impressive calling card. Delivered with a laid-back confidence and technique honed from years of 8mm experience, Spielberg constructs the slight, picaresque journey with a loose structure and improvisational editing strategies yet combines this with a classical, lucid sense of composition that gives the film a unique feeling of being both spontaneous yet formal, spirited yet mature. Without ever resorting to the directorial fireworks that often mar the work of new film-makers, Spielberg allows time for the characters to breathe, drawing naturalistic performances from McMyler and Levin, the latter's separation from the prevailing hippie spirit reinforcing the film as a portrait of the director as a young man. In its mere 26-minute running time, Spielberg displays the affectionate sense of character towards his two drifters that has often gone unnoticed in many of the feature films that have followed. A classic example of the short film format.

SPIELBERG ON SPIELBERG: 'I can't look at it now. It really proved how apathetic I was during the 60s. When I look back at that film, I can easily say, "No wonder I didn't go to Kent State," or "No wonder I didn't go to Vietnam or I wasn't protesting when all my friends were carrying signs and getting clubbed at Century City." I was off making movies and *Amblin'* is the slick by-product of a kid immersed up to his nose in film.'

TV Work as a Director

Night Gallery (1969)
'Eyes'

(Colour, 26 mins)

Network NBC
Producer William Sackheim
Screenplay Rod Serling
Director Of Photography Richard Batcheller
Associate Producer John Badham
Music William Goldenberg
Art Director Howard E Johnston
Film Editor Edward M Abroms

CAST: Joan Crawford (*Claudia Menlo*), Barry Sullivan (*Dr Heatherton*), Tom Bosley (*Stanley Resnick*), George MacCready (*Hendricks*), Garry Goodrow (*Louis*), Shannon Farnon (*1st Nurse*), Richard Hale (*Doctor*)

TRANSMISSION DATE: 8 November, 1969.

PLOT SUMMARY: Blind, coldhearted millionaire Claudia Menlo lives a secluded existence in a New York tower block she built for herself. She blackmails a doctor into performing an operation that will give her sight for around thirteen hours. The operation is a success but, as Menlo removes the bandage to experience the world visually for the first time, New York is hit by an all consuming power blackout and all she can see is blackness, eventually plummeting to her death through her apartment window.

BACKSTORY: First published in a 1967 short story anthology 'The Season To Be Wary' by *Twilight Zone* creator Rod Serling, 'Eyes' was originally intended to be a theatrical feature before it wound up in this pilot for Rod Serling's *Night Gallery*, a blatant attempt to replicate the magic of the *Zone*. Overly talky and riddled with plot inanities, Spielberg was not impressed with the raw material but was desperate for his first pro directorial assignment.

CASTING: The original choice for 'Eyes' was Bette Davis, who flatly refused to work for a 22-year-old neophyte. So, displaying immense

13

faith in Spielberg, Universal fired Davis and hired Joan Crawford. Only really knowing her through *Mildred Pierce* (1945) and *What Ever Happened To Baby Jane* (1962) when she signed on for the assignment, Spielberg took a crash course on Crawford's career before their first meeting. This took on a bizarre twist: as Spielberg walked into her apartment, Crawford was stumbling about her flat wearing a blindfold, to replicate blindness. Still, the neophyte and the veteran struck an unlikely, fruitful relationship.

PRODUCTION: 'Eyes' started filming on 3 February 1969 with only a seven-day shooting schedule. As the crew of seasoned veterans believed the young director to be a publicity stunt, Spielberg had a hard time proving himself as the man in control. Due to his elaborate shooting methods and Crawford's reliance on cue cards to remember her lines, the first two days moved at a snail's pace. To add insult to injury, the third day saw Crawford laid low by an ear infection, forcing Spielberg to improvise around her absence. Nevertheless, Spielberg finished the episode only two days behind schedule.

TICS OF THE TRADE: In an attempt to pep up a leaden script, Spielberg laced 'Eyes' with a number of striking shots and precocious techniques; Spielberg shoots Dr Heatherton's entrance into Menlo's apartment through a bauble in a chandelier, rendering the image upside down; the flashy editing that extends the removal of Menlo's bandages in multiple angles; the impressionistic collage of images as Menlo stumbles around in the dark; glass shattering across a portrait of Menlo in slow motion as she falls out of the window. Dated certainly, but still a remarkable display of filmic fireworks.

FINAL ANALYSIS: Because of its reliance on showy technique for effect, Spielberg was branded an experimental director within the TV system and failed to work for almost a year. The youngster learned his lessons well: his later TV work finds much more restrained but effective methods of storytelling, and he also gained valuable lessons in keeping on schedules and dealing with temperamental actors. As a piece of drama, 'Eyes' is overblown and leaden, hamstrung by stilted dialogue and stagey acting. But it still remains an interesting illustration of Spielberg's innate visual sophistication and imagination.

SPIELBERG ON SPIELBERG: 'That show put me through dire straits. It was good discipline but a very bad experience.'

Marcus Welby MD (1970) 'The Daredevil Gesture'

(Colour, 52 mins)

Network ABC
Producer David J O'Connell
Screenplay Jerome Ross
Director Of Photography Walter Strenge
Assistant Director Joseph E Boston

CAST: Robert Young (*Marcus Welby*), Frank Webb (*Larry Bellows*), James Brolin (*Dr Steven Kiley*), Marsha Hunt (*Mrs Bellows*).

TRANSMISSION DATE: 17 March 1970.

PLOT SUMMARY: In the popular series revolving around a Santa Monica physician, 'The Daredevil Gesture' concerns Welby's involvement with Larry Bellows, a teenage haemophiliac who insists on joining a high school field trip despite the protestations of his overly protective mother. With Welby's help, Larry, also the subject of a broken home, finally gets to act like a regular kid.

TICS OF THE TRADE: A sinuous tracking shot through a high school locker room is the only real Spielbergian touch.

FINAL ANALYSIS: Despite the sensitive depiction of a teen outsider – Spielberg draws a manic performance from young Webb – there is little to distinguish this as a Spielberg production.

Night Gallery (1971) 'Make Me Laugh'

(Colour, 24 mins)

Network NBC/Universal
Producer Jack Laird
Teleplay Rod Serling
Music Robert Prince
Theme Gil Melle
Director Of Photography Richard C. Glouner
Art Director Joseph Alves Jr
Film Editors Bud Hoffman, James Ceilesie

CAST: Godfrey Cambridge (*Jackie Slater*), Tom Bosley (*Jules*), Jackie Vernon (*Miracle Maker*), Al Lewis (*Mishkin*), Sidney Clute (*David Garrick*).

TRANSMISSION DATE: 6 January 1971.

PLOT SUMMARY: Down-on-his-luck comedian Jackie Slater is granted one wish by a mysterious wishmaker – that everything Slater utters produces uproarious laughter. Slater becomes a big success but loses the the thrill of creating genuine laughter. His move into dramatic theatre is thwarted as no one takes him seriously. Slater's subsequent demand to reverse his power ends in tragic consequences.

FINAL ANALYSIS: Lacking the visual sophistication and dramatic subtleties of Spielberg's other small screen outings, 'Make Me Laugh' is the director's least interesting televisual offering. Yet the portrait of an artist who wants to be popular (then serious) does have a certain amount of resonance across his feature film career.

The Name Of The Game (1971) 'LA 2017'

(Colour, 74 mins)

Network NBC/Universal
Producer Dean Hargrove
Screenplay Philip Wyle
Executive Producer Richard Irving
Music Score Billy Goldenberg, Robert Prince
Theme Dave Grusin
Director Of Photography Richard A Kelley
Set Decorations Bert F Allen
Film Editor Frank Morriss

CAST: Gene Barry (*Glenn Howard*), Barry Sullivan (*Dane Bigelow*), Sharon Farrell (*Sandrell*) Edmund O'Brien (*Bergman*), Severn Draden (*Cameron*), Paul Stewart (*Dr Rubias*), Louise Latham (*Helen Bigelow*) Regis J. Cording (*Chairman*)

TRANSMISSION DATE: 15 January 1971.

PLOT SUMMARY: Falling asleep at the wheel while driving down LA desert roads, environmental spokesperson/publisher Glenn Howard crashes his car, and wakes up, *Twilight Zone*-style, in the future. Escorted to a subterranean compound by armed guards, Howard learns he is in LA in the year 2017, where toxic air has forced life underground. Realising the new LA is a thinly-disguised police state, Howard joins a band of revolutionaries and breaks to the surface. However, as Howard begins to choke on the polluted atmosphere, he is saved by the LAPD in 1971. It was all a dream.

TICS OF THE TRADE: Without ever resorting to expensive production design, Spielberg evokes a credible, claustrophobic vision of a world underground; for subterranean scenes, lengthy tracking shots following menacing militia mark out the confined spaces: for the brief view of the world above, Spielberg effectively utilises distorted lenses, bizarre framings and colour filters to make his location look ravaged and barren.

FINAL ANALYSIS: At some 72 minutes long, 'LA 2017' became Spielberg's first professional feature-length effort in Hollywood. Perhaps mired down by too many stale sci-fi cliches and static plotting, the movie allowed Spielberg a wide scope for generating scary, compelling, expressionistic imagery. For hints of his future work, 'LA 2017' has a chapel that consists of flashing lights and bleeps – a precursor of the *Close Encounters* brand of religiosity – and some of the angles in the climactic car chase prefigure *Duel*. But, independently, this remains a vivid slice of atmospheric science fiction on the cheap.

Columbo
'Murder By The Book' (1971)

(Colour, 76 mins)

Network Universal/NBC
Produced by Richard Levinson, William Link
Screenplay Steven Bochco
Music by Billy Goldenberg
Cinematography Russell Metty
Film Editing John Elias, John Kaufman
Set Decoration Richard Friedman
Costume Design Burton Miller

CAST: Peter Falk (*Lieutenant Columbo*), Jack Cassidy (*Ken Franklin*), Jim Ferris (*Martin Milner*), Rosemary Forsyth (*Joanna Ferris*), Barbara Colby (*Lily La Sanka*).

TRANSMISSION DATE: 15 September 1971.

PLOT SUMMARY: The first regular episode of Columbo after two pilots, 'Murder By The Book' sees the dishevelled 'tec investigate the death of one half of America's most popular crime writing partnership.

TICS OF THE TRADE: Some of 'Murder By The Book's' most inventive touches come on the soundtrack. The only noise in the opening scene is the clattering of the typewriter hitting the paper – giving the opening a portentous chilling quality removed from reality.

FINAL ANALYSIS: Generally considered among the best *Columbo* episodes, 'Murder By The Book' sees Spielberg honing his ability to draw out performances and develop a visual style all in the service of a strong story. Showing the kind of narrative patience that would serve him well in his big screen thrillers, Spielberg spends a long time building up the first murder, which pays off as Columbo fits the puzzle together. Television murder mystery at its best.

The Psychiatrist (1971) 'The Private World Of Martin Dalton'

(Colour, 52 mins)

Network ABC
Producer Jerrold Freeman
Screenplay Bo May
Director Of Photography Lloyd Ahern

CAST: Roy Thinnes (*Dr James Whitman*), Jim Hutton, Kate Woodville, Stephen Hudis (*Martin Dalton*), Pamelyn Ferdin

TRANSMISSION DATE: 10 February 1971.

PLOT SUMMARY: A medical drama series built around an idealistic LA shrink and his older, more world-weary partner. This episode (the first in a short-lived series) concerns a young boy who withdraws into a fantasy world of TV and comic books to escape his troubled existence.

FINAL ANALYSIS: Marked out by extraordinary dream sequences and a sensitive portrait of a child ill at ease with the world, 'The Private World Of Martin Dalton' is among the strongest TV antecedents to Spielberg's theatrical work.

The Psychiatrist (1971) 'Par For The Course'

(Colour, 52 mins)

Network NBC
Producer Jerrold Freedman
Teleplay Thomas Y Drake, Herb Berrman, Jerrold Freedman, Bo May
Story Thomas T Drake
Director Of Photography Lloyd Ahern

CAST: Roy Thinnes (*Dr James Whitman*), Clu Gulager, Joan Darling, Michael C. Gwynne.

TRANSMISSION DATE: 10 March 1971.

PLOT SUMMARY: A golf pro comes to terms with his imminent death from duodenal cancer. As his wife slowly becomes unhinged, the golfer's buddies, who have previously been unable to face his death, return to the golf course, dig up the eighteenth hole, put it in a shoebox (complete with flag) and bring it to the hospital. The delighted pro squeezes the dirt all over his head and thanks them for the greatest present he has ever received.

TICS OF THE TRADE: When the golfer's wife (played by Joan Darling) phones her mother in tears, rather than Spielberg moving in for the big close-up of her emotional face, Darling turns her back to camera and the camera begins to withdraw slowly away from her as she utters a solitary word ('Mama'). The less-is-more approach exemplified to the full.

FINAL ANALYSIS: With the director allowed more input into the script than usual, 'Par For The Course' is a benchmark in Spielberg's career. Proving he was more than just an artful technobrat, it established Spielberg's credibility within the television community, opened numerous doors for broader material and marked his maturation as a fully fledged film-maker.

Owen Marshall, Counselor At Law (1971) 'Eulogy For A Wide Receiver'

(Colour, 52 mins)

Network ABC
Producer Jon Epstein
Executive Producer David Victor
Created by Jon Epstein
Writer Richard Bluel
Music Elmer Bernstein
Director Of Photography Harkness Smith
Art Director John J. Lloyd
Film Editor Milton Shifman
Set Decorations George Mild

CAST: Arthur Hill (*Owen Marshall*), Lee Majors (*Jess Brandon*), Joan Darling (*Freda Klause*), Stephen Young (*Dave Butler*), Brad David (*Martin Cardwell*), Lou Frizzell (*Sam Miller*), Anson Williams (*Steve Baggott*).

TRANSMISSION DATE: 30 September 1971.

PLOT SUMMMARY: In a series concerning a warm, compassionate, small-town defence attorney and his young partner Joss Brandon, this episode sees the pair defend a high-school football coach who is accused of feeding drugs to his team following the death of a star player.

TICS OF THE TRADE: More subtle than most of Spielberg's TV work, 'Eulogy For A Wide Receiver' contains a visual tension during seemingly simple dialogue scenes with intent faces big in the foreground as a character talks in the background. Eschewing the usual static mosaic of close-ups that pass for courtroom dramas, Spielberg draws on subtly unnerving camera moves and even has the audacity to frame through a projector spool to the quarterback's intent expressions as he understands the win-at-all-costs mentality that engulfs him.

FINAL ANALYSIS: An engaging courtroom drama, 'Eulogy For A Wide Receiver' reconfirmed to industry movers and shakers that there was more to Spielberg than dazzling technique – that he was capable of building character while making subtle points about the spirit-crushing importance of American high school sports. Indeed, its condemnation of a jock-fuelled ethos is its most Spielbergian trait.

Duel (1971)

(Colour, 73 mins)

Network ABC
Producer George Eckstein
Screenplay Richard Matheson (based on his published story)
Director Of Photography Jack A Marta
Film Editor Frank Morriss
Music Billy Goldenberg
Art Director Robert A Smith
Sound Edwin Shall
Stunt Coordinator Cary Loftin
Supervising Sound Editor James Troutman
Sound Re-recording Robert Hoyt

CAST: Dennis Weaver (*David Mann*), Jacqueline Scott (*Mrs Mann*), Eddie Firestone (*Cafe Owner*), Lou Frizzell (*Bus Driver*), Gene Dynarski (*Man In Cafe*), Lucille Benson (*Lady At Snakearama*), Cary Loftin (*Truck Driver*), Dale VanSickle (*Car Driver*)

TRANSMISSION DATE: 13 November 1971.

MPAA: PG

UK: AA

BUDGET: $750,000

TITLE SEQUENCE: Over a black screen we hear the sounds of someone entering a car and starting up the engine. Taking a point of view from the car's bonnet, the camera reverses back into a suburban street to reveal the black screen as the darkness of a garage. Over broadcasts from the car radio – traffic news, jazzy music, ads for haemorrhoid medication – a series of shots, linked by dissolves, plot a progression through a busy city and on to the open freeways.

PLOT SUMMARY: On his journey to keep an unspecified business appointment, mild-mannered suburbanite David Mann takes a country route to short circuit the heavy traffic warnings. His journey is slowed down when he finds himself behind a dilapidated petrol tanker, spewing exhaust and hogging the open road. Mann easily passes the truck yet, moments later, the truck roars past Mann in a dangerous overtaking manoeuvre.

Rising to the challenge, Mann goes all out and passes the vehicle, putting as much distance between himself and the lorry as possible. Following a brief pit stop in a garage where Mann is informed his radiator hose needs replacing, the journey continues with the tanker driver quickly overtaking the helpless Mann and teasing him with dangerous road games – for example waving Mann into oncoming traffic – which culminate with Mann being run off the road. Cleaning up in a cafe where the truck is parked outside, Mann deliberates over what to do, eventually picking on the wrong driver and getting beaten up for his troubles.

Back on the highway, the deadly game continues to the point where Mann pulls into a snake farm to phone the cops. His call is cut short as the truck ploughs into the phone box, demolishing the ramshackle farm. Mann makes a break into quarry country, yet, as he tries to power up a steep incline, his radiator hose conks out, the engine starting to overheat. Snapping on his seat belt like a gunslinger ready for action, Mann drives towards the truck, bailing out at the point the truck impacts on the car, which sees both vehicles plunge over a cliff. Placed in silhouette by the setting sun, Mann sits alone, contemplating his survival.

BACKSTORY: A celebrated science fiction author (*The Incredible Shrinking Man*, *I Am Legend*) and contributor to *Twilight Zone* and *Night Gallery*, Richard Matheson was inspired to write *Duel* after a similar, if less sustained, run-in with a truck. Jotting down the incident on the back of an envelope, Matheson tried to hawk it around as a TV plot, trying to sell it to various series including *The Fugitive*. Spielberg first came across the idea when his secretary Nona Tyson handed him the April '71 issue of *Playboy* and he saw Matheson's short story, written some seven years after its genesis. Spielberg's enthusiasm for the project encouraged producer George Eckstein – who had been led to the story by future TV mogul Steve Bochco, then a writer on *Columbo* – to give him his shot. Although mooted as a potential feature film, there was so much concern that the slight storyline could hold a lengthy running time that it ultimately remained small screen.

CASTING: During the period when *Duel* was considered as a theatrical venture, Gregory Peck was the first choice to play David Mann. After Peck turned the movie down, Spielberg went to Dustin Hoffman and David Janssen who also passed. Eventually Universal closed down production on cowboy cop show *McCloud* to free up Dennis Weaver to take the role. Although best known for TV favourite *Gunsmoke*, Weaver had proved in Orson Welles' *Touch Of Evil* (1958) he could portray a nervy coward à la David Mann.

PRODUCTION: *Duel* started filming on 13 September 1971, shooting much of the film on Highway 14, thirty to forty miles North of Los Angeles. To keep to the tight sixteen-day schedule and ensure that the film became a protean visual experience, Spielberg storyboarded the film on IBM cards. Yet, unusually, he also went one stage further; commissioning an entire map proffering a bird's eye view of the intended shooting circuit. Wrapping the blueprint around the location motel room, Spielberg created an easy way to plan multiple set-ups at a time and gauge a geography of which terrain offered the most fruitful dramatic possibilities. Other unusual practices during the shoot went back to the silent days. Just as actors in the pre-sound era acted and reacted to piano music played on set, so Spielberg played a tape recording of Dennis Weaver reading Mann's voice-over so the actor could time and pull appropriate expressions on his face.

TICS OF THE TRADE: From the very first image outside Mann's viewpoint – the car driving by framed menacingly against barbed wire – the technique in *Duel* is geared to creating visual and storytelling tension. Peppered with exaggerated framings, elaborately choreographed camera moves from car to truck (and vice versa) and skewwhiff angles more common in cinema than TV, Spielberg uses wide-angled shots looking down at Mann's car and up at the hurtling truck to emphasise the difference in scale of the road warriors. Much was made of Spielberg's decision to offer only partial glimpses of the truck driver to enhance the sense of mystery and suggest a world of machinery run rampant. The director, however, underplays the master stroke. 'That was not intentional . . . at first. I was not trying to mislead you by asking the driver to pose that way, to be blocked by the bulkhead.'

SOUND EFFECTS: Although *Duel* could easily play as a silent movie, Spielberg creates fantastic impact throughout with his deployment of sound. In particular by juxtaposing the sound of the two engines – the sad whine of Mann's car, the low and menacing rumble of the truck – the sense of Godzilla versus Bambi is made palpable. To create the final death moans of the truck, Spielberg's initial idea was to mix truck effects with the voice of a woman treated with distortion. One of the sound editors suggested to Spielberg that the roar of the Gil-Man from *The Creature From The Black Lagoon* (1954) might be effective. The end result is positively Jurassic.

WHAT'S THE SCORE? Provided by Universal contract composer Billy Goldenberg, the score for *Duel* owes much to Bernard Herrmann's music for Alfred Hitchcock. A mixture of frenzied over-excited strings, driving percussion and random dissonant effects, the score is used sparely throughout the film – the first cue arrives around twenty minutes in – often used in the form of random strings to punctuate specific moments.

CUT SCENES: When *Duel* was theatrically released overseas in 1972, four sequences were added, two created by Spielberg, two written by George Eckstein. Spielberg's contribution saw the opening gambit from the point of view of Mann's car and the truck attempting to push Mann into an oncoming train. Eckstein's scenes saw the truck come to the aid of the stranded school bus and a completely superfluous scene in which Mann phones his wife from a laundrette, the latter accusing him of cowardly behaviour after a man 'practically raped her' at a party. Despite being overly literal, the scene manages to display some typical directorial flourishes: as Mann speaks on the phone in long shot, a woman enters the laundrette, moves to the foreground and opens a dryer, framing Weaver perfectly through the little round window. The scenes added another $100,000 to the original budget.

For the international release, Spielberg also managed to excise much of the narration and extraneous dialogue. It is this 91-minute version that has become the edit left for posterity; the original TV cut is no longer on release.

UNSUNG HERO(ES): Dilys Powell, the *Sunday Times* film critic who got behind *Duel* to such an extent that Spielberg often cites Powell's influence as a prime mover in his career. To wit her review: 'Mr Spielberg comes from television (*Duel* was made for television), he is only twenty-five. No prophecies, but I fancy this is another name to look out for.'

THE CRITICAL FACULTY: 'Film buffs will rightfully be studying and referring to *The Duel* [sic] for some time . . .' (Tony Scott, *Daily*

Variety) . . . 'Best TV movie of 1971 . . . a classic of pure cinema.' (Cecil Smith, *Los Angeles Times*).

BOX OFFICE: While *Duel* performed only moderately well in the US TV ratings, the film received a theatrical outing in Europe, Australia and Japan where it grossed around $8 million. The film received a belated stateside theatrical outing in 1982, where moviegoers proved reluctant to go out and see it.

AWARDS: *Duel* won an Emmy, the big US TV award, for Outstanding Achievement in Film Sound Editing. The film's only other nomination came in the best cinematography category. The film was much better received in Europe. In Avoriaz, France, the film earned the Grand Prix of the first Festival de Cinema Fantastique in January 1973 and the best first film at Italy's Taormina Film Festival.

GEDDIT! As Mann passes a parked sedan that resembles a police car, the vehicle actually turns out to belong to a pest exterminator named Grebleips – Spielberg backwards!

Eagle-eyed viewers may notice that the truck has seventeen notches on its bumper, an indication that killing motorists is just a way of life.

FACTOID FRENZY: Promoting *Duel* in Rome, Spielberg's failure to acknowledge the film was a metaphor for the struggle between the upper and working classes made four Italian journalists walk out of the press conference.

Making the movie, Weaver drove over 2,000 miles in the red Valiant.

FINAL ANALYSIS: The effect of *Duel* on Spielberg's career was instant and monumental: it turned him from an up-and-coming TV player into a hot-to-trot movie-maker courted by the studios for feature work. Relying on his trusted method of storyboarding to make a logistically complex film on time and budget, Spielberg created the perfect showcase for his growing understanding of using taut technique to turn a slender story into a gripping, exhilarating experience.

While *Duel* is an obvious precursor of the car-bound antics of *The Sugarland Express* and the machine-like menace of *Jaws*, its sense of a suburban everyman challenged by large forces is an idea that Spielberg has played out over his whole career, especially in *Close Encounters*.

Some thirty years on, *Duel* holds up remarkably well – the film's only flaw is Weaver's explanatory voice-over which feels embarrassingly redundant – and remains Spielberg's leanest, most unsentimental work to date. What still impresses is Spielberg's mature handling of the one note premise, building the conflict up gradually and realistically, then spicing it up with ingenious strategies – the scene in which Mann tries to guess which cowboy drives the malevolent rig is as neatly worked as anything on the road – and fantastically engineered surprise and suspense. Here lies the significance of *Duel* within Spielberg's career: it confirmed that such a sense of story-spinning savvy, formal control and cinematic imagination was never going to be contained within a small box in the corner of the living room.

SPIELBERG ON SPIELBERG: '*Duel* is an indictment of machines. And I determined very early on that everything about the film would be the complete disruption of our whole technological society. Keys falling out of locks. Kids playing wind-up toys. And especially, where the truck was concerned, I wanted to be the true, perfect, perpetual-motion machine.'

Something Evil (1972)

(Colour, 72 mins)

Network CBS
Producer Alan Jay Factor
Screenplay Robert Clouse
Music Wladimir Selinsky
Cinematographer Bill Butler
Film Editor Allan Jacobs
Production Design Albert Heschong

CAST: Sandy Dennis (*Marjorie Worden*), Darren McGavin (*Paul Wooden*), Ralph Bellamy (*Harry Lincoln*), Jeff Corey (*Gehrmann*), Johnny Whitaker (*Stevie Worden*), John Rubinstein (*Ernest Lincoln*), David Knapp (*John*), Laurie Hagan (*Beth*), Herb Armstrong (*Schiller*), Margaret Avery (*Irene*), Debbie Lempert (*Laurie*), Sandy Lempert (*Laurie*).

TRANSMISSION DATE: 21 January 1972.

PLOT SUMMARY: Paul and Marjorie Worden, with adolescent son Stevie and baby Laurie, escape the rigours of city life by purchasing a farmhouse in rural Pennsylvania. Increasingly spooked by a child's voice crying out in the night. Marjorie befriends local occult buff Harry Lincoln who provides cautionary tales of a devil in the farmhouse and suggests she paints a pentacle on the floor of her kids' bedroom. As the supernatural activity increases – both Marjorie and Harry suffer attacks from unseen forces – Marjorie locks her children in their bedroom only to learn from Lincoln that the devil is seeking to take possession of Stevie. With Paul breaking down the door to the kids' room, Marjorie grabs Stevie up into the pentacle and forces the evil away by outpourings of love.

TICS OF THE TRADE: Many of the techniques that Spielberg would develop in his feature work are present in rough-hewn form: the rapid camera moves and repeated action editing that depict Marjorie's fright in the vineyard pre-empt Dieter's attack by the compies in *The Lost World*. Similarly, the cutting strategy that juxtaposes Marjorie destroying her collection of pentacles with Stevie bouncing a basketball against the house wall is an early incarnation of the cross-cutting bravura that marks out many later Spielberg films, particularly *The Color Purple* and *Schindler's List*. *Something Evil* is also one of the first movies in which Spielberg uses camerawork to delineate a child's point of view. Depicting little Stevie at play – chasing frogs or kicking a ball – Spielberg angles the shots from Stevie's level, a technique that was developed even further with *E.T.*.

FINAL ANALYSIS: It is easy to see Spielberg's attraction to *Something Evil* as his first effort, post *Duel*. Allowing a lot of scope for visual pyrotechnics and virtuoso set pieces, it also created more space for him to demonstrate and hone his skills with character and performance. The resulting picture is high on atmosphere and the kind of thrill that comes with a film-maker finding his feet, but is low on scares and emotional pull for an audience. However, *Something Evil* does preface some ideas that Spielberg will return to throughout his career, particularly in *Poltergeist*: the family terrorised by supernatural forces, a child as a conduit for the supernatural, the mother of the family taking a much more dominant role than the father (see also *The Sugarland Express*, *Close Encounters*, *E.T.*) and even right down to the distorted child's voice to provide a focus for the fear. Yet, that *Something Evil* prefigures the boon in the diabolical genre that exploded with *The Exorcist* and *The Omen* a few years later, hints at another talent that Spielberg developed over the ensuing years – an uncanny knack to predict what audiences want.

Savage (1973)

(Colour, 76 mins)

Producer Paul Mason
Teleplay Richard Levinson, William Link, Mark Rodgers
Story Mark Rodgers
Executive Producers Richard Levinson, William Link
Music Gil Melle
Cinematography Bill Butler
Film Editing Edward M Abroms
Art Direction William H Tuntke

CAST: Martin Landau (*Paul Savage*), Barbara Bain (*Gail Abbott*), Will Geer (*Joel Ryker*), Paul Richards (*Peter Brooks*), Michele Carey (*Allison Baker*), Susan Howard (*Lee Raynolds*), Barry Sullivan (*Judge Daniel Stern*).

TRANSMISSION DATE: 31 March 1973.

PLOT SUMMARY: Joel Ryker is a wealthy Bel-Air party-giver who has a stable of girls on call whom he uses to blackmail prominent figures. When one of his girls, Lee Raynolds, goes to TV reporter Paul Savage with news of her 'friendship' with Judge Daniel Stern, a nominee to the supreme court, Ryker has Raynolds killed by henchman Paul Brooks. Savage solves the murder but has his ethics called into question after Stern's wife pleads with him not to reveal the findings and ruin her husband's career.

FINAL ANALYSIS: Somewhat of a disappointment after the razzle-dazzle of *Duel* and *Something Evil*, *Savage* is a staid conventional piece of work that fully displays lack of interest in the material. There are a few nifty directorial strokes – a scene set in a TV studio is played out in menacing silhouette – but for the most part, this is formulaic, leaden stuff.

Stories (1985–7)

Obviously inspired by shows such as *Twilight Zone*, *Alfred Hitchcock Presents* and *Night Gallery*, *Amazing Stories* was originally conceived as a fertile ground for all the plots and ideas that sprung from Spielberg's head but never made it on to a movie screen. The result was a series of uneven adventures that came nowhere near the beguiling qualities of his theatrical outings. Spielberg personally directed the following two entries.

Ghost Train (1985)

(Colour, 25 mins)

Network NBC
Supervising Producers Joshua Brand, John Falsey
Executive Producer Steven Spielberg
Production Executives Kathleen Kennedy, Frank Marshall
Produced by David E Vogel
Developed by Steven Spielberg, Joshua Brand, John Falsey
Teleplay by Frank Deese
Story by Steven Spielberg
Story Editor Mick Garris
Director Of Photography Allen Daviau
Production Designer Rick Carter
Editor Steve Kemper
Music John Williams

CAST: Robert Blossoms (*Old Pa*), Scott Paulin (*Mr Globe*), Gail Edwards (*Jolene Globe*), Lukas Haas (*Brian Globe*), Renny Roker (*Dr Steele*)

TRANSMISSION DATE: 28 September 1985

PLOT SUMMARY: Brought back into the fold of his family after time in a retirement home, an eccentric old timer, known to his family as Old Pa, makes an immediate connection with his young grandson Brian, telling the youngster a tale about how he narrowly escaped death by not boarding the doomed train, the Hardball Express. Believing the phantom train is returning to collect him, Old Pa gathers together his things, much to the consternation of his family. Yet the old timer is proved right as a locomotive powers into his living room and Old Pa boards the train for his journey to the other side.

FINAL ANALYSIS: Although perhaps too low key to be a great series opener, 'Ghost Train' is a poignant little tale, far better than many of the entries that followed. Drawing great performances from Blossoms and Haas, Spielberg doesn't overegg the emotional content, sketching a warm, affectionate relationship in minimum screen time. It does have its big Spielberg moments – the train crashing into the house is a bigger set piece than usually seen on the box – but this gets by more on character and feeling rather than filmic fireworks.

The Mission (1987)

(Colour, 50 mins)

Network NBC
Supervising Producers Joshua Brand, John Falsey
Executive Producer Steven Spielberg
Production Executives Kathleen Kennedy, Frank Marshall
Produced by David E Vogel
Developed by Steven Spielberg, Joshua Brand, John Falsey
Teleplay by Menno Meyjes
Story by Steven Spielberg
Associate Producer Steve Starkey
Story Editor Mick Garris
Director Of Photography John McPherson
Film Editor Steve Kemper
Music John Williams

CAST: Kevin Costner (*Captain Spark*), Casey Siemaszko (*Jonathan*), Kiefer Sutherland (*Static*), Jeffrey Jay Cohen (*Jake*), John Philbin (*Bullseye*), Gary Mauro (*Sam*), Glen Mauro (*Dave*), Karen Kopins (*Liz*), Nelson Welch (*Father Mckay*).

TRANSMISSION DATE: 15 May 1985.

PLOT SUMMARY: The crew of a World War Two American bomber embark on their 23rd and final mission. Tragedy strikes when belly gunner Jonathan, a wannabe cartoonist, gets trapped in the floor gun turret during aerial combat. With the landing gear damaged, all looks bleak as the plane comes into land until Jonathan sketches a doodling of the plane with its wheels down causing a set of cartoon wheels to appear and magically bring in the plane to safety.

FINAL ANALYSIS: 'The Mission's' combination of two great Spielberg passions – aviation and animation – is enjoyable but ultimately unsatisfying TV. Spielberg has loads of fun playing with the clichés of World War Two bomber flicks – the priest and Jonathan's pregnant wife waiting at the control tower – and expertly wracks up the tension before the film's final moments. Undone by the concluding element of supernatural whimsy that proves unsatisfying, 'The Mission' embodies the strengths and weaknesses of the series as a whole: imaginative directing, good acting and excellent production value let down by a weakness in the yarns themselves.

Spielberg also provided the story ideas for the following *Amazing Stories* episodes: 'Mummy Daddy', 'The Amazing Falsworth', 'Alamo Jobe', 'Remote Control', 'Santa '85', 'Fine Tuning', 'Dorothy And Ben', 'The Main Attraction', 'Mirror, Mirror', 'One Amazing Night', 'The Wedding Ring', 'The Greibble', 'What If', 'Blue Man Down', 'You Gotta Believe Me'.

Feature Films

The Sugarland Express (1974)

(Colour, 109 mins)

Studio Universal
Screenplay Matthew Robbins, Hal Barwood
Story by Steven Spielberg, Matthew Robbins, Hal Barwood
Producers Richard D Zanuck, David Brown
Director of Photography (Panavision) Vilmos Zsigmond
Production Executive William S Gilmore
Edited by Edward M Abroms ACE (American Cinema Editors), Verna Fields
Art Director Joseph Alves Jr
Music by John Williams
Assistant Director James Fargo
Stunt Co-ordinator Carey Loftin
Sound John Carter, Robert Hoyt
Special Effects Frank Brendel
Unit Production Manager William S Gilmore
Second Assistant Director Thomas Joyner
Transportation Manager Alby Thomas
Harmonica solos 'Toots' Thielemans

CAST: Goldie Hawn (*Lou Jean Poplin*), William Atherton (*Clovis Poplin*), Ben Johnson (*Captain Tanner*), Michael Sacks (*Officer Maxwell Slide*), Harrison Zanuck (*Baby Langston*), Steve Kanaly (*Officer Jessup*), Gregory Walcott (*Officer Mashburn*), Louise Latham (*Mrs Looby*), AL Camp (*Mr Knocker*), Jessie Lee Fulton (*Mrs Knocker*).

BUDGET: $3 million

MPAA: R

BBFC: AA

TITLE SEQUENCE: After a simple black-and-white title card – 'This film is based upon a real event which happened in Texas in 1968' – we start close up on a cluster of Texas road signs, moving down to reveal a coach pulling up at the side of a desolate crossroads. Lou Jean Poplin steps off, gains her bearings and, accompanied by John Williams's simple guitar/harmonica theme, walks towards the Texas

Pre-Release Center to visit her incarcerated husband Clovis. (Interestingly, she passes a hollowed-out car – a subtle allusion to her fate at the film's end). The white credits (speared with a black line) take a break as Lou Jean has her belongings checked by a security guard, but resume with a complex tracking shot following Lou Jean through the detention centre – the convoluted tricksiness of the camera move strangely mirroring the duplicity of her intentions to spring Clovis free.

PLOT SUMMARY: Texas, 1974. Newly released from prison, Lou Jean Poplin helps her husband Clovis to escape from a minimum-security prison. Driven by a desire to be reunited with her baby son Langston, who has been placed with foster parents because Lou Jean's ex-con status makes her an unfit mother, the couple hitch a ride with an elderly couple, subsequently steal their car and become engaged in a high-speed chase with a patrol car that leads the Poplins to crash in the woods. The rookie officer in pursuit, Maxwell Slide, checks out the scene of the crash but is taken hostage by the Poplins and forced to drive them in his patrol car 2311 all the way to Sugarland to pick up the toddler.

With a police officer in danger, a veteran Department of Public Safety officer, Captain Tanner, is assigned to apprehending the outlaws and securing Slide's safe release. As the journey progresses, the Poplins' flight becomes a *cause célèbre*, joined by an ever-growing cavalcade of police cars, TV crews and small-town well-wishers caught up in the couple's plight. En route, we are treated to comedic vignettes, great car smash-ups, terrifying violence and subtly drawn relationships: a believable friendship between the Poplins and Slide and a touching relationship between the outlaws and Captain Tanner conducted entirely over CB and megaphones.

As the procession arrives in Sugarland, Tanner realises there is only one way out of the situation: while making a deal with Clovis that he will be able to pick up Langston in Sugarland, Tanner orders two sharpshooters to wait in the foster home to pick off the couple. Despite Slide's protestations that all is not well, Clovis approaches the house and is shot by the marksmen. A title card informs us that Lou Jean and Langston were eventually reunited and that Slide and Tanner are still serving on the force.

BACKSTORY: Ironically, for a director continually associated with fantasy, the impetus for Spielberg's first feature film was culled straight from the newspaper headlines. NEW BONNIE AND CLYDE, screamed the Los Angeles *Citizen News* in its 2 May 1969 edition, referring to the escapades of an ex-convict, Robert Samuel (Bobby) Dent, and his wife

Ila Faye Dent. Just released from a conviction for shoplifting, Ila coerced her husband into kidnapping a Texas highway patrolman, J Kenneth Crone, and forcing him at (shot)gunpoint to drive across Texas to retrieve their two-year-old daughter from foster parents. While the *Citizen News* reported 'a high-speed chase that ended seven hours later in a gunfight with lawmen', in actuality, Dent was tailed across the Lone Star state by a hundred cop cars and struck a deal with the Texas Department of Public Safety's Captain Jerry Miller: Dent would be allowed to see his kids at the home of his father-in-law at Wheelock in exchange for Crone's safe release. As he entered the house, the children were nowhere to be seen. Crone dived for cover and Dent was killed by two riflemen after failing to obey a command to drop his gun.

Spielberg proposed the idea to Universal in 1969, but they nixed the project, saying it was too downbeat. Yet refusing to let the story go, Spielberg developed the idea with two writers, Hal Barwood and Matthew Robbins, contemporaries of George Lucas at the University of Southern California's film school, forging an outline entitled *Carte Blanche*, a reference to the freedom given to the outlaw couple by the Texas lawmen. United Artists showed an interest in the outline but got cold feet, so the project returned to Universal, where it was put on the fast track: on 11 April 1972, Spielberg showed the outline to an MCA exec, Jennings Lang, who ushered the project into development that day. A week of research in Texas saw the first-draft screenplay generated in a further thirteen days.

Then the project stalled until it was revived by the production team of David Brown and Richard D Zanuck. The two men had formed an alliance at Twentieth Century Fox in the 60s, where Brown was an executive vice-president and Zanuck, the son of the mogul Darryl F Zanuck, rose up the ranks to be Motion Pictures President, responsible for such hits as *Butch Cassidy and the Sundance Kid* (1969), *Patton* (1970) and *M*A*S*H* (1970). Yet, after a string of Fox flops, the pair were unceremoniously fired (by Zanuck Sr!) and formed an independent production company. While still an exec at Fox, Zanuck had denied Spielberg the chance of making his feature debut by turning down the Spielberg script, *Ace Eli and Rodger of the Skies* (1973) – the first time Zanuck had dealings with the young film-maker.

Announced in the Hollywood trade press as the first Steven Spielberg film on 17 October 1972, *Sugarland*'s second-draft screenplay was delivered that day. Two months later the film found its final title – the name conjuring up images of a fairy-tale land – having gone through *American Express* and plain ol' *Sugarland* in the interim.

ORIGINS: Despite the hundreds of chase movies, from the Keystone Kops to Spielberg's own *Duel*, the most pervasive influence on *The Sugarland Express* can be found in Billy Wilder's *Ace in the Hole* (UK title: *The Big Carnival*, 1951). Starring Kirk Douglas as a down-on-his-luck reporter, Chuck Tatum, who prolongs the rescue of a man trapped in a mining disaster to grab bigger headlines, the film shares many of the themes that underpin Spielberg's road movie: the way in which the media can shape and participate in an event as opposed to merely reporting on it; how private tragedy can become public property; the clamour for 'ordinary heroes' as a focus for shared sentimentality.

Lovers on the lam on the open road can be found in numerous places: Fritz Lang's *You Only Live Once* (1937), Nicholas Ray's *They Live By Night* (1949), *Gun Crazy* (1949) and Arthur Penn's *Bonnie and Clyde* (1967) are the most famous examples of picaresque couples taking flight, all sharing decidedly doomed outcomes.

As we shall see with Spielberg, cartoons are a recurrent inspiration. *Sugarland* is nothing if not the Chuck Jones's *Road Runner* cartoons transformed into live action, the episodic structure and the road-centric imagery more than recalling the bird-versus-coyote showdowns. Indeed, using a *Roadrunner* clip within *Sugarland*, Spielberg acknowledges the debt with touching, chilling ends (see **Sound effects**).

Visually, *Sugarland* owes most to the films of Robert Altman, which is not surprising considering Spielberg hired Altman's cinematographer, the Hungarian Vilmos Zsigmond. In Altman films such as *McCabe and Mrs Miller* (1971) and *The Long Goodbye* (1973), Zsigmond established a look that was both naturalistic and stylised, employing diffused light (aeons away from the overlit brightness of studio lighting) and long lenses to flatten the imagery.

Finally, *Sugarland*'s closing image of a lone figure in silhouette against blazing sunshine is traceable not only to Spielberg's own *Duel* but also to George Lucas's *THX-1138* (1970) – obviously early-70s shorthand for quasi-heroism.

CASTING: Considering the downbeat nature of the material, it was imperative for Spielberg to find a big name for Lou Jean. After the director had met with various actresses, it was the producer Richard D Zanuck who suggested Goldie Hawn. Having begun her career in a chorus-line cancan troupe at the 1964 World's Fair, Hawn found fame as a ditzy blonde on the wacky TV show *Laugh-In* before moving on to movies, bagging a Best Supporting Oscar for *Cactus Flower* (1969). At the time of *Sugarland*, Hawn had an exclusive production deal at Universal and had passed on a number of projects before signing on for *Sugarland* for $300,000 in December 1972. Interestingly, Lou Jean is the first in a long line of similar Spielberg heroines – women who are tousled, unkempt, vaguely tomboyish and very happy in the company of men. *Close Encounters*' Jillian Guiler, *Raiders*' Marion Ravenwood, *Always*' Dorinda Durston, *Jurassic Park*'s Ellie Sattler, even *Hook*'s Tinkerbell come from the same mould as Lou Jean.

For Lou Jean's likable dimwitted husband Clovis, Spielberg selected William Atherton, who had two credits to his name at that point – *The New Centurions* (1972), *Class Of '44* (1973) – and would later become better known as the stuffy bureaucrat in *Ghostbusters* (1984) and the pushy reporter in the *Die Hard* series. It was Atherton's wild eyes yet quiet intensity that won the day with Spielberg. As if to emphasise the similarity between Clovis and Officer Slide – Spielberg's intention was to suggest that both men had the same start in life but took different turns – Michael Sacks was cast as the kidnapped patrolman partly because of his resemblance to Atherton. Sacks was a hot property after an eye-catching turn in *Slaughterhouse 5* (1972).

A former rodeo champion and Hollywood stuntman, Ben Johnson was part of John Ford's stock company of actors, appearing in *Three Godfathers* (1949) and *She Wore a Yellow Ribbon* (1949) and taking the lead in *The Wagonmaster* (1950). Specialising in Westerns – he also appeared in *Shane* (1953) and *The Wild Bunch* (1969) – Johnson won an Oscar for his performance in *The Last Picture Show* (1971). As a cowboy born out of time, Johnson's Captain Tanner is full of dignity, compassion and humanity, the perfect melding of actor, persona and role.

PRODUCTION: Steven Spielberg's first feature film began shooting on 15 January 1973. To intensify the harshness of the story, Spielberg opted to shoot in winter – he actually wanted rain in order to set up compositions through moving windscreen wipers – partly in order to diminish Goldie Hawn's sunny disposition.

'I was thinking, Well, let's take it easy,' recalled Zanuck. 'Let's get the kid acclimated to this big-time stuff. But when I got there the first day he was about ready to get the first shot, and it was the most elaborate fucking thing I've ever seen in my life. I mean tricky: all-in-one shots, the camera going and stopping, people getting in and out. But he had such a confidence in the way that he was handling it.'

Only towards the end of the shoot did Zanuck and Brown need to protect their young charge – from himself. Worried that the downbeat ending might prove uncommercial, Spielberg got cold feet and lobbied that the young runaways should live at the end of the movie. However, in a reversal of usual director–producer roles, it was Zanuck and

Brown who persuaded the film-maker to remain true to the integrity of the story and let the kids meet their sealed fate.

Shot entirely on location, *Sugarland* began filming for ten days in Richmond, Clodine, Sugar Land (not to be confused with the fictional Sugarland) and the Beauford Jest Farm, which doubled as the opening scene's correctional facility. The unit moved on to six and a half weeks' work in San Antonio (the car-lot shoot-out was staged here) before a brief stint in Texas's Universal City, then moving to the border town of Del Rio for the last week.

As with *Duel*, Spielberg plotted out the events of the chase on a mural and storyboards, the auto action being captured by a Corvette camera car initially constructed for the filming of *Bullitt* (1968). The unit production manager, Bill Gilmore, not only sweet-talked the Texas Department of Public Safety into allowing the *Sugarland* production to shoot along Texas highways despite the fact that the film, for the most part, depicts the Texas law enforcers as inept and heartless, but he also secured the supporting cast of police cars against incredible odds. Prior to *Sugarland*'s shoot, Sam Peckinpah's *The Getaway* (1972) had been shot in similar locations, the crew participating in bar-room brawls and stealing car radios from vehicles hired out by local authorities. Hence the *Sugarland* unit were denied access to the authorities' motor pool. To fill out the four-wheeled extras, Gilmore moved quickly and bought 23 cars at a police auction, then acquired seventeen more cars from other sources (although Universal publicity boasted 250), still some 60 short of the real-life 100-strong procession.

The Sugarland Express finished filming in late March 1973, just five days over its 55-day schedule.

TICS OF THE TRADE: Eschewing the late 60s Hollywood practice of filming car interiors in a studio against a back projection, Spielberg and his cinematographer, Vilmos Zsigmond, took to real wheels with numerous innovations to give the car sequences a previously unrealised authenticity combined with a sense of grace and fluidity. Slide's patrol car 2311 had the wheels removed and was mounted on a low-slung trailer, which in turn was fitted with a small platform that allowed the camera crew to perform tracking shots alongside the car while it was in motion.

For shots within the car interior, Zsigmond utilised the new, highly compact Panaflex camera, which accommodated stunning handheld shots. It was now possible to do a 360-degree pan inside the car, and fitting the camera to a board to create a makeshift tracking device allowed smooth dolly shots from front seat to back within a moving car at 35 m.p.h.! As the Panaflex camera arrived late in the day – *Sugarland* was its first professional outing – Spielberg scheduled the most difficult shots towards the end of the shoot. The planning paid off. If nothing else, *The Sugarland Express* is an object lesson in how to make conversations in cars entirely cinematic.

Away from the open road, Spielberg energises the storytelling through constant camera arcs, cranes and moves, always keeping the emphasis on *motion* pictures. He even adds his own imprint on the 70s penchant for zoom shots by combining them with pans and tracking shots, not only to conceal the zoom but also to add a subtle sense of disorientation. *Sugarland* also sees Spielberg utilise the dolly-zoom trickery made famous one movie later by *Jaws*: as a sharpshooter takes aim at 2311 while the car moves towards the foster parents' home, the camera zooms out from the car but tracks in towards the rifleman's shoulder – the effect is to elongate, almost freeze, the action, creating a heightened moment of suspense before the carnage begins. The film's mixture of a loose handheld approach combined with a more formal style contributes a unique feel to the movie – at once sloppy yet controlled – and (unconsciously) mirrors the film's central dynamic between the naïveté of the runaways and the stern authority of the Texan bureaucracy.

COMIC RELIEF: Unlike the later heavy-handed *1941*, Spielberg plays the car carnage exactly right, proving that cars careering into each other can be funny when this grows organically from the situation. En route, Spielberg laces the yarn with perfectly played comedic set pieces (Clovis flushing the marksman out of the portaloo) and some lovely observational gags (the kids miscounting the parade of police cars), as well as visual comedy born out of whimsical composition: the Elmer Thud-style hats of the vigilantes bobbing up and down behind the fence; the shot of 2311 moving up the hill, then slowly rolling back down as it has run out of gas. The interplay between Lou Jean, Clovis and Slide – Lou Jean's insistence that she has to pee, Slide teaching Clovis how to drive cop-style – is also neatly judged, building up character as well as comedy.

SOUND EFFECTS: Coupled with the documentary style of the images, Spielberg sought a raw, real quality for the soundtrack. Because the Panaflex camera was so quiet, it meant that the sound recordist, John Carter, could record sound live – the cars were kitted out with multiple microphones rigged into the police walkie-talkies – giving the film a veracity that could not have been achieved with actors redubbing their lines. In the end, only ten lines were looped at a later date.

Occasionally Spielberg heightens the sound for lyrical effect (a patrol car CB singsong against a beautiful twilight sky) or dramatic bluntness (the gunshot that nails Clovis is suitably far reaching), but for the most part the cacophony of police sirens, tyre screeches and radio traffic is subtly, naturally layered. Again using an Altman speciality, Spielberg also employs overlapping dialogue, especially to link scenes and speed up the action.

Perhaps the most interesting scene aurally in the film occurs as Lou Jean and Clovis break into a motor home on a used-car lot. Daydreaming about being reunited with baby Langston, they can see – but cannot hear – a Chuck Jones *Road Runner* cartoon playing in a nearby drive-in. With the animated antics appearing across the couple's face in the window, we watch Clovis improvising the comedy sound effects – Roadrunner's 'beep beep', fizzing dynamite – as the action unfurls. When Wile E plunges off the cliff, Clovis's face goes from joy to despair as he registers the coyote's demise as a precursor of his own fate. A homespun sound-effects-spotting session, it is one of the most moving scenes in any Spielberg film.

WHAT'S THE SCORE? An avid collector of movie soundtracks since his teens, Spielberg discovered John Williams listening to the score for a Steve McQueen movie, *The Reivers* (1969). Finishing up *Sugarland*, Spielberg called Williams, who was by then an Oscar winner for adapting *Fiddler on the Roof* (1971) and a leading composer in the disaster-movie genre (for example, *The Poseidon Adventure* (1972), *Earthquake* (1974)), and invited him to look at this picture. It was a low-key start to the director's most enduring creative relationship.

Spielberg had originally conceived the score for *Sugarland* as a broad, big symphonic piece in the vein of *The Reivers* – very bold, very sweeping, very American. After seeing the film, Williams (for the first but not last time) persuaded the director to go another way: for the small-scale, human story, Williams suggested an intimate, tender sound created by a small orchestra. To locate the movie firmly in Texas, Williams used harmonica as the dominant voice in the composition and utilised the celebrated Dutch harmonica maestro 'Toots' Thielemans as his musical conduit.

Shot through with a folksy simplicity, the score is used sparingly in the film, to heighten the verisimilitude: the main theme is haunting and direct (the first few notes are very similar to 'The Twelve Days of Christmas') and spun out in various guises across the movie – most poignantly as Lou Jean writes 'Hi' on the back window to Captain Tanner. Williams also concocted a soft drumming rhythm that has a backwoodsy feel to it (it accompanies Captain Tanner pushing 2311 up the hill) and, to underline the more dynamic aspects of the story, an almost military snares'n'string motif that joins the patrol cars on the chase.

UNSUNG HERO: The stunt co-ordinator, Carey Loftin, who not only choreographed (and on occasion improvised) the mêlée of motor action along the Texan highways but also ensured that not one stunt person in his charge suffered any injury. As well as designing the carnage, Loftin drove in many of the key sequences, in particular the night-time collision sequence in which 2311 is sideswiped by an oncoming police car. Realising that hitting the principal vehicle would require a delicate touch, Loftin opted to drive the careering police car, hitting his mark to perfection. A veteran of *Duel*, Loftin displays an ability to create exciting stunt work that never stretches the bounds of credibility and gives *Sugarland* some of its most impactful, memorable moments. Consider the TV crew van capsizing, sending six reporters flailing into the air, or the police car scramble out of the football stadium, which mixed eleven stuntmen with 43 police officers who drove like maniacs because they had been riled by the film crew.

GEDDIT! In *Sugarland*'s true-life inspiration, Bobby Dent was shot by a Robertson County sheriff named ET Elliott. Both those initials and that surname would play pivotal roles in a later Spielberg blockbuster.

At one point during a nocturnal pursuit, a bored Clovis holds a torch under his face, creating a classic horror-film lighting strategy. This echoes a childhood prank Spielberg used to play on his sisters, while intoning 'I am the mooon!' for added scare value.

Baby Langston is played by Harrison Zanuck, Richard D Zanuck's son.

The foster father of baby Langston is played by Merrill L Connally, who went on to work with Spielberg again as the Team Leader in *Close Encounters*.

Ted Grossman, who plays Metz in *Sugarland*, later became a stuntman on *Jaws*.

The final scenes of the movie were shot adjacent to the Amistad Dam – coincidentally, the title of Spielberg's slave epic some 24 years later.

FACTOID FRENZY: Scouting for locations on *Sugarland*, Spielberg checked into an antiquated hotel in Jefferson, Texas. As he got ready for bed, the director kept glimpsing a figure out of the corner of his eye which disappeared on closer scrutiny. Moments later, the entire room went cold. After quickly firing off snapshots, Spielberg scarpered to the nearby Holiday Inn. *Poltergeist*, anyone?

With the crew away from home, holed up in motels, nookie with the indigenous populace was rife among the *Sugarland* unit. Indeed, four of the crew ended up staying on in Texas and marrying local girls.

Keep 'em peeled for the actor Steve Kanaly as Officer Jessup. Kanaly found fame later in the 70s as Ray Krebbs in *Dallas*.

At one point, half the crew were incapacitated by a flu bug from London. Indeed, there was a hiatus in production as Goldie Hawn was left stricken in bed for two days.

Spielberg brought back two mementos from the location – the revolving chicken sign from the scene at the drive-in, which was installed at his quarters at Universal, and the Poplins' bullet-ridden police car 2311, which he drove around town before donating it to a museum.

Sugarland's assistant director, Jim Fargo, went on to direct *The Enforcer* (1976) and *Every Which Way But Loose* (1978) for Clint Eastwood.

THE CRITICAL FACULTY: 'Spielberg could be that rarity among directors, a born entertainer – perhaps a new generation's Howard Hawks . . . In terms of the pleasure that technical assurance gives an audience, the film is one of the most phenomenal debut films in the history of movies.' (Pauline Kael, *The New Yorker*.) 'The arrival of an extraordinarily talented new filmmaker.' (Paul D Zimmerman, *Newsweek*.) 'One is apt to fear for the second film of a promising young director, but for once the anxiety was unnecessary.' (Dilys Powell, *The Times*.) 'A prime example of the new style factory movie: slick, cynical, mechanical, empty . . . Everything is underlined: Spielberg sacrifices narrative logic and character consistency for quick thrills and cheap laughs.' (Stephen Farber, The *New York Times*.)

BOX OFFICE: Delayed from a Thanksgiving opening to avoid more heavyweight releases such as *The Exorcist* (1973) and Zanuck and Brown's *The Sting*, *The Sugarland Express* opened on 5 April in 250 theatres, grossing a modest $7.5 million in the USA, earning an additional $5.3 million in overseas revenues. Spielberg heard about the film's failure to hit big at the most inopportune moment – the day he started filming on *Jaws*.

AWARDS: Pretty much neglected in its homeland, *The Sugarland Express* won its only major award abroad: Best Screenplay at the Cannes Film Festival. Spielberg was also nominated in the Best Director category.

JOIN THE DOTS: Kids – *Jaws, Close Encounters of the Third Kind, 1941, E.T. The Extra-Terrestrial, Twilight Zone: The Movie, Indiana*

Jones and the Temple of Doom, The Color Purple, Empire of the Sun, Hook, Jurassic Park, Schindler's List, The Lost World: Jurassic Park, Amistad. **Kidnapped kids** – *Close Encounters of the Third Kind, Indiana Jones and the Temple of Doom, Empire of the Sun, Hook, Schindler's List, Amistad.* **Suburbia** – *Close Encounters of the Third Kind, E.T. The Extra-Terrestrial, Empire of the Sun, The Lost World: Jurassic Park.* **Dolly zoom** – *Jaws, E.T. The Extra-Terrestrial, Indiana Jones and the Last Crusade.* **Contemporary setting** – *Jaws, Close Encounters of the Third Kind, E.T. The Extra-Terrestrial, Twilight Zone: The Movie, Always, Hook, Jurassic Park, The Lost World: Jurassic Park.* **Based on real-life events** – *1941, Empire of the Sun, Schindler's List.* **Movies within movies** – *Close Encounters of the Third Kind, 1941, E.T. The Extra-Terrestrial.* **Absent fathers** – *Close Encounters of the Third Kind, E.T. The Extra-Terrestrial, The Color Purple, Empire of the Sun, Indiana Jones and the Last Crusade, Hook.*

SEND IN THE CLONES! On its release, *The Sugarland Express* was flanked by two other movies in which criminal lovers take to the open road. Robert Altman's *Thieves Like Us* (1974) was a typically (for Altman) loose remake of *They Live By Night* (1948) with Keith Carradine and Shelley Duvall taking flight, whereas Terrence Malick's *Badlands* (1973) starred Martin Sheen and Sissy Spacek in a lyrical retelling of the Charles Starkweather killing spree (Spielberg would go head to head with Malick again with the face-off between *Saving Private Ryan* and *The Thin Red Line*). Although all three films were critically praised, none did well at the box office – Spielberg is a firm believer that all three films nullified each other's chances in the marketplace. Other subsequent films that can be located in this 70s obsession with the open road include *Citizen's Band* (1977), *Smokey and the Bandit* (1977) *Corvette Summer* (1978), *Convoy* (1978) and *The Driver* (1978).

While hardly carbon copies of *The Sugarland Express*, 90s films and couples that have taken a similar route include *Kalifornia* (1993, Brad Pitt and Juliette Lewis), *True Romance* (1993, Christian Slater and Patricia Arquette), *Natural Born Killers* (1994, Woody Harrelson and Juliette Lewis, again). Clint Eastwood's *A Perfect World* (1993) plays similar riffs, particularly in its complex relationship between kidnapper (Kevin Costner) and captive (TJ Lowther) and the sense of the police procession in pursuit.

FINAL ANALYSIS: While many first films of great directors tend to be uneven affairs graced by flashes of brilliance, *The Sugarland Express* is the genuine article. Marking a seamless transition from TV to movies, all the hallmarks that would later define Spielberg's genius are not only present but fully formed: skilful story construction, an unerring correctness in the camera placement and editing, superbly marshalled action, empathy towards fundamentally likable human beings, a clutch of great performances – Johnson and Atherton in particular shine – all coalesce to create a gem of a debut movie.

In fact, the only thing keeping *Sugarland* from being archetypal Spielberg was its complete failure at the box office. Theories have abounded about why the film never caught the public imagination: the title made it sound too much like a children's flick; audiences failed to accept fluffy Goldie Hawn in a serious role; the whole story arc was just too much of a downer. But, released in an age where movie marketing was just starting to come into its own, *Sugarland* failed to reach an audience because it was a difficult film to sell to the public; it was an anti-establishment stance that presented its authority figures as rounded and sympathetic; a lovers-on-the-lam frolic that was marinated in melancholy. While its contradictions and complexity are among its most interesting aspects, these were never going to translate into long lines around the block.

Steven Spielberg's least-seen film is the most underrated picture of his career. Striking a perfect balance between character and action without a shred of sentimentality in sight, *Sugarland* has much more thematic density than many of the movies that have followed it and it doesn't ever resort to heavy-handed direction in order to make a point. The intrusive nature of the media, the public craving for celebrity, the American fascination with guns, the pervasive influence of car culture – the low-speed chase of OJ Simpson is nothing if not *Sugarland* writ real – are all invoked and dissected with a gossamer touch. If Spielberg had stayed closer to the interests and subtleties of his first film rather than focusing on more spectacle-derived moments, the world might have a completely different perception of him as a film-maker today.

SPIELBERG ON SPIELBERG: 'It's a terrible indictment of the media more than anything else. It was a circus on wheels . . . Also, I liked the idea of here is the American condition of today, that people want to be part of the Walter Cronkite seven o'clock news. They don't just want to watch it, they want to be in it. And I like the idea that today any one of us can create a major news story by doing the smallest, most simple neurotic act – which is sort of what this picture's about. It's really an act of the heart. It's an errand of mercy but it is so simplistic that it had to develop, it had to mushroom into something that fucked up.'

Jaws (1975)

(Colour, 124 mins)

Studio Universal
Music John Williams
Editing Verna Fields
Director of Photography Bill Butler
Written by Peter Benchley, Carl Gottlieb (based on the novel by Peter Benchley)
Produced by Richard D Zanuck, David Brown
Production Design Joseph Alves Jr
Special Effects Robert A Mattey
Production Executive William S Gilmore Jr
Underwater Photography Rexford Mex
Camera Operator Michael Chapman
Sound John R Carter, Robert Hoyt
Unit Production Manager Jim Fargo
First Assistant Director Tom Joyner
Second Assistant Director Barbara Bass
Script Supervisor Charlsie Bryant
Location Casting Shari Rhodes
Set Decorator John M Dwyer
Technical Adviser Manfred Zendar
Live-Action Shark Footage Filmed by Ron and Valerie Taylor

CAST: Roy Scheider (*Martin Brody*), Richard Dreyfuss (*Matt Hooper*), Robert Shaw (*Quint*), Lorraine Gary (*Ellen Brody*), Murray Hamilton (*Vaughn*), Carl Gottlieb (*Meadows*), Jeffery C Kramer (*Hendricks*), Susan Backlinie (*Chrissie*), Jonathan Filley (*Cassidy*), Chris Rebello (*Michael Brody*), Jay Mello (*Sean Brody*), Ted Grossman (*Estuary Victim*), Lee Fierro (*Mrs Kintner*), Jeffrey Voorhees (*Alex Kintner*), Craig Kingsbury (*Ben Gardner*), Dr Robert Nevin (*Medical examiner*), Peter Benchley (*Interviewer*).

BUDGET: $9/10 million

MPAA: PG

BBFC: A

TITLE SEQUENCE: The principal cast names appear simply white on black accompanied by John Williams's inimitable cello E notes. As the music breaks into a run, an underwater camera probes through seaweed, past coral, exploring the mysteries of the deep. This not only produces instant tension but also immediately keys the audience into the shark's calling card – a zigzag camera movement accompanied by that primal theme. As the music reaches its climactic shrill, the images switch to a nocturnal beach party, the soundtrack to a harmonica. The rest of the credits play out against a background of hippie-esque revellers, canoodling couples, a bonfire and a young woman chased into the water for a skinny dip . . .

PLOT SUMMARY: *Jaws* begins with one of the most memorable, powerful, celebrated opening sequences in movie history: Chrissie Watkins, a party girl out for a good time, goes for a midnight dip off the coast of the fictional Long Island resort of Amity Island. As she treads water waiting for her drunken suitor, she is pulled below the surface by an unseen force that proceeds to thrash her through the water with a savage ferocity. Almost as soon as it has begun, the attack is over, the victim's remains washed ashore.

After a coroner's examination confirms that the cause of Chrissie's death is a shark attack, the chief of police, Martin Brody, who has fled with his family to the calm of Amity to escape the hell-hole of New York, attempts to close the beaches. Pressured by town officials, chiefly by the altruistic Mayor Vaughn, and local businesses who rely on summer dollars for their livelihoods, Brody is coerced into keeping the beaches open. In a scene of brilliantly orchestrated terror, his worse fears are realised, however, as the shark takes the life of young Alex Kintner, ensuring a 24-hour closure of the beach.

With a $10,000 reward posted for the capture of the shark, all of Amity's local sportsmen take to the water in search of the killer. Now joined by Matt Hooper, a shark expert from the Oceanographic Institute, Brody watches some amateur fishermen bring home a tiger shark that Hooper believes is too small to be the killer fish. Later that night, Brody and Hooper perform an autopsy and their suspicions are confirmed – it's the wrong shark. A late-night foray into the sea reveals the shark has attacked a local fisherman's boat. A tooth tells Hooper that Amity Island is being targeted by a great white shark – a fact that Mayor Vaughn ignores in order to capitalise on the upcoming Fourth of July tourist trade.

The Fourth of July weekend arrives. Brody ups the safety ante on the beach with guards on towers and Hooper patrolling the waters. Still, after the shark manages to strike in a nearby estuary, Brody forces Vaughn into hiring Quint, a foul-mouthed veteran shark hunter, to catch the shark. Brody (overcoming his fear of the water) and Hooper join Quint aboard his vessel, the *Orca*, to begin the hunt.

Whereas other film directors may have opted to occasionally return to land (e.g., cloying scenes with Brody's wife and kids), Spielberg has the confidence to play the rest of the movie out at sea. In between the shark's infrequent appearances, conflicts are developed (a growing antagonism between Quint and Hooper), motivations revealed (Quint's shark vendetta emerges from being stranded in shark-infested waters after the torpedoing of the USS *Indianapolis*) – and a believable bond is formed as the men unite to quell the force of nature. Although the trio succeed in slowing the shark down by slugging barrels into its side, the hunters soon become the hunted as the great white launches various assaults on the *Orca*.

With no options left, Hooper goes underwater in an anti-shark cage with the vague hope of shooting a poison-tipped spear into the fish's mouth. The shark rips the cage to pieces before moving on to the *Orca*, gobbling up the boat and Quint in huge chomps. With barely any piece of wreckage above water, Brody contrives to shove a compressed-oxygen tank into the shark's mouth, then blows it up by shooting at the tank with his rifle. A presumed dead Hooper joins a relieved Brody and the two paddle home on a makeshift float, Brody's fear of the water a long-distant memory.

BACKSTORY: *Jaws* was Peter Benchley's first novel. An associate editor at *Newsweek*, Benchley had based his book on an item in the *New York Daily News* about a Long Island fisherman, Frank Mundus, who harpooned a shark weighing an estimated 4,400 pounds (Mundus became the obvious inspiration for Quint). A lifelong shark obsessive, Benchley fashioned the raw material into an *Enemy of the People*-style thriller, concluding with an elongated sea hunt. Very quickly, the property became the subject of a film-industry feeding frenzy: Universal wanted the book for Alfred Hitchcock; Columbia sought *Jaws* for Stanley Kramer. Yet the producers Richard D Zanuck and David Brown won out, paying $175,000 for the rights. Considering the logistics, Zanuck and Brown initially thought an experienced action director was needed – *The Great Escape*'s (1963) John Sturges was considered, as was Dick Richards, who talked himself out of the gig at a lunch with Benchley by continually referring to the shark as 'the whale'.

Jaws entered Steven Spielberg's life after he stole the manuscript from Zanuck and Brown's office as reading material for the weekend. Although he was concerned at being stereotyped a 'truck and shark director', Spielberg's keenness for the project extended to producing storyboards from sequences in the novel and even producing *Jaws* T-shirts in an effort to convince Zanuck and Brown that he was the man for the job. However, his enthusiasm backfired on him: when Spielberg announced he was jumping ship to direct the Paul Newman adventure *Lucky Lady* (1975), Zanuck and Brown turned up to the meeting wearing their Spielberg-gifted *Jaws* T-shirts. The shaming ploy worked and Spielberg signed on the proverbial dotted line in June 1973.

Spielberg's first task was to streamline the novel, excising the sordid affair between Hooper and Brody's wife, Mayor Vaughn's underworld dealings with the mafia and the film's overt *Moby Dick* correlations. After Benchley had produced two draft screenplays, Spielberg turned to the Pulitzer prizewinning playwright and screenwriter Howard Sackler, who spent five weeks on an uncredited script polish. Following Spielberg's own unsatisfactory attempts to rewrite the script – one of his more outlandish notions included ending the movie with a swarm of shark fins approaching Amity – the director turned to his old pal Carl Gottlieb, a comedy writer and TV script consultant, to punch the script up on location, producing new scenes on a daily basis.

One enduring piece of *Jaws* mythology that remains a mystery is who actually penned Quint's chilling tale of the USS *Indianapolis*. Based on a real-life event that happened on 29 July 1945, Quint tells the story of a US military cruiser that was sunk by six torpedoes, sending 800 crew into the water who began floating in linked clusters. Around fifty died overnight (from drowning, torpedo injuries and hydrophobia), but then, for three days until the rescue, sharks picked off around five hundred sailors. For years it was thought that the writer–director John Milius – a mine of military yarns – had supplied the tale, as he claimed he had dictated it over the phone to Spielberg on location. While it is indisputable that Milius wrote the scar-comparing scene that precedes the *Indianapolis* speech, others have disputed his sole authorship of the latter. The writer Carl Gottlieb has stated that the seed of the scene was sown with Howard Sackler and was developed by Robert Shaw, who performed the speech one night at dinner. Spielberg further complicates this by adding all three to the mix: Sackler wrote it, Milius embellished it and Shaw revised it. Whoever wrote it – Shaw later claimed sole responsibility while Roy Scheider has said many people on the set chipped in with contributions – the scene resonates through the rest of *Jaws*, layering Quint with extra dimensions of motivation and upping the dramatic (and horrific) ante of the rest of the sea hunt.

ORIGINS: For such a populist blockbuster, *Jaws* has surprising roots in a troika of classic literature: as the critic Nigel Andrews, among others, has outlined, the notion of a small town riddled with underhand double dealing and moral subterfuge belongs to Ibsen's *An Enemy of the People*; the elevating of a sea beast to almost mythic status can be traced to the heart of Melville's *Moby Dick*; and Coleridge's *The Rime of the Ancient Mariner* is a poetic encapsulation of *Jaws*' final act, depicting how the solitude of a life on the ocean can diminish the hardest souls.

Charting its influences from the big screen – anything from *King Kong* (1933) to *The Beast From 20,000 Fathoms* (1953) to *Godzilla* (1954) – *Jaws* is a 'monster' movie writ aquatic. It also has its foot in the 70s trend of disaster movies – see *Airport* (1970), *The Poseidon Adventure* (1972), *Earthquake* (1974), *The Towering Inferno* (1974) – where a force of nature picks off hapless victims one by one until the indominatable human spirit prevails.

CASTING: *Jaws* is positive proof that the cast lists that become enshrined in movie history often bear little resemblance to the first names scribbled on paper napkins. For Hooper, Spielberg first considered Jon Voight, Timothy Bottoms, Jeff Bridges and *Cabaret*'s Joel Grey before plumping for Richard Dreyfuss. Hot after George Lucas's *American Graffiti* (1973), Dreyfuss originally turned the role down, stating that it was a film he'd much rather watch than make. The actor changed his mind after catching his own performance in *The Apprenticeship of Duddy Kravitz* (1974) – believing he was so dreadful and fearing future lack of employment, Dreyfuss called Spielberg immediately and begged for the part.

Charlton Heston campaigned vigorously for the role of Brody, yet Spielberg wanted a more human, vulnerable presence. The role was offered to Robert Duvall – who really wanted to play Quint! – until David Brown talked Spielberg into using the Chicago actor Roy Scheider, who had received plaudits for *The French Connection* (1971).

For the pivotal role of Quint, Lee Marvin turned down Spielberg's offer point-blank. Sterling Hayden declined because he couldn't leave Paris owing to insurmountable tax problems. Finally Robert Shaw, fresh from a performance in Zanuck and Brown's Oscar-winning *The Sting* (1973), won out – yet, like Hayden, he was also beset with tax issues, avoiding the IRS by spending his non-filming days in Montreal or Bermuda.

Yet, before the inimitable trio were in place, the first role to be cast was Ellen Brody. Richard Zanuck wanted his wife Laura Harrison to play the role but Spielberg went one better, offering the role to Lorraine Gary, wife of the then Universal president Sid Sheinberg. Not only did he have a credible actress in a potentially bland role, but the inexperienced director had an insurance policy against getting fired.

PRODUCTION: Misguidedly, Zanuck and Brown believed it would be possible to train a real shark to perform for the camera. From a shopping list of sixteen shots prepared by Spielberg, two Australian shark documentarians, Ron and Valerie Taylor, were hired to capture shots of the shark circling and attacking Hooper's cage. The shoot was embellished by a genius idea from the producer Richard D Zanuck: to make the shark look even more imposing, Zanuck hired the four-foot-eleven midget stuntman Carl Rizzo to double as Richard Dreyfuss while the actor would shoot reaction shots in the safety of a tank at a later date.

Dropping anchor just off the Great Barrier Reef, the crew were ready to film when a great white, responding to the horse-meat bait, surfaced and mangled the empty metal cage to a wiry mess. Rizzo immediately scarpered and locked himself in the ship's loo. Although Spielberg never got any shark-versus-Rizzo footage, the shots of great whites circling and devouring the empty cage were so great he decided to accommodate them: in the book, Hooper went the way of Quint; now he would swim to safety.

Principal photography began at Martha's Vineyard on 2 May 1974. The challenges were virtually insurmountable: an unfinished script, changeable weather, a failing mechanical shark, keeping the horizon clear from pleasure boats and tourists plus the sheer logistics of filming at sea (for instance, a squall toppled the camera into the drink and the film was emergency-helicoptered to New York and salvaged) saw the schedule escalate from 55 days to 159. Working under the constant threat of being fired, Spielberg had to contend with studio discontentment over the rushes – where *was* the action? – and more frequent visitations from suits, one uncharitable exec suggesting Universal could earn back their investment by displaying the shark on the Studio Tour and charging an extra nickel.

With the crew dubbing the film 'Flaws', the elongated shoot saw scenes set at the height of summer now shot in the depths of winter. Tensions ran high. Scheider went crazy one night, inaugurating a massive food fight. Shaw and Dreyfuss began a running feud – Shaw gave the youngster insulting advice and blasted him with cold water, Dreyfuss poured away Shaw's whiskey – although many claim it was the belligerent Shaw's way of generating the fictional antipathy between Hooper and Quint. Yet somehow Spielberg harnessed the siege mentality to his advantage. The escalating schedule meant the actors had time to find their characters and develop a rapport that adds dimension to potentially cardboard characterisations.

On the last day of shooting – 17 September 1974 – Spielberg sported his most expensive denim outfit to stave off a dunking from the mutinous crew. As the last shot was in the can, he jumped into a waiting speedboat and sped shorewards yelling, 'I shall not return.' After the shoot had finished, Spielberg and Dreyfuss spent a night cutting loose in a Boston hotel. Indeed they swore so loudly they were thrown out by the management. Spielberg subsequently suffered anxiety attacks and experienced dreams of Martha's Vineyard a full three months after finishing his *Jaws* tour of duty.

TICS OF THE TRADE: While Spielberg's early plan was to bathe the Amity scenes in an enveloping sunshine – a look based on the art of the painter Andrew Wyeth – and have the last act with the hunt descend into a more foreboding feel, the weather and a temperamental shark dictated a more ad hoc approach. Yet, once again, the minuses were turned into pluses. Forced into shooting the sea-set scenes in a handheld style, the camera operator, Michael Chapman, under the guidance of the cinematographer, Bill Butler, gave the movie a direct, realistic, fresh look. Considering all the limitations – physical, mechanical, financial – Spielberg's control of the film-making elements is astonishing: from colour (the only red in the film is the scarlet of blood) to the use of the widescreen format (as Chrissie is tugged from left to right, Spielberg uses the whole frame for dynamic ends); from the implication of menace to the music (the famous two-note cello leitmotif accompanies only the actual shark, not the various red herrings), the movie-making guile is seamless, never calling attention to itself. It is always at the service of the story.

Spielberg does, however, allow himself an audacious moment of directorial virtuosity. As a nervous Brody watches little Alex Kintner being swallowed by the shark, Spielberg performs a dolly zoom (the camera is pushed towards a subject while simultaneously zooming out), which means that Roy Scheider stays the same size in the frame while the background explodes backwards – a stunning visual embodiment of Brody's anxiety and horror. Subsequently overused by almost everyone, the effect was appropriated from the bell-tower finale of Hitchcock's *Vertigo* (1958). The 27-year-old Spielberg had the confidence to practically throw it away on a scene twenty minutes in.

CLASSIC LINES:
Hooper: 'What we are dealing with here is a perfect engine – an eating machine. It's really a miracle of evolution. All this machine does is swim and eat and make little sharks.'

Brody: (after witnessing the shark for the first time): 'You're gonna need a bigger boat.' (This line, never in the original script, was an ad-lib by Scheider.)

Hooper: 'That's a twenty-footer.'
Quint: 'Twenty-five.'

COMIC RELIEF: Like the best of Hitchcock, *Jaws* finds its humour at the height of its suspense. Sly red herrings occur prior to both the second and third shark attacks that drop the guard for the real shock tactics: the former has Brody mistake an elderly bather's black hat for the shark; the latter has the beach evacuated over two kids peddling a fake fin. Yet, more than providing respite from the tension, *Jaws'* humour grows from and helps to define its characters: the classic moment in which Hooper squashes a plastic beaker in response to

Quint's crushing a beer can comments more about the characters – their class differences, attitudes to machismo – than reams of dialogue ever could (the scene was cooked up by Spielberg, Dreyfuss and Gottlieb in a Boston hotel room). Similarly, a pissing contest in which the pair compare scars prior to the USS *Indianapolis* story is a funny indication that the men are slowly finding common ground.

VISUAL EFFECTS: After plans to train real sharks to perform movie stunts were jettisoned, the *Jaws* production decided to go the mechanical route. Spielberg had been very impressed by the squid in Disney's *20,000 Leagues Under the Sea* (1954) and lured the veteran mechanical-effects expert Robert A Mattey out of retirement. Housed in a workshop dubbed Shark City, Mattey and his crew built three mechanical great whites, collectively nicknamed Bruce after Bruce Ramer, Spielberg's particularly rapacious lawyer. The first two Bruces – one that could be filmed only from the left, the other exclusively from the right – were mounted on a crane-like arm which ran on submerged steel rails allowing a run of seventy feet in a straight line. The third Bruce was life size, photo-realistic from every angle and attached to a sea sled operated by scuba divers. Each one had skin made of polyurethane, motors and pneumatic rams to operate the eyes, mouth and tail, weighed half a ton and cost around $200,000 to build.

Bruce had never been tested under construction in LA, and his first outing in the real ocean proved both problematic and costly: barnacles gathered on the substructure and had to be constantly scraped off; the corrosive effects of salt water meant that Bruce needed a new skin and running repairs every week; the shark's first attempts to leap on to the *Orca* (and eat Quint) saw the boat begin to sink; Bruce even whacked his nose on the towing platform. Perhaps all the technical nightmares would have been worthwhile if the results had looked great on film. But they didn't. 'Bruce's eyes crossed and his jaws wouldn't shut right,' noted the director Brian De Palma on seeing early footage.

Yet it is precisely this hokey, rubbery quality – watch the teeth bend back as the shark chomps into Quint – that endears Bruce (and *Jaws*) to film fans. On its twentieth anniversary Spielberg announced (as yet unfulfilled) plans to revisit *Jaws* with computer-generated imagery to spruce up Bruce's performance. Yet, in this case, the pursuit of perfection misses the point – there is something homespun about *Jaws'* title star that makes it more fun than pixels could ever muster.

SOUND EFFECTS: As well as a great film to watch, *Jaws* is a unique movie to listen to. From Quint's attention-grabbing introduction as he drags his fingernails down the blackboard to the carefully placed ringing buoys after each death to the clicking of Quint's fishing reel as the great white runs with the line, the film boasts a richly detailed soundtrack that adds texture and meaning to the unfolding drama.

Some sound-effects trivia: Chrissie's screams in the opening attack are the actual cries of the actress Susan Backlinie as she was pulled in all directions at once by the crew (see **factoid frenzy**); the fizzing sound of the shark skimming through water was achieved by shaking up a large Coca-Cola bottle, spraying it on to concrete and then mixing the result with zip and water effects; and finally the death cries of the great white shark are the ones that accompany the death of the truck in *Duel*, itself appropriated from the roar of the Gil-Man from *The Creature From the Black Lagoon* (1954).

WHAT'S THE SCORE? Originally Spielberg had conceived the theme music for *Jaws* as something melodic and gentle that would stand in direct contrast to the shark's malevolent menace. Yet John Williams had other ideas: with one hand, he played the director a chugging two-note theme that slowly gathered momentum, describing the effect as akin to a shark – 'instinctual, relentless, unstoppable'. Subsequently, the theme has become the most instantly recognisable of all film themes – Spielberg believed it accounted for around a third of the movie's box-office takings – yet it should not detract from the rest of the score: *Jaws* is full of jaunty jigs (to represent Quint's seafaring saltiness), high drama (check out the fugue that underscores the building of the anti-shark cage) and spirited adventure music (reminiscent of the 30s pirate scores by Erich Korngold) that make scenes between three men and a plastic shark soar.

CUT SCENES: Many of the scenes that Spielberg jettisoned during the cutting of *Jaws* were intended to expand on the character of Quint yet were lost to keep the story moving. These scenes include: a shot of Quint's truck emblazoned with his monicker and the white outline of a shark; a scene depicting Quint's shipmate telling him he won't go on the shark hunt (scenes of Quint's accomplice walking the streets of Amity were also excised); and, best of all, a terrific sequence in which Quint enters a music shop to buy piano wire and ends up ridiculing a small boy playing the clarinet – the scene has an added poignancy if you consider that a young Steven Spielberg was very fond of playing the clarinet. (Spielberg also played third clarinet at the *Jaws* recording session.)

Missing scenes away from Quint include Hooper relating a dirty phone call he once made as he performs the autopsy on the tiger shark, Ellen feeding the Brody mutts and the shark pursuing Brody's son Michael during the Fourth of July celebrations.

When Spielberg was happy with the final cut, *Jaws* was first tested with a real audience in Dallas's Medallion Theater on 26 March 1975. As Spielberg paced in the shadows, an audience member ran out from the auditorium (the Kintner death was exploding on the screen), vomited in the lobby, then immediately returned to his seat. 'That's when I knew we had a hit,' noted the director. Indeed, *Jaws* went down so well that night that a second screening had to be arranged.

A screening in Long Beach two days later confirmed everybody's hopes – *Jaws* was going to go ballistic. As a result of that preview, Scheider's classic line, 'You're gonna need a bigger boat', was given more emphasis in the sound mix, as it was often drowned by audience reactions to the shark's big entrance. Yet the biggest change to emerge from this screening was in the discovery of the dead fisherman, Ben Gardner. Feeling it didn't have enough impact, Spielberg restaged the scene in the swimming pool of the editor, Verna Field, throwing a tarpaulin over the top to simulate night conditions and adding half a gallon of milk to the water to make it more photogenic. With camera equipment secretly borrowed from the studio, the restaging included just a severed dummy head to scare the bejesus out of Richard Dreyfuss. The scene is probably the most effective scare of the movie but it does beg a question: what sort of man-eating shark spits a head back into the hull of a boat?

UNSUNG HERO: The film editor Verna Fields, who not only managed to edit a whole movie around a fake-looking shark while still keeping the suspense credible but also juggled shots that would never match – sunny days next to cloudy, choppy seas next to calm – with such rhythm that even the most anal of continuity spotters does not notice/care. Nicknamed 'Mother Cutter' by the younger generation of 70s directors (she also presided over *The Last Picture Show* [1971] and *American Graffiti* [1973]), Fields edited the movie on location, often badgering Spielberg to get the footage she needed. Be it individual sequences (each shark attack is exemplary engineered tension) or the ebb and flow of the story as a whole (slow, patient, no shark build-up seguing into full-steam-ahead action) the result is a masterclass in movie editing.

GEDDIT! The author Peter Benchley plays a newscaster reporting on the shark attacks.

The screenwriter Carl Gottlieb plays Amity's newspaper editor, Harry Meadows.

The Brodys' dog is played by Spielberg's mutt, Elmer.

The voice heard over Quint's radio introducing Ellen Brody is Spielberg's.

Ben Gardner, the fisherman who first greets Hooper on dock and later has his severed head pop out of a chewed-up hull, is played by Martha's Vineyard's legendary shark hunter Craig Kingsbury. To nail Quint, Spielberg ordered Shaw to spend as much time as possible with Kingsbury.

Jaws is the first movie to feature Spielberg's fascination with shooting stars – watch one fly over the *Orca*. See also *Close Encounters*, *E.T. The Extra-Terrestrial* and *Temple of Doom*.

FACTOID FRENZY: Amid much Island brouhaha, the Vineyard police chief, Jesse Oliver, was caught taking handouts from the film company. He was subsequently demoted to the lowly status of the town's fourth cop.

For the opening Chrissie attack, the actress Susan Backlinie was placed in a harness and pulled around by groups of crew members in a human game of tug of war.

The lovely moment where Brody's son mimics his father at the dinner table came about after Spielberg noticed that Jay Mello was copying the actor's every move. A replay of the moment later found its way into *E.T.*

Spielberg brought his own pillow with him on location and filled it with celery because he found the smell comforting. Ah, bless!

When Spielberg's film-making friends, including George Lucas, John Milius, Hal Barwood and Matthew Robbins, visited the director on set, Lucas decided to crawl into the mouth of the mechanical shark – and broke it.

Before *Jaws* opened, Spielberg had suggested that Universal market little chocolate sharks which, when bitten into, squirted cherry juice. The studio rejected the idea.

The week *Jaws* opened a great white shark bit a bather in San Diego, putting a shark on the cover of *Time* magazine and into the general consciousness. Spielberg, Zanuck and Brown insist to this day that the attack was not a publicity stunt.

Fidel Castro released pirate prints of *Jaws* into Cuban cinemas, saying, 'It's a Marxist picture. It shows that businessmen are ready to sell out the safety of the citizen rather than close down against the invasion of sharks.'

To celebrate Universal's 25th anniversary in 1989, a time capsule was buried to be opened on the 50th anniversary. Among the items included was a tooth from Bruce the shark.

THE CRITICAL FACULTY: 'A coarsegrained and exploitative work which depends on excess for its impact. Ashore it is a bore, awkwardly staged and lumpenly written.' (Charles Champlin, *Los Angeles Times*.)

'The ads show a gaping shark's mouth. If sharks can yawn that is presumably what this one is doing. It's certainly what I was doing all through this picture.' (Stanley Kauffman, *New Review*.) 'I discerned a tendency to cheer when the shark ate Mr Shaw. By then, sympathies, mine at any rate, were with the fish.' (Dilys Powell, *Sunday Times*.) A thriller of an exactly calculated effect, and a brisk old-fashioned efficiency that is almost forgotten now.' (David Robinson, *The Times*.) 'One hell of a good story, brilliantly told.' (Roger Ebert, *Chicago Sun Times*.) 'Perhaps the most perfectly constructed horror story in our time.' (*Hollywood Reporter*.) 'A production-problem-plagued film turning out beautifully. (*Variety*.) 'One of the most cheerfully perverse films ever made . . . The director, identifying himself with the Dreyfuss character, sets up barechested heroism as a joke and scores it off through the movie.' (Pauline Kael, *The New Yorker*.) 'You feel like a rat being given shock treatment.' (Molly Haskell, *The Village Voice*.)

BOX OFFICE: Released in America on 20 June 1975, *Jaws* chomped a massive $8 million in four days (from 408 theatres). Turning a profit in just fourteen days, it became the most successful film at the US box office in just eleven weeks, having grossed $458 million. This success was accompanied by the biggest merchandising/marketing ballyhoo ever to surround a movie: T-shirts, beach towels, inflatable sharks and shark-tooth jewellery became all the rage – one plucky entrepreneur even tried flogging Styrofoam shark fins; for one summer only, ice-cream flavours became Jawberry, Sharkalate and Finnila; animal-rights activists successfully put a stop to the Universal Studio Souvenir Shop flogging real shark foetuses housed in formaldehyde. Such was the *Jaws* phenomenon that, on 10 July 1975, Universal took out a full-page in the *Wall Street Journal* reminding America: 'It's a movie, too'.

AWARDS: Nominated for four Academy Awards: Best Picture, Editing, Music, Sound. *Jaws* scooped three out of the four, losing out on Best Picture to *One Flew Over the Cuckoo's Nest* (1975). In one of the more humiliating episodes of his career, Spielberg invited an LA TV news crew in to capture his reaction as the nominations were announced, confidently predicting a clean sweep for *Jaws* across the board. To his embarrassment and chagrin, Spielberg was not even nominated. Subsequently, the director has been much more reserved around Oscar time.

John Williams also picked up a BAFTA, a Golden Globe and a Grammy for his score. Verna Fields nabbed the American Cinema Editors' award for Best Edited Feature Film. And the movie itself won a People's Choice award as the 'favorite motion picture' of 1975.

THE SIZZLE! Unusually for a Spielberg production, *Jaws* was marked by a war of words – between the director and Peter Benchley. The tussle began after Spielberg had badmouthed the novel in a *Newsweek* article. Benchley retorted in the *Los Angeles Times*: 'Spielberg needs to work on character. He knows, flatly zero. Consider: He is a twenty-six-year-old who grew up with movies. He has no knowledge of reality but the movies.' Then came the killer conclusion: 'Wait and see, Spielberg will one day be known as the greatest second unit director in America.' Thankfully, way before the shoot ended, the two men made peace.

JOIN THE DOTS: Kids – *The Sugarland Express, Close Encounters of the Third Kind, 1941, E.T. The Extra-Terrestrial, Twilight Zone: The Movie, Indiana Jones and the Temple of Doom, The Color Purple, Empire of the Sun, Hook, Jurassic Park, Schindler's List, The Lost World: Jurassic Park, Amistad.* **Roller-coaster plotting** – *1941, Raiders of the Lost Ark, Indiana Jones and the Temple of Doom, Indiana Jones and the Last Crusade, Jurassic Park, The Lost World: Jurassic Park.* **Dolly zoom** – *The Sugarland Express, E.T. The Extra-Terrestrial, Indiana Jones and the Last Crusade.* **Contemporary setting** – *The Sugarland Express, Close Encounters of the Third Kind, E.T. The Extra-Terrestrial, Twilight Zone: The Movie, Always, Hook, Jurassic Park, The Lost World: Jurassic Park.* **Based on a book** – *The Color Purple, Empire of the Sun, Hook, Jurassic Park, Schindler's List, The Lost World, Amistad.*

SEND IN THE CLONES! Spielberg toyed with the idea of directing a *Jaws* sequel, tampering with scripts involving the Scheider and Dreyfuss characters and even considering a full-blown reenactment of the *Indianapolis* yarn. Yet sanity returned and Spielberg wisely left the franchise in Universal's hands; the eventual Jeannot Szwarc-directed sequel, surprisingly titled *Jaws 2* (1978), paired a contractually obligated Scheider with a group of unappealing teens to risible ends. The sequel improved on the swiftness of the shark and the tagline – 'Just when you thought it was safe to go back in the water' – but nothing else.

Things went from bad to worse with *Jaws 3-D* (1983), directed by the original film's art director Joe Alves, in which a great white attacks a marine theme park. The final harpoon in the *Jaws* thorax was *Jaws 4: The Revenge* (1987). Lorraine Gary returns as Ellen Brody, who believes the shark has developed a personal vendetta against the Brody family, so heads to the Caribbean, romantically hooks up with Michael Caine only to have the tenacious great white trace her to the island hideaway. The rest is really too awful to contemplate.

Much more enjoyable was the slew of animal-on-the-loose imitations that followed in *Jaws*' wake: *Orca* (1978 – whales), *Grizzly* (1976 – bears), *Squirm* (1976 – worms), *Tentacles* (1977 – octopus), *Cujo* (1983 – St Bernard), *Alligator* (1980 – self-explanatory) and *Piranha* (1978), Joe Dante's witty exploitation film that is Spielberg's personal favourite of the *Jaws* rip-offs. *Blood Beach* (1981) takes *Jaws* one step earlier by locating the horror beneath the sand. It also features the immortal tagline, 'Just when you thought it was safe to go back in the water, you can't cross the goddam beach.'

Peter Benchley tried (and failed) to repeat the success with *The Deep* (1977), featuring a killer manta ray, drugs, Jacqueline Bisset in a wet T-shirt, lost treasure and Robert Shaw reprising his Quint schtick. *Jaws* paved the way for the slasher genre and *Alien* (1979) is a sci-fi variant. The 1991 TV movie *Mission of the Shark* did finally get to dramatise the *Indianapolis* disaster. More recently, *Deep Blue Sea* (1999) replayed *Jaws*' licks with genetically modified sharks (earning the nickname 'Jaws Indoors') and *Lake Placid* (2000) saw a crocodile go on the rampage to comedy-horror effect.

JAWS GOES POP: One of the most parodied scenes of all time, *Jaws*'s opening der-dum der-dum gambit has found its way into a variety of movies: *Caddyshack* (1980), *The Secret Of My Success* (1987), *Top Secret* (1984), *Swingers* (1996) all riff on *Jaws*'s shark attack set-pieces. But the king of all *Jaws* opening scene skits must go to *Airplane!* (1980): as the music builds, an aircraft tail fin cuts through the clouds like a shark fin through water, before roaring over the camera.

Also, see the referential moment in *Stakeout* (1987) where Emilio Estevez and Richard Dreyfuss play a 'guess the movie' quote game: as Estevez utters 'You're gonna need a bigger boat', Dreyfuss hasn't got a clue. *The Simpsons* episode 'Radio Bart' features a guy with a fishing hook and chocolate bar clearly modelled on Quint.

More subtle allusions can be found in the movies of Kevin Smith. *Clerks* (1994) replays *Jaws* moments with a corn chip fin in a sea of salsa. *Chasing Amy* (1997) features a very funny skit riffing on the Quint–Hooper scar comparing scene with Jason Lee and Joey Lauren Adams trying to outdo each other with injuries gained during oral sex. Another indie film-maker obsessed with *Jaws* is Steven Soderbergh, who used the famous dolly zoom technique as Laura San Giacomo in *sex, lies and videotape* (1989) experiences a full-throated orgasm.

Jaws also spawned probably the most famous movie theme park attraction on the Universal Studios Tour in which the Shark attacks the studio train.

FINAL ANALYSIS: Decidedly its director's movie, *Jaws* established Spielberg as a master movie architect and a box-office heavy hitter in a single bite. It whetted Spielberg's appetite for big budgets and large-scale visual effects, elements that would dominate most of the ensuing films; it also introduced Richard Dreyfuss as a kind of Spielberg alter ego, all childish wonder and nerdy energy. Finally, it showed Spielberg the practicality of test screenings and the importance of marketing and merchandising towards a film success.

Few films are as ruthlessly effective as scaring the bejesus out of audiences than *Jaws*. Operating on a manipulation of suspense and surprise, Spielberg's mastery at guiding the audience exactly where he wants to take them is nothing short of spellbinding. Yet, bridging the gap between *Boy's Own* adventure and adult drama better than any other Spielberg film, *Jaws* is so much more than the efficient thrill machine it is often dismissed as. Building on the technical command he displayed in *Duel* and the humanity of *The Sugarland Express*, Spielberg's direction displays a typical richness of character, attention to nuance and a pervading sense of warmth that is missing from most blockbusters.

On its release, weirdy-beardy theorists doctored up all sorts of long-winded theories to define and pigeonhole *Jaws'* success: an embodiment of post-Watergate anxieties; a metaphor for male castration fears; a re-enactment of Freudian thinking (The shark is a phallic symbol – discuss). Yet, some 25 years on, the phenomenon seems easier to explain: a simple, potent tale perfectly told by a director working at the top of his game.

SPIELBERG ON SPIELBERG: 'Sometimes you can be a movie. Other times you have to pretend a movie. *Jaws* is a side of me I pretended to be. I don't really think that's who I am. I look at it now and it kind of turns my stomach.'

Close Encounters of the Third Kind (1977)

(Colour, 135 mins)

(Special Edition: released 1980, 132 mins)

Studio Columbia
Written by Steven Spielberg
Director of Photography Vilmos Zsigmond ASC
Producers Julia and Michael Phillips

Director of Photography of Additional American Scenes William A Fraker ASC (American Society of Cinematographers)
Director of Photography of Additional Indian Scenes Douglas Slocombe BSC (British Society of Cinematographers)
Production Designer Joe Alves
Special Photographic Effects Douglas Trumbull
Music John Williams
Editing Michael Kahn ACE
Visual Effects Concepts Steven Spielberg
Unit Production Manager Clark Paylow
Additional Directors of Photography John Alonzo ASC Laszlo Kovacs ASC, Frank Stanley (uncredited)
Directors of Photography – Special Edition Michael Butler, Allen Daviau
Realisation of Extra-terrestrial Carlo Rambaldi
Technical Adviser Dr J Allen Hynek
Art Director Dan Lomino
Assistant Director Chuck Myers
Supervising Sound Effects Editor Frank Warner
Production Illustrator George Jensen
Production Sound Mixer Gene Cantamessa
Special Effects Consultant Roy Arbogast
Re-recording Mixers Buzz Knudsen, Don MacDougall, Robert Glass
Costumes Jim Linn
Make-up Supervisor Bob Westmoreland
Casting Shari Rhodes, Julliette Taylor
Stunt Co-ordinator Buddy Joe Hooker
UFO Photography Dave Stewart
Chief Model Maker Gregory Jein

CAST: Richard Dreyfuss (*Roy Neary*), François Truffaut (*Claude Lacombe*), Teri Garr (*Ronnie Neary*), Melinda Dillon (*Jillian Guiler*), Cary Guffey (*Barry Guiler*), Bob Balaban (*David Laughlin*), J Patrick McNamara (*Project Leader*), Warren Kemmerling (*Wild Bill Walsh*), Roberts Blossom (*Farmer*), Philip Dodds (*Jean Claude*), Shawn Bishop (*Brad Neary*), Adrienne Campbell (*Sylvia Neary*), Justin Dreyfuss (*Toby Neary*), Lance Henriksen (*Robert*), Merrill Connally (*Team Leader*), George Dicenzo (*Major Benchley*).

BUDGET: $19 million

MPAA: PG

BBFC: A

TITLE SEQUENCE: Once again highlighting Spielberg's skill at establishing mood and securing audience involvement from the start, *Close Encounters*' title design is a fantastic parlour trick. The titles fade in and out while an unnerving ethereal shimmer begins on the soundtrack. Fuelling anticipation, the hum, augmented by eerie vocals, builds gradually to an ear-piercing crescendo as the black screen erupts into the blinding brightness of a desert sandstorm. Eagle-eyed viewers will spot that, between the blackness and the sandstorm, there are a few frames of white to heighten the effect.

PLOT SUMMARY: The present day. In the Sonora Desert, Mexico, an international team, led by a Frenchman, Claude Lacombe, discover Flight 19, a World War Two squadron believed missing in the Bermuda Triangle but still in pristine condition; in Indianapolis air-traffic control, an aircraft reports a near miss with a bright light; in Muncie, Indiana, the toys in four-year-old Barry Guiler's bedroom almost magically spring to life and he is chased into the night by his mother, Jillian.

Elsewhere in Indiana, Roy Neary, a power repairman, is called out to investigate a city-wide blackout. Stopping to look at directions, Neary finds his truck hit by a cone of intense light, the gravity in his cab going haywire. He follows the light source – a clutch of UFOs – in a high-speed nocturnal pursuit along Indiana highways, nearly running over young Barry, equally enraptured by the flying lights. Energised and half sunburned, Roy returns home and drags his bemused wife Ronnie and three kids to the scene of the sighting. All are decidedly nonplussed. Over the next few days, Roy becomes increasingly drawn into UFOmania; seeing strange visions of a mountain in pillows, shaving cream and mashed potato. He also loses his job, much to Ronnie's annoyance.

Spielberg interweaves the personal stories – the familial conflicts increase as Neary's mountain (and mounting) obsession grows stronger, Barry Guiler is kidnapped by aliens in a harrowing abduction – with the broader picture as the international team piece together the UFO puzzle. In Northern India, Lacombe witnesses a large crowd chanting a five-note sequence that they tell him came from the sky. The five tones translate mathematically into map co-ordinates to Devil's Tower, a locale in Wyoming that is hastily prepared as a UFO landing site.

While Neary constructs his most elaborate mountain structure yet (his wife has left him over it), the original structure appears on the TV news in relation to an evacuation of Wyoming due to a nerve-gas scare. Realising this is a ruse set up by the military to clear the area of the civilian populace, Neary drives to Devil's Tower, where he hooks up with Jillian, who has been having the same visions. After a brief capture by troops – Neary is interrogated by Lacombe – Neary and Jillian escape deportation to scale the mountain, an army helicopter in hot pursuit, and find the landing site on the other side.

In the last forty minutes of the film, plot in the traditional sense is jettisoned as a fantastic display of light and sound take centre stage. Heeding the call of the five tones, a cluster of small UFOs dance around Devil's Tower to scintillating effect. Yet all this is a prelude to a jaw-dropping mothership, a kind of majestic flying jukebox that enthralls all who witness it. The mothership and Earth's computers communicate through a maelstrom of music and light; the result is that a ramp opens, emitting a bright, blinding light, and various returnees emerge, chiefly the pilots of Flight 19, and Barry Guiler, who runs into the arms of an emotional Jillian.

As aliens mingle with humanity for the first time, Lacombe argues the case that Neary should be among the select group to board the mothership. Quickly suited up, Neary approaches the ship and is singled out by the ETs, who usher him aboard the spacecraft. (In the Special Edition, we see Neary inside the ship gazing in awe at the inner workings.) The ship moves up into the starry sky, the world (well, America) watching with wonder.

BACKSTORY: The genesis of *Close Encounters* can be traced through a number of events in Spielberg's formative years. Key among these is the night Spielberg's father Arnold pulled the young Steven from his slumber to watch a meteor shower career across Arizona. The scene is replayed as Roy Neary drags his wife and kids to witness the locale of his first UFO encounter. Moreover, *Close Encounters* is nothing if not a big-budget remake of the sixteen-year-old's *Firelight*, encompassing ideas of alien intruders in the heart of suburbia, the (typically for Spielberg) broken family and the thrill of scientific adventure.

In between the two in 1970, Spielberg wrote a short story entitled *Experiences* about lights in the sky which occurred over a lovers' lane while teens made out in cars. Renaming the project *Watch the Skies*, Spielberg then gave the movie a more adult spin: perhaps pitched as UFOGate, the script was couched as a political thriller in which the notion of government cover-ups and Project Blue Book – the real-life *X Files* – were much more to the fore.

The switch from conspiracy theories to the more spiritual quest that exists in the finished film was facilitated by Paul Schrader, the writer of *Taxi Driver* (1976), who was introduced to Spielberg by *Close Encounters*' producers, Julia and Michael Phillips. Entitled variously *Pilgrim* and *Kingdom Come*, Schrader's scenario was a typically religious take centred on a forty-five-year-old Air Force officer, Paul Van Owen, who, hired by the government to debunk UFO mythology, goes through a kind of enlightenment after experiencing his own encounter. Van Owen threatens to blow the lid on the existence of extra-terrestrial life. To keep him quiet the US government secretly fund his research. He then spends the next fifteen years looking for proof, only to realise that the truth isn't out there but in the elevated consciousness of his head.

With Spielberg and Schrader ultimately not seeing eye to eye (see The sizzle!), Walter Hill, then David Giler, subsequently took a crack at *Close Encounters*. The *Sugarland Express* writers, Hal Barwood and Matthew Robbins, were next up, adding the crucial element of the aliens kidnapping the child (very *Sugarland*!). Developing the project visually with the production illustrator, George Jensen, Spielberg then produced a number of drafts himself – the first time aliens were visualised in the script – calling upon Jerry Belson to hang around on location and help define the characters.

Still a few elements stuck from the Schrader scenarios, particularly the notion of a mountain vision implanted in the hero's head (the re-creation of that image in the Neary living room is also a Schrader conceit) and elements of the ending. Yet the most significant contribution Schrader made to *Close Encounters* was to find the film's unwieldy yet strangely memorable title. The phrase comes from the ufologist Dr J Allen Hynek's 1972 book *The UFO Experience: A Scientific Enquiry.* Hynek, very much a model for Paul Van Owen, defined 'Close Encounters of the First Kind' as sightings of a UFO, 'Close Encounters of the Second Kind' as physical evidence left by a UFO and 'Close Encounters of the Third Kind' as contact with alien beings.

ORIGINS: Perhaps because Spielberg, the ultimate film geek, penned the screenplay himself, the film is crammed full of references to movie history. Although the opposite of the paranoid Cold War sci-fi of the 50s – see *The Thing From Another World* (1951), *The War of the Worlds* (1953), *Them!* (1954) – *Close Encounters*' benevolent view of alien visitors is traceable to flicks such as *The Day the Earth Stood Still* (1951) and *It Came From Outer Space* (1953); the latter even has children witnessing the spacecraft land outside their bedroom. A further infant–alien interface is present in Don Siegel's *Invasion of the Body Snatchers* (1955), as it is only the kids who can spot the otherworldly visitors in human form. Kubrick's *2001: A Space Odyssey* (1968) inscribed *Close Encounters*' view of aliens as spiritual vessels. Indeed, Spielberg dipped liberally into the Kubrick film, particularly in terms of its quasi-religious tone.

Cartoons also play a prominent part in the fabric of *Close Encounters*. The UFOs chasing the police cars down the highways mirror Chuck Jones's *Road Runner* antics; the lightstorm over Devil's Tower closely resembles the terrifying phantasmagoria of the *Night On Bald Mountain* sequence from *Fantasia* (1940). *Bambi* (1942) is also alluded to, both in Jillian chasing Barry through dark woodland and in the five-tone motif, which is not a million miles from the beginning of 'April Showers'.

Yet the biggest Walt influence on the movie is *Pinocchio* (1940): while Neary's rush towards Devil's Tower is akin to Pinocchio's escape from Pleasure Island, it is Spielberg's quotation from Pinocchio's calling-card 'When You Wish Upon a Star' (as sung by Cliff 'Ukelele' Ike) that is the film's most blatant appropriation. A celebration of belief, optimism and dream fulfilment, the song appears on a musical box in the Neary household and Spielberg originally planned to have the song play over the film's finale, but the idea was scuppered after it split audience opinion at a test preview. Spielberg subsequently had John Williams integrate the song into the score of 1980's Special Edition, featuring a more full-blown orchestral rendition.

Away from Disney, the abduction of Barry recalls the plot of *The Searchers* (1956 – Spielberg watched it twice on location) and the house under siege in Hitchcock's *The Birds* (1963). Another Hitchcock film important to *Close Encounters*, particularly during the climb up Devil's Tower, is *North By Northwest* (1959) – the helicopter spraying nerve gas being an allusion to the crop-duster set piece, and Roy reaching for Jillian's hand mirrors Cary Grant and Eva Marie Saint atop Mount Rushmore. Moreover, *Close Encounters* plays on the 'ordinary man in extraordinary circumstances' motif that is at the basis of much of Hitchcock's work. Capra's *It's A Wonderful Life* (1946) is another telling touchstone: not only in terms of the affirmation of magic and optimism within ordinary America, but also the darker scenes of family tension that are often overlooked in both films.

CASTING: Originally, Spielberg wanted Jack Nicholson to play Roy Neary. Nicholson was keen but wanted to direct *Goin' South* (1978) first. The Phillipses sought Gene Hackman and Al Pacino. However, Dreyfuss had heard about *Close Encounters* all through *Jaws* and, after some pleading by the actor and financial juggling by the producers, the *Jaws* alumnus got the nod. Building on the boyish impetuosity of his *Jaws* persona, Dreyfuss complicates it with a convincing sense of obsession and despair while never losing his eminent likability.

Working his way through the Hollywood French Actors Handbook, Spielberg met all the usual suspects on a trip to Paris – Lino Ventura, Yves Montand, Jean Louis Trintignant, Phillipe Noiret and a very young Gerard Depardieu – before coming up with the inspired idea of the French film director François Truffaut to play the scientist Claude Lacombe (who was probably modelled on the real life UFO experts Aime Michel and Jacques Vallee). Best known for directing classics such as *Les Quatre Cents Coups* (1959), *Jules et Jim* (1961) and *La Nuit Americaine* (1973) Truffaut gave a performance in *L'Enfant Sauvage* (1969), in which he sensitively portrayed a nineteenth-century doctor who tries to communicate with an infant raised in the forest, that conveyed a gentleness and patience that was perfect for Lacombe.

Probably best known for her role in *Young Frankenstein* (1974), Teri Garr was cast as Neary's wife Ronnie after Spielberg spotted her in a TV coffee commercial. The role of Jillian was yet to be cast 72 hours before Spielberg was scheduled to shoot her first scene. Then the director Hal Ashby sent Spielberg ten scenes from his unfinished movie *Bound For Glory* (1976), suggesting he keep his eye on Melinda Dillon. Bowling over Spielberg, the actress was hired on the spot.

After looking at around two hundred kids, Spielberg found his Barry Guiler in a school in Douglasville, Georgia, a suburb of Atlanta. Four-year-old Cary Guffey had not only never been in front of a camera before, he had never even seen a movie.

PRODUCTION: Although scenes were shot at the Air Traffic Control Center in Palmdale, California, for two days during December 1975, *Close Encounters*' principal photography started in earnest near Gilette, Wyoming, on 16 May 1976. After Spielberg had looked at and rejected Ship Rock in Oregon, Devil's Tower National Monument, a 885-foot-high volcanic monolith, was selected as the locale for the first meeting between human and alien life. Following a two-week shoot, the crew decamped to a disused World War Two hangar in Mobile, Alabama. Having struggled with the elements on *Jaws*, Spielberg wanted to map out his story in a controlled environment – the set was six times bigger than the largest Hollywood soundstage – yet the sheer scale of the set brought its own headaches: the humidity inside the hangar generated artificial clouds and resultant drizzle; an occasional hurricane would lift the tarpaulin off the roof, making filming impossible. The movie finished up filming by travelling to Bombay for Lacombe's investigation of Indian sightings (the crowd of extras continually failed to memorise the five-note chant) and the Mojave Desert for the discovery of Flight 19 (the first scene in the movie, one of the last to be shot) before returning to Los Angeles to tie up some loose ends.

TICS OF THE TRADE: From the toys coming to life in Barry's bedroom to Neary's first 'Close Encounter', *Close Encounters* is filled with set pieces that allow a director to show off his virtuosity. Possibly because *Jaws* allowed Spielberg creative carte blanche, *Close Encounters* is significant within the director's career as establishing many of the stylistic traits that have dominated that career. Chief among these is the wielding of light to participate in the drama. 'I have always loved what I call "God light", shafts coming out of the sky, or out of a spaceship or out of a doorway. It's just been very romantic and extremely wondrous to me, light.' Light is everything in *Close Encounters*: creating mystery (the appearance of the aliens is shrouded in backlight), red herrings (the UFO that turns out to be a helicopter), terror (the orange glow that knifes through the keyhole of the Guiler household) and wonder (the spectacle of the mothership).

Following the fluid hand-held camera shots that characterised *Jaws*, *Close Encounters* is dominated by tracking (or dolly) shots, usually towards a character looking up in awe at something bigger than life. A kind of visual shorthand for impending wonder or doom, it is an image that has recurred in practically every Spielberg film since.

Close Encounters also fully announced Spielberg's genius as a director of children, capturing them with maximum spontaneity yet minimum sickliness. While it is evident in scenes within the Neary household, it is the performance of four-year-old Cary Guffey that really steals your breath. For the moment in which Barry's expression transforms from trepidation to a quizzical look, to outright delight as he follows aliens around his house, Spielberg hatched a nifty plan, dressing the make-up man, Bob Westmoreland, and himself as the Easter Bunny to elicit reactions of surprise, wonder and curiosity.

CLASSIC LINES:
Roy: 'I guess you noticed something a little strange with Dad. But it's OK, I'm still Dad. It's just that something is happening to me I can't describe.'

Team Leader: 'If everything is ready here on the dark side of the moon, play the five notes.'

Team Leader: 'They haven't aged.'
ARP Project Member: 'Einstein was right.'
Team Leader: 'Einstein was probably one of them.'

COMIC RELIEF: As ever with Spielberg, *Close Encounters*' funniest moments come from pure visual invention. Such as when the UFO investigators search frantically for a map. Cutting through the confusion with the *thwack!* of a door being kicked through, Spielberg segues to the team breaking into a darkened office and awkwardly rolling a massive globe like a beach ball. Yet the most inspired moment of visual comedy occurs as Neary, stopping in the middle of the road to check map directions, waves a car that has pulled up behind him, headlights blazing, to swerve around him. As a second car pulls up behind him, he blithely repeats the gesture, only to have the headlights of the 'car' rise up behind him – his first Close Encounter with a UFO. Sly, elegant, hilarious.

VISUAL EFFECTS: To create the most credible UFOs ever depicted on screen, Spielberg turned to the visual effects supremo Douglas Trumbull. A former technical illustrator who graduated to making animated promotional films for the Air Force and NASA, Trumbull had become the cutting-edge exponent of visual effects after his pioneering work on Kubrick's *2001: A Space Odyssey*. However, having directed his own sci-fi opus *Silent Running* (1971), Trumbull had retired as an effects-hand-for-hire and was creating state-of-the-art projection systems until Spielberg's challenge to create the unreal in a real (as opposed to outer space) environment piqued his pride.

The original conception for the mothership depicted a *2001*-esque monolithic black shape blocking out the stars, then emitting an intense white light from an opening in its underbelly. Yet two separate incidents changed Spielberg's thinking. Every day on location in India, the director was struck by a gigantic oil refinery, lit up at night by thousands of small lights and draped with pipes, tubing and walkways. This image, compounded by a barmy evening when a slightly stoned Spielberg did a handstand on the bonnet of his car and viewed the sprawl of LA upside down, transformed the idea that the mothership would have the appearance of a 'city of light'.

The resulting model was six feet in diameter, weighed forty pounds and was an intricate structure of Plexiglas, steel and plywood graced with neon and quartz bulbs. Powered by twelve motors, the model was a flat circular disc that could be fitted with a variety of shapes – cones, pyramids etc. – and rigged with neon. The mothership remains one of the most stunning visual effects in movie history. Its grace, attention to detail and majesty would be incredibly difficult to attain with contemporary CGI techniques – once seen, it immediately takes up a space in your movie memory bank.

The smaller UFOs, unlike the flying-saucer clichés of 50s sci-fi, were conceived as small clusters of bright, shining, silent lights in keeping with the majority of reported sightings. They were created through a mixture of fibre-optic and light-scanning techniques plus miniature UFO models running up and down horizontal and vertical tracks in a blacked-out studio.

Spielberg's initial idea for the creation of the aliens ranks among the most ridiculous in his whole career. To get away from the man-in-the-suit cliché, one hundred chimpanzees were dressed in tutus, adorned with fake alien heads, then pushed on roller skates through the frame – the result was apparently a scene from the golden age of slapstick. In the end, Spielberg dressed six-year-old dance students in ET costumes and shot them against a bright white light using massive overexposure techniques to give them a spindly, mysterious appearance.

For the alien emissary who communicates with humankind, Spielberg rejected initial concepts from make-up gurus Frank Griffin and Tom Burman and the puppeteer Bob Baker. Instead he hired Carlo Rambaldi, then best known as the architect behind the mechanical *King Kong* (1976). Spielberg described the alien, nicknamed Puck, as a cross between a 'foetus and a Dickens character', the idea being that, as their intellect grew (hence the big head), the ETs' use for their muscles and senses would decrease (hence the thin arms and small eyes and nose). The mechanical creation took three months to build at a cost of $30,000 and consisted of a fibreglass head and a steel and aluminium framework covered in thin polyurethane. It took a crew of fifteen to operate all the levers – like a big kid, Spielberg operated the smile function himself.

SOUND EFFECTS: With little actual reference to how UFOs and aliens actually sound, Spielberg and his supervising sound-effects editor Frank Warner were forced to get creative. Determined not to get over-cartoony, they used everyday sounds in unconventional ways, generally to create an unsettling effect: a UFO's presence is usually heralded by a cessation of all natural sounds – crickets, birds, highway ambience – which slowly fade up after the shattering experience is over. At other times, it could mean that everyday noises might be reversed, slowed down or mixed with other sounds in bizarre combinations.

'Creating the sounds for The Mothership called for a lot of discussion,' Warner told *American Cinematographer* magazine. 'We didn't want a pulsating sound, because we were trying to stay away from typical outer space pulsations. We went for a heavy low-end sound, like the sound of a big heavy furnace or a big swarm of mosquitoes.'

WHAT'S THE SCORE? The score for *Close Encounters* has the most pivotal musical role in any Spielberg film. With the screenplay dictating that man and alien communicate through lights, colours and chiefly music, Spielberg and Williams's major musical task was coming up with the memorable musical message. Williams originally wanted to use seven notes – the same as in 'When You Wish Upon a Star' – but Spielberg insisted on just five, which sounded more like a greeting than a melody. Eventually, the pair went through around three hundred five note combinations before they chose one.

With hindsight, the resulting phrase seems the only choice, perfect both in its primitive synthesiser form or in the full-blown orchestral statement, subsequently entering the *Zeitgeist* as an all-encompassing theme for alien activity. Williams composed much of the music from the script and storyboards as most of the special effects were not in place. This blind approach to composing resulted in a much more adventurous score than *Star Wars:* the score covers many musical bases charting a musical progression from atonal terror (the abduction of Barry) to lyrical majesty (the first sighting of Devil's Tower) that leaves no section of the orchestra untapped in a riveting display of symphonic virtuosity.

UNSUNG HERO: The remarkable character actor Roberts Blossom makes an indelible impression as the wild-haired, crazy-eyed farmer who watches UFOs whizz down the Indiana highway. Blossom's short time on screen is full of magical moments: his observation as the cops chase the alien vehicles, 'They can fly rings around the moon but we're years ahead of 'em on the highway'; his admission at the UFO symposium that he has also seen Bigfoot and the 'STOP AND BE FRIENDLY' sign that he holds up for the aliens.

CUT SCENES: 'Filming should never be a dry-cement process. I have the luxury of retouching the painting,' Steven Spielberg said, embarking on the Special Edition of *Close Encounters.* Given $2 million by Columbia, Spielberg was granted a further opportunity to resculpt his vision through re-editing and reshooting, but at a price – he had to show the inside of the mothership.
Scenes excised for the Special Edition included:
• Following the first scene in Neary's house, the original version followed Neary to work at the power plant where an argument is in progress about electrical havoc wreaking across the city.
• The farmer's line: 'They can fly rings around the moon but we're years ahead of them on the highway.'
• Neary lying on his bed staring at a pillow resembling the shape of Devil's Tower, while Ronnie's voice grilling him over finding a job fades out.
• A scene where Roy and Jillian attend a press conference at an air force base, whose participants deny the existence of UFOs. The farmer tells everyone he saw Bigfoot and Neary scribbles a drawing of Devil's Tower on a napkin.
• A shot showing Roy joining the table before the mashed-potato sequence.
• The hilarious scene that sees Roy throw bricks and plants through his window to create Devil's Tower in his living room. The moment where Roy climbs through the window on a small ladder is also missing from the Special Edition.
• On arriving at Devil's Tower, Roy is turned back by a guard (played

by Carl Weathers, Apollo Creed in *Rocky*) who threatens to shoot Neary if he doesn't move back.

Scenes shot omitted from the original version but returned for the Special Edition:

- After Barry runs off into the night, the Special Edition cuts to a shot of Neary's neighbourhood, then inside the house with Neary using railroad cars to explain fractions to his son. A row ensues about the family going to play goofy golf or see *Pinocchio*. The scene picks up the original version as Neary's boss calls him.
- During Roy's truck chase with the flying saucers, a shot with a UFO hovers in front of a McDonald's sign.
- A powerful sequence with Roy freaking out, taking a shower with his clothes on. Ronnie yells at him for destroying her family as the kids look on in horror, calling their father a 'crybaby'.

Completely new scenes created for the Special Edition included:

- A scene in which the International Investigation Team discover the *Cotopaxi*, a ship, in the middle of the Gobi Desert. Shot by Allen Daviau with a miniature boat by Greg Jein, the scene features Bob Balaban and J Patrick McNamara but crucially not François Truffaut. An interesting scene in itself, it adds little to the story – save broadening the search to a more global level – which the opening discovery of Flight 19 has already suggested.
- Neary entering the mothership. Combining model work by Robert Swarthe and new material with a now permed Richard Dreyfuss gazing in awe at the spacecraft interior, the resulting scene, revealing some colourful machinery, celestial 'energy' and rows of tiny little aliens, is pretty but ultimately dissipates the wonder and magic of its progenitor.

Scenes that never made it to any version of *Close Encounters* included:

- The original opening scene in which Lacombe and Laughlin arrive at an airport to investigate a commercial jet that has just passed a UFO.
- Extra footage with the aliens – aliens flying and a distorted ET-point-of-view shot.
- A scene in which Neary rewires the government building so the window lights spell out U-F-O.
- A special effect seen involving cuboids – little white boxes that emanate from the mothership and dance around like fireflies.

The Special Edition opened on 31 July to a mixed critical response and a muted public response, the net result sacrificing spectacle for character and diluting some of the original's mystery.

GEDDIT! 'Watch the Skies', the working title for *Close Encounters*, is actually the last line from Howard Hawks's sci-fi classic *The Thing From Another World* (1951).

Dr J Allen Hynek, the movie's technical adviser, has a small cameo in the film – he is the white-haired scientist who moves through the crowd as the mothership lands.

Roy Neary's son Toby is played by Justin Dreyfuss, nephew of Richard. Spielberg picked him for his strong family resemblance.

The US Air force official who misleads the group of UFO observers is named Major Benchley – a nod to the *Jaws* author, Peter Benchley.

As the TV in the Neary living room blares out *The Ten Commandments* (1956), the music that is audible is not the Elmer Bernstein score but a specially commissioned John Williams replica appropriately entitled 'The Eleventh Commandment'.

Phillip Dodds, who plays Jean Claude, the technician who actually plays the five tones, arrived on set merely to install the synthesiser. Spielberg felt he had the right look so cast him.

Among those playing returnees leaving the mothership are the *Sugarland Express* writers Hal Barwood and Matthew Robbins, and Bruce Davison, who at that time was Spielberg's next-door neighbour.

The four-legged returnee is Spielberg's cocker spaniel Elmer (now commanding an agent after his cameo in *Jaws*) – *Close Encounters of the Furred Kind*, anyone?

Keep 'em peeled for the following glued on to the side of the mothership: a 1945 aircraft (neatly tying up with the film's opening scene), Darth Vader's TIE fighter, a Volkswagen van and, visible in the scene in which the spacecraft rises above Jillian's head, an upside-down R2-D2 and C-3P0.

FACTOID FRENZY: Spielberg means 'play mountain' in German. How apt.

To achieve the moment where the UFO causes gravity to go A.W.O.L. in Neary's truck cab, Spielberg strapped Richard Dreyfuss to the seat and revolved the cab and camera 180 degrees, forcing everything – maps, torches, glove compartment contents – to fall downwards in reality but upwards on screen. The trick had been previously used in *Royal Wedding* (1951) by Fred Astaire to dance on the ceiling.

For the scene in which Lacombe and Laughlin argue with Major Walsh over Neary's right to be at Devil's Tower, François Truffaut had so much difficulty remembering his lines that he had them placed on cue cards around the set – he even pasted one on the actor Warren Kemmerling's chest.

To avoid continuity errors, Dreyfuss's digital watch revealed the time only at the press of a button.

Columbia refused to stump up extra cash for the moment where the tones of the mothership blow out the glass of a landing-site module.

Rather than lose the effect, Spielberg stumped up several thousand dollars from his own pocket for the sugar glass himself.

During one take of the mashed-potato-building sequence, Dreyfuss started pawing through the mound of carbohydrate asking, 'Is Victoria Principal in here?', the reference being that Spielberg had previously dated the soon-to-be *Dallas* star for a while.

On location in Alabama, filming halted while everybody rushed outside to witness a UFO. In reality, the light in the sky was an Echo Satellite.

When filming had finished, Spielberg presented Cary Guffey with a cup inscribed, 'Cary Guffey, Best Actor, 1976 by Steven Spielberg, Director, *Close Encounters Of The Third Kind*'.

THE CRITICAL FACULTY: 'A celebration not only of children's dreams but also of the movies that help find those dreams.' (Frank Rich, *Time*.) 'It has a visionary magic and a childlike comic spirit, along with a love of comic surprises, and a skeptical let's-go-try-it spirit. It sends you out in a state of blissful satisfaction.' (Pauline Kael, *New Yorker*.) 'The Dumbest Story Ever Told.' (Molly Haskell, *New York*.) 'This might be the most expensive gibberish ever put on screen.' (Rex Reed, *Los Angeles Times*.) 'The one salient feature of Spielberg's script is that it makes no sense whatever . . . the most monumental molehill in movie history, conveniently cone-shaped to serve as a dunce's cap for an extremely swollen head.' (John Simon, *Esquire*.) 'The most important film of our time . . . For unlike *2001* which almost knew what it wanted to say but faltered in its conclusion, unlike *Star Wars* which had little to say but said it with great technical flair and proficiency, *Close Encounters* knows exactly where the center of the universe is . . . We are, after all, the star children.' (Ray Bradbury, *Los Angeles Times*.)

BOX OFFICE: Released in America on 16 November 1977, *Close Encounters* grossed $72 million in just three weeks – making it the ninth-biggest film of 1977 after barely a month on release – on its way to a worldwide gross of $270 million.

AWARDS: Nominated for eight Academy Awards: Best Director, Supporting Actress (Melinda Dillon), Cinematography, Art Direction/Set Decoration, Music, Film Editing, Visual Effects, Sound. In the end, *Close Encounters* followed through on one of its nods – Vilmos Zsigmond for Best Cinematography – but Frank Warner was deservedly awarded a Special Achievement Oscar for Sound Effects. At the BAFTAs, Joe Alves won for Best Production Design/Art Direction and the film was also cited for Best Film, Direction, Screenplay, Supporting Actor (François Truffaut), Cinematography, Music, Film Editing and Sound. The film was also cited for four Golden Globes – Best Motion Picture, Director, Screenplay, Score – but won zilch. Finally, John Williams picked up a Grammy for the soundtrack of the score.

THE SIZZLE! After reading the screenwriter Paul Schrader's first draft of the *Encounters* screenplay, the two men had an unresolvable conflict over the direction the script should take: Schrader wanted to make a movie about a flawed, tragic, religiously driven figure; Spielberg wanted to make a movie about his favoured everyman hero. 'That was my argument with him,' Schrader noted at the time. 'Who the fuck wants to see *that*? This is supposed to be the greatest event in the history of the Earth! But Steve wanted to make a movie about the porter – about a guy who would go off to Mars and start a chain of McDonald's.' Yet, despite his initial input, Schrader withdrew from Writer's Guild negotiations over a screen credit – a move that probably cost him a cool couple of million dollars.

Controversy followed *Close Encounters* to the set: giving a radio interview in Alabama about the movie, Richard Dreyfuss launched into an attack on the Ku Klux Klan who were marching in Mobile on the Fourth of July weekend. Death threats immediately swamped the station and Dreyfuss was flown out of Alabama that same day. Assigned two redneck bodyguards, he finished the shoot under constant supervision.

JOIN THE DOTS: Kids – *The Sugarland Express, Jaws, 1941, E.T. The Extra-Terrestrial, Twilight Zone: The Movie, Indiana Jones and the Temple of Doom, The Color Purple, Empire of the Sun, Hook, Jurassic Park, Schindler's List, The Lost World: Jurassic Park, Amistad.* **Kidnapped Kids** – *The Sugarland Express, Indiana Jones and the Temple of Doom, Empire of the Sun, Hook, Schindler's List, Amistad.* **Aliens** – *E.T. The Extra-Terrestrial.* **Aircraft** – *1941, Raiders of the Lost Ark, Indiana Jones and the Temple of Doom, Empire of the Sun, Indiana Jones and the Last Crusade, Always, Hook, Saving Private Ryan.* **Suburbia** – *The Sugarland Express, E.T. The Extra-Terrestrial, Empire of the Sun, The Lost World: Jurassic Park.* **Contemporary setting** – *The Sugarland Express, Jaws, E.T. The Extra-Terrestrial, Twilight Zone: The Movie, Always, Hook, Jurassic Park, The Lost World: Jurassic Park.* **Movies within movies** – *The Sugarland Express, 1941, E.T. The Extra-Terrestrial.* **Absent fathers** – *The*

Sugarland Express, E.T. The Extra-Terrestrial, The Color Purple, Empire of the Sun, Indiana Jones and the Last Crusade, Hook.

SEND IN THE CLONES! Obviously the biggest influence *Close Encounters* wielded over Spielberg's career would be detected in *E.T. – The Extra-Terrestrial* five years later. Other Spielberg-produced films that rode in on the back of *Close Encounters'* interest in alien life forms include the sickly *Batteries Not Included* (1987), in which aliens rejuvenate an ailing tenement block, and *Men In Black* (1997), in which Will Smith and Tommy Lee Jones kicked otherworldly butt to comedic, hugely lucrative ends (*Strange Invaders* (1983) also played comic riffs on extraterrestrial tourists). Away from Spielberg, Ron Howard's *Cocoon* (1985), Randall Kleiser's *Flight of the Navigator* (1986), James Cameron's *The Abyss* (1989) and Robert Zemeckis's *Contact* (1997) all share the *Close Encounters* worldview that alien life will be benign, the last two trading in a similar sense of wonder and quasi-religious overtones. Displaying the polar opposite view, Roland Emmerich's jingoistic *Independence Day* (1996) and Tim Burton's subversive *Mars Attacks!* (1987) depicted their off-planet visitors as destruction-crazed warmongers. Taking real-life experiences as their starting point, both *Communion* (1990) and *Fire in the Sky* (1993) treated ET visitation with a similar straight-faced tone that infuses *Close Encounters*. For the record, the latter features an appearance by *E.T.*'s Henry Thomas. On TV, *Dark Skies* (1990s) and, most successfully, *The X Files* (1990s onwards) have reproduced *Close Encounters* storylines (visitations, military cover-ups, lead characters obsessed with aliens) and motifs (the lighting in *The X Files* rips off Spielberg wholesale) in small-screen versions.

CLOSE ENCOUNTERS GOES POP: One of the earliest references to *Close Encounters* found its way into the James Bond flick *Moonraker* (1979) – as 007 punches in a key to open a door, the famous five notes play to signal entry. The dreadful *Morons from Outer Space* (1985) features an alien ship communicating through light, colour and five note patterns – the twist comes as it is revealed to be a Wurlitzer. In *Independence Day* (1996), Steven Hillier (Will Smith) punches out an alien, quipping, 'Now that's what I call a Close Encounter!'

In *Toy Story* (1995), Buzz Lightyear is surrounded by the three-eyed aliens in a manner similar to Roy Neary as he is welcomed on board the mothership – the scene also sees the aliens point to the sky in a parody of *Encounters'* Indian scene.

Movies that have riffed on the title include: Cheech and Chong's *High Encounters Of The Ultimate Kind* (1980); *Dangerous*

Encounters Of The First Kind (1980); *Close Encounters Of The Spooky Kind* (1980); sex romps *Close Encounters Of A Handyman* (1978), *Erotic Encounters Of The Fourth Kind* and *Very Close Encounters Of The Fourth Kind* (1978), an Italian soft porn about three nerds trying to get their astronomy teacher into the sack.

Away from movies, *The Simpsons* had fun at *Close Encounters'* expense in the episode entitled 'Homie The Clown' in which a preoccupied Homer begins to build a circus tent out of mashed potato in a similar vein to Neary crafting Devil's Tower. Electronic guru Meko created a disco version of the main theme and dance group Hot Gossip had a hit with 'I Lost My Heart To A Starship Trooper' which sampled the five notes. Yet perhaps the strangest way that *Close Encounters* became part of the culture was the appropriation of its two-lane poster image for a Durex advertising campaign – Close Encounters of The Sensitive Kind.

FINAL ANALYSIS: Of course, *Close Encounters* was not the only science-fiction film to hit the screens in 1977. But, if *Star Wars* remains a masterpiece of comic-book dynamism and mythic potency, it is *Close Encounters* that has aged more gracefully, providing a deeper, more sophisticated and ultimately more rewarding cinematic experience. Indeed, considering Spielberg's reputation for infantilism, it is also a resoundingly adult, non-campy take on science-fiction staples, injecting the drama with a human element – the scenes of Neary and family falling apart are raw and bleak, hardly the stuff of cosy fantasy – and an emotional uplift that is rare for the genre.

The technical proficiency that marked, say, *Duel* or *Jaws* is still intact but there is an added dimension here that lifts *Close Encounters* to another plane. The difference is in Spielberg's personal investment in the story he is telling: ripped from the fabric of his life, embroidered by the fantasies of his youth, *Close Encounters* was the first Spielberg film to map out the preoccupations that would be played out over the rest of his career, identifying a set of themes and ideas that have rightfully been dubbed Spielbergian. It is also a film that changed the perception of Spielberg: before *Close Encounters*, he was seen as a masterful (albeit mechanical) manipulator of audience emotions; after *Close Encounters*, he was a poet of Suburbia and the cinema's most persuasive cockeyed optimist.

What emerges most strongly for the first time in *Close Encounters* is an insider's fascination with suburbia. The rites and rituals of lower-middle-class America are charted with an almost documentarian's eye for detail; it is present in the meticulous set decoration, the Neary family argument over goofy golf versus *Pinocchio*, the constant presence of the TV as an extra character in the scene. However, the Spielberg attitude towards Suburbia is much more ambivalent than his detractors give him credit for, at once affectionate and seductive (especially for non-American audiences – who hasn't wanted to live in a Spielberg neighbourhood?), yet also wary, realising it is something that must be escaped. As Neary, building his replica Devil's Tower in the living room, gazes out on his neighbourhood, he watches over an idyll of garden sprinklers, children playing and Dad cleaning the car. Yet almost immediately he closes his curtain, blocking out the humdrum world, knowing that the confines of such conformity must be transcended. Critics have often noted that Spielberg's favourite theme is 'ordinary people in extraordinary situations' and *Close Encounters* is the ultimate encapsulation of that theme. But actually this (by now hackneyed) conceptualisation of Spielberg's scenarios falls short: be it mild-mannered motorist, aquaphobic police chief or UFO-obsessed power worker, Spielberg's everyman (or -woman) is often confronted with the limitations of the everyday, yet he (or she) exceeds those limitations to become a hero.

Also new in *Close Encounters* is a sense of gentleness and benevolence that has continued to course throughout Spielberg's career. There are no villains (the closest thing the film comes to a bad guy is Neary's put-upon wife, Ronnie) or traditional storytelling conflicts at play. Instead the film is propelled by a yearning for comprehension, a faith in something beyond the everyday and, most pervasively, a sense of wonder, both at the unknown delights that populate the night sky and also in Spielberg's unshakeable belief that the goodness in humanity will prevail. Like the best of Spielberg, *Close Encounters* is profoundly, unfashionably anti-cynical, exposing a film-maker unabashedly wearing his soul on his sleeve.

A stunning confection of innocent charm, infectious optimism, suburban autobiography and cathedral-like beauty, *Close Encounters* ranks among the most personal blockbusters ever released by a Hollywood studio. And one of the finest.

SPIELBERG ON SPIELBERG: 'My feeling has always been that I would have to see it for myself to really believe it, to make a statement that I believe that UFOs are here and watching us as we are watching them. I'd have to see it for myself – not just make movies about it. But I give credence to all the witnesses all over the world, all these different cultures and languages, who see the same thing over and over again. And that's kept my interest in UFOs high ever since.'

1941 (1979)

(Colour, 146 mins)

Studio Columbia/Universal
Screenplay by Robert Zemeckis & Bob Gale
Story by Robert Zemeckis & Bob Gale and John Milius
Producer Buzz Feitshans
Executive Producer John Milius
Director of Photography William A Fraker
Production Designer Dean Edward Mitzner
Edited by Michael Kahn ACE
Music by John Williams
Unit Production Managers Chuck Myers, Herb Willis
First Assistant Directors Jerry Zeismer, Steve Perry
Special Effects Created by AD Flowers
Miniature Supervisor Gregory Jein
Costumes by Deborah Nadoolman
Art Director William F O'Brien
Matte Paintings by Matthew Yuricich
Visual Effects Supervisor Larry Robinson
Casting by Sally Dennison
Production Illustrator George Jensen
Production Sound Mixer Gene S Cantamessa
Supervising Sound Effects Editor Fred J Brown MPSE
Make-up Supervisor Bob Westmoreland
Hairstyles by Susan Germaine
Stunt Co-ordinator Terry Leonard
Camera Operation Dick Colean
Re-recording Mixers Buzz Knudson, Robert Glass, Don MacDougall, Chris Jenkins

CAST: Dan Aykroyd (*Sgt Tree*), Ned Beatty (*Ward Douglas*), John Belushi (*'Wild' Bill Kelso*), Lorraine Gary (*Joan Douglas*), Claude Crumn (*Murray Hamilton*), Christopher Lee (*Von Kleinschmidt*), Tim Matheson (*Birkhead*), Toshiro Mifune (*Commander Mitamura*), Warren Oates (*Colonel Maddox*), Robert Stack (*General Stilwell*), Treat Williams (*Sitarski*), Nancy Allen (*Donna Stratton*), Lucille Benson (*Gas Mama*), Jordan Brian (*Macey Douglas*), John Candy (*Foley*), Elisha Cook (*the Patron*), Eddie Deezen (*Herbie Kazlminsky*), Bobby DiCicco (*Wally Stephens*), Dianne Kay (*Betty*), Perry Lang (*Dennis DeSoto*), Patti LuPone (*Lydia Hedberg*), J Patrick McNamara (*DuBois*), Frank McRae (*Ogden Johnson Jones*), Stephen Mond (*Gus Douglas*), Slim Pickens (*Hollis Wood*), Wendie Jo Sperber (*Maxine Dexheimer*), Lionel Stander (*Angelo Scioli*), Dub Taylor (*Mr Malcomb*), Ignatius Wolfington (*Meyer Mishkin*), Christian Zika (*Stevie Douglas*), Joseph Flaherty (*USC MC*), David Lander (*Joe*), Michael McKean (*Willy*), Hiroshi Shimizu (*Ito*).

BUDGET: $31.5 million

MPAA: PG

BBFC: A

TITLE SEQUENCE: Over John Williams slow, distinctively martial music, the credit 'Universal And Columbia Pictures Present' and the film's title (written numerically) appear in bold white lettering against black. As the music builds in excitement, an introductory scroll describes the sense of panic that gripped the west coast of America following the attack at Pearl Harbor.

PLOT SUMMARY: It's 13 December, 1941 on the coast of Santa Monica. A young woman is going for an early-morning dip. As the familiar theme from *Jaws* emerges, she swims out to sea, yet is caught in a sudden frenzy of panic. However, rather than a shark taking bites out of her, she is elevated into the air by the periscope of a surfacing Japanese submarine. As the girl watches down the periscope the submarine commander, Mitamura, is joined by Nazi kommandant Von Kleinschmidt as they discuss their plan of action: to strike a blow at the heart of America – Hollywood (or 'Horrywood' as the sub crew have it).

This planned invasion sparks off a nexus of paranoia from which a number of storylines spring: the desire of a crazed P-40 Warhawk pilot, 'Wild' Bill Kelso, to be the first American to take down an enemy fighter; the abduction of 'Holly' Wood by the Japanese crew in order to find their way to his geographical namesake; the instalment of an antiaircraft gun by Sgt Tree and crew in the backyard of Ward Douglas; civilian Wally's dream of winning the big jitterbug contest at the USO, only to find the dance and his girl Betty have been seconded to the military; the attempts of General Joseph Stilwell to watch *Dumbo* in peace; the manoeuvrings of Captain Birkhead to get Stilwell's secretary Donna Stratten up in an aircraft as Donna will become aroused only when airborne.

The disparate storylines begin to coalesce as the antagonism between Wally and Sitarski escalates into a full-scale riot involving soldiers, sailors and zoot-suiters. The mêlée is broken up by Tree with a rousing speech, yet the tank commander is knocked unconscious, forcing Wally to take charge (don't ask). Borrowing a Beechcraft Trainer from psychotic Colonel 'mad man' Maddox, Loomis does get off the ground with Donna but is mistaken for the enemy by Kelso, who chases them across the skies above Hollywood Boulevard. The ground forces, thinking an invasion has begun, start shooting and take down the two aircraft – Loomis and Donna landing in the prehistoric theme park La Brea Tar Pits, Kelso belly-flopping on to Hollywood Boulevard. Meanwhile, Ward spots the lurking sub – Hollis Wood long since escaped after pretending he was constipated (don't ask) – and decides to commandeer the antiaircraft gun himself. Back on Hollywood Boulevard, Kelso instructs the tank crew to take out the sub. Ward engages with the enemy, resulting in the total destruction of his house – though more courtesy of himself than the Japanese.

Under the misapprehension that the amusement park is an industrial facility, the sub turns its arsenal towards the fairground attractions, knocking the Ferris wheel off its moorings and into the sea. Hoping to sink the sub (as it were), Wally and crew follow suit as torpedoes knock the tank into the drink. Bobbing up and down, the tank personnel are amazed to see Wild Bill career on a motorbike into the waves and become a war criminal aboard the submarine, Tokyo-bound.

The following morning, Stilwell arrives to survey the scene at the Douglas household. Making a stirring speech about 'facing the enemy in their own backyard', Ward knocks a wreath of peace on to the front door of his semi-demolished house. Rather than the expected door-falls-down gag, the whole house begins to roll, falling off a cliff face and into the ocean.

BACKSTORY: As difficult as it may be to believe, the inspiration for *1941* is based on a semblance of reality. On 22 February 1942, a Japanese submarine fired off twenty shells at oil fields off the coast of California, near Santa Barbara. While the shells did virtually zero damage, a projectile hit an oil-well derrick and an unexploded shell injured an army officer attempting to diffuse it. As Los Angeles went on a state of alert, two nights later around 3 a.m., unidentified aircraft were spotted over the coastline inducing an hours' worth of antiaircraft fire. LA RAIDED! screamed the *Los Angeles Times*. The city was subsequently caught in the grip of bogus aircraft sightings and shootings – exploding shrapnel from 1,440 rounds of antiaircraft ammo rained down on blacked-out streets – the frenzy reaching such a fever pitch that one civilian was injured due to an exploding shell and five people died due to traffic accidents caused by the lights-out policy or heart attacks.

Also conflated into the fabric of *1941* is the zoot-suit riot of 1943, in which scores of sailors fought running battles with Hispanics wearing zoot suits, the former, who were about to go off to war, angry with the latter for their flouting of wearing a uniform.

Uncovering these story strands while researching a subversive screenplay entitled *Tank!*, Robert Zemeckis and Bob Gale, both USC film school graduates, pitched the story to their film school tutor John Milius. An admirer of the *Tank!* screenplay, Milius, under the banner of his A Team Productions, commissioned the Two Bobs (as they were widely called) to fashion a screenplay around the air raid as a satire on anti-Japanese hysteria and paranoia run rampant. With the Two Bobs' first draft finished in just under a month, the fervent liberal goader Milius dubbed the script *The Night The Japs Attacked*, a title that changed to *The Night The Japanese Attacked*, then *The Great Los Angeles Air Raid* in the name of political correctness. Originally planning to direct the movie, Milius jumped ship in order to helm his pet project, the surfing buddy movie *Big Wednesday* (1978).

The 'how' of Spielberg's involvement with *1941* is easy to explain. A long-time compadre of Milius, Spielberg developed his interest in the screenplay over 'male bonding' sessions at LA's Oak Tree Gun Club. 'Steven had this cheap Super-8 camera and he had all this film of us eating at Tommies (a hamburger joint) and covering ourselves in chilli and throwing up all over the car, doing imitations of Bigfoot, wonderful stuff,' Milius observed. 'Great howling mad evenings out there at the range, out of which came *1941*.' The 'why' of Spielberg's involvement, however, is more difficult to comprehend.

In July 1976, Zemeckis and Gale holed up with the director for two months at the Wyoming location of *Close Encounters*. They retitled the screenplay *The Rising Sun* and *Hollywood '41* before landing on *1941*, and the story was backdated to the day and night of 13 December 1941 to bolster the proximity to Pearl Harbor and tap into a Christmassy milieu. From a core group of teenaged protagonists, the cast of characters was embellished to accommodate big-name stars. Spielberg also talked Zemeckis out of a dark *Dr Strangelove*-ish ending in which Wally became a bombardier on the *Enola Gay*, the aircraft that dropped the atomic bomb on Hiroshima. The idea that the city was wasted because the Japanese spoiled a dance contest was deemed too dark for public consumption.

Originally, Milius had set up *1941* with MGM, yet Spielberg's involvement with the movie saw it switch studios to become a co-production between Universal and Columbia. With a provisional budget around the $6 million mark, the film actually entered production bankrolled to the tune off $26 million – the final film came in at $31.5 million, some five times the original guesstimate.

ORIGINS: Among the best films prior to *1941* that have found humour in the follies of war, and all the macho bravado and gung-ho patriotism that goes with conflict, are Preston Sturges's *Hail The Conquering Hero* (1944), *Dr Strangelove* (1964), *M*A*S*H* (1970) and *Catch 22* (1970) – but all these films found far more humour than *1941* managed to locate. There is also something of Orson Welles's radio broadcast of *The War of the Worlds* in the sense of a country caught in the grip of a manufactured panic.

The biggest influence on *1941* (one invoked a lot by Spielberg at the time) was HC Potter's *Hellzapoppin'* (1941). A kind of *Airplane!* of its day, this was a showcase for the comics Ole Olson and Chic Johnson and was a revised version of a popular burlesque review, filled to the brim with sight gags, Frankenstein's monster, 40s tunes and a send-up of romantic craziness. The irreverent tone and the scattershot aesthetic can be found at the heart of *1941*. The film also has a foot in other multi-cast broad comedies, particularly of the 60s. Released in 1966, Norman Jewison's *The Russians Are Coming, The Russians Are Coming* sees a stranded Russian submarine crew land on a Connecticut holiday island and instil a sense of panic, all very *1941*. Similarly, Stanley Kramer's *It's A Mad, Mad, Mad, Mad World* (1963) is a direct antecedent of *1941*. Common to both films is a heavy reliance on slapstick, fist fights, elaborate pratfalls and a cast of loony characters working within a single story framework.

Other strands of comedy that can be detected in the film are American institution *MAD* magazine, cartoons – Chuck Jones was brought in as a consultant and many of the gags have his sense of timing and meticulous construction – and the golden age of comedy from the silents of Buster Keaton and Mack Sennett, to the physical horseplay of Laurel and Hardy and, in particular, the Three Stooges, a touchstone for Zemeckis and Gale as well as the director.

Other specific references include the centrepiece brawl of John Ford's *The Quiet Man* (1952), the father of *1941*'s full-blown punch-up – the start of the USO mêlée is even marked by the traditional reel *The Rakes of Mallow*. Spielberg has also taken the fast pace and faster dialogue delivery from directors such as Preston Sturges and Frank Capra – a technique dubbed by Spielberg 'cut time' – if little of the wit.

CASTING: Filling the huge ensemble that made up the dramatis personae of *1941* started with the casting of John Belushi as 'Wild' Bill Kelso. A fan of the *Saturday Night Live* star following a *Jaws* skit called 'Victims of Shark Bite', Spielberg brought up the subject of *1941* over dinner which sparked Belushi into an improvisation involving a Japanese submarine commander not unlike his *SNL* Samurai baker character. Spielberg promised Belushi that, if the movie was made, the part was his. While Spielberg remained resolute about Belushi's comedic genius, he changed his mind about the role, offering the actor the larger part of Kelso. The actor's fee: a cool $350,000.

At their next meeting, Belushi suggested to Spielberg that the *SNL* alumnus and fellow Blues Brother Dan Aykroyd would be ideal for Tank Commander Frank Tree. There and then, Aykroyd slipped into character, deadpanning a litany of military/artillery stats. Spielberg hired the Canadian on the spot, not only for his laugh-making ability but also as a security blanket for the volatile Belushi.

Initially, Spielberg offered the role of General Joseph Stilwell to John Wayne. Wayne spent an hour reading the script, then spent the following hour trying to dissuade Spielberg from doing the movie. 'I'm surprised at you,' Wayne barked. 'I thought you were an American and I thought you were going to make a movie to honour the memory of World War Two. But this dishonours the memory of what happened.' Next on the list, Charlton Heston passed for similar reasons. The B-movie director Sam Fuller was the next to refuse on the grounds that he bore no resemblance to Stilwell whatsoever (see **Geddit!**). It was John Milius who suggested Robert Stack, best known as the indefatigable Elliot Ness on TV's *The Untouchables*, who lends Stilwell and the film a quiet shred of dignity.

For the role of Commander Mitamura, the Japanese subcommander left vacant by Belushi, Spielberg sought and garnered the legendary Toshiro Mifune. Best known for his performances in the films of Akira Kurosawa – *Rashomon* (1950), *Seven Samurai* (1954), *Throne of Blood* (1957), *Yojimbo* (1961) – Mifune told Spielberg at their first meeting that the behaviour of the Japanese crew was inappropriate. Christopher Lee was cast as the Nazi officer Von Kleinschmidt seconded to the sub mission.

PRODUCTION: After the rigours of location shooting on his previous movies, *1941* marked the first time Spielberg made a movie in a Hollywood studio.

Whether it was the luxury of working within a controlled environment or the hubris of two successive blockbusters, Spielberg soon developed eyes that were way too big for his budget. 'We would have been better off with $10 million less,' Spielberg later observed, 'because we went from one plot to seven subplots. But at the time, I wanted it – the bigness, the power, hundreds of people at my beck and call and millions of dollars at my disposal and everybody saying, yes, yes, yes.' Unhappy with the first take of Kelso's P-40 skidding on to Hollywood Boulevard, Spielberg ordered another take at the cost of $400,000 a go. The film's final gag saw a full-sized house built and pushed off a beach-front cliff with seven cameras filming its fall. A mere snip at $260,000.

Partly because Belushi and Aykroyd could work only three nights a week due to commitments to *Saturday Night Live* and partly because

Spielberg's imagination kept running away with him – towards the end of the schedule he added a dreadfully unfunny thirty-second vignette which saw the tank crash through a paint factory at an equivalent cost of a three-bedroom Californian home – *1941* took an astonishing 247 days to shoot, filming finally concluding on 16 May 1979.

TICS OF THE TRADE: The look of *1941*, which is among the most stylised (and stylish) films in the director's back catalogue, is probably its most successful element. To make the miniature work appear realistic, the director of photography William A Fraker shrouded the set in fog effects. Being the first material shot, it dictated the visual style of all the scenes that followed. Subsequently, *1941* has wisps of smoke or dust blowing through practically every frame – the fact that it appears (without motivation) in normal interiors as well as exteriors gives the film a hazy, unreal sheen. Add lighting that is by turns gaudy and intentionally overexposed and cyclorama backgrounds that are obviously fake (witness the Ferris wheel), the result is a unique dreamlike texture.

On a promotional tour in Europe to publicise *Close Encounters*, Spielberg fell in love with the Louma crane at the Deauville Film Festival. Invented by Jean-Marie Lavalou and Alain Masseron, the Louma is a lightweight, remote-controllable camera perched at the end of an extendible fifteen-foot boom that made the trickiest camera moves achievable while the director watched the results on a monitor. First used effectively by Roman Polanski on *The Tenant* (1976), the Louma became Spielberg's pet plaything and, although originally scheduled for just a few key shots, it became Spielberg's main camera on *1941*.

Hired out for a whopping $8,000 a week, the Louma crane lends *1941* a stunning visual kineticism. This dynamism reaches its apex in the astonishing jitterbug set piece in which Wally is chased round the USO by Sitarski, all the while trying to win the dance contest with Betty. Full of back flips, great hoofing and beautifully realised cartoony capers, the choreography between the actors, the dancers and the camera is stunning in its planning and intricacy – the moment where the camera does a 360-degree take of the hall as the dancers peel like an orange to reveal Wally and Betty is miraculous – and remains one of the greatest sequences within the Spielberg canon.

CLASSIC LINES:
General Stilwell: 'This isn't the state of California. It's a state of insanity.'

Hollis Wood: 'Oh no you don't. You thought you were going to let me show you where Hollywood was, didn't ya? Try to sneak up on me like you did Pearl Harbor. Bet you're gonna bomb John Wayne's house, ain't ya?'

'Wild' Bill Kelso: 'My name is "Wild" Bill Kelso, and don't you forget it.'

General Stilwell: (*last line*): 'It's gonna be a long war.'

COMIC RELIEF: It may seem strange to talk about comic relief in a film that purports to be an out and out comedy, yet, amid the carnage and frenzy that is often passed off as humour, this is how the smattering of *1941*'s genuinely funny moments sometimes feel. Of the big gags, the opening *Jaws* riff comes off a treat – although some critics found it audacious that Spielberg was referencing himself so early in his career. However, it is the smaller moments that really land: the incongruity of the Japanese sub crew finding a compass within Hollis Wood's candy packet when their own hi-tech compass is on the blink; Stilwell crying at *Dumbo*; Wynowski kicking Birkhead in the shins to check he is not a Japanese infiltrator wearing stilts; Herb's ventriloquist's dummy spotting the sub before
his human counterparts. Some of Dan Aykroyd's monologues find knowing laughs in the out-and-out patriotism of 40s war movies and Lionel Stander provides that *1941* rarity – underplaying: his gestures to Lorraine Gary to move out of the sight of the antiaircraft gun are priceless. Actually funnier than its reputation suggests, but not much.

VISUAL EFFECTS: Exasperated by the experience of *Close Encounters*, Spielberg dictated that *1941*'s effects would take place before the camera, using effects techniques that were available to film-makers working in the year 1941. To handle the physical effects, Spielberg hired the Hollywood veteran AD Flowers, who had demolished Pearl Harbor for *Tora! Tora! Tora!* (1970). Among the full-scale challenges facing Flowers and his crew, few caused more headaches than landing Kelso's aircraft in the middle of Hollywood Boulevard. To launch the aircraft, a 140-foot wooden ramp was constructed across the Columbia parking lot. The plane rode on an underbelly cart along the ramp's track with a cable attaching the aircraft to a truck. After falling disastrously short on the first take, the P-40 performed perfectly second time around, even managing to hit a traffic signal changing the sign to STOP!

Aircraft miniatures were flown using a sophisticated wire system that allowed the models to fly upside down and perform barrel rolls.

Adding an extra frisson of excitement, the Louma crane was mounted on a tracking device and followed alongside the planes in midair. In addition, a low-running camera cart motored down the streets as fast as the planes were flying – the result was a thrilling perspective that might have been taken from a speeding car. For the showstopping Ferris wheel rolling into the sea, a catwalk was constructed in the studio rafters suspending the miniature big wheel by cables. The model was spun by hand, the cables were cut and, still attached to the tracks, the wheel spun wildly down the pier and into the water.

SOUND EFFECTS: Everything about *1941* is loud! The music, the explosions, the car crashes, the gunshots. Even the costumes are loud! The penchant for high volume, however, should not detract from the fact that *1941* is a superbly, meticulously constructed soundtrack.

Occasionally, the sound design does opt for the funny touch – listen out for the traffic-light ping that, like a boxing match bell, starts off a new round of rioting – but generally *1941* eschews the use of overtly comic sound effects in favour of something hyperreal: this is a world where every tyre has a screech, every bullet a ricochet and every Ferris wheel that rolls off a pier must be accompanied by an almighty splash.

WHAT'S THE SCORE? Dominating the score (and film) more than any other Williams theme, the *1941* march, all snare drums and stirring brass, treads a barely perceptible line between an actual military march and being a parody of one. Lacking the richness and diversity of Williams's best work, the rest of the score is equally bombastic and obvious – the first sight of the Japanese sub is accompanied by a heavy-handed rising-sun motif – baring a brazen gusto that eventually wares the listener down. Much more successfully, Williams also contributes a spot on pastiche of Benny Goodman's 'Sing, Sing, Sing' (entitled 'Swing, Swing, Swing' on the original soundtrack) for the USO jitterbug, the track buzzing with bold brass, pounding percussion – lots of cymbal hits to help punctuate the Wally–Sitarski chase – and soaring clarinets.

CUT SCENES: The first preview of *1941* took place on 19 October 1979 at the Medallion Theater in Dallas – where *Jaws* and *Close Encounters* had been previewed to such acclaim. Subsequently, gala openings on 16 November were cancelled as the movie underwent a rejig, the release date pushed back to 14 December. Following a second preview in Denver, *1941* finally emerged from the cutting room seventeen minutes shorter than the 146-minute version screened in

Dallas. Reinserted for a 1996 laserdisc director's cut, the excised scenes are as follows:

- Miss Fitzroy (Penny Marshall) lectures a group of young women (including Betty and Maxine) about that evening's USO dance, which is broken by a posse of carousing military men eager to find some action.
- Wally and his pal Denny losing their jobs at the diner, thrown out by Mr Malcomb after they have started a fight with the military.
- Wally in a department store deliberates over buying an expensive zoot suit. Denny sounds a fake air-raid siren causing major-league panic – a gun-toting Santa starts bellowing out evacuation orders – and Wally walks out of the store wearing the natty threads; the plan has worked to perfection. This scene ends with Dennis meeting the twin girls we see him with later in the USO club.
- Scioli argues in Italian with his wife about converting the family car into an armoured vehicle. Later, he explains to Claude his duties as a lookout at the top of the Ferris wheel. Another excised scene sees Scioli further explaining to Claude, now joined by Herb, his late-night watch. The scenes really bolster Scioli's character – he is a shadow in the finished film – and display Lionel Stander's light comedy touch.
- An excellent scene in which Ito (Hiroshi Shimizu) leads a crack team of Japanese assailants to shore disguised as Christmas trees, taking pictures of themselves. We also see a drunken Hollis Wood attempting to chop them down, resulting in his capture.
- A dinner in the Douglas household that sees Ward outlining to Betty her duties when meeting servicemen at the USO dance. The scene includes a nifty moment in which Macey wears a gas mask to the dinner table, sucking up the pea soup through the hose attachment, the goggle lenses slowly filling with green liquid.
- A scene in which Ogden Johnson Jones arrives at the barracks and begins arguing with the racist Foley about property lines in their quarters. A further excised scene sees Sgt Tree break up a fist fight between the pair, informing them that a riot is in progress on Hollywood Boulevard. We see the crew climb aboard Sgt Tree's tank, Lulubelle, and start her up.
- Outside the USO, Wally meets his fellow zoot-suiter Martinez and compadres. They are denied access to the club and, adding insult to injury, Sitarski promptly sets fire to Wally's suit. A riot nearly ensues. We subsequently see the civilian Dennis dressed as a marine with his arm around the twins.
- There is an additional scene of Captain Birkhead making out with a journalist. We also get more dialogue between Birkhead and Donna

Stratton as Birkhead drives to the Pomona airfield trying to convince her the car feels just like a plane.

- The interceptor commander gives the order to go to condition blue – in the theatrical print, there are only conditions 'yellow' and 'red'.
- Stilwell watching *Dumbo* and his altercation with the messenger Mizerant is extended.
- A scene of the Japanese sub arriving off the coast by the Douglas house and the sub's entire crew watching Joan Douglas take a bath through the window. There is also more of Ward and Joan arguing about the gun in the yard.
- Wally rides Lulubelle down a residential street, shooting up Officer Miller's police car to smithereens. Pedestrians run for their lives.

While the longer version restores a greater semblance of character than the released one, it is unlikely the film would have been much better received at the greater length. A scene that was shot but does not appear in any version of the movie is an addendum to the Hollis Wood pocket-emptying scene – Wood produces a condom from his pocket, confusing the Japanese, who start to blow it up as a balloon.

UNSUNG HERO: The miniatures supervisor, Gregory Jein, whose extensive model work is the real joy of the film. In a smooth transition from *Close Encounters*, where Jein had supervised the creation of the mothership, his workload included rendering the Ocean Pier Amusement Park, Hollywood Boulevard, La Brea Tar Pits and the vast landscape of the Los Angeles basin, all in scaled down form. For the beleaguered Amusement Park (based on buildings from the Santa Monica Pier and the Long Beach Pike), the model maker's loving attention to detail is astonishing: tiny pieces of furniture, gumball machines, bicycles in racks, prizes for the game booths, even newspapers adorned with headlines screaming WAR! became bite-sized props in buildings carved out of balsa wood to explode easily, then weathered with oil and thinner for a dirtied-down, realistic finish. The centrepiece Ferris wheel was a twelve-sided polygon, eleven feet in diameter, weighing 160 pounds, and peppered with over 2,000 bulbs. Yet that was not the extent of Jein's exquisite minutiae: for sitting atop the big wheel were one-and-a-half-inch, animatronic versions of Claude and Herb, including a version of the ventriloquist's dummy that was the size of a paper clip. Having begun eight months before principal photography started, yet among the last to finish, Jein's model work is simultaneously stylised yet realistic, perhaps the most impressive ever to fill a feature film. And, in these days of digital dominance, it is something all the more to be cherished.

GEDDIT! For the *Jaws* skit that kicks off the movie, the actress Susan Backlinie reprised her role as the nude bather. Spielberg also replays some of the framing and camera moves to the very letter.

Spielberg also references *Duel* – as Belushi stops to refuel his plane at a desert gas station. The scene was shot in the same location in Aqua Dunce where the truck haunted Dennis Weaver – Spielberg also brought back Lucille Benson to reprise her role as the gas station owner.

Penny Marshall, Laverne from *Laverne And Shirley*, and the director of *Big* (1988), *Awakenings* (1990) and *A League of Their Own* (1992), plays the small role of Mrs Fitzroy, the cheerleader for the USO girls.

Speaking of *Laverne And Shirley*, the actors David Lander and Michael McKean, Lenny and Squiggy in that series, portray two soldiers named Willy and Joe, aping famous wartime cartoon characters by Bill Mauldlin. A second pairing of flak gunners were called Hanley and Saunders, names culled from the TV series *Combat*.

The cigar-chomping commanding officer of Interceptor Command is played by Sam Fuller, the legendary B-movie director responsible for cult classics such as *Park Row* (1952), *Shock Corridor* (1963) and *The Naked Kiss* (1964).

Sgt Tree's tank is nicknamed Lulubelle, a reference to Humphrey Bogart's tank in *Sahara* (1943).

After Sitarski fails to hitch a ride to chase the tank, Betty's friend Maxine hikes up her skirt, flashes a bit of leg and gets 'Wild' Bill Kelso to pull over on his motorbike. The scene replays a classic Clark Gable–Claudette Colbert ruse from Frank Capra's *It Happened One Night* (1934).

Delirious from having a chandelier fall on his head, Wally sits on the dance floor muttering, 'There's no place like home, there's no place like home.' This apes Judy Garland's classic dialogue from Victor Fleming's *The Wizard of Oz* (1939).

Playing the dusty motorcycle messenger Mizerany is John Landis, director of *National Lampoon's Animal House* (1978) and *The Blues Brothers* (1980), the latter starring Belushi and Aykroyd.

Slim Pickens's collection of things in his pockets – rabbit's foot, knife – resembles the moment in Stanley Kubrick's *Dr Strangelove* (1964), where playing Major 'King' Kong, he reels off the contents of a survival kit.

Young Stevie Douglas wears the uniform of the Boy Rangers – a reference to the boys' club in Frank Capra's *Mr Smith Goes to Washington* (1939).

1941 proved to be the final note in the glittering career of Spielberg's cocker spaniel, Elmer. Here, he movingly takes on the role of the Douglas family pet.

J Patrick McNamara, who plays DuBois, has a similar role as a supporting military type in *Close Encounters*.

1941 ends with a dedication 'For Charlsie Bryant', a reference to Spielberg's script supervisor, who died shortly after *Close Encounters*.

FACTOID FRENZY: Look out for a very young-looking Mickey Rourke playing Reese, a member of Aykroyd's tank crew.

At the instigation of John Landis, the make-up effects guru Rick Baker dressed up in a gorilla suit and trashed the miniature sprawl of buildings and vehicles à la King Kong.

The moment depicting 'Wild' Bill Kelso slipping off the wing of his plane was not a preplanned stunt: Belushi fell from the wing, knocking himself unconscious in the accident.

If you look closely, it is James Caan who throws the very first punch that ignites the USO fracas. Caan happened to be passing the set, was rushed into a sailor's costume and invited to start the mêlée.

Continuity spotters should keep a close eye on the seating positions of Herb and Claude. As Wild Bill Kelso's P-40 comes in to attack, the pair have swapped sides.

THE CRITICAL FACULTY: 'The most conspicuous waste since the last major oil spill, which it somewhat resembles.' (Charles Champlin, *Los Angeles Times*.). 'A celebration of the gung ho silliness of old war movies, a celebration of the Betty Grable–Betty Hutton period of American pop culture. In this movie, America is still a very young culture – foolish, violent, casually destructive but not venal. That we joke about a moment of national crisis shows that we are still young and sane.' (David Denby, *New York*.) 'A comedy completely devoid of humour, one of the most crashingly inept comedies of the past decade.' (Bruce Williamson, *Playboy*.) 'A movie that will live in infamy . . . *1941* isn't simply a silly slur against any particular race, sex, or generation – it makes war against all humanity.' (Michael Sragow, *Los Angeles Herald Examiner*.) 'Technically accomplished as the effects are, it is Spielberg's characteristic childlike glee that ignites these scenes.' (Frank Rich, *Time*.) 'A hectic smug, self-destructive farce, an appalling waste of filmmaking and performing resources . . . pointless, hateful, an artistic disgrace.' (Gary Arnold, *Washington Post*.) 'The most appalling piece of juvenilia foisted on the public.' (Stephen Farber, *New West*.) 'What *1941* proves finally is that the Japanese didn't have to worry about destroying Hollywood. All they had to do was wait years and let Steven Spielberg do it for them.' (Neal Gabler, *Weekly News*.)

BOX OFFICE: Despite its reputation as the flop of Spielberg's career, *1941* was not the box-office disaster it is often perceived as. Opening in the US on 14 December 1979, the film actually turned a small profit, taking in a worldwide gross of $90 million. The film's negative press was compounded by the seizure of American hostages in Teheran by the Khomeini regime – the prevailing sense of national outrage rendered a film that mocked the military, patriotism and other such all-American values an unlikely candidate to be widely embraced. Conversely, the film fared a little better in Europe, where its brazen attacks on Yank jingoism were always more likely to be more welcome.

AWARDS: Nominated for three Academy Awards, Best Cinematography, Sound and Visual Effects, *1941* walked away empty handed.

THE SIZZLE! Cocaine use was widespread on the *1941* set – some 25 members of the cast and crew were reputedly users. The biggest indulger was John Belushi, who could do lines of coke but not lines of dialogue, according to the book *Wired* by Bob Woodward. Things came to a head on 5 December when Belushi annoyed Spielberg by turning up to the set an hour late – dropped off by the actress Lauren Hutton, he fell out of a car – and the sober director unleashed his fury at the incapacitated actor in the confines of his trailer. Spielberg subsequently assigned the associate producer, Janet Healy, to nursemaid the actor for the rest of the shoot. As a black comment on both the film's box-office chances and Belushi's on-set behaviour, a *Saturday Night Live* writer Michael O'Donoghue, created badges that read 'John Belushi: 1952–1941'.

JOIN THE DOTS: Kids – *The Sugarland Express, Jaws, Close Encounters of the Third Kind, E.T. The Extra-Terrestrial, Twilight Zone: The Movie, Indiana Jones and the Temple of Doom, The Color Purple, Empire of the Sun, Hook, Jurassic Park, Schindler's List, The Lost World: Jurassic Park, Amistad.* **Roller-coaster plotting** – *Jaws, Raiders of the Lost Ark, Indiana Jones and the Temple of Doom, Indiana Jones and the Last Crusade, Jurassic Park, The Lost World: Jurassic Park.* **World War Two** – *Raiders of the Lost Ark, Empire of the Sun, Indiana Jones and the Last Crusade, Schindler's List, Saving Private Ryan.* **Aircraft** – *Close Encounters of the Third Kind, Raiders of the Lost Ark, Indiana Jones and the Temple of Doom, Empire of* *the Sun, Indiana Jones and the Last Crusade, Always, Hook, Saving Private Ryan.* **Historical setting** – *Raiders of the Lost Ark, Indiana Jones and the Temple of Doom, The Color Purple, Empire of the Sun, Schindler's List, Amistad, Saving Private Ryan.* **Based on real-life events** – *The Sugarland Express, Empire of the Sun, Schindler's List, Saving Private Ryan.* **Movies within movies** – *The Sugarland Express, Close Encounters of the Third Kind, E.T. The Extra-Terrestrial.*

SEND IN THE CLONES! *Used Cars* (1980), Robert Zemeckis's second feature as a director, shares many traits with *1941*, particularly a large-ensemble cast, multiple plots vying for attention, a strain of black comedy and a high percentage of physical comedy. John Landis's *The Blues Brothers* (1980), featuring John Belushi, Dan Aykroyd and, in the film's final moments, Steven Spielberg, also laboured under the delusion that having vehicles crash into each other was a substitute for real wit. Although no one in their right mind would set out to duplicate *1941*, it appears that a few films were ushered into production to jump on the expected comedy-military bandwagon: Howard Zieff's *Private Benjamin* (1980) and Ivan Reitman's *Stripes* (1981).

FINAL ANALYSIS: If Spielberg put one foot wrong in the making of *1941*, it was deciding to take on the project in the first place. *1941* is probably best perceived as a regrettable necessity in the Spielberg canon. Necessary in that its artistic failure purged the young director of his growing sense of hubris; regrettable in that it was such a regressive step after the personal preoccupations that coursed through *Close Encounters of the Third Kind*.

Indeed, it is interesting to see how much of Spielberg there is in *1941*. In a certain sense, the film can be taken as a comic replaying of the themes that underpin *Close Encounters*: regular Americans take on a heightened fear of alien invasion and unidentified flying objects (Ward's destruction of the interior of his own house bares a passing resemblance to Roy Neary trashing his living room in *Close Encounters*). Also, the film reconfirms Spielberg's affinity with the outsider – not only in the nominal hero Wally, who would rather dance than serve his country, but also in his sympathetic portrayal of the Japanese, who are allowed much more dignity than any of the Americans. Moreover, *1941* is the first full-blown pronouncement of Spielberg's fascination with World War Two in general and aircraft in particular – there are lingering, loving camera shots of aircraft (usually from Donna's point of view) that foreshadow *Empire of the Sun* – an interest born out of stories regaled by his father, a radio operator on B-52 bombers.

Like the rest of Spielberg, *1941* is profoundly in love with movies. If the moment as Stilwell cries quiet tears at the baby Dumbo being caressed by his mother is a funny, charming blip in an otherwise unfunny, charmless film, it also points to Spielberg's firm commitment to the notion of movies as a great escape, evoking the power of cinema to provide comfort in conflict.

The biggest problem with the movie as a slice of entertainment – and this is fundamental for a film boasting the tagline 'A comedy spectacular' – is that there are sustained periods that are completely laughter-free zones. Trading on the misguided belief that wanton destruction, manic shouting and John Belushi are actually funny, *1941* amazes but rarely amuses. Breaking all the strictures that had previously served Spielberg well – tell a linear story, put character before effects – the film never gels into a coherent whole, being populated with too many characters, all of them thinly drawn, and any sense of audience involvement or gradually mounting hysteria is overwhelmed by the sheer relentlessness of its carnage.

That said, there are many films that don't have a fiftieth of its craftsmanship or imagination that did not get as mercilessly vilified in the press. And taken dispassionately, its individual components – Michael Kahn's slick editing, Deborah Nadoolman's protean costume design, Dean Edward Mitzner's stunning period evocation, Terry Leonard's out-on-a-limb stuntwork – are more than just the best that money can buy, displaying a depth of proficiency that would have been Oscar-worthy if allied to a different script. The same can be said for Spielberg's film-making, which is just as inventive and adroit as the successes that bookend it. If his control over the comedy had matched his execution of technique, *1941* would have been a masterpiece.

SPIELBERG ON SPIELBERG: 'Power can go right to the head. I felt immortal after a critical hit and two box-office hits, one being the biggest hit in history up to that moment. But *1941* was not a screw-you film: I can do anything I want, watch me fail upward. I was very indulgent on *1941*, simply because I was very insecure with the material. It wasn't making me laugh, or any of us laugh, either in dailies [rushes] or on set. So I shot that movie every way I knew how to try and save it from what I thought it actually became, which is a demolition derby.'

Raiders of the Lost Ark (1981)

(Colour, 115 mins)

Studio Paramount/Lucasfilm
Production Design Norman Reynolds
Director of Photography Douglas Slocombe
Associate Producer Robert Watts
Editing Michael Kahn ACE
Music John Williams (performed by the London Symphony Orchestra)
Executive Producers George Lucas, Howard Kazanjian
Screenplay Lawrence Kasdan
Story by George Lucas and Philip Kaufman
Produced by Frank Marshall
Casting Mike Fenton and Jane Feinberg, Mary Selway
Second Unit Director Michael Moore
Stunt Co-ordinator Glenn Randall
Costume Design Deborah Nadoolman
Visual Effects Supervisor Richard Edlund
Mechanical Effects Supervisor Kit West
First Assistant Director David Tomblin
Production Supervisor Douglas Twiddy
Operating Cameraman Chic Waterson
Art Director Leslie Dilley
Production Illustrator Ed Verreaux
Production Artists Michael Lloyd, Ron Cobb
Sketch Artists Roy Carnon, Dave Negron
Chief Make-up Artist Tom Smith
Stunt Arranger Pete Diamond
Animal Handlers Michael Culling, Steve Edge, Jed Edge
Production Sound Roy Charman
Special Sound Effects Editing and Rerecording Ben Burtt
Supervising Sound Effects Editor Richard Anderson
Re-recording Bill Varney, Steve Maslow, Greg Landaker
Special Visual Effects by Industrial Light and Magic
Stunts Terry Leonard, Martin Grace, Vic Armstrong, Wendy Leach, Sergio Mione,
Rocky Taylor, Chuck Waters, Bill Weston, Paul Weston, Reg Harding, Billy Horrigan

CAST: Harrison Ford (*Indiana Jones*), Karen Allen (*Marion Ravenwood*), Paul Freeman (*Rene Belloq*), Ronald Lacey (*Toht*), John Rhys-Davies (*Sallah*), Denholm Elliott (*Marcus Brody*), Wolf Kahler (*Dietrich*), Anthony Higgins (*Gobler*), Alfred Molina (*Satipo*), Vic Tablian (*Barranca*), Don Fellows (*Colonel Musgrove*), William Hootkins (*Major Eaton*), Fred Sorenson (*Jock*), Tutte Lenkow (*Iman*), Kiran Shah (*Abu*), Souad Messaoudi (*Fayah*), Vic Tablian (*Monkey Man*), Terry Richards (*Arab Swordsman*), Pat Roach (*1st Mechanic*), Steve Hanson (*German Agent*), Frank Marshall (*Pilot*), George Harris (*Katanga*), Eddie Tagoe (*Messenger Pirate*), Ted Grossman (*Peruvian Porter*).

BUDGET: $22.8 million

MPAA: PG

BBFC: A

TITLE SEQUENCE: *Raiders of the Lost Ark* opens with the slyest in-joke in movie history: the mountain of the Paramount logo almost imperceptibly transforms into a real mountain, cleverly clueing us in that this, above all, is a movie *about* movies. Accompanied by John Williams's probing, foreboding music and Tarzan-esque sound effects, we follow a fedora-clad figure leading a group of hired hands through a Peruvian jungle. Passing through shafts of light, crossing a stream and encountering an Aztec gargoyle, we catch only glimpses of the leader, his identity shrouded in mystery. The titles end as the man in the hat – who turns out to be Indiana Jones, of course – pulls a poisoned dart from a tree. For the record, the titles are in a vaguely exotic white font, not the comic-strip orange-to-crimson lettering that became the film's logo.

PLOT SUMMARY: *Raiders* begins with a barnstorming opening sequence, quickly establishing the film's tone, tempo and the intrepid qualities of its hero. It's South America, 1936. An archaeologist Indiana 'Indy' Jones, is leading an expedition to find a priceless Aztec relic. As Indy's companions disappear one by one, he enters a temple riddled with booby traps – tarantulas, giant spikes, flying darts, rolling boulders – and purloins the golden statuette. Yet his efforts are in vain, because the booty is quickly taken from him by his arch rival, a French archaeologist, René Belloq. Fleeing Belloq's band of marauding natives, Indy makes his getaway in a waiting seaplane, sharing the cockpit with his one and only phobia – a snake!

Having returned to his day job as a college professor, Indy is recruited by US Army Intelligence to find the lost Ark of the Covenant, the casket containing the fragments of the Ten Commandments. It seems that the Nazis, believing the Ark has mystical, all-conquering powers, are near to recovering the artefact in Tanis, Egypt, and Jones is the perfect man to foil their plan for world domination.

Indy's first port of call is Nepal, where he is reunited with Marion Ravenwood, a former flame and now hard-drinking barkeeper. Indy believes Marion has the headpiece to the Staff of Ra, a medallion-cum-crystal that, if placed in a map room adorned with a miniature model of Tanis, can pinpoint the Well of Souls, the resting place of the Ark. Before Jones can secure the headpiece, the Nazis, led by a sadistic agent, Toht, raze the bar to the ground in a ferocious shoot-out and fist fight. After Toht is burned attempting to grab the headpiece through licking flames, Indy and Marion escape with the vital medallion, agree to become partners and make their way to . . . Cairo. Almost immediately the couple are pursued by enemy agents in a busy bazaar with Marion apparently killed in a truck explosion. Indy discovers not only the location of the Well of Souls and that Belloq is heading up the Nazi excavation, but, later, that Marion is actually alive and being held hostage by the Germans. Much to her annoyance, he decides to leave her tied up, fearing her escape will scupper his chances of plundering the Ark.

The action subsequently intertwines Belloq's seduction/interrogation of Marion (he fails on both counts) with Indy, aided by his friend Sallah, penetrating the Well of Souls. The cavernous pit may be filled wall to wall with snakes, but Indy overcomes his greatest fear to gain possession of the magnificent Ark. However, the Nazis discover the American's exploits, steal the Ark and seal him in the tomb, with a distraught Marion for company.

At this point the film moves up a gear into overdrive: Indy breaks free by using his sheer strength to topple a thirty-foot jackal statue through a wall. Following two spectacular set pieces – a fist fight around an out-of-control aircraft segues into a breathless horse-versus-truck chase – Indy regains control of the Ark and escapes aboard the *Bantu Wind*, a pirate steamer bound for England.

On board, Indy and Marion rekindle their romance, but love is interrupted by the Nazis' U-boat. The Ark, and Marion, change hands once more as the baddies travel to an unnamed Greek Island with Indy, disguised in a stolen Nazi uniform, in wet pursuit. Forced to surrender, Indy and Marion are tied up as Belloq performs the opening-of-the-Ark ritual: cue a maelstrom of supernatural power that leaves the bad guys wasted yet Indy and Marion unscathed. The couple return to Washington, where Indy is dismayed to learn that the Ark has been sectioned for government research. Finally, we (but not Indy) watch the Ark being packed up and left to rot in a warehouse full of identical wooden crates.

BACKSTORY: The pairing of the director of *Star Wars* (1977) and the director of *Jaws* may have been a marketing man's dream but the collaboration between Steven Spielberg and George Lucas has its roots way beyond a quick dollar. Spielberg first met Lucas in 1967 at a student film festival at the University of California (Los Angeles) where Lucas, then a hot-shot film-school graduate, was showing his sci-fi short *THX-1138: 4EB (Electronic Labyrinth)*. After being blown away by the movie, the twenty-year-old Spielberg 'was jealous to the very marrow of my bones', yet the pair struck up what has become one of moviedom's most enduring friendships, built on a love of cinema, a similar optimistic worldview and a total respect for the audience in the film-making equation.

Spielberg's induction into the exploits of Indiana Jones famously began over a sand-castle-building session. On holiday in Hawaii with George Lucas, who was vacationing only to escape the opening of *Star Wars*, Spielberg spun his yarn of a university professor/derring-do archaeologist on the beach outside the Mauna Kea hotel. Lucas had initially dreamed up the idea in 1973, outlining four plots concerning a hero who, when not obtaining rare antiquities, took on the demeanour of a suave Cary Grant type, using the riches from his expeditions to fund a penchant for top hats, the finest champagnes and the slinkiest blondes.

Lucas first hatched the story to his fellow San Franciscan film-maker Philip Kaufman, who proceeded to add a vital element. Drawing on a childhood memory of his GP, who was obsessed with the Ark of the Covenant and its supernatural potential, Kaufman wrote the search for the gold-encrusted cabinet into the plot, bolting it to Hitler's obsession with the occult and religious artefacts. Working only on *Raiders* for two weeks, Kaufman left to pursue other projects. Three years and one gigantic sand castle later, enter Spielberg.

With Lucas's agreement, Spielberg drafted in Lawrence Kasdan, a young advertising copywriter, to write the screenplay. Kasdan's on-spec screenplays *The Bodyguard* (1992, then tailored for Steve McQueen rather than Kevin Costner) and *Continental Divide* (1981) displayed an intuitive understanding of movie history and the spirit of old-school Hollywood that was the essence of *Raiders*.

In January 1978, Spielberg, Lucas and Kasdan held a week of story conferences in which the threesome argued, acted, baited and hammered the story into shape. While there were some sticking points – Spielberg and Kasdan were against the Indy-as-playboy element – all three men agreed on a characterisation of Jones as a dark figure who had fallen from the archaeological faith to become little more than a grave robber. Maybe through the decency inherent in Harrison Ford's persona, Jones emerges as a much more straight-arrow hero on screen.

Out of these story sessions emerged many of the movie's signature touches: Spielberg came up with the idea of the hero being chased by the boulder; Lucas invented the monkey giving a Nazi salute, a submarine sequence and the heroine slugging the hero on their first meeting; Kasdan added Indy being chased through a jungle by restless natives – a scene from one of his favourite movies, *Too Hot To Handle* (1938) starring Clark Gable – and created 'Indy' as an endearing abbreviation of Indiana. By the way, Indiana Jones was initially Indiana Smith until Spielberg thought that Smith was too common!

ORIGINS: Without doubt the most overt influence on *Raiders of the Lost Ark* is the adventure serials of the 30s and 40s. Famously produced by Republic Studios, serials such as *Flash Gordon Conquers the Universe* (1940), *Don Winslow of the Navy* (1942) and *Black Hawk* (1952) were cut to a precise formula: corny dialogue, cheap sets, no mushy stuff and contrived action all over fifteen episodes that always ended on a cliffhanger, forcing thrill seekers to come back next week.

Although *Raiders* invokes the spirit of the serials rather than containing slavish imitation, there are specific antecedents to Indy's adventures. The battle against the Nazis was taken up by *The Masked Marvel* (1943) and *The Spy Smasher* (1942). The figure of a whip-cracking hero can be traced to *Lash La Rue*, *Man With the Steel Whip* and various Zorro adventures such as *Zorro Rides Again* (1937) and *Zorro's Black Whip* (1944) – moreover, *Zorro's Fighting Legion* (1939) also included a truck chase in Episode 8 that bares comparison to *Raiders*. The Flying Wing – the disc-shaped aircraft that menaces Indy with its propellers – also played a prevalent part in serials such as *Fighting Devil Dogs* (1938) and *King of the Mounties* (1942). To trace *Raiders'* treasure-hunt plotting, we can look to *The Perils of Nyoka* (1942), a fifteen-chapter struggle centred on the Golden Tablets of Hippocrates, upon which – believe it or not – the cure for cancer is inscribed!

For Spielberg and Kasdan, however, *Raiders* stemmed more from classic A-list Hollywood adventure movies. Indy himself is an amalgam of numerous movie heroes: Humphrey Bogart's gruff cynic Fred C Dobbs in *The Treasure of Sierra Madre* (1948); Errol Flynn's derring-do swashbuckler in *The Adventures of Don Juan* (1949) and the cool of Sean Connery's James Bond – a debt acknowledged by the casting of Connery as Indy's father in *Indiana Jones and the Last Crusade*. The battered fedora, khaki pants and leather jacket are a reference not only to *The Treasure of Sierra Madre* but also to Charlton Heston's Brad in *The Greatest Show On Earth* (1952), the first film Spielberg ever saw. Similarly, Indy dressed as an Arab in the map room is a direct nod to David Lean's hero in *Lawrence of Arabia* (1962), another Spielberg favourite.

Of the supporting characters, Marion Ravenwood is a tough talker type beloved by the revered director Howard Hawks – most closely modelled on Jean Arthur's Bonnie Lee in Hawks's *Only Angels Have Wings* (1939) – whereas Belloq and Toht could have walked straight out of Rick's bar in *Casablanca* (1942), one of untold movies aped by *Raiders* that utilise maps to pinpoint exotic locales.

CASTING: After a countrywide search for an unknown (or 'Johnny, a construction worker from Malibu', as Spielberg was apt to say) to play

Indiana Jones, the role was offered to Tom Selleck, then the Marlboro Man on countless billboards. Yet, in the kind of cruel twist of fate that quashes careers, CBS TV picked up the option to a pilot that Selleck had just starred in, *Magnum PI*, preventing him from donning the fedora and bullwhip. The final irony, of course, was that an actors' union strike delayed the start of *Magnum*'s filming, meaning that, because *Raiders* was shooting in Europe far away from union restrictions, Selleck could have done the role after all.

With less than six weeks to go before shooting, Spielberg found the solution to his problem at the London premiere of *The Empire Strikes Back* (1980): Harrison Ford. Working hard to distinguish the grown-up Indiana Jones from the boyish Han Solo, Ford eschewed the one-liners and provided the perfect blend of reluctant heroism and roguish charm.

The casting of Indy's love interest, Marion, was equally tough. The first choice, Amy Irving, lost the role after her relationship with Spielberg ended. Debra Winger passed due to a scheduling conflict. Then, following a series of auditions held in the kitchen of Lucas's company Lucasfilm – if actors were scheduled in the morning they prepared food, if they tested in the afternoon, they *ate* food – Spielberg found his Marion in the New York stage actress Karen Allen, best known at that point for *National Lampoon's Animal House* (1978).

Originally conceived as a small comic sidekick character, the role of Sallah was initially offered to Danny DeVito, who proved too expensive. Seeing a reel of the TV miniseries *Shogun*, Spielberg subsequently cast the Welsh actor John Rhys-Davies, rethinking the part as a robust pirate figure. Other roles were filled out by excellent British character actors: Denholm Elliott as Indy's mentor Brody, Ronald Lacey as Gestapo agent Toht and, after Spielberg rejected the crooner Jacques Dutronc and the Italian Giancarlo Gianni, Paul Freeman filled the white threads of the suave archaeologist Belloq.

PRODUCTION: Kicking off in June 1980, *Raiders*' globetrotting production schedule encompassed La Rochelle, France (the Nazis' submarine pen), EMI Elstree (studio interiors), Tunisia (Egypt exteriors) and Kuai, Hawaii (the exteriors of the Peruvian temple). The shoot was marked by a dynamic between Spielberg's big-budget appetite (he deemed the 2,500 snakes hired to fill the Well of Souls were not enough, so ordered a further 4,000) and Lucas's frugal cost cutting: Spielberg's 200 acres for the Tanis dig site became 70 (saving $7,500); Spielberg's four engines from the Flying Wing became two (saving a further $250,000).

Yet drawing on his experience of working fast and loose in American TV, Spielberg infused *Raiders* with a shoot-from-the-hip sensibility that lent itself to the fast-paced yarn, giving the film a palpable sense of energy and staving off any hint of indulgence. While *Raiders* had officially been scheduled for 85 filming days, Spielberg, Lucas and key personnel were working to a clandestine schedule that saw the film steered home under budget and eleven days ahead of schedule. The ghost of *1941* had been well and truly laid.

TICS OF THE TRADE: Inspired by comic books such as *The Green Lantern* and *Sgt Rock*, Spielberg's original visual game plan for *Raiders* was to shoot it in an expressionistic manner full of exaggerated framings and dramatic lighting effects – a kind of black-and-white movie in colour. 'I orgasmed in the first two months of my preparation,' Spielberg noted, 'and then I essentially tore it up and just told the story.' Yet some vibrant traces of the approach remain: the clearly defined shadows that announce Indy's entrance at Marion's bar; hands passing guns menacingly across the foreground as Belloq and Indy face off in an Arab bar; Indy running into a big close-up during the bazaar foot chase. Elsewhere, Spielberg energises the action through trademark camera moves – for instance, a bravura spiralling camera crane down towards Marion in the Well of Souls – but for the most part, his direction is a model of stylish economy. This is perhaps typified by the moment Marion is shoved into the Well of Souls: to stress the threat of the snakes, Spielberg cuts away from her dangling to a close-up of an asp slithering through the open toe hole of her fallen shoe. Confident, simple, unforgettable.

CLASSIC LINES:
Belloq: 'Jones, do you realise what the Ark is? It's a transmitter. It's a radio for speaking to God. And it's within my reach!'
Indy: 'You wanna talk to God? Let's go see him together. I've got nothing better to do . . .'

Marion: 'You're not the man I knew ten years ago.'
Indy: 'It's not the years, honey, it's the mileage.'

Indy: 'Meet me at Omar's. Be ready for me. I'm going after that truck.'
Sallah: 'How?'
Indy: 'I don't know. I'm making this up as I go.'

COMIC RELIEF: Although elements of *Raiders'* humour suggest that Spielberg hadn't got the slapstick of *1941* out of his system – Marion decking Indy by upturning a steamed-up mirror, assorted villains getting whacked on the head – most of the comedy stems seamlessly from the action, leavening but never destroying the surrounding action/tension. *Raiders* abounds in carefully plotted lightness: as Indy teaches his archaeology class, a besotted student bats her eyes revealing 'I Love You' scrawled on the lids – Indy stutters and stammers but is saved by the bell; Indy trying to put on a stolen Nazi uniform, yet, unlike the case with every other World War Two movie, it is too small; in a gag originally intended for *1941*, Toht marches in on Marion and Belloq, opens an officious-looking case and pulls out what looks like an instrument of torture – then proceeds to hang his coat up on it. Genius.

An integral part of *Raiders*' mythology, the film's most inspired piece of visual comedy was born on location. Frantically searching the dusty Cairo streets for the kidnapped Marion, Indy arrives in a crowded marketplace. The assembled throng parts to reveal a black-clad swordsman (Terry Richards), who threatens Indy with a nifty display of scimitar twirling. Pulling a pained do-I-really-have-to-do-this? expression, Jones simply draws his revolver and shoots the assailant. Cue one unanimous bout of audience applause.

However, this – one of the most magical moments in movie history – never appeared in Lawrence Kasdan's original screenplay. Kasdan's script outlined a three-page whip-versus-sword fight, but there are differing accounts about who actually came up with the moment of inspiration. Harrison Ford claimed he came up with the idea the night before, figuring it would add credence to Jones's motivations – his priority is saving Marion, so he doesn't have time for another protracted battle. Spielberg's take is slightly different: 'We were all tired. It was toward the end of the schedule. I said, "Look, let's all be heroes. Shoot the guy and save the girl."'

But perhaps such questions of authorship miss the point – great cinema is born out of genius like this.

VISUAL EFFECTS: As expected, Spielberg turned to George Lucas's effects house Industrial Light and Magic (ILM) to provide *Raiders*' spectacle. While most of the effects workload involved subtle creations of locations through models and glass paintings (Marion's bar exterior, the concluding warehouse), the opening of the Ark sequence gave ILM the chance to flex their muscles. The Ark's guardian ghosts were created using a mixture of animation techniques and bits of silk fabric fastened to wire armatures dragged through a tank full of water. For the hair-raising moment where an angelic-looking spirit transforms into a ghoulish apparition, the actress Greta Hicks was caked all in white and filmed suspended against a black background. The shot was then mixed with a perfectly matched skeletal dummy, then projected through water and rephotographed to produce the ghostlike distortion effect.

The spectacular deaths of the villainous trio began with fake heads being generated through plaster-cast sessions with the actors: packed with blood bags and latex flesh, Toht's melting visage was accomplished by blasting the prosthetic bonce with three heaters and filming the result with time-lapse photography; Dietrich's imploding head was achieved through fully inflated bladders acting as cheeks which, once the air was let out, deflated into a perfectly wrought mummified effect; Belloq's exploding head was detonated by an air cannon and *two* shotguns. The effect was so gruesome that flames were superimposed over the shot to detract from the gore!

SOUND EFFECTS: Often held up and dissected in film schools as the perfectly constructed soundtrack, much of *Raiders'* power to enthral and excite comes from its audio wizardry. The effects were designed by Richard L Anderson and the *Star Wars* sound supremo Ben Burtt, and are marked by Burtt's renowned desire to create new sounds rather than utilise stock library effects: Indy's whip is the treated sound of a jet taking off; the punches in fist fights are the result of bashing leather jackets with baseball bats; and the rolling-boulder rumble is a Honda station wagon coasting down a gravel road mixed with a rocket blast-off. From the newly recorded gunshots to the flying darts in the Peruvian temple – Burtt loved the arrow sounds in *The Adventures of Robin Hood* (1938) so much he tracked down the film's sound designer to find out how they were done – *Raiders* still sounds fresh, dynamic and alive some twenty years on.

WHAT'S THE SCORE? Described by Spielberg as 'something you can walk out of the theatre whistling', 'The *Raiders* March' is among the most popular Spielberg/Williams themes. Combining a pulpy parody of 30s adventure scores with a warm. sincere, feel-good dynamic, the joyous brass captures both Indy's brazen dramatics and the film's cocksure ability to deliver a fun time – like most Williams themes, it is also malleable enough to be turned into sweeping, reflective and comedic variations. Elsewhere, Marion's theme is perhaps more delicate than the character herself would like – its slightly melancholy romanticism is straight out of a Warner Bros melodrama – and the score overflows with exciting fight/chase music and an imaginative use of the whole orchestra to render the mystery and power of the Ark. An object lesson in how to mirror screen action in memorable music.

CUT SCENES: A scene in which a German soldier deliberates over executing Sallah was excised partly due to excess smoke clogging up the shot and partly because it slowed down the story. The role of the

Nazi was played by a young German tourist whose performance apparently took Spielberg's breath away.

Originally, Indy's first meeting with Marion at her bar was a lot longer yet much of the character exposition – e.g., how she became the owner – became a cutting-room casualty, much to the writer Lawrence Kasdan's chagrin.

To explain how Indy rode the Wurfler submarine to the desert island, a scene was shot with Harrison Ford whipping himself on to the periscope as the vessel submerges. Apart from explaining a lapse in story logic, the fantastical scene displayed an inventive use of Indy's whip.

UNSUNG HERO: The stunt co-ordinator, Glenn Randall, who not only taught Harrison Ford how to use a whip but who marshalled his team of twelve stunt men through breathtaking fire sequences, punch-ups and high falls. The zenith of their achievement is the eight-minute chase in which Indy steals a steed to pursue the Ark on a heavily guarded truck. Riffing on a stunt created by the legendary stunt man Yakima Canutt for John Ford's *Stagecoach* (1939), Indy works his way into the cabin, out of the windscreen, then under the speeding truck, whipping himself on to the axle, which results in his being dragged along at full pelt. Directed by the second unit director, Michael Moore, from meticulous Spielberg storyboards (the first time, incidentally that Spielberg had used a second unit), the stunt was performed by a heavily protected Terry Leonard, who just months earlier had been seriously injured performing a similar stunt on *The Legend of the Lone Ranger* (1981) – if you watch closely you'll notice that, once under the vehicle, Leonard is being dragged along a shallow ditch to give him more breathing space. Hats off to Randall, who not only devised the gig but had the nerve-racking experience of driving the truck with Leonard underneath. Hats on to Indy who, in true serial tradition, never loses his fedora once during the spectacular sequence.

GEDDIT! That Indiana was named after the Lucas family dog, an Alaskan Malamute, is among the best-known movie in-jokes in the world (the trivia was woven into the fictional story in *Indiana Jones and the Last Crusade*).

Star Wars' lovable droid duo R2-D2 and C-3PO are carved into stone walls of the Well of Souls as hieroglyphics. The biplane that spirits Indy away from the tribesman reads OB-3PO. Moreover, the gully in which Indy threatens to blow up the Ark is the same locale in which R2-D2 gets zapped by the Jawas.

Look out for the actor Vic Tablian, who has two roles in the movie:

he is the treacherous tracker Barranca, who tries to shoot Indiana Jones in the back during the opening sequence; then, with a beard and an eye patch, he plays the motorcycle-riding owner of the Nazi-saluting monkey.

Another actor who appears twice is Pat Roach, initially as a Sherpa in the Nepal bar-room fight, then as the bald-headed mechanic who fights Indy between the propellers of the Flying Wing. He is killed both times. Roach also appears in *Temple of Doom* and *Last Crusade*.

The producer Frank Marshall has a small role as the Nazi pilot who tries to shoot Indy during the Flying Wing punch-up. ILM's visual-effects supervisor, Dennis Muren, also pops up as a Gestapo agent reading *Life* magazine, who gives Jones the evil eye as he boards the plane bound for Nepal.

Raiders 'borrows' two shots from other movies: a DC-3 flying through the Himalayas was appropriated from *The Lost Horizon* (1973); the Washington street scene towards the end was lifted from *The Hindenburg* (1975).

The final shot of the movie – the Ark being stored in a warehouse full of similarly crated-up artefacts – is a reference to the final moments of *Citizen Kane* (1941). It was thought up by Philip Kaufman.

FACTOID FRENZY: George Lucas actually shot some second-unit sequences on *Raiders*, including the shot of the monkey giving the Nazi salute, a moment that Frank Marshall had spent days trying to capture.

To shoot Indy's submarine exploits, the *Raiders* production sourced the submarine used in Wolfgang Petersen's *Das Boot* (1981) until the U-boat's agent would not allow his 'client' to go out in waves above three feet.

Marion is Lawrence Kasdan's wife's grandmother's name. Ravenwood comes from a street name in Los Angeles.

Spielberg's original intention for Toht was to give him a light emanating from his eye and a metal arm that doubled as a machine gun firing off bullets through his finger. Lucas nixed the idea.

Among the rats used to react to the throbbing sounds of the Ark in the hold of the *Bantu Wind* is a rodent turning around in circles. Rather than acting on cue, it turned out the little critter was deaf and had an equilibrium problem.

As Belloq and the Ark are held hostage by Indy and his bazooka, look out for the actor Paul Freeman swallowing a fly but not fluffing a line.

Indy's sprint from a giant boulder, made from 300 pounds of fibreglass, wood and plaster, was achieved by mounting the free-spinning rock on a retractable arm – every retake meant numerous stalactites had to be re-glued.

The penultimate scene in which Marion greets a sulky Indy on the steps was an afterthought. It was Lucas's then wife Marcia (herself an editor) who noted that the film lacked emotional resonance because the fate of Marion was not addressed. So Spielberg quickly shot the steps sequence outside the mayor's office in San Francisco.

THE CRITICAL FACULTY: 'Slam Bang! A movie, movie . . . One leaves *Lost Ark* feeling, like the best films of childhood, it will take up permanent residence in the memory.' (Richard Schickel, *Time*.) 'Out-Bonds Bond.' (Dilys Powell, *Sunday Times*.) 'It's hats-in-the-air, heart-in-the-mouth time at the movies again.' (Sheila Benson, *Los Angeles Times*.) 'One of the most deliriously funny, ingenious and stylish American adventure movies ever made.' (Vincent Canby, *New York Times*.) 'Kinesthetically, the film gets you but there's no exhilaration and no surge of feeling at the end.' (Pauline Kael, *New Yorker*.) 'Indy the hack adventurer is a bit of a [Spielberg] self-portrait, with touches of both vanity and self-loathing.' (Victoria Geng, *Film Comment*.)

BOX OFFICE: Released in America on 21 June 1981 on eight hundred screens, *Raiders* grossed a whopping $81 million in just three days and easily ended up as the US box-office champion of 1981 at $242 million. In the UK, opening the day after the Prince Charles–Diana Spencer wedding and against Bond number 12 *For Your Eyes Only*, *Raiders* wound up a close second to 007. In Paris, *Les Adventurers de l'Arche Perdue* (as *Raiders* translated) saw five hundred people turned away on its opening day, holing up in one Champs Elysées cinema for 89 weeks. To date, *Raiders of the Lost Ark* has grossed $363 million worldwide and is the second-highest grossing film in Paramount's history – just behind *Forrest Gump* (1994).

AWARDS: Nominated for eight Academy Awards: Best Picture, Director, Cinematography, Editing, Original Score, Art Direction, Visual Effects, Sound, *Raiders* grabbed gongs for art-direction, editing, visual effects and sound and also won a special-achievement award for Sound Effects Editing (Ben Burtt, Richard L Anderson). Nominated for the second time as Best Director – the first was for *Close Encounters* – Spielberg lost out to Warren Beatty for *Reds* (1981). *Raiders* also won a BAFTA for Art Direction plus seven awards at the Academy of Science Fiction Fantasy and Horror Films Awards.

THE SIZZLE! Following Philip Kaufman's two-week collaboration in the early days of *Raiders'* script development, Lucas suggested

Kaufman take profit percentage points as gratitude for his contribution. Although Kaufman initially agreed, his lawyers insisted he have a story credit. Lucas was reluctant to grant this, feeling he had written story outlines before Kaufman became involved. Yet, after some protracted negotiations, Kaufman won both his credit and the promised percentage of the profits.

Also on the legal front, Lucas, Spielberg, Kasdan and Paramount Pictures were hit by a $210 million law suit filed by Robert L Kuhn, claiming the film-makers stole the idea for *Raiders*. Kuhn charged that he had written a 900-page novel called *Ark* centred on a modern-day forty-year-old archaeology professor and his lost love searching to keep the Ark's mystical powers from a European conglomerate of Germans and Russians. The suit was quickly thrown out.

Elsewhere, *Raiders* came under criticism for perpetuating racial stereotypes and reinforcing old prejudices: be it filling up the bad-guy roster with spineless South Americans, vicious Arabs and Caribbean pirates or transforming Nazis into cartoony relief. At the time Spielberg remained unrepentant – 'The thing you have to keep in mind about *Raiders* is that it's only a movie' – but, in the light of later films, it is something he now regrets: '*Schindler's List* was a bit of an epiphany for me. I look back on *Raiders of the Lost Ark* and wish that I hadn't turned Nazis into figures that entertain you.'

JOIN THE DOTS: Roller-coaster plotting – *Jaws, 1941, Indiana Jones and the Temple of Doom, Indiana Jones and the Last Crusade, Jurassic Park, The Lost World: Jurassic Park*. **World War Two** – *1941, Empire of the Sun, Indiana Jones and the Last Crusade, Schindler's List, Saving Private Ryan*. **Aircraft** – *Close Encounters of the Third Kind, 1941, Indiana Jones and the Temple of Doom, Empire of the Sun, Indiana Jones and the Last Crusade, Always, Hook, Saving Private Ryan*. **Historical Setting** – *1941, Indiana Jones and the Temple of Doom, The Color Purple, Empire of the Sun, Schindler's List, Amistad, Saving Private Ryan*.

SEND IN THE CLONES! Among the most successful of *Raiders* imitators, *Romancing The Stone* (1984), directed by Robert Zemeckis, starred Michael Douglas as a soldier of fortune, Jack Colton, helping a romantic novelist, Joan Wilder (Kathleen Turner), find her kidnapped sister. A spirited, more adult adventure than *Raiders*, the film spawned a lacklustre sequel, *Jewel of the Nile* (1985). Brian Hutton's *High Road to China* (1983) gave Tom Selleck a role almost identical to the part he lost out on.

FINAL ANALYSIS: Still the yardstick by which all summer blockbusters should be measured, *Raiders* is the movie experience popcorn was invented for. Re-establishing the golden touch at the box office that went missing in action with *1941*, it also saw Spielberg fine-tuning his working practices and shooting style, paving the way for the kind of energy that saw *Jurassic Park* and *Schindler's List* made *in the same year*. Finding inventive solutions to Lucas's hard-nosed limitations, Spielberg also showed that he could collaborate with a long-time friend with both the creativity flourishing and the relationship remaining intact.

For all the perfectly staged action, quickly etched characters, relentless momentum and incessant fun, Spielberg's biggest coup is maintaining a brisk, light, tongue-in-cheek tone that never descends into camp. As with *Jaws*, he took pulp material and invested it with a lucid, compelling quality that lifted it from the efficiently entertaining to the truly memorable.

Critics have argued that, unlike *E.T.*, *Raiders* is an impersonal work, sharing few of Spielberg's recurring interests – a sense of wonder, big emotions – yet few concerns are closer to Spielberg than film lore, and it is this respect and passion for the craft that gives *Raiders* its soul. Indeed, what ultimately separates *Raiders* from the action pack is affection, not only for the genres and staples it is parodying but for the sheer delight in yarn spinning. The mark of all great cinema, *Raiders* joyously reaffirms why we love movies in the first place.

SPIELBERG ON SPIELBERG: 'When people were just discovering *Raiders* and throwing up their hats, I was exhausted from the experience of having made the movie. I never saw *Raiders* with the general public until it opened at the Cinerama Dome after its forty-fourth week in movie theaters. This was the first time with the public, and almost a year had passed since I'd last seen it. I was able to watch the picture semi-objectively and to enjoy the film as entertainment. But there was still a feeling of "Why did I do it that way? Why didn't I do it this way? Gee, why did I use those syphilitic camels?"'

E.T. The Extra-Terrestrial (1982)

(Colour, 115 mins)

Studio Universal
Music by John Williams
Edited by Carol Littleton
Written by Melissa Mathison

Producers Steven Spielberg, Kathleen Kennedy
Director of Photography Allen Daviau
Production Designer James D Bissell
Production Supervisor Frank Marshall
Associate Producer Melissa Mathison
Production Manager Wallace Worsley
First Assistant Director Katy Emde
E.T. created by Carlo Rambaldi
Visual Effects Supervisor Dennis Muren
Casting Mike Fenton, Jane Feinberg, Marci Liroff
Set Designer William Teegarden
Set Decorator Jackie Carr
Camera Operators John Fleckenstein, John Connor
Production Illustrator Ed Verreaux
Sound Mixer Gene Cantamessa
Costume Design Deborah Scott
Supervising Sound Effects Editor Charles L Campbell
E.T.'s Voice Design Ben Burtt
Re-recording Mixers Buzz Knudson, Robert Glass, Don Digirolamo
Optical Effects Co-ordinator Mitchell Suskin
Additional E.T. Effects Robert Short
Special Artistic Consultant Craig Reardon
Communicator Design Henry Feinberg
Special Visual Effects by Industrial Light and Magic
Spaceship Design Ralph McQuarrie

CAST: Dee Wallace (*Mary*), Henry Thomas (*Elliott*), Peter Coyote (*Keys*), Robert MacNaughton (*Michael*), Drew Barrymore (*Gertie*), KC Martel (*Greg*), Sean Frye (*Steve*), Tom Howell (*Tyler*), Erika Eleniak (*Pretty Girl*), David O'Dell (*Schoolboy*), Richard Swingler (*Science Teacher*), Frank Toth (*Policeman*), Robert Barton (*Ultra Sound Man*), Michael Darrell (*Van Man*).

BUDGET: $11.5 million

MPAA: PG

BBFC: U

TITLE SEQUENCE: Following the spinning globe of the Universal logo, violet credits are set against black. The letters 'E.T.' appear in a handwritten, almost childish style with subtitle 'The Extra-Terrestrial' in a more formal font. The soundtrack breathes quiet, dissonant, spooky noises, finally halted by the 'Directed By Steven Spielberg' credit – the film-maker as a reassuring, paternal presence. Lacking the grandiose flash and thunder of, say, *Close Encounters*' opening gambit, the titles are among the most modest in the Spielberg collection, pre-empting the story about to unravel – small and intimate.

PLOT SUMMARY: The opening wordless eleven minutes of *E.T.* showcase Spielberg's complete mastery as a visual storyteller to the full. Under the lights of a seemingly antiquated spacecraft, a team of alien botanists investigate a nocturnal forest on the outskirts of a Los Angeles suburb. As the call is given to return to the ship, one of their number is inadvertently left behind. A team of mysterious, shadowy figures led by a man identified only by his large set of keys are in hot pursuit, so the squat alien takes shelter in a suburban garden shed.

Inside the house, a game of dungeons and dragons is in full swing. Sent out to the pizza delivery van to pay, ten-year-old Elliott Taylor (not only are his initials ET but so are the first and last letters of his first name, further linking the two soul mates together) is drawn to the shed and a simple game of catch reveals it to be occupied. As he grabs his mother Mary (who has recently separated from Elliott's father) and his older brother Michael, further investigation throws up nothing – except for some footprints – and Elliott is ridiculed for his conviction. Later that night, Elliott encounters the creature and the pair startle each other, the creature fleeing into the night.

The following morning, Elliott leaves a trail of candy in the woods leading back to his house and, sure enough, the alien finds his way back into Elliott's life. Introducing him to both Michael and his smaller sister Gertie (but keeping him a secret from his mom), Elliott dubs the creature E.T., slowly developing an empathetic relationship emphasised as E.T. drinks beer and Elliott gets sozzled. With the alien's pursuers drawing ever nearer, E.T. says he wants to return home and the kids find odds and ends to help him construct a communication device to contact his own planet. On Hallowe'en, Elliott smuggles E.T. (disguised as a ghost) out of the house and heads for the forest, their journey taking in a magical flying bike-ride silhouetted by the moon.

However, as the squat creature becomes increasingly sick in the foreign environment, Elliott becomes sick too, and returns home to find the house invaded by Keys and his squad of government officials. Equipment is set up by the unit to help save both boy and alien, but, as E.T. withers, the symbiotic bond between the two is broken, leaving a heartbroken Elliott to watch E.T. die. Elliot is left alone with his friend to grieve, but his sobs turn to joy as a message from his own planet rejuvenates the ailing alien, his trademark heartlight burning bright. Elliott and Michael spring E.T. from quarantine with the help of their BMX biker buddies and head towards the landing site, with the law in hot pursuit. All seems lost as the police create an impenetrable barricade. E.T. saves the day by lifting the bicycles into the air and over a blazing sunset to his waiting spacecraft. Bidding Elliott an emotional farewell, E.T. returns aboard his transport, which leaves a stunning rainbow across the night sky.

BACKSTORY: *'Keeds!'* François Truffaut told Spielberg, watching him direct Cary Guffey on the set of *Close Encounters*. 'You must make a movie with keeds!' If the advice was followed to the letter, the antecedents that inform Steven Spielberg's most personal project are more convoluted. Of course, perhaps the biggest influence is the Spielberg childhood: *E.T.* is shot through with the pain of his parents divorcing when he was seventeen and the separation pangs Spielberg endured in a family constantly on the move; and the Los Angeles suburb where *E.T.* is set closely resembles the curving streets and hillsides of the Saratoga neighbourhood where he spent his teen years. As he told *Rolling Stone*'s Michael Sragow on *E.T.*'s release: 'I'm not into psychoanalysis but *E.T.* is a film that was inside me for many years and could only come out after a lot of suburban psychodrama . . . *E.T.* was about the divorce of my parents, how I felt after my parents broke up. I responded by escaping into my imagination to shut down all the nerve endings, crying "Mom, Dad, why did you break up and leave us alone?" My wish list included having a friend who could be both the brother I never had and a father I didn't feel I had anymore.'

As well as the underlying emotions, the script is peppered with specific incidents drawn from Spielberg's life: Elliott feigning illness by heating up a thermometer against a light bulb was a trick employed by the young Spielberg; the scene in the school biology lab is another direct reference to Spielberg's youth: when the class began to dissect a frog, little Steven became nauseated and had to run outside.

The initial impetus to make the movie was light years away from the Disney-esque fable it eventually became. Spielberg had been developing *Night Skies* with the writer John Sayles – author of the *Jaws* rip-off *Piranha* (1978) and *Alligator* (1980). Concerning a band of eleven malevolent aliens who terrorise the inhabitants of an isolated farmhouse, the script had a number of scenes that were a jumping-off point for *E.T.*: in *Night Skies*' opening scene, the gang leader, Scar, kills farm animals merely by touching them with his long bony finger. Moreover, Sayles had included a sensitive alien named Buddy, who strikes up a partnership with an autistic child. Spielberg briefly toyed with the idea of directing the movie himself. Yet, possibly predicated on his firm belief that aliens wouldn't travel all that way just to be hostile, Spielberg opted for a more gentle route. *E.T.* was going to start where *Close Encounters* left off.

It took *Raiders of the Lost Ark* in general and the Tunisian desert in particular to coalesce the disparate elements in Spielberg's mind. He related an outline of a young boy befriending a stranded alien to the screenwriter Melissa Mathison, who was on location accompanying her partner Harrison Ford. The writer of two underrated children's movies, *The Black Stallion* (1979) and *The Escape Artist* (1980), which pointedly explored the mindset of disenfranchised kids, Mathison at that time was considering giving up writing and the idea of penning science fiction was even more unappetising. Still, cajoled by Spielberg and Ford during a bumpy Tunisian car trip, she became intrigued by the idea of a sweet boy-meets-alien love story and agreed.

Taking weekly collaborations with Spielberg during the editing of *Raiders*, Mathison started work on the screenplay on 8 October 1980 and produced a first draft within a speedy two months. If the story was Spielberg's pet project, Mathison made some telling contributions to its development. Early drafts of her script, for instance, talked up E.T.'s relationship with plants – in one scene E.T. communicates with tomatoes and artichokes in Elliott's garden regarding whether he should make contact with humans. A scene that was retained in the final version – the initial game of catch between Elliott and E.T. – was played out with an orange rather than a baseball. Most surprisingly, it was Mathison's idea to have E.T. abandoned in a magical *Bambi*-esque forest – Spielberg's (in hindsight prosaic) notion for the alien's landing was in a vacant parking lot. Spielberg also gave the script to his regular ghostwriter Matthew Robbins, who made some distinctive revisions, subtracting a storyline about Elliott's best friend who threatens to blow E.T.'s cover but adding the notion that the whole house is covered and hermetically sealed by a tarp.

As a project *Night Skies* was in development with Columbia and Spielberg gave the studio first refusal on the kinder, gentler update, at this point called *E.T. And Me*. But, in one of those decisions that haunt executives to the grave, Columbia passed on the opportunity to bankroll one of the most lucrative movies in film history, so Spielberg took the project back to his old stamping ground, Universal. Bizarrely, due to the *Night Skies* deal, Columbia retained five per cent of *E.T.*'s net profits, meaning the film was the studio's most lucrative film of 1982 without ever really being a Columbia film.

ORIGINS: More than science fiction, *E.T.* stems from a tradition of small-child-loves-animal flicks, ranging from *My Friend Flicka* (1943) centred on a boy and his colt, to Disney's *Pete's Dragon* (1977), concerning a boy and his badly animated dragon – for the record, the dragon was also called Elliott. Yet, the most famous of these movies is the MGM Lassie franchise running from 1943 (the first movie, *Lassie Come Home*, starred Roddy McDowell and Elizabeth Taylor) to 1951.

Films that have informed *E.T.*'s view of childhood include Truffaut's *L'Argent de Poche* (1976), a charming yet unsentimental view of a kid-only universe; *The Night of the Hunter* (1955), Charles Laughton's only film as a director, which not only influenced the kids of *E.T.* but also its striking imagery and sense of forest atmosphere; *The Blue Bird* (1940), in which Shirley Temple and Johnny Russell go after the bluebird of happiness in a fairy-tale milieu, again placing hardened kids in a fantastical context; *Whistle Down the Wind* (1961), which sees three youngsters – mirroring *E.T.*'s brood – finding a criminal in a barn – mirroring *E.T.*'s set-up – and being taken in by his claims that he is Jesus Christ, the kids sharing the *E.T.* clan's fascination with the outsider; and *Our Mother's House* (1967), which is built around seven kids who bury their mother's body in the garden to avoid going to an orphanage. Carlos Saura's *Spirit of the Beehive* (1973) focuses on two kids whose imagination runs riot after watching *Frankenstein*. The sense of the inner workings of the childish imagination provided a strong antecedent to Spielberg's visions.

Away from movies, classics of children's literature, including Frank Baum's *The Wonderful Wizard of Oz*, Rudyard Kipling's *Kim* and the fairy tales of George MacDonald (*The Princess and the Goblin*), have also impacted heavily on *E.T.* in numerous ways from the simple linear storytelling to the pervasive tone of innocent adventure. Yet the real touchstone in this respect is *Peter Pan* – *E.T.* borrows liberally from the JM Barrie landmark, citing everything from flying kids, to death followed by resurrection, Spielberg even casting Keys as a contemporary Captain Hook. To acknowledge the debt, the film also includes a direct quotation with Mary reading a passage to Gertie ('Clap your hands if you do believe in fairies'), an enraptured E.T. listening from the hallway.

CASTING: One of the many positive influences *E.T.* exerted over modern movies was raising the ante for children's performances in movies. The director found his Elliott after the film editor Ed Warschilka Jr sent Kathleen Kennedy a reel of Sissy Spacek's directorial debut *The Raggedy Man* (1981). The oldest of Spacek's sons was played by Texan Henry Thomas, a ten-year-old from San Antonio. Spielberg hardly had to make a great leap of imagination to envision Thomas as Elliott: in *The Raggedy Man*, he played a fatherless kid who wanders around in the yard with a torch. Aeons away from the sickly tots that populated child flicks, Thomas invests Elliott with a remarkable reserve and gravitas that does little to ingratiate and is all the more moving for it.

For sweet, precocious Gertie, Spielberg discovered sweet, precocious Drew Barrymore. The third generation of the Barrymore acting clan – daughter of John Barrymore Jr and the actress Idiko Jaid, granddaughter of the silent-movie star John Barrymore – Drew had started in commercials aged two and a half, and would have come to Spielberg's attention playing William Hurt's daughter in Ken Russell's

Altered States (1980). Originally interviewed for *Poltergeist*, Barrymore won Spielberg over at her screen test by concocting tales of being in a punk-rock band.

Elliott's older brother Michael was the first film role for sixteen-year-old Robert MacNaughton. Previously, he had received huge plaudits for his off-Broadway role as an idiot with water-divining powers in *The Diviners*. If Thomas and Barrymore got all the attention, MacNaughton is the unsung hero of the *E.T.* trio: on paper, he seemed the bland brother; on film, he turns in an understated transition from cynical teen to true believer.

Shelley Long was Spielberg's original choice for the role of Mary, the brood's separated mom. After the *Cheers* star proved unavailable Spielberg spotted Dee Wallace in the little-known TV show *Skag* opposite Karl Malden. Prior to that, Wallace had caught the eye in a cameo in Blake Edwards's *10* (1979) and as the heroine of Joe Dante's *The Howling* (1981). Spielberg knew all about Peter Coyote, as the actor had tried out for Indiana Jones after Tom Selleck fell out. A skilled resourceful performer, he was winning attention at the time for his role in Walter Hill's *Southern Comfort* (1981). A kind of American version of *Close Encounters*' Claude Lacombe, Coyote handles Keys's shift from mysterious authoritarian to sensitive father figure with gentle aplomb.

PRODUCTION: For the first time in his feature-film career, Steven Spielberg did not storyboard *E.T.*. He started but, around 40 per cent of the way through the script, the director jettisoned his *de rigeur* visual blueprinting process, sketching out only the effects shots. For his pet project, Spielberg would be flying without a safety net.

'I had the feeling the boards might force the child actors into stiff, unnatural attitudes and I didn't want that. I wanted them to be so spontaneous that if something natural did come up – something that was a gift from the gods – then we'd be able to use it without the boards saying we couldn't.'

Shot under the faux title of *This Boy's Life* – described as 'a comedy about antics and lifestyles of boys living in Southern California today' – *E.T.* began production shooting scenes of Elliott's high school on Tuesday, 8 September 1981. Having finished at Culver City High School, the production shot for eleven days in the Southern California districts of Tujunga (Elliott's house exteriors) and Northridge (Elliott's neighbourhood exteriors) before finishing the rest of the shoot over 42 days at the Laird International Studios in Culver City – the home of *King Kong* and *Gone With the Wind*. Amid fears that *E.T.* would be leaked to the press, security was a major concern on set with every cast and crew member required to sign a confidentiality agreement.

Facilitated by the creature's proficiency, the breakneck shooting undoubtedly influenced the spontaneity and brisk coherence that courses through *E.T.* In the brave new world after *Raiders*, Spielberg completed the 65-day schedule four days ahead of time.

TICS OF THE TRADE: 'I think as a director I was more conscious of lighting on *E.T.* than on any movie I've ever done before,' Spielberg told *American Cinematographer* in 1982. By creating the exterior forest and backyard in the malleable environment of a studio, Spielberg and his cinematographer Allen Daviau were able to control the look of the movie, using the twin Spielberg arsenal of diffuse fog effects and backlighting. The resulting movie not only defines the trademark Spielberg look more than any other film, but has an imagination, subtlety and boldness that are rare in American film.

Foremost in everyone's mind was the lighting of the creature. 'If you got too much light on him, particularly in the early scenes, it was a disaster,' Daviau explained. 'One iota too little, and there was nothing there. So it was all like that riding on a knife edge: it was very tricky stuff.' Yet Daviau worked wonders. Using aluminium foil as a means to bounce and create small pockets of light, Daviau's interplay of silhouette and backlight creates a wonderful sense of mystery around E.T. in the early scenes, adding emotional textures as the character grows more visible through the course of the film.

Perhaps the trickiest challenge was to create visual variety in the cramped quarters of a child's bedroom. Spielberg wanted to create an inner sanctum that was believable, yet somehow safe and magical. In a similar approach to that used in *Close Encounters*, Daviau opted to ground the fantasy in absolute realism, justifying every illumination with a light source, even hustling Spielberg for the exact time of day the scene took place in order to determine the exact direction of light. The magic comes in the form of Elliott's toy cupboard, E.T.'s home and sanctuary for most of the movie. Again, the unreal feel is painted with logical light sources: the yellow kerchief draped over a lamp bathes the room in an artificial sunset but the masterstroke is the stained-glass window, the spreckled colour lending the room a wonderland feel – the paintings of Maxwell Parrish had a strong impact on these scenes. The warmth in the house is played in direct contrast to the antiseptic feel once the Government agents move in: pale machinery and clear plastic shower curtains turn the place of sanctuary into a cold, fluorescent clinic.

As with the lighting, the framing also takes an up-front role in emphasising dramatic beats. To underline the fact that the movie is

113

taking place in a child's universe, the camera is placed very low – *E.T.* is abundant with ceilings – and the adult characters (e.g., the biology teacher) are painted as marginal, often faceless figures – most notably the leader of the hunt, identified only by his keys. As ever, Spielberg turned to the world of animation for his inspiration.

'It was very important to me that adults not be part of this children's world – visibly,' Spielberg noted. 'That they have no identity until it's crucial to the story. I remember the cartoons of Warner Bros and MGM, of Chuck Jones, of Friz Freleng and Tex Avery, of all the great cartoonists of the 40s . . . you never see the adults . . . You saw the hands. You saw the stockings. You saw the high-heeled shoes. You saw the tight-fitting dress. You never saw the character!'

It should also be marked that Spielberg returns to the bravado of the dolly zoom for the first time since *Jaws*: the camera tracks towards and zooms out from an overview of Elliott's neighbourhood. As the movement concludes, a still camera lens is forced into shot, snapping away, the camera panning right to a huge close-up of that bunch of keys. If not as dramatic as the Roy Scheider moment, the technique serves to disorientate a simple surveillance scene and key us in to the danger that looms over Elliott's household.

CLASSIC LINES:
Michael *(trying to explain away Elliott's first encounter with E.T.)*:
  'Maybe it was a pervert or a deformed kid.'
Gertie: 'A deformed kid.'
Michael *(sarcastically)*: 'Maybe an elf or a leprechaun.'
Elliott: 'It was nothing like that, penis breath!'

Elliott: 'I'm keeping him.'

Elliott: 'How do you explain school to a higher intelligence?'

E.T.: 'E.T. phone home.'

Elliott: 'He's a man from outer space and we're taking him to his spaceship.'
Greg: 'Well, can't he just beam up?'
Elliott: 'This is reality, Greg.'

E.T.: 'Come.'
Elliott: 'Stay.'
E.T.: 'Ouch.'
Elliott: 'Ouch.'
E.T.: 'I'll be right here.'
Elliott (last line): ''Bye.'

COMIC RELIEF: Delivered with the deftest touch by both director and cast, *E.T.* has a generous sprinkling of hilarious scenes. Best of all is the priceless moment in which Gertie's high-pitched scream startles E.T., his neck extending in fear, the chase through the house that follows building up the laughter. More sly, if equally funny, is the sequence in which Mary explores the kids' toy cupboard, the camera panning round the array of toys passing an impassive E.T. inconspicuous in the mix. This is a perfectly executed piece of visual humour. Elsewhere, Spielberg scores laughs by using E.T. as a comedy stooge: dressed up as a bag lady, bumping into work surfaces when drunk or falling flat on his face as when Mary knocks the creature over with the fridge door – it was Spielberg's idea to get the character inebriated.

VISUAL EFFECTS: A perfect example of how effects can grace and embellish a story without dwarfing it, *E.T.* saw Spielberg return to George Lucas's Industrial Light and Magic facility after the fruitful collaboration on *Raiders*, the effects team headed up by the movie's visual effects supervisor Dennis Muren. Although the film contained only around fifty effects shots, ILM's shot roster ran the gamut of the company's effects arsenal, including miniature work, matte paintings, stop-motion and motion-control camerawork. The two central flying-bike set pieces – one iconic moment involving Elliott and E.T. traversing the night sky, the other seeing E.T. spirit the five cyclists away from the encroaching authorities – were achieved by a technique known as go-motion, a variation on the traditional stop-motion technique, that uses a computerised system to add realistic motion blurring to puppets and models.

To a scale of four inches per foot, three immaculately detailed miniature bikes were created – even the brakes worked on Elliott's – along with three fully articulate bodies and five interchangeable heads which were repainted/redressed to represent different characters. To add a human presence into the scene, live-action shots of the actors on bikes were shot against a blue screen and inserted into footage shot from a helicopter.

Landing in a miniature forest, 13 feet by 14 feet, adorned with two-foot-tall redwoods (created from Juniper sprays), E.T.'s spaceship, designed by the *Star Wars* visionary Ralph McQuarrie, was originally conceived as a flat saucer-shaped craft but ultimately resembled an antiquated, Jules Verne-type diving bell. Standing 24 inches high, weighing around 45 pounds, the model was one of the most mechanically complex items created for a movie at the time. As the spaceship leaves the Earth's atmosphere for the last time, the storyboards dictated that the ship leave a vapour trail. However, ILM went one better, creating a rainbow. That is so Spielbergian that you wonder how he didn't think of it himself. It is the perfect sign-off for E.T.'s first adventure on Earth.

SOUND EFFECTS: It is one of the myths that surround *E.T.* that Debra Winger provided the voice for the title star. While Winger did deliver some of the character's pivotal lines – including 'E.T. phone home' – the bulk of E.T.'s utterances were delivered by Pat Welsh, a 65-year-old Marin County housewife. The sound designer, Ben Burtt, overheard her distinctive vocals in a camera store and cheekily asked the retired elocution teacher to remove her dentures and talk without her teeth. Convinced that her screechy voice was ideal for the role, Burtt paid her $350 to spend a day recording E.T.'s minimal dialogue. Subsequently, her voice was enriched by watery textures. A Lucasfilm employee, Howie Hammerman, had the dubious honour of providing E.T.'s belch during the beer frenzy, whereas other sounds were grabbed from the animal world – the scream E.T. gives out after seeing Elliott for the first time is an otter shriek that has been electronically processed. Moreover, the alien's purring sounds that lull Elliott to sleep are actually dog growls played at a slower speed.

Elsewhere, the film demonstrates Spielberg's use of sound to underscore plot points and emotions. This is most vividly demonstrated in the the high-pitched jangling of keys that gives the leader of the E.T. pursuit team his monicker. 'Keys have always scared me,' Spielberg told Barry Norman. 'I had a friend in college who wore a very large keyring, with thirty, forty keys on it. We could hear him coming a hundred yards away. Down the hallways, against the tiles, the floor of the school halls, you'd hear these keys get louder and louder. And I thought that would be a frightening image, especially to a space creature who doesn't know what keys are.'

WHAT'S THE SCORE? Now working on their sixth film together, the collaboration between director and composer was as smooth as ever. In a modus operandi that was rapidly becoming the norm since *Close Encounters*, Williams composed the score before the effects sequences were finished, often creating music to missing scenes on pure instinct. Flitting between delicate lyricism, portentous malevolence and lush, occasionally operatic romanticism, Williams, as ever, plays, works and reworks numerous themes across the story: the ethereal flute theme that sets the story in motion; the menacing music that accompanies Keys and co. – as Keys becomes a more friendly figure, this music is cleverly recast in a lighter, gentler mode; the Elliott–E.T. love theme with its gentle interplay between strings, woodwind and harp – a blissfully dreamlike variation occurs as the impressionistic lullaby that lulls Elliott and E.T. to sleep; the piece generally referred to as 'The Theme From *E.T.*', which accompanies the flight over the moon, an exhilarating piece of wholesome feel-good scoring. The score is as emotionally resonant as film scores get, and, unlike the case with, say, *Jaws* or *Raiders*, no theme is given any more precedence than any other, the music dovetailing together into a beautifully realised whole. In short, *E.T.* represents John Williams's best work for Spielberg.

CUT SCENES: With Spielberg's regular editor Michael Kahn on loan to *Poltergeist*, the director turned to Carol Littleton to cut *E.T.* into shape. Scenes shot but deleted include:

Extra footage inside E.T.'s spacecraft. Here we see more of the intergalactic nursery: bizarre vegetation such as a four-foot root with a human face, the botanist's gardening tools and two cobra plants (actually hand puppets) battling each other.

A small scene in which Elliott moves around the room basically relighting the space to his satisfaction while receiving a lecture from his mother. Although the scene would have helped establish a lighting schema to Elliott's room, it was removed as it slowed the story down.

The next deleted moment occurs just after Elliott has shown E.T. his *Star Wars* toys. The phone interrupts the guided tour and Elliot goes to answer it. While Elliott talks to his mom, E.T. explores and falls into a full bath. Feigning vomiting to get off the phone, Elliott sprints into the bathroom. But the little alien likes water, gently pushing the boy away, lying in the bath and blowing bubbles.

Following Elliott's liberation of the lab frogs, he begins filling his textbook with diagrams of electronic circuitry. In telepathic contact with E.T., who is constructing his communicator device, he sees his scribbling going off the edge of the paper, on to the desk and continuing in midair before he begins writing with chalk on the blackboard and all over the walls.

Next to go was probably the most famous of all *E.T.*'s cut scenes. Elliott is dragged before the school principal, played by no less than Harrison Ford! As with other shots of authority figures in the film, we never see Ford's face – only the back of his head, his shoulders and his hands. Melissa Mathison also appeared in the scene as the school nurse.

Other scenes dropped:
- A small scene where E.T. creeps into Mary's bedroom as she sleeps and places an M&M sweet on her pillow. Maybe this moment was excised as Mars wouldn't play ball with the product-placement fee.
- At Hallowe'en, Elliott and E.T. run into the neighbourhood nerd, Lance. Elliott passes E.T. off as his cousin.
- In the prerelease version, the quintet-of-flying-bikes sequence

actually ran longer than in the finished print. To add a sense of purpose to the scene, Spielberg took out about a third of the live-action chase preceding the flight and a shot of a Go-Motion puppet sightseeing from his midair status.

- Finally, there are two different shots of E.T.'s spaceship coming out of clouds that appear in trailers for *E.T.* but not the final movie.

UNSUNG HERO: Carlo Rambaldi, creator of the mechanical E.T., for pulling off the astonishing trick of making the audience forget that the star of the movie is a special effect. Taking up the baton from Spielberg's visualisation process – which included the normal (conceptual drawings by Ed Verreaux) and the abnormal (sticking pictures of the poet Carl Sandburg's and Albert Einstein's eyes on to the faces of infants), Rambaldi created a full-size clay version for videotape testing, the final ugly face based on a character from a Rambaldi painting, *Ladies of the Delta*, and the eyes of his Himalayan cat.

The full-size E.T. was three feet tall and capable of 85 different moves, worked by a dozen operators using a complex series of hydraulic, mechanical and electrical cables. As it was not feasible to house all the innards in one body, three different versions were built with four changeable heads, the favoured one being an electronic model competent in 35 different facial tics.

To enhance E.T.'s dexterity, Rambaldi created a pair of latex, four-fingered gloves that were pasted on to the hands of the mime artist Caprice Roth. On her first day of shooting, a nervous Roth drank gallons of coffee, the excessive caffeine causing her hands to shake on camera. Amid jokes about E.T.'s DTs, the cautious hand moves were worked in as a character trait.

Supplementing the Rambaldi creation, three actors played E.T. in the walking scenes. Matthew De Merrit, legless since birth, was discovered by Spielberg at the UCLA Medical Center in Los Angeles, and portrayed E.T. in the knockabout drinking scene. Yet the role proved too physically taxing for the twelve-year-old, so Pat Bilon, a two-foot-ten nightclub bouncer (!), handled the lion's share of E.T.'s walking and running scenes – he also plays E.T. under the sheet on Hallowe'en. On the film's release a two-foot-eleven, 22-year-old actress, Tamara de Treaux, gained talk-show notoriety as the woman who brought E.T. to life. In actuality, she was E.T.'s stand-in and doubled for the alien only in the concluding walk up the spacecraft gangplank.

GEDDIT! In the early scenes within E.T.'s spacecraft, among the flora is a replica triffid from Phillip Yordan's *The Day of the Triffids* (1962). As the kids move out of the house to check Elliott's claims of an intruder, one of the group sings the theme to *The Twilight Zone* ('Deedle-deedle, deedle-deedle') – aptly enough, Spielberg's next film as a director.

Separated from his landing party, E.T. surveys a city sprawl. In actuality this is an ILM matte painting littered with in-jokes such as a street lined with fast-food joints (McDonald's, Taco Bell, KFC) and a drive-in movie theatre showing *Star Wars*.

Other *Star Wars* references in *E.T.* include Elliott showing the alien his action figures, Michael doing a Yoda impression and E.T. chasing after a Yoda lookalike on Hallowe'en – John Williams interpolates a snatch of Yoda's theme to underline the joke.

The science-fiction movie that E.T. watches on TV is *This Island Earth* (1955).

The movie Elliott re-enacts and E.T. watches is John Ford's *The Quiet Man* (1952), starring John Wayne and Maureen O'Hara. As Elliott kisses the girl, John Williams replays the love theme from Victor Young's score. The girl whom Elliott kisses after liberating the amphibians is played by Erika Eleniak, who found fame as Shauni McClain in *Baywatch*.

Also in the Hallowe'en scene, an unbilled Debra Winger (who provided the voice for some of E.T.'s dialogue) plays a heavily disguised hatchet victim.

The optical supervisor, Mitchell Suskin, plays one of the medical team who battle to save E.T.'s life.

The breathtakingly lucid image of Elliott and E.T. flying in front of the moon became the logo for Spielberg's production company Amblin.

FACTOID FRENZY! To create a huge blossom on one of the alien trees, the effects crew inflated condoms and covered them in molten polyfoam. Once the creation had cooled, the prophylactics were deflated resulting in a perfect alien flower.

Such was the demand to see *E.T.* that Spielberg showed the film to President Reagan at the White House, Javier Perez at the United Nations (Spielberg was awarded a UN Peace Medal) and Prince Charles at the Empire, Leicester Square.

In Sweden, Finland and Norway, under-twelves were banned from seeing *E.T.* because of 'the portrayal of adults as the enemies of children.'

In 1985, Spielberg filed a claim against the *Los Angeles Times*, who printed a caricature of E.T. as an LA hipster sporting decadent rings, a coke spoon and a razor blade hanging from his telescopic neck.

Spielberg plans to reissue the film on its twentieth anniversary in 2002. Although some of the missing scenes will be reinstated, *E.T.* won't suffer the ignominy of undergoing a CGI makeover.

THE CRITICAL FACULTY: 'Watching this vibrantly comic, boundlessly touching fantasy, you feel that Spielberg has, for the first time, put his breathtaking technical skills at the service of his deepest feelings.' (Michael Sragow, *Rolling Stone*.) 'A triumph almost beyond imagining.' (Kenneth Turan, *California*.) 'A dream of a movie, a bliss-out . . . Genuinely entrancing movies are almost as rare as extra-terrestrial visitors.' (Pauline Kael, *New Yorker*.) 'The best Disney movie Walt Disney never made' (*Variety*.) 'E.T. is as contemporary as laser beam technology but it's full of the timeless longings expressed in children's literature of all eras.' (Vincent Canby, *New York Times*.) 'A fabulous masterpiece that leaves all who see it with a warm and radiant glow of optimism and joy.' (Rex Reed, *New York Daily News*.) 'One of the most beautiful fantasy adventures ever made. The millions who see it will stay rooted in their seats, astonished what movies can do.' (David Denby, *New York* magazine.) 'A miracle movie and one that confirms Spielberg as a master storyteller of his medium . . . A perfectly poised mixture of sweet comedy and ten-speed melodrama, of death and resurrection, of a friendship so pure and powerful it seems like an idealised love.' (Richard Corliss, *Time*.)

BOX OFFICE: Opening on 11 June 1982, *E.T. The Extra-Terrestrial* grossed $11.8 million in its first weekend of release, then bucked the trend by actually increasing its grosses over the next 21 days: $12.4 million the next week, $12.8 million the second and $14 million the third. In that first week of release, Spielberg was personally earning half a million dollars a *day* as his cut of the profits. The film remains Spielberg's biggest hit in the US to date, raking in a jawdropping $399.8 million. Elsewhere, the film enjoyed a Christmas roll-out – *E.T.* is nothing if not a Christmas movie – earning $301.2 million, the worldwide gross totalling $701 million.

A by-product of the unparalleled popularity was the merchandising onslaught: although Spielberg wanted to preserve some of the purity around the character, MCA/Universal hurriedly licensed around two hundred spin-offs in an attempt to cash in. E.T.'s image subsequently appeared on dolls, chocolate cereals, books, ice cream (in actuality, vanilla, coloured an otherworldly green), picture-disc records, even adorning women's undergarments. To halt the progress of the unlicensed bandwagonning, Universal spent around $2 million filing two hundred lawsuits in pursuit of bogus merchandising.

Tie-in deals made before the film came out started to look very canny. Melissa Mathison had specified in her script that Elliott would lead E.T. back to the house using a trail of M&Ms. However, Mars chose not to co-operate with the production, believing E.T. to be an ugly creature who would frighten young children. At that time, Jack Dowd, vice-president at Hershey's Chocolate, was seeking to create a high profile for his new confectionery line, Reese's Pieces. Hershey's bankrolled a joint campaign to the tune of $1 million – the poster features the squat alien munching the chocolate underscored with the slogan 'E.T.'s Favorite Candy' – and sales of Reese's Pieces jumped by 65 per cent.

AWARDS: Nominated for nine Academy Awards, *E.T.* picked up Oscars for Best Music, Visual Effects, Sound and Sound Effects Editing. It was also nominated for Best Picture, Director, Screenplay, Cinematography, Film Editing, losing out on everything to Richard Attenborough's *Gandhi*. At the BAFTAS, the film was nominated for Best Film, Director, Screenplay, Outstanding Newcomer (Henry Thomas, Drew Barrymore), Cinematography, Music, Film Editing, Make-Up Artist, Production Design/Art Direction, Sound and Visual Effects, with John Williams the only winner on the night for Best Music. Williams also picked up a Golden Globe (where the film won the gong for Best Motion Picture – Drama) and a Grammy for his score.

THE SIZZLE! As *E.T.* ruled the world's box office, a very public dispute arose over patenting the image of the creature. Credited as the sole writer of *E.T.*, Melissa Mathison took Universal to arbitration via the Writer's Guild of America, arguing that, as the first written description of the alien character appeared in her screenplay, she was entitled to a slice of the merchandising revenue. Universal countered, affirming that Spielberg and Sayles had outlined the description in the *Night Skies* script, but the arbitration found in favour of Mathison: the look of the alien was all outlined in Mathison's drafts long before Carlo Rambaldi's work had started.

Spielberg came into more legal hot water after a 38-year-old playwright, Lisa Litchfield, filed a $750 million lawsuit against him. She claimed the director had ripped *E.T.* off from her 1978 one-act play, *Lokey From Maldemar*. Barry Price, a writer, made similar claims that *E.T.* more than resembled a story idea he had pitched to Disney. Both suits were thrown out.

Around that time, Spielberg was also accused of plagiarism by a more respected source: the legendary Indian film-maker Satyajit Ray contended that Spielberg had stolen the story from an unproduced screenplay, *The Alien*, which Ray had circulated around Hollywood in the late 70s – he even cited specific scenes that had been pilfered wholesale, like the alien bringing dead plants back to life. While Spielberg's lawyer's eventually persuaded the director to back off, the story hit around Oscar time and, some believe, seriously dented Spielberg's chances of winning.

JOIN THE DOTS: Kids – *The Sugarland Express, Jaws, Close Encounters of the Third Kind, 1941, Twilight Zone: The Movie, Indiana Jones and the Temple of Doom, The Color Purple, Empire of the Sun, Hook, Jurassic Park, Schindler's List, The Lost World: Jurassic Park, Amistad.* **Aliens** – *Close Encounters of the Third Kind.* **Suburbia** – *Close Encounters of the Third Kind.* **Dolly zoom** – *The Sugarland Express, Jaws, Indiana Jones and the Last Crusade.* **Contemporary setting** – *The Sugarland Express, Jaws, Close Encounters of the Third Kind, Twilight Zone: The Movie, Always, Hook, Jurassic Park, The Lost World: Jurassic Park.* **Movies within movies** – *The Sugarland Express, Close Encounters of the Third Kind, 1941.* **Absent fathers** – *The Sugarland Express, Close Encounters of the Third Kind, The Color Purple, Empire of the Sun, Indiana Jones and the Last Crusade, Hook.* **Ordinary people in extraordinary situations** – *The Sugarland Express, Jaws, Close Encounters of the Third Kind, 1941, Twilight Zone: The Movie, Empire of the Sun, Hook, Jurassic Park, Schindler's List, The Lost World: Jurassic Park, Amistad, Saving Private Ryan.*

SEND IN THE CLONES! Although Spielberg has resolutely resisted making a sequel to *E.T.*, certain ideas for a follow-up have been thrashed about. In 1985, William Kotzwinkle wrote a novel, *E.T., The Book of the Green Planet*, based on a story idea from Spielberg. More interestingly, basking in the glow of the film's success, Spielberg reunited with Melissa Mathison to work through ideas on a filmic sequel. Entitled *ET II: Nocturnal Fears*, it has a plot that turns the tables on the original as Elliott and friends are kidnapped by extra-terrestrials and contact E.T. to rescue them. Nothing ever came of the idea. But, if there is any sequel to *E.T.*, it is the Spielberg-devised Universal Studio Tours ride, a $40 million attraction that opened in 1991.

John Carpenter's *Starman* (1984) saw a fish-out-of-water love story develop as an alien in human form (Jeff Bridges) fell for an earthling (Karen Allen). *D.A.R.Y.L.* (1985) mined *E.T.*-style 'emotional sci-fi' in the yarn as a young robot begins to develop feelings. *Flight of the Intruder (1986)* and *Batteries Not Included* (1987) once again pitched aliens within a friendly family environment. *Mac and Me* (1988) followed a group of aliens trying to survive in California, sharing many parallels with *E.T.*'s plot. Subsequent films that have pitted lonely children with 'magical' buddies include *Short Circuit* (1986), *Star Kid* (1998) and *The Iron Giant* (1999). Movies such as *Splash!* (1984), *Free Willy* (1993) and *Flipper* (1996) would have also been easier to obtain a green light for the glow of *E.T.*'s success.

E.T. GOES POP: Probably the first *E.T.* in-joke in a movie appeared in *Young Doctors In Love* (1982) just six weeks after *E.T.* opened – *E.T.*'s catchphrase 'Phone home' can be heard on the hospital tannoy. *Airplane II: The Sequel* (1982) saw E.T. phone from an airport payphone – cost: $6 million! *Gremlins* (1984) sees one of the mischievous creature reach out for a phone line, also growling 'Phone Home'. In *Naked Gun 2½: The Smell Of Fear* (1991), Leslie Nielsen's Frank Drebin flies across the moon in a parody of *E.T.*'s famous shot. While playing Captain Steve Hillier, Will Smith makes a simple threat in *Independence Day* (1996): 'I'm just a little anxious to get up there and whoop E.T.'s ass'. *Star Wars: Episode 1 – the Phantom Menace* (1999) clearly features a delegation of E.T.s in the galactic senate sequence.

'Flying' (the theme from *E.T.*) reached number eighteen in the UK chart. *The Simpsons* episode 'The Springfield Files' sees Reverend Lovejoy lecture on a visitor from the heavens who brings a message of peace and love: 'E.T. The Extra-Terrestrial, I loved that little guy.'

Since April 1999, *E.T.* has been the star of a string of British Telecom commercials where he helps a family overcome their communication problems. Fortunately, we've yet to see Spielberg's cherished creation blighted by being 'on the mobile'.

FINAL ANALYSIS: Perhaps the most unassuming blockbuster ever to create queues snaking outside cinemas, *E.T.* represents a landmark movie in the Spielberg canon. Building on the poet-of-suburbia mantle that started with *Close Encounters*, Spielberg continued his unique fascination with science fiction as autobiography. That he emerged from the film perceived as a spinner of shiny new fairy tales spells the crucial difference between *Close Encounters* and *E.T.*: if the former is a resolutely adult take on family dysfunction and otherworldly delights, the latter is located firmly within a child's worldview.

The success of *E.T.* ensured Spielberg an unparalleled creative carte blanche and financial autonomy embodied by the creation of his production outfit Amblin Entertainment in 1984. A further byproduct of the film's popularity was the cementing of Spielberg's status as a recognisable celebrity: a slew of biographies appeared, and his life story was mythologised in countless magazine features.

As a piece of film-making, *E.T.* taught Spielberg that his instincts and impulses were the equal of any storyboard. Much more

importantly, it is a film that will pass the test of time and find
a new abode in the affections of each successive generation. The
film is a simple parable, lyrically told, and its underlying messages –
that strangeness is only skin-deep, that love conquers all – are
certainly well-worn themes, but they are so seductively argued and
beautifully wrought that watching *E.T.* is like hearing them for the
first time.

If the surfeit of exposure and tie-in merchandising has seen the little
critter become a much-abused icon, it should not detract from the
tangible sense of innocence that imbues every frame. There is a purity
about *E.T.* that is unparalleled in modern movies, its ability to
bedazzle and beguile remaining untarnished. Graced with a simple,
affecting screenplay, performed with an astonishing naturalism, shot
with a careful attention to detail and delicacy, then embellished by the
subtlest special effects, *E.T.* gambled on the hope that beneath a
culture of highly developed cynicism beat sensitive, open hearts. And
in daring to be tender, in daring to be emotional, Spielberg created his
most perfectly formed film to date. A magical magnum opus to sit
atop any career.

SPIELBERG ON SPIELBERG: 'When I started *E.T.* I was fat and
happy and satisfied with having the films I had on my list. And I
just didn't feel I had anything to lose. I had nothing to prove to
anybody except me – and any people who might have wondered if
I ever had a heart beating beneath the one they assumed that ILM
built for me.'

Twilight Zone: The Movie (1983)

(Colour, 102 mins)
Kick the Can (23 mins)

Studio Warner Brothers
Producers Steven Spielberg, John Landis
Executive Producer Frank Marshall
Screenplay George Clayton Johnson, Richard Matheson, Josh Rogan
Story George Clayton Johnson
Director of Photography Allen Daviau
Production Design James D Bissell
Music Jerry Goldsmith
Editing Michael Kahn ACE
Associate Producer Kathleen Kennedy
Casting Mike Fenton and Jane Feinberg, Marci Liroff
Project Consultant Carol Serling

Production Manager Dennis E Jones
First Assistant Director Pat Kehoe
Second Assistant Director Dan Attias
Script Supervisor Katharine Wooten
Location Manager Richard Vane
Auditor Bonne Radford

CAST: Scatman Crothers (*Mr Bloom*), Bill Quinn (*Mr Conroy*), Martin Garner (*Mr Weinstein*), Selma Diamond (*Mrs Weinstein*), Helen Shaw (*Mrs Dempsey*), Murray Matheson (*Mr Agee*), Peter Brocco (*Mr Mute*), Priscilla Pointer (*Miss Cox*).

BUDGET: $10 million

MPAA: PG

BBFC: AA

TITLE SEQUENCE: 'Kick the Can' is the second instalment in a four part anthology (the other three directed by John Landis, Joe Dante and George Miller). In the true tradition of the *Twilight Zone* TV series, the camera tilts down from the sky to the entrance of the Sunnyvale Rest Home. Underscored by gentle, nostalgic harp music, a voice-over intones: 'It is sometimes said that, where there is no hope, there is no life. Case in point: the residents of Sunnyvale Rest Home, where hope is just a memory. But hope just checked into Sunnyvale disguised as an elderly optimist who carries his magic in a shiny tin can . . .'

PLOT SUMMARY: For the residents of the Sunnyvale Rest Home, life is a staple diet of lectures about vitamins and watching the game show *Jeopardy* on TV. The status quo is disrupted by Mr Bloom, an elderly black gentleman who encourages the residents to recall their favourite childhood games and fantasies. Mrs Dempsey recollects her dreams of being a dancer; Mr Weinstein relates his love of climbing; Mr Agee speaks of his desire to be the silent matinée star Douglas Fairbanks. When the tables are turned on him, Mr Bloom recalls his love of the playground game, kick the can, and, producing a shiny tin can, suggests everyone join him for a game that evening. All are enthused except the miserable Mr Conroy, who refuses to take part.

With Bloom waking everyone from their midnight slumber, the Sunnyvale residents gather in the garden to play kick the can, a variation on hide and seek in which the winner is the person who can kick the tin can without being spotted. The game gets under way and the can is quickly kicked – with surprising, magical results. The OAPs have returned to their childhood selves running around the garden, reciting nursery rhymes, climbing walls and dancing. At the height of the reverie, the kids ask Bloom why he has opted to stay old, He tells them that he has kept his age the same but his mind young, an insight that causes the group to ponder on the ramifications of being young again; reliving school, losing loved ones and the general hardships of life are deemed too tough to go through again and the kids decide to return to their real ages – except Mr Agee, who takes off into the night in full Douglas Fairbanks swashbuckling mode.

The following morning, the group are refreshed – even Mr Conroy is seen furiously kicking the can in search of some rejuvenation. Mr Bloom leaves Sunnyvale and walks down the street to a nearby convalescence home, presumably to work his magic on a new set of ageing hearts.

BACKSTORY: Airing on CBS from 1959–64, *Twilight Zone* was the brainchild of Rod Serling, a prolific TV writer who wrote half the episodes and acted as the on-screen Master of Ceremonies. Running to 150 episodes, the surreal twist-in-the-tale yarns worked through absurd premises and nifty plotting (plus a classic theme tune by Marius Constant), rather than any reliance on special effects, garnering a cult following.

Although Serling had plans for a movie version himself – first as a three-part anthology movie, then as a feature-length episode – *Twilight Zone: The Movie* did not move towards reality until after his death in 1975. The idea was resurrected at Warner Bros, who were anxious to draw wunderkind directors into their fold, believing a new, improved *Twilight Zone* anthology would be too difficult for any baby-boomer film-makers to resist. Once Spielberg signed on – the first time he had worked with WB – others soon followed: John Landis (*National Lampoon's Animal House, The Blues Brothers*) came aboard as writer-director-co-producer; Joe Dante (*Piranha, The Howling* (1980)) and George Miller (*Mad Max* (1979), *Mad Max II* (1981)) were brought in for their first Hollywood studio assignments.

John Landis was to write and direct the only fresh story idea, revolving around a modern-day bigot who becomes a victim of persecution in various time frames by the Nazis, the Ku Klux Klan and the Americans in Vietnam; Dante was to remake the episode 'It's A Good Life', embellishing the slender tale of a small boy with malevolent mind-bending powers with typical cartoon-style wackiness and mischievous humour; Miller was to update perhaps the best-remembered of all *Zone* episodes, 'Nightmare At 20,000 Feet', in which an aircraft passenger is driven increasingly crazy by a gremlin ripping to pieces the wing of a plane.

For his own segment, Spielberg hired Richard Matheson, the

architect of *Duel* and a guiding creative force behind the original *Zone* series, for scripting duties. The first treatment Matheson attacked was an idea Spielberg was originally going to direct for MGM. At Hallowe'en, a bully sets about all the kids, who are dressed up for trick-or-treating, only to find that supernatural creatures dish out payback – the story ends with the thug unable to take off his own horrific mask.

However, this story was dropped when Spielberg turned his attention to 'The Monsters Are Due on Maple Street', a 1960 *Zone* episode penned by Serling himself. This story sees a typical Spielbergian neighbourhood turned into disarray after a series of inexplicable power failures. Heightened by rumours from a local sci-fi fan (a young Spielberg?) that aliens have infiltrated their number, all hell breaks loose in true *War of the Worlds* style and the idyllic community disintegrates into anarchy. In a chilling coda, aliens watch from a nearby hill, chuckling at the ease with which they have set human beings against each other, and begin their preparations for invasion.

Following the death of the actor Vic Morrow and two children in a helicopter accident during the shooting of John Landis's segment (see **The sizzle!**), Spielberg canned 'The Monsters Are Due on Maple Street', perhaps because the story dictated that a child actor work late nights with dangerous special effects, which would be inappropriate in the wake of the accident, and perhaps because Spielberg wanted to soften the tone of the film with a less macabre tale. Opting to direct the most gentle and mellow of *Zone* tales, Spielberg switched to 'Kick the Can'. Airing on 2 September 1962, 'Kick the Can' was directed by George Clayton Johnson and starred Ernest Truex as Charles Whitley, the man-child who starts an OAP insurrection via the childhood game. Best known for scripting the first broadcast *Star Trek* episode, 'Man Trap', and writing the novel *Logan's Run*, George Clayton Johnson wrote the yarn in his final script for the series.

Although Richard Matheson rewrote the original episode, Johnson himself suggested a pivotal change for the movie version. On TV, the kids scoot off into the night; in the movie, however, they opt to return to decrepitude. 'You're provoked into a lot of thought once you see these children running off into the night,' Johnson argued. 'What are they going to do? The story has really just opened when that happens. That had been on my mind for years, so I had worked out another half-hour teleplay that took off at the end of that.'

Ultimately, Spielberg brought in Melissa Mathison under the pseudonym 'Josh Rogan' to polish the final script, adding the character of Agee who does actually choose to leave the adult world behind.

ORIGINS: There are many precedents of the anthology form utilised by *Twilight Zone: The Movie*. Often cited by Spielberg and Landis as the biggest influence, Ealing Studios' excellent *Dead of Night* (1945) sees an architect (Mervyn Johns) driven mad by an endless rondelet of recurring dreams in which supernatural tales are related to him. It employs many *Zone* attributes: a framing device, a cache of quality directors (Cavalcanti, Charles Crichton, Robert Hamer, Basil Dearden) and a host of star names. Other portmanteau pictures include *Dr Terror's House of Horror* (1965), *Asylum* (1972), EC Comics' *Tales From the Crypt* (1972) and the Stephen King–George Romero collaboration *Creepshow* (1982).

The swashbuckling antics of Mr Agee have their roots not only in Douglas Fairbanks but also in the heroics of Errol Flynn, particularly *The Adventures of Robin Hood*. Also, perhaps the success of *Star Trek: The Motion Picture* (1979) – another favourite baby-boomer TV show blown up for the big screen – influenced Warner Bros execs to turn their attention to the *Zone*.

CASTING: For the role of the sprightly Mr Bloom, Spielberg chose Scatman Crothers, whom he had seen on the set of Kubrick's *The Shining* (1980) while shooting *Raiders* at Elstree. Crothers, whose real first name is Benjamin, gained the nickname Scatman from his skill at scatting, the ability to improvise sounds to jazz melodies. He was a jazz singer-drummer-guitarist before moving into acting in the early 50s. Résumé highlights include *The Aristocats* (1970), *Lady Sings the Blues* (1972), *One Flew Over the Cuckoo's Nest* (1975) and *Bronco Billy* (1980) but he will be chillingly remembered as the hotel psychic Halloran in *The Shining*. His trademark was a toothy, winning smile.

Eschewing the Hume Cronyn–Jessica Tandy school of obvious octogenarians, Spielberg rounded out the home's residents with fresh old faces: Bill Quinn (Mr Conroy) featured in *The Birds* (1963) and, bizarrely enough, also had a part in *Ace Eli and Rodger of the Skies* (1973), the film that gave Spielberg his first big-screen credit; Martin Garner (Mr Weinstein) had appeared in *The Big Fix* (1978), *The Frisco Kid* (1979) and *Airplane II* (1982); prior to the *Zone*; Murray Matheson (Mr Agee) began his film career in *The Way to the Stars* (1945); taking in *The Bamboo Prison* and *Love Is a Many Splendored Thing* (both 1955) along the way; Helen Shaw (Mrs Dempsey) went on to star in *Parenthood* (1989); Selma Diamond (Mrs Weinstein) started out as a comedy writer for magazines and TV before switching to acting – she featured in *It's A Mad, Mad, Mad, Mad World* (1963), *Bang the Drum Slowly* (1973) and *My Favorite Year* (1982).

Also, keep 'em peeled for Priscilla Pointer as Miss Cox, the

Sunnyvale orderly. Best known to audiences as Amy Irving's mother in *Carrie* (1976), Pointer is Amy Irving's real-life mother and was Spielberg's mother-in-law at the time.

PRODUCTION: With a schedule that encompassed one day on location in an old people's home plus five days on the Warner Brothers lot, 'Kick the Can' began its six-day shoot on 26 November 1982. Lacking his customary zeal to personally supervise every detail, Spielberg failed to attend preproduction meetings, allowed the script supervisor Katharine Wooten to stage scenes for him and even let 'Josh Rogan' work on dialogue readings with the actors.

TICS OF THE TRADE: Reunited with many of his *E.T.* collaborators – the cinematographer Allen Daviau, production designer James D Bissell, editor Michael Kahn – Spielberg seems to have taken the stylistic traits of his masterpiece and, while they're beautifully rendered, redeployed them without the same thought or care. Early scenes of the rest home are bathed in warm, nostalgic tones which, once the game of kick the can is under way, give way to the diffuse lighting and heavy backlight that have become Spielberg's trademark. Moreover, Spielberg's staging of the action lacks the dynamism of his top form, the imagery and camera movement nowhere near as compelling as usual.

CLASSIC LINES:
Mr Conroy: 'I like being old. My son has already promised to have me frozen.'
Mr Weinstein: 'You're already frozen, popsicle head.'

Mr Bloom: 'The day we stop playing is the day we start getting old.'

WHAT'S THE SCORE? Among the most interesting things about *Twilight Zone: The Movie* is that it represents the first time (of two so far) Spielberg has not worked with John Williams as his feature-film musical collaborator. Perhaps the only rival to Williams in the modern movie music stakes, Jerry Goldsmith, had previously contributed to the *Zone* TV series as well as classic scores to the horror fantasy genre: *Planet of the Apes* (1968), *The Omen* (1976, for which he won an Oscar), *Alien* (1979), *Star Trek: The Motion Picture* (1979), even the Spielberg-produced *Poltergeist* (1982).

Needing a tougher edge to counterbalance the sentimental scenario, Goldsmith's soundtrack for 'Kick the Can' is overly twee, despite pretty scoring. He lacks Williams's skill at energising the pictures through careful spotting, and the mixture of real instruments and synthesisers – such as the faux trumpet fanfare that accompanies young Mr Agee as Douglas Fairbanks – is at its best in the piano-dominated melancholy passages and the joyous waltz that accompanies the Mr Agee–Mrs Dempsey dance. Elsewhere, the score is so light it practically floats away.

GEDDIT! The Actor Richard Swingler plays the role of Mr Gray Panther in 'Kick the Can'. He also portrayed Elliott's science teacher in *E.T. The Extra-Terrestrial*.

Warner Bros wanted to warm Spielberg's ego by calling the movie *Steven Spielberg Presents The Twilight Zone*. Spielberg preferred the TV title.

Utilising special effects and sound overdubbing, Spielberg considered using Rod Serling introductions that had never been seen to preface each segment. But the idea was scrapped.

After *Twilight Zone: The Movie*, the actor Scott Nemes (young Mr Weinstein) opened Spiral West, a club that *didn't* sell alcohol.

Although credited as project consultant, Carol Serling, widow of Rod, was less than impressed with the finished movie: 'Rod's stories were about people. They weren't about spaceships and green-eyed monsters. The movie, on the other hand, placed an emphasis on special effects. How could it be otherwise with Spielberg?'

Part of Rod Serling's original conception of the *Twilight Zone* anthology movie was the story called 'Eyes', eventually included in the *Night Gallery* series directed by Spielberg.

THE CRITICAL FACULTY: 'A lump of ironic whimsy . . . The tone here is sentimental-comic, horribly slick. It's as if Steven Spielberg had sat down and thought out what he could do that would make his detractors happiest.' (Pauline Kael, *New Yorker*.) 'Kick the Can' is lugubrious self-parody set to a raging torrent of sappy music. Spielberg has become the King Midas Of Candyland – from space monsters to senility, everything he touches turns to icky goo.' (J Hoberman, *Village Voice*.) 'The theme is echt-Spielberg and his technique is as stylish as ever but here it is dangerously close to self-parody. What was innocent, wondrous and charming in *E.T.* here looks like an advertisement for innocence, wonder and charm. Alas, hardsell whimsy is a contradiction in terms.' (David Ansen, *Newsweek*.)

BOX OFFICE: Opening in the US on 24 June 1983, *Twilight Zone: The Movie* grossed a disappointing $42 million worldwide. Yet perhaps this figure is not so bad when you consider the above reviews.

THE SIZZLE! On 23 July 1982, during the filming of John Landis's segment at the Indian Dunes Park, north of Los Angeles, the actor Vic Morrow and two Vietnamese children, six-year-old My-Ca Dinh Le and seven-year-old Renee Shin Yi Chen, were thrown into a lake after a ground-based explosion sent a chopper whizzing across a mock Vietnamese village, crashing to the ground: the helicopter skid crushed Chen to death and the flailing rotor decapitated Morrow and Dinh Le.

As it emerged that the two children were hired illegally and employed in a dangerous scene that contravened child-safety laws, Landis was pulled over the coals, first by the Director's Guild of America, who rebuked the film-maker for 'unprofessional conduct'; then the California Labor Commission fined Landis (plus the associate producer George Folsey Jr, the unit production manager Dan Allingham and Warner Bros) $5,000, the strictest penalty for transgressing labour laws, with the California Occupational Safety and Health Administration stepping in with 36 citations and some $1,350 in fines.

Yet the most serious charge levelled at the production saw Landis, Folsey, Allingham, the special-effects co-ordinator Paul Stewart and the helicopter pilot Dorcey Wingo charged with involuntary manslaughter resulting from 'child endangerment' (and three additional manslaughter charges resulting from 'gross negligence'), the first time a major Hollywood director was ever indicted on criminal charges resulting from an on-set fatality. In 1985, facing a possible six years in prison, Landis, Allingham and Folsey suggested a plea bargain that meant admitting to charges of 'conspiracy to illegally employ children' in exchange for dropping the manslaughter charge. The LA county DA's office rejected the bargain and a long, controversial, media-saturated trial raged over ten months before Landis and his co-defendants were acquitted in May 1987.

The only mention of Spielberg in any legal citations came in the civil lawsuits by the families (these included Vic Morrow's daughter, the actress Jennifer Jason Leigh) of the three victims which resulted in a number of multimillion-dollar settlements. Despite a claim by one of the team, Carl Pittman, that he saw Spielberg at the location on the night of the accident (later retracted), Spielberg was not present on that night and there has never been any evidence to link the film-maker to any criminal act. But, surprisingly enough, considering his status as producer of the film, Spielberg was never interviewed by any government agency throughout the five-year investigation of the incident.

JOIN THE DOTS: Kids – *The Sugarland Express, Jaws, Close Encounters of the Third Kind, 1941, E.T. The Extra-Terrestrial,*

Indiana Jones and the Temple of Doom, The Color Purple, Empire of the Sun, Hook, Jurassic Park, Schindler's List, The Lost World: Jurassic Park, Amistad. **Contemporary setting** – *The Sugarland Express, Jaws, Close Encounters of the Third Kind, E.T. The Extra-Terrestrial, Always, Hook, Jurassic Park, The Lost World: Jurassic Park.*

SEND IN THE CLONES! While the Spielberg-produced *Batteries Not Included* (1988) played similar riffs on the rejuvenation of the old by mysterious forces, and *Hook* revisited the idea of grown-ups finding their lost childhoods, the biggest influence *Twilight Zone: The Movie* had on the Spielberg output is present in the *Amazing Stories* TV series (1985–87), a Serling-like collection of surreal tales that lacked the *Zone*'s inspiration, edge and storytelling smarts. The Rob Bottin-designed creature that pulls the wing to pieces in *Nightmare At 20,000 Feet* can be seen as a precursor for Joe Dante's *Gremlins* (1984). Other horror anthology movies to follow in *Twilight Zone: The Movie*'s wake (if hardly clones) include *After the Midnight* (1989), *Tales From the Darkside: The Movie* (1990), *From a Whisper To a Scream* (1986), *Grim Praerie Tales* (1990) and *Tales From the Hood* (1995).

FINAL ANALYSIS: In many respects it is obvious why making a segment of an anthology movie appealed to Spielberg: apart from acknowledging a debt to a prime influence in his youth, adapting a short story and being cosseted around other talented film-makers offered a way of easing back into movie directing after the phenomenon of *E.T. The Extra-Terrestrial*. The finished article, however, falls a long way short of the promise. Perhaps because he was numbed by the helicopter tragedy, there is little of the telling nuance, and genuine sense of innocence and feeling that mark out his best work. It is not completely without interest – given Spielberg's affinity for childhood, it is surprising the wrinklies opt for old age again – and it makes for an early sketch piece to the premise of *Hook*. But, for the most part, 'Kick the Can' is heavy-handed and saccharine-dominated, dwarfed by the Dante and Miller segments that follow it. As Spielberg's penchant for the sentimental got the better of him, remaking 'The Monsters Are Due on Maple Street' might have been a more rewarding option.

SPIELBERG ON SPIELBERG: 'A movie is a fantasy – it's light and shadow flickering on a screen. No movie is worth dying for. I think people are standing up much more now than ever before to producers and directors who ask too much. If something isn't safe, it's the right and responsibility of every actor or crew member to yell "Cut!"'

Indiana Jones and the Temple of Doom (1984)

(Colour, 118 mins)

Studio Paramount/Lucasfilm
Executive Producers George Lucas, Frank Marshall
Produced by Robert Watts
Associate Producer Kathleen Kennedy
Written by Gloria Katz, Willard Huyck
Story by George Lucas
Music John Williams (performed by the London Symphony Orchestra)
Costume Design Anthony Powell
Production Design Elliott Scott
Director of Photography Douglas Slocombe BSC
Editing Michael Kahn ACE
Casting Mike Fenton and Jane Feinberg, Mary Selway Buckley, Marci Liroff
Second Unit Director Michael Moore
Choreography Danny Daniels
Assistant Director David Tomblin
Production Supervisor John Davis
Sound Design Ben Burtt
Visual Effects Supervisor Dennis Muren
Mechanical Effects Supervisor George Gibbs
Visual Effects by Industrial Light and Magic
Stunt Arranger (studio) Vic Armstrong
Stunt Arranger (location) Glenn Randall
First Assistant Director David Tomblin

CAST: Harrison Ford (*Indiana Jones*), Kate Capshaw (*Willie Scott*), Ke Huy Quan (*Short Round*), Amrish Puri (*Mola Ram*), Roshan Seth (*Chatter Lal*), Phillip Stone (*Captain Blumburtt*), Roy Chiaq (*Lao Che*), David Yip (*Wu Han*), Ric Young (*Kao Kan*), Chua Kah Joo (*Chen*), Rex Ngui (*Maître d'*), Phillip Tann (*Chief Henchman*), Dan Aykroyd (*Weber*), Akio Mitamura (*Chinese Pilot*), Michael Yama (*Chinese Co-Pilot*), DR Nanayakara (*Shaman*), Dharmadsasa Kuruppu (*Chieftain*), Stany De Silva (*Sajnu*), Dharshana Panangala (*Village Child*), Raj Singh (*Little Maharajah*), Frank Olegario (*Merchant 1*), Ahmed El-Shenawi (*Merchant 2*), Art Repola (*Eel Eater*), Nizwar Karanj (*Sacrifice Victim*), Pat Roach (*Chief Guard*), Moti Makan (*Guard*), Mellan Mitchell, Bhasker Patel (*Temple Guards*), Arjun Pandher (*1st Boy In Cell*), Zia Gelani (*2nd Boy In Cell*).

BUDGET: $28 million

MPAA: PG

BBFC: PG

TITLE SEQUENCE: Playing a neat variation on *Raiders*' opening gag, *Temple of Doom* opens with the Paramount mountain logo, which dissolves through to a mountain etched into a giant gong, the camera moving back to reveal an Asian servant striking the instrument. We are in a Shanghai nightclub and the floor show is about to begin: the inept *chanteuse* Willie Scott's rendition of Cole Porter's 'Anything Goes' (a pretty good summation of the film's ethos) in Cantonese. As Willie moves through the smoke emanating from a theatrical dragon's mouth, we enter the MGM version of the number playing in Willie's head. A line of chorus girls, decked out in eye-catching silver, work through a highly choreographed routine captured with all the style and glamour of a big production number. The sequence ends as Willie runs back into the Chinese nightclub and into a big close-up. For the record, the title appears in the infamous *Raiders* comic-strip orange-to-crimson lettering.

PLOT SUMMARY: While it continues the *Raiders* tradition of beginning the film with the concluding moments of a previous Indiana Jones adventure, *Temple of Doom*'s opening salvo actually beats *Raiders*' for nutty invention and manic energy. It's 1935 in this prequel (the year before *Raiders*) in a Shanghai nightclub. Attempting to secure the diamond he has been promised by a Chinese mobster, Lao Che, as payment for the recovery of a Manchu dynasty urn, the archaeologist Indiana 'Indy' Jones is double-crossed and drugged by the gangster. What follows is one of the most inspired set pieces in Spielberg's career as Indy searches frantically for the antidote, his new-found companion Willie Scott searching desperately for the diamond in a frenzy of machine-gun fire, dancing girls, spilling ice, falling balloons and kung fu killers. The sequence concludes as Indy and Willie jump out of the window, through various canopies and into a waiting car driven by Indy's orphaned sidekick Short Round, who speeds them through Shanghai streets to the airport.

Once midair, the threesome find themselves in more trouble as the crew (it is a Lao Che-owned aircraft) bail out over the Himalayas. Improvising a dinghy into a parachute, Indy, Willie and Short Round crash-land on a mountainside and plunge perilously into running rapids before arriving in an Indian village. They are welcomed as saviours, and the village elders ask Indy to find the sacred Sankara stone, whose theft, along with the disappearance of all the children, has condemned the village to poverty and misery.

Despite protestations from Willie, Indy drags his companions to Pankot Palace to investigate the villagers' claims that the sinister Thuggee cult is on the rise. Although he's made welcome by the pubescent Maharajah and his prime minister Chatter Lal, who dismiss the rise of the Thuggee as folklore, Indy's suspicions are confirmed after he is attacked in his quarters by a Thuggee assassin. Seeing off the assailant, Indy and Short Round investigate a tunnel: as the pair become trapped in a room full of slowly descending spikes, Spielberg skilfully hikes up the tension by intercutting Jones's struggle to escape the chamber with Willie's attempts to get into it to flee death by a thousand bugs.

Following a hair's-breadth escape, the trio move out of the frying pan but into the fire as Indy discovers the Temple of Doom itself and a human sacrifice presided over by the High Priest, Mola Ram. Indy moves down to recover the Sankara stone that enables the ritual but is captured along with Willie and Short Round. Indy is forced to drink the blood of the Kali, which turns him into an evil zombie-like presence. After preparing Willie as a sacrificial victim, Indy is brought to his senses by Short Round just in time to save Willie from certain death. Back to his regular self, Indy discovers the village children are being used to dig for the remaining two Sankara stones and leads a slave revolt, freeing the children to run out into the light.

What follows is the equivalent of *Raiders*' Flying Wing punch-up/truck-versus-horse spectacular: to make good his escape, Indy baffles a hefty guard on a rocky conveyor belt, then speeds away in a breathless mine-car chase before being pursued on to a cliff face by gushing water coursing through the tunnels. After a tense face-off on a severed rope bridge, which sees Mola Ram plunge to his death, Indy saves the final Sankara stone to return prosperity and children to rejuvenate the village.

BACKSTORY: To write the screenplay for *Temple of Doom*, Lucas turned to his *American Graffiti* (1973) cohorts Willard Huyck and Gloria Katz. Once again Spielberg, Lucas and the screen scribes holed up for a week of script meetings *chez* Lucas in Northern California. Katz and Huyck polished off the first draft of their script in six weeks, completing two further drafts within the next three weeks (once in London, Spielberg turned to John Milius for an over-the-phone transatlantic dialogue spin). Not wishing to merely retread *Raiders* glories, all agreed that *Temple of Doom* – originally titled *Indiana Jones and the Temple of Death* until 'Death' was decreed too grim for summer thrill-seeking audiences – would be a darker, more nightmarish adventure for the archaeologist. The other decision ensured that Jones should appear less the mercenary grave robber, more the benevolent hero. Spielberg himself added the character of the child sidekick Short Round to help refocus and humanise Indy's motives and quest.

Certain elements from the *Raiders* script meetings re-emerged: Lucas's conception of Indy as a tuxedo-clad, champagne-drinking hero found its way back into the opening nightclub scene, for instance. Moreover, scenes and ideas from Lawrence Kasdan's screenplay that were excised for budgetary reasons took up residence in the new movie. For example, Kasdan's original screenplay had Indy impregnating the museum of an evil warlord and included a moment where the archaeologist strangles a samurai warrior with his whip and severs a gong from its hinges and uses it as a shield against machine-gun fire. This nifty action lick found its way into *Temple of Doom*'s opening. Similarly, the *Temple of Doom* moment where Indy escapes an empty aircraft aided by an inflatable raft was originally dreamed up for *Raiders*, as was the mine-car chase. Lucas also appropriated the opening dance number from the Huyck–Katz screenplay for *Radioland Murders* (1994).

ORIGINS: The comedic striking of a gong that starts *Temple of Doom* echoes the opening of *Gunga Din* (1939), which in itself was a parody of the J Arthur Rank logo – hence a movie image that parodies a movie image that parodies a movie image! The *Gunga Din* resonances do not stop there, however: from the plot details (a forbidden temple, the Thuggee sect, the worship of Kali) to the broad strokes of action and comedy, *Temple of Doom* resembles *Gunga Din* to a large extent.

Although an anthology of numerous Hollywood musical moments, the 'Anything Goes' routine – orderly lines of dancing girls captured by a highly mobile camera – owes most to the choreography of Busby Berkeley, the visionary behind *42nd Street* and *Golddiggers of 1933* and *Footlight Parade* (all 1933).

As with *Raiders*, the substance of *Temple of Doom* owes much to the low-budget serials made by Republic Studios in the 30s and 40s: the Chamber of Spikes can be found in equally relentless form in Chapter 4 of *Perils of Nyoka* (1942). The Temple of Doom itself can be directly traced to *Tiger Woman* (1944) where the victims of the eponymous tribe leader were suspended from above, then lowered into a pool of boiling lava. A la *Doom*, the sacrificial acts were accompanied by a booming drumbeat. The chicanery of bad guys leaving good guys in a pilotless aircraft occurred in *Drums of Fu Manchu* (1940). *King of the Mounties* (1942) saw the hero bail out only to fortuitously land in a Canadian haystack. *Jungle Girl* (1941),

Spy Smasher (1942) and *King of the Forest Rangers* (1946) saw conveyor belts used as agents of danger. Mine-car chases were a staple of Republic fodder – the studio had its own 'mine-car set' in the valley – as were scenes in which heroes were chased down tunnels by rushing water (*Manhunt of Mystery Island* (1945), *Jungle Girl* (again) and *Zorro's Fighting Legion* (1939) not only featured torrents of running aqua but also rope-bridge set pieces similar to the conclusion of *Temple of Doom*).

CASTING: With *Temple of Doom*'s prequel status precluding the return of *Raiders*' Karen Allen, the search was on for a new Indy love interest. Sharon Stone was among the hundreds of actresses Spielberg saw for the part before settling on a then brunette Kate Capshaw – Lucas was adamant that Willie was blonde to contrast with Marion. Born Kathy Sue Nail, Capshaw, a graduate from the University of Missouri with a master's degree in learning disabilities, progressed from modelling to TV ads to US daytime soap (*Edge of Night*) before making her movie debut in *A Little Sex* (1982) opposite *1941*'s Tim Matheson. Seven years after *Temple of Doom*, Capshaw became Spielberg's second (and current) wife.

After a worldwide search for Short Round encompassing 6,000 children, Ke Huy Quan was found, ironically enough, in Los Angeles. The seventh of nine children born to Chinese parents, Ke spent the first six years of his life in Saigon before the family relocated Stateside. During his audition, Ke struggled over his English, so Spielberg set up an improvisation with Harrison Ford in which Short Round would accuse Indy of cheating at cards. Played around a jungle campfire, the scene actually wound up in this movie.

As with *Raiders*, the supporting actors were culled from UK casting directories: Phillip Stone could well have come to Spielberg's attention after his work with Stanley Kubrick – *A Clockwork Orange* (1971), *Barry Lyndon* (1975), *The Shining* (1980) – for the role of Captain Blumburtt; Amrish Puri (Mola Ram), a big star in Indian movies, and Roshan Seth (Chatter Lal), who played Nehru in *Gandhi* (1982), filled the villainous roles.

PRODUCTION: 'Indy II' (as it read on the clapperboard) started filming on 18 April 1983. The production had originally wanted to shoot in the Rose Palace of Jaipur in the Indian state of Rajasthan, yet government officials were offended by what they perceived as the racist nature of the script and denied the film-makers access, forcing the filming to Sri Lanka instead. As the main unit shot scenes of Indy discovering the Indian village in Kandy, a second unit, once again headed up by Michael Moore, travelled to Macao in Hong Kong to film the opening car chase set in the streets of Shanghai.

The two units joined forces back at Elstree over the ensuing three months. Working with newcomers to the Indiana Jones fold – the production designer Elliott Scott, the costume designer Anthony Powell and the mechanical effects supervisor George Gibbs – Spielberg continued his penchant for cheap, effective solutions to potentially expensive problems.

After additional filming in Northern California (the cliffhanger), Arizona, Idaho and Florida (the crocodiles), filming was completed on 8 September, a week behind schedule.

TICS OF THE TRADE: Whereas *Raiders* was a sunny, outdoor, sweeping adventure movie, *Temple of Doom* is dark, internal and claustrophobic. 'In many ways, the visual style of the film was conceived when George [Lucas] told me the story,' Spielberg told *American Cinematographer*. 'I heard Kali Cult and Thuggees. I heard temple of doom, black magic, voodoo and human sacrifice. What came to my mind immediately was torchlight and shadows and red lava light. I felt that dictated the visual style of the movie.'

With the storyline working in his favour, Spielberg developed the stylised film-noir look that he hinted at in *Raiders*. Starting from the bright gaudy sheen of an old Hollywood movie – the opening dance number, the banquet scene, the love tease between Indy and Willie – the movie descends in style to very dark, very low-key imagery. The expressionistic lighting created by a knocked-over lamp as Indy grapples with the garrotting assassin, the wild framings and bizarre lighting that mark the Temple of Doom and the candlelight that illuminates Indy as he spasms under the blood of the Kali really push the envelope on what is possible in a mainstream Hollywood blockbuster.

CLASSIC LINES:
Indy: 'I suggest you give me what you owe me or anything goes.'

Short Round: 'You call him Dr Jones, doll!'

Chatter Lal: 'Dr Jones, the eminent archaeologist?'
Willie: 'Hard to believe isn't it?'

Mola Ram: 'You do not believe me. You will, Dr Jones. You will become a true believer.'

COMIC RELIEF: While resembling *1941* in its frenetic attempts to grab laughs, *Temple of Doom* comes off much more smartly. Acting as a counterpoint to the darkness that lies at the heart of its plot, *Temple* *of Doom* is a veritable compendium of movie comedy styles working through slapstick (the opening nightclub mêlée), gross-out (the banquet) and wordplay (Indy's cries of 'Water! Water!' to cool his feet are met with a torrent of the stuff rushing through the tunnel).

VISUAL EFFECTS: Once shooting had finished, the main item on the effects agenda at Industrial Light and Magic included a scaled-down version of the mine-car chase to capture the steep drops, sharp curves and the shots that were well nigh impossible to do in live action. With the miniature set being well over fifty feet in length, two sizes of mine car were created: small ones for stop-motion photography and larger-scale ones for high-speed shots in which the models fly through the air. To keep the scale of the set as small as possible, the visual effects supervisor Dennis Muren adapted 35mm Nikon cameras to take magazines of thirty feet of film rather than bulky conventional movie cameras. The action was subsequently shot one frame at a time by the animator Tom St Amand, then enhanced optically by adding 'shake' to give the impression the footage was shot by a live-action camera. Other optical additions included, as a lump of wood is dropped in front of the mine car, sparks at the bottom of the truck in order to draw the eye to the threat.

The other main tasks for ILM included the miniature plane that crash-lands in the Andes, the molten lava pit that plays host to the Temple of Doom sacrifices and the creation of various locales through matte paintings; these included the Indian village, the exteriors of Pankot Palace, cave interiors and the cliff face that rounds off the mine-car chase.

WHAT'S THE SCORE? Again joined by the London Symphony Orchestra, John Williams does a neat job of reinventing the old theme while creating new, more disturbing material. Spielberg relies on bold statements of the *Raiders* march to punctuate the heroics – we get blasts of the familiar tune as the airborne dinghy inflates or when Indy and Short Round start picking off the Thuggee guards – but, as if to emphasise the more human dimension to Indy, the theme has a less brassy, warmer feel to it this time round. Other themes include a grandiloquent romantic motif for Willie and a catchy, jaunty, Oriental melody for Short Round. Yet Williams saves his best music for inside the Temple of Doom itself: a rollicking march to accompany the slave children's revolt; grinding, pounding rhythms to illustrate the inexorable descent of the chamber of spikes; and a nightmarish choral chant to accompany the Temple of Doom's sacrificial rituals that, as Spielberg suggests in the CD liner notes, 'could be the only music in the world effective to knock the hat off Indiana Jones' head'.

UNSUNG HERO: The production illustrator Ed Verraux, an ILM art director, Joe Johnston, and the production designer Elliott Scott, who made Spielberg's movie on paper during the four months of *Temple of Doom*'s preproduction stage. Working from Spielberg thumbnail sketches, the trio created 4,000 storyboards mapping out the movie for both logistical and budgetary as well as creative reasons.

Yet the previsualisation process went way beyond sketching. Scott built elaborately detailed seventeen-inch cardboard mock-ups (peopled by half-inch characters) of all the major sets – Indy's quarters, the crusher set, the quarry cavern – which Spielberg photographed with his 35mm Nikon to determine the most dynamic angle. Moreover, Johnston shot video footage of a mini mine-car chase (again rendered in cardboard), which was transferred to film and then cut into the live action.

Perhaps the most extensively preplanned of all Spielberg movies, *Temple of Doom* is such a finely honed, perfectly dovetailing, beautifully crafted visual experience, and that is down to the work generated before even a frame of film was exposed.

GEDDIT! As every film geek knows, the nightclub in which Willie Scott performs is named Club Obi Wan after *Star Wars*' Jedi Knight.

As Indiana Jones, Willie and Short Round arrive at the airport to be greeted by Dan Aykroyd, keep an eye out for Steven Spielberg, George Lucas and (the then Lucasfilm publicity director) Sydney Ganis dressed as missionaries in the background. The Executive Producer Frank Marshall is also spottable pulling a rickshaw.

Indiana Jones may be named after Lucas's dog, but Willie Scott is named after Spielberg's cocker spaniel and Short Round is named after the writer Gloria Katz's pooch who, in turn, was named after a character in Sam Fuller's *The Steel Helmet* (1951).

Pat Roach, who appeared in *Raiders* as the Nepalese Sherpa and bald mechanic, reprises his role as a hulking Indy nemesis by battling with Jones on a moving conveyor belt.

In an obvious reference to *Raiders*, two Arab swordsmen jump out to halt Indy's path. Looking smugly confident, Indy goes for his gun, only to find it missing from the holster. A nice throwback to a classic *Lost Ark* moment, it does represent a break in the space-time continuum if you consider that *Temple of Doom* is set before *Raiders*.

FACTOID FRENZY: As he strained his back riding elephants in Sri Lanka, Ford's commitment to stuntwork led to his suffering from a ruptured disc. To treat the injury, surgeons injected Ford's spine with a solution concocted from green papaya, a well-known meat tenderiser. The actor was back on set in six weeks.

Among *Temple of Doom*'s credits reads 'Physical Conditioning for Mr. Ford by Body by Jake, Inc'. This refers to Jake Steinfeld, a personal trainer to the entertainment industry, who whipped Harrison Ford (and Spielberg) into physical shape before and during the shoot.

Matte photography on *Temple of Doom* is credited to one David Fincher, the director of *Se7en* (1995) and *Fight Club* (1999).

To keep the snakes within his own care, UK animal handler Mike Culling booked his pythons into the Sri Lankan hotel under the name Mr and Mrs Longfellow.

The sheep's-eyeball soup was a regular tomato soup with fake eyeballs stuck to the bottom of the dish with putty – until Kate Capshaw dislodged them. The modelled monkey heads were filled with whipped cream and vegetable colouring to represent chilled simian brains.

For the climax where the rope bridge collapses, look closely for the layer of multicoloured dust designed to leave a residue or shadow of the bridge's former self to help sell the fall.

THE CRITICAL FACULTY: 'This is brilliance that rides on narrow-gauge tracks. You don't fault a theme park for not being a cathedral.' (Richard Corliss, *Time*.) 'One of the most sheerly pleasurable comedies ever made.' (Pauline Kael, *New Yorker*.) 'Spielberg has gone to such great lengths to avoid boredom that he has leaped squarely into the opposite trap: this movie has such unrelenting action that it jackhammers you into a punch drunk stupor.' (Jack Kroll, *Newsweek*.) 'That Spielberg should devote himself to anything so debased in imagination is unbearably depressing.' (David Denby, *New Yorker*.) 'The most cheerfully exciting bizarre, goofy romantic adventure movie since *Raiders*, and if it's high praise to say that it's not so much a sequel as an equal.' (Roger Ebert, *Chicago Sun Times*.) 'A two hour series of none too carefully linked chase sequences . . . sitting on the edge of your seat gives you a sore bum but also a numb brain.' (Derek Malcolm, *Guardian*.)

BOX OFFICE: Released in America on 23 May 1984, *Indiana Jones and the Temple of Doom* notched up $180 million at the US box office alone, some $60 million short of *Raiders*.

AWARDS: Nominated for two Academy Awards: Best Original Score (which it lost to *A Passage To India*) and Best Visual Effects – step forward, Denis Muren, George Gibbs, Michael J McAllister, Lorne Peterson – which it won. The *Temple of Doom* visual-effects crew also picked up a BAFTA, where the film was also nominated for Best Cinematography, Editing and Sound.

The other honour bestowed on Spielberg at the opening of *Temple of Doom* was to have his hand and footprints set in cement outside Mann's Chinese Theater on Hollywood Boulevard. Yet Spielberg (and Lucas) arrived ninety minutes late, by which time the cement had virtually hardened.

THE SIZZLE! Actually living up to the severity of its title, *Temple of Doom* provoked much furore from critics, parental groups and religious organisations who felt it overstepped the violence yardstick acceptable in a film predominantly aimed at children. On the back of special pleadings from both Paramount and the Lucas–Spielberg camp, the film garnered a PG certificate, backed by a poster campaign that stated 'This may be too intense for younger children'. Despite the disclaimer, the press used the film as a clarion call for responsible film-making and the resultant controversy saw Spielberg publicly apologise for the movie. The upshot of *Temple of Doom*'s graphic qualities – along with a similar reaction to the Spielberg-produced *Gremlins* – saw the introduction of the PG-13 rating to the American certification system. In the UK, *Temple of Doom* achieved a PG rating but only after the BBFC had made 25 cuts (the most important excision involved Mola Ram pulling out a human heart from the sacrificial victim).

JOIN THE DOTS: Kids – *The Sugarland Express, Jaws, Close Encounters of the Third Kind, 1941, E.T. The Extra-Terrestrial, Twilight Zone: The Movie, The Color Purple, Empire of the Sun, Hook, Jurassic Park, Schindler's List, The Lost World: Jurassic Park, Amistad.* **Kidnapped kids** – *The Sugarland Express, Close Encounters of the Third Kind, Empire of the Sun, Hook, Schindler's List, Amistad.* **Roller-coaster plotting** – *Jaws, 1941, Raiders of the Lost Ark, Indiana Jones and the Last Crusade, Jurassic Park, The Lost World: Jurassic Park.* **Aircraft** – *Close Encounters of the Third Kind, 1941, Raiders of the Lost Ark, Empire of the Sun, Indiana Jones and the Last Crusade, Always, Hook, Saving Private Ryan.* **Historical setting** – *1941, Raiders of the Lost Ark, The Color Purple, Empire of the Sun, Schindler's List, Amistad, Saving Private Ryan.*

SEND IN THE CLONES! *King Solomon's Mines* (1985) leaped on to the post-*Temple of Doom* adventure bandwagon with Richard Chamberlain as Allan Quatermain (this even had the cheek to purloin *Raiders'* John Rhys-Davies), followed by a sequel, *Allan Quatermain and the Lost City of Gold* (1987). Both featured Sharon Stone fresh from her failed Willie audition. An Australian effort, *Sky Pirates* (1985), also served up an Indy clone in search of a mystical stone.

FINAL ANALYSIS: Following the controversy surrounding *Indiana Jones and the Temple of Doom*'s shadowy, violent tone, Spielberg offered numerous public retractions for the nightmare he created. In actuality, he needn't have apologised. Boasting the squirm factor that squarely appeals to kids (if not overprotective parents), *Temple of Doom* is the perfect encapsulation of childish nightmares, served up with devilish glee within an obviously fantastic milieu. Moreover, Spielberg often being painted as a director with an overly sentimental, optimistic worldview, the albeit comic-book darkness of *Temple of Doom* highlights a shaded flipside to his universe that was present in *The Sugarland Express* and emerges more fully in *Empire of the Sun*, *Schindler's List*, *Amistad* and *Saving Private Ryan*.

Inevitably, *Indiana Jones and the Temple of Doom* falls slightly short of the standard set by *Raiders of the Lost Ark*, yet remains superior to 1989's *Indiana Jones and the Last Crusade*. While *Temple of Doom* replicates *Raiders*' sense of mounting momentum and nonstop fun, it is in the sections in between the action sequences where *Doom* loses out, lacking the well-realised characters (Willie is no Marion, Mola Ram no Belloq), the inventive wit and the sharpness of script that made the original outstanding: *Raiders* saw Indy use both brain and brawn to track down his prize; second time out (or, considering its prequel status, should that be first time out?), Indy uses only muscle and the film is poorer for it.

That said, *Temple of Doom* often surpasses *Raiders* as adroitly assembled action cinema. The set pieces, particularly the chamber of spikes and mine-tunnel pursuit, fit together with deft precision and jaw-dropping bravura. Spielberg's marshalling of the opening nightclub mêlée, building up information (the whereabouts of the antidote/diamond) and incident (the human shish kebab, the chorus girls, the rolling gong) at a dizzying rate, is nothing short of miraculous. And, if nothing else, the dazzling opening song-and-dance number is the ultimate confirmation that Spielberg has to revive the full-blown musical before he stops directing.

SPIELBERG ON SPIELBERG: 'The picture is not called *The Temple of Roses*: it's called *The Temple of Doom*. I can remember as a child at the movies my parents used to cover my eyes in the cinema when they felt I should not be exposed to what was coming out of the screen: it was usually two people kissing innocently. There are parts of this film that are too intense for younger children but this is a fantasy adventure. It is the kind of violence that doesn't really happen, will not really happen and cannot really be perpetuated by people leaving the cinema and performing these tricks on their friends at home.'

The Color Purple (1985)

(Colour, 152 mins)

Studio Warner Bros
Produced by Steven Spielberg, Kathleen Kennedy, Frank Marshall, Quincy Jones
Executive Producers Jon Peters, Peter Guber
Screenplay by Menno Meyjes
Based upon the novel by Alice Walker
Director of Photography Allen Daviau
Production Designer J Michael Riva
Edited by Michael Kahn ACE
Music Quincy Jones
Costume Design Aggie Guerard Rodgers
Casting Reuben Cannon and Associates CSA
Unit Production Manager Gerald R Molen
First Assistant Directors Pat Kehoe, Richard Alexander Wells
Art Director Robert W Welch
Music Supervision Tom Bahler
Make-up Design Ken Chase
Project Consultant Alice Walker
Set Designer Virginia L Randolph
Production Sound Mixer Willie Burton
Illustrators John C Johnson Jr, Ed Verraux
Special Effects Supervisor Matt Sweeney
Stunt Co-ordinator Greg W Elam
Supervising Sound Editor Richard L Anderson
Re-recording Mixers Buzz Knudson, Robert Glass, Don Digirolamo
Second Unit Director Frank Marshall

CAST: Danny Glover (*Albert*), Whoopi Goldberg (*Celie*), Margaret Avery (*Shug Avery*), Oprah Winfrey (*Sofia*), Willard Pugh (*Harpo*), Akosua Busia (*Nettie*), Desreta Jackson (*Young Celie*), Adolph Caesar (*Old Mister*), Rae Dawn Chong (*Squeak*), Dana Ivey (*Miss Millie*), Leonard Jackson (*Pa*), Bennet Guillory (*Grady*), John Patton Jr (*Preacher*), Carl Anderson (*Reverend Samuel*), Susan Beaubian (*Connie*), James Tillis (*Buster*), Phillip Strong (*Mayor*), Larry Fishburne (*Swan*), Peto Kinsaka (*Adam*), Lelo Masamba (*Olivia*), Margaret Freeman (*Odessa*), Howard Starr (*Young Harpo*), Daphaine Oliver (*Young Olivia*), Jadili Johnson (*Young Adam*), Lillian Njoki Distefano (*Young Tashi*), Donna Buie (*Daisy*), Leon Rippy (*Store Clerk*), John R Hart (*Mailman*), David Thomas (*Road Gang Leader*), Carrie Murray (*Loretta*).

BUDGET: $15 million

MPAA: PG

BBFC: 15

TITLE SEQUENCE: Over the Warner Bros logo, the busy sounds of insects and birds increase in volume and continue over the credits, purple lettering in an elaborate, flowery handwritten style against a black screen. The arrival of Whoopi Goldberg's credit kick-starts the sounds of children singing, playing a clap-hands game, subliminally linking the actress to the action in progress. The soundtrack becomes even more enriched as a shimmer of strings leads us into the first image: a big close-up of a flower tilting up to reveal two black girls – Celie and Nettie – playing in a field. As a pretty version of what will become the main theme takes off, the credits carry on as the camera follows the kids joyously running through high flowers in a series of tracking shots. The pair exit the flowers, revealing one of them – Celie – to be pregnant. The sequence ends as the 'Directed by Steven Spielberg' credit appears in a perfectly composed shot of Celie surveying the sky, taking in the beautiful day.

PLOT SUMMARY: In 1909 Georgia, Celie, a young black girl, sees her two children Adam and Olivia (both sired by her father) sold at birth to the Reverend Samuel. Celie's only comfort comes courtesy of her close relationship with her sister Nettie, a bond that is broken when Celie is forced into a loveless marriage with a widower, Albert Johnson, a.k.a. Mister. Violently abused by Mister, and attacked by his kids, Celie becomes a long-suffering obedient wife (chief among her chores is shaving Mister), her gloom lifted only when Nettie comes to stay. Yet, after Nettie resists Mister's sexual advances, she is banished from the farm and Celie's life, Mister stating that Celie will never hear from Nettie again.

Seven years on, Celie still hasn't received word from Nettie but life in the Johnson family has moved on: first in the brief marriage of Mister's son Harpo to the formidable Sofia – Celie is amazed by her spirit – and, second, the arrival of a blues singer, Shug Avery, the real love of Albert's life, at the household. Shug struts her stuff at Harpo's Juke Joint, where she performs a song dedicated to Celie, who is transfixed by her openness. Escaping a bar-room brawl started by Sofia, who has punched out Harpo's new girl Squeak, Shug teaches Celie the meaning of tenderness by gently kissing her. Celie attempts to leave for Memphis with Shug (who has been unable to reconnect with her preacher father) but Mister returns, quashing her escape.

Picking up after a subplot involving Sofia being arrested for squaring up to the mayor, and her becoming a downtrodden maid, Celie is delighted to see Shug return with a new husband in tow. As the two men swap Shug stories, the singer discovers that Mister has been hiding Nettie's letters, a correspondence that details Nettie's life in Africa as a missionary with the Samuels, and that Celie's children are alive and well. Seething, Celie contemplates cutting Mister's throat during his ritual shaving session but Shug stops her with news that Nettie, Adam and Olivia are returning to America. In a powerful scene set around a dinner table, Celie tells Mister exactly what she thinks of him and this time does leave for Memphis with Shug and Grady.

Inheriting the family home from her mother (it transpires the man she thought was her father was actually her stepfather), Celie runs a successful dress shop. Singing at the Juke Joint, Shug hears the music from her father's church and leads the party revellers to sing in unison with the choir, resulting in a reconciliation with her father. A lonely, chastened Mister brings Celie the letter that confirms her estranged family are coming home. The subsequent reunion redefines 'ecstatic'.

BACKSTORY: Steven Spielberg started reading *The Color Purple* at the suggestion of his collaborator, Kathleen Kennedy, not as a potential directing assignment but as a rattling good read.

'If she'd presented it to me as a potential project, I think I'd have felt challenged and defensive,' Spielberg recalled. 'But I started reading it and I couldn't stop.'

As a movie project, *The Color Purple* was placed with the then production duo of Peter Guber and Jon Peters at Warner Bros, who had engaged the legendary film composer and Michael Jackson producer, Quincy Jones, as a collaborator on the project. It was Jones who sought out Spielberg as the director, feeling he was the best bet not only to get the movie made but also to get it to the widest possible audience.

On the surface, Alice Walker's Pulitzer Prize-winning novel seemed an unlikely source material for a Spielberg film. Constructed as a series of letters from a young black girl to her sister and God, Walker's earthy, conversational, 'womanist' prose encompassed physical abuse, incest, bigotry and lesbianism all within a historical black milieu far removed from Spielberg's white middle-class suburbia. Yet Celie is an outsider trying to make sense of an alienated reality and *The Color Purple* shares the reconstruction of a family motif that lies at the centre of many of Spielberg's stories.

Yet before Spielberg got the gig, he had to meet with Alice Walker's approval. It was the first time he had been interviewed for a job since *Jaws*, and the pair met at Walker's home in San Francisco on 20 February 1984. Walker knew little of Spielberg's reputation but the surprising ace in the hole was *The Sugarland Express*: Walker had caught some of it on late-night TV and admired its passionate intensity and empathy with its characters. This, allied with his deep understanding of the book, saw Spielberg given the go-ahead.

While the relationship between Spielberg and Walker was for the most part a fruitful one, the collaboration did induce some anxieties within Walker. The first arose as Spielberg, early in the production phase, announced his admiration for *Gone With the Wind* (1939) in general and the childlike slave Prissy (played by Butterfly McQueen) in particular – a sentiment that sent alarm bells ringing in Walker, who detested the simplistic stereotypes depicted in the film. Moreover, at a preproduction meeting, Spielberg suggested that Walker take a cameo role in a street scene holding Spielberg's newly born baby Max. The racial naïveté inherent in the idea upset Walker deeply.

As a sign of Spielberg's and Jones's desire to retain Walker's input, the pair invited the author to write the screenplay. Although exhausted by the project after an eighteen-month publicity tour promoting the book, Walker turned in a first-draft screenplay that was much more sexually explicit regarding Celie and Shug's relationship. After Walker vetoed Spielberg's choice of Melissa Mathison to carry on the redrafting of the screenplay, the Dutch-born writer Menno Meyjes was brought in after Spielberg was impressed with Meyjes's script for *Lionheart*. Hammering out a first draft in three weeks, Meyjes's most important addition to the script was to introduce voice-over to reproduce the epistolary nature of the novel. Meyjes completed five drafts in five months before the director was satisfied. The resulting screenplay is pretty faithful to its source material, but one addition for the movie is Shug's quest to reconcile with her father. It was also Spielberg's idea for the young Nettie and Celie to be reading *Oliver Twist*, a book that had a bigger bearing on his next project *Empire of the Sun*.

By far, the most controversial adaptation decision concerned the toning down of Celie and Shug's lesbian love act. Not only did Spielberg excise the explicit language – the book is full of references to 'titties' and 'pussies' – but also a scene in which Shug holds up a mirror to Celie's private parts to teach her about the beauty of her own body and sexuality. In the finished film, the couple share a smattering of chaste kisses in a scene tentatively played by Goldberg and Avery.

'It was an artistic decision,' Spielberg explained at the time. 'I didn't categorise it as a lesbian relationship so much as a love relationship of great need. No one ever loved Celie other than God and her sister. And here, Celie is being introduced to the human race by a person full of love. I didn't think a full-out love scene would say it better.'

147

ORIGINS: Stylistically and emotionally, *The Color Purple* draws much of its influence from two of Spielberg's cinematic heroes: John Ford and David Lean. From Ford, Spielberg sequestered the simplicity and lucidity of composition as well as the semi-realistic depiction of a rural idyll that was a trademark of numerous Ford films from *Tobacco Road* (1941) to *The Searchers* (1956). Indeed, the final moments of *The Color Purple* – Celie and her family gathered on the porch – has a number of visual reference points in the opening and closing moments of the latter, with Debbie (Natalie Wood) returning to the Jorgensen family fold displaying a similar thematic thread. Spielberg has also cited the influence of *The Grapes of Wrath* (1940) on the deeply emotional tone of *The Color Purple* as well as the cinematography: the scene in which Celie gives birth in the foreground with Pa pacing up and down outside in the background is a nod to the style of deep-focus photography made famous by the *Wrath* cameraman, Gregg Toland.

From Lean's filmography, *Dr Zhivago* (1965) is the key work in relation to *The Color Purple*. Celie and Nettie peering at Mister through small clear circles in otherwise frosted windows and the artful dissolve from railway tracks to tyre tracks owe a big debt to Lean's work on *Zhivago*, as does the graceful crane shots that follow Celie running across the farmstead. A more specific reference occurs as Celie walks behind her mother's hearse, a clear echo of *Zhivago*'s opening.

CASTING: Whoopi Goldberg (real name: Caryn Johnson) came to Spielberg's attention via Alice Walker. A huge fan of the novel, Goldberg wrote to Walker offering to play 'dirt on the floor' if any movie adaptations were in the pipeline. Walker was already a fan of Goldberg's character-driven one-woman show and recommended her to Spielberg. The director invited Goldberg to perform her act at his screening for some friends – who turned out to be Walker, Quincy Jones, Lionel Richie and Michael Jackson. Bravely (or stupidly), she even included a skit on *E.T.* in which the alien is a dope fiend who ends up in an LA jail. While Spielberg subsequently offered her the role of Celie, Goldberg privately wanted to play Sofia, believing the character had more heart. She decided not to argue.

Following supporting roles in *Escape From Alcatraz* (1979), *Witness* (1985) and *Silverado* (1985), Danny Glover earned his biggest role to date. (He would gain much more popularity as the affable Roger Murtaugh, Mel Gibson's partner in the *Lethal Weapon* franchise.) Tina Turner was at the top of the casting director Reuben Cannon's list to play Shug Avery, but the legendary singer turned down the role – much to the relief of Alice Walker, who believed that Turner brought too much real-life baggage to the role. The executive producer Peter Guber suggested Diana Ross, an idea that similarly filled Walker with anxiety and dread. Eventually, Margaret Avery won out as the sensuous singer.

Another first-timer on *The Color Purple* was Oprah Winfrey. Quincy Jones had caught her as host of *AM Chicago* on a hotel room TV and, recognising her feisty, self-respecting sensibilities, suggested to Spielberg she would be ideal for Sofia. The success of the movie introduced Winfrey to a national audience, paving the way for TV superstardom with her self-monickered talk show.

PRODUCTION: *The Color Purple* started its eight-week shooting schedule in midsummer 1985 in Universal Studios before moving on location to Monroe, North Carolina. As with *E.T.*, Spielberg didn't storyboard the screenplay, not wishing to pin ideas or emotions to a preconceived plan. Unusually for the director, this ad hoc approach occasionally meant that scenes – in particular Celie's uprising at the dinner table – were shot from manifold angles with no real plan in Spielberg's head about how it would fit together. As a kind of safety net, Alice Walker was ever present on set, writing lines of dialogue, advising on the accuracy of costume and set design, even reading aloud from the book to duplicate Celie's voice-over.

The first scene to go before the camera was Celie flowering at the sight of Shug's show-stopping performance at the Juke Joint. Starting with this scene was a canny decision by Spielberg: just as Celie transforms, witnessing a life she never knew existed, so the lens catches Whoopi Goldberg's very first time before the camera, drinking in the wonder that surrounds her. Noticing Goldberg's reticence around the rest of the cast in rehearsal, Spielberg carefully nurtured her performance, referencing scenes from other films to explain the expressions he wanted her to achieve. Equally intimidated on her first movie, Oprah Winfrey worked in a constant state of insecurity – her on-set journal revealed she believed Spielberg hated her – until the dinner scene in which the director encouraged her to improvise her dialogue. After the scene ended, Whoopi Goldberg rose at the table and declared, 'My sister today became an actress.'

TICS OF THE TRADE: Spielberg's visual construction of *The Color Purple* is classical, enveloping the action in strikingly simple compositions, sumptuous lighting and lyrical camera moves. Yet, for once, the style works against the content, taking something that should be raw and real, transforming it into something picturesque and movie-like: the kind of 'God light' that worked so well for *Close Encounters* or *E.T.* here adds a sentimental patina – see the light pouring through the window as Celie and Shug discover Nettie's letters – that dilutes the drama.

However, *The Color Purple* is also a vehicle for some textbook editing. As Celie reads Nettie's letters from Africa, a flurry of crosscutting transplants the African plain into Georgia: so as Celie looks up from her reading by a riverside, an elephant storms through the bushes, seemingly towards her; as Celie surreptitiously hides Nettie's letters in a hymn book, we seamlessly switch to a bulldozer crashing through the chancel in Nettie's church thousands of miles away. While the effect not only speeds up the drama considerably, it makes the potentially dull act of a character reading letters entirely cinematic. This crosscutting technique reaches its zenith as Spielberg juxtaposes Celie shaving Mister, Shug running to stop Celie slitting Mister's throat and an African sacrificial ritual to dazzling ends, hiking up the excitement into a frenzy while always retaining clarity within the drama. The scene is an early incarnation of the set piece in *Schindler's List*, which contrasts Goeth's beating of Helen with a party in full swing.

Allied to the film-making fireworks, Spielberg also finds powerful moments in restraint. A sequence in which Mister playfully rides alongside Nettie with every intention of raping her is a superbly assembled montage, contrasting and building Mister's playfulness with Nettie's ever-increasing fear – however, as Mister drags Nettie off into the woods, the camera does not follow the pair, suggesting the struggle through sound. An even more powerful sense of Spielberg's dramatic suggestion sees Sofia square up to the mayor: rather than depict the punch in big close-up, Spielberg cuts to a wide shot as Sofia draws back her fist and our view of the blow is obliterated by a yellow truck that roars across the frame. Once the vehicle has passed by, we see the mayor falling to the ground.

CLASSIC LINES:
Shug Avery: 'I think it pisses God off when you walk by the colour purple in a field and don't notice it.'

SOUND EFFECTS: The aural design of *The Color Purple* is sensitive, rarely obtrusive, achieving some powerful effects through subtlety: the buzz of a fly hovering as Celie shaves Albert is unnerving, an embodiment of her irritation with him; the jangling of the horse's bridle that becomes almost a musical motif, scoring Celie's hope for the potential arrival of Nettie's letters. When the story moves to 1936, the motif is retained by the jangle of an ornamental tree on the bonnet of the mailman's car replacing the bridle. Spielberg also used some bold cross-mixing to help link scenes: this is most prevalent in the sounds of Celie and Nettie clapping hands that fades almost imperceptibly into the clop of a horse's hooves as Mister goes on the prowl for Nettie – that childish innocence is under threat from animalistic menace is hinted at on the soundtrack.

WHAT'S THE SCORE? Of all the criticisms surrounding *The Color Purple*, little generated more flak than Quincy Jones's music. This was only the second time a Spielberg feature had not featured John Williams, and Jones's score was heavily attacked for surpassing even Williams in the syrup stakes. While the main theme is pretty and there is an effective cue that melds the sound of rain in Georgia with the sounds of percussion in Africa, the score flits between a twee Americana (Nettie teaching Celie, the comedy stomp following Sofia's walk towards Mister's house) and unbearable saccharine (the potentially moving scene of Celie discovering and reading Nettie's letters is trounced by a swell of strings) that dissipates any sense of emotional truth.

Yet where Jones does come into his own is supervising the songs that play a pivotal role in the movie. Celie's flowering is mirrored by the evolution of black music as the film traverses African music, church spirituals, earthy blues numbers and jazz. As well as the original recordings, Jones created a number of songs from scratch. Created for Shug's leading of the Juke Joint rabble to church, 'Maybe God Is Trying To Tell You Something' is spirited, authentic-sounding gospel, but the real showstopper is 'Miss Celie's Blues', a soulful number that first expresses Shug's love for Celie. The first time Alice Walker heard the song – a prominent part of the book – she felt 'annoyed at first that brothers [i.e. men] wrote it.'

CUT SCENES: When Oprah Winfrey complained to Spielberg that a fight scene between Sofia and Harpo was too slapstick, the director barred her from watching rushes. However the actor's instincts proved correct when Spielberg excised the scene.

GEDDIT! Way down the cast list playing Swan is one Laurence Fishburne back in the days when he was plain old Larry.

The cries dubbed over the birth scene are the actual cries of Spielberg's baby son Max playing in the bath.

More sound-effects trivia: the dejected sounds of Harpo whistling as Sofia leaves him were provided by Spielberg himself.

Margaret Avery, who plays Shug, had previously worked with Spielberg in a small role on his TV movie *Something Evil*.

Oprah Winfrey's production company is named Harpo after Sofia's spouse. Coincidentally, Harpo is Oprah backwards.

FACTOID FRENZY: The cast and crew of *The Color Purple* had to endure the odour of frankincense throughout the shoot, used to add atmosphere to each shot.

Alice Walker's contract stipulated that half of the crew would be women or from an ethnic minority.

To help keep costs down, Spielberg took the Directors Guild of America minimum fee of $40,000, which was subsequently put towards the film's budget.

In a strange but true slice of Spielberg history, Spielberg's son Max was born on 13 June just as Spielberg was shooting Celie's childbirth scene.

Color Purple's African scenes were re-created in Newhall, California, and on location in Kenya, with Frank Marshall in the role of Second Unit Director.

THE CRITICAL FACULTY: 'Mr Spielberg has looked on the sunny side of Miss Walker's novel, fashioning a grand multi-hanky entertainment that is as pretty and lavish as the book is plain.' (Janet Maslin, *New York Times*.) 'Spielberg is still magnificently Spielberg.' (Nigel Andrews, *Financial Times*.) 'Spielberg leaves us clutching the 154 [sic] minute chain of slick mostly shallow set-pieces, staged with an eye to prettification.' (Geoff Brown, *The Times*.) 'The movie is faithful to the events of the novel but it sees those events through lavender-colored glasses that transform them into fiction of an entirely different order.' (Vincent Canby, *New York Times*.) 'Inauthentic and unconvincing. At times it seems we're watching an angry feminist tract made in the style of a Disney animal story . . . the most painfully square movie about black people ever made.' (David Denby, *New York Times Magazine*.) 'As shoddy as it is uplifting . . . Even before the credits have ended, Spielberg is waving pink flowers in your face and boosting the music. In a word *The Color Purple* is overwrought. It does for tearjerking what *1941* does for slapstick. (J Hoberman, *Village Voice*.) 'It's all very pretty but it's cinematography, not cinema.' (Richard Corliss, *Time*.)

BOX OFFICE: Opening on 18 December 1985 – Spielberg's 39th birthday – *The Color Purple* earned $94 million in the US, growing to $142 million worldwide.

AWARDS: When Academy Award nominations were announced on 5 February 1996, *The Color Purple* was cited in eleven categories – Best Picture, Actress (Whoopi Goldberg), Best Supporting Actress (both Margaret Avery and Oprah Winfrey), Screenplay Based on Writing from Another Medium, Cinematography, Editing, Art Direction/Set

Above *Duel*: The killer truck bears down on David Mann (Dennis Weaver)
(© Universal Pictures)

Above *The Sugarland Express*: Lou Jean Poplin (Goldie Hawn) in a rare contemplative mood (© Universal Pictures)

Above *Jaws*: 'That's a twenty-footer!' 'Twenty-five.' (©Universal Pictures)

Left *Close Encounters of the Third Kind*: Barry Guiler (Cary Guffey) bathed in Spielbergian 'God light' (© Columbia Pictures)

Below *1941*: The jitterbug riot in full swing (©Universal Pictures)

Above *Raiders of the Lost Ark*: Archaeologist Indiana Jones (Harrison Ford) doing what he does best (© Lucasfilm/Paramount)

Below *Indiana Jones and the Last Crusade*: Indy and Dr Elsa Schneider (Alison Doody) – tomb raiders (©Lucasfilm)

Above *E.T. The Extra-Terrestrial*: The defining image of Spielberg's career
(© Universal Pictures)

Below *E.T. The Extra-Terrestrial*: 'I'm keeping him.' (© Universal Pictures)

Above *Twilight Zone: The Movie*: Mr Bloom (Scatman Crothers) ends the game of Kick the Can (© Warner Bros)

Right *The Color Purple*: Sisters doin' it for themselves (© Amblin Entertainment)

Right *Empire of the Sun*: Jim Graham (Christian Bale) gets separated from his parents (© Warner Bros)

Above *Always*: Pete
Sandich (Richard Dreyfuss)
realises he is surplus to
requirements
(© Amblin Entertainment)

Left *Hook*: Captain Hook
(Dustin Hoffman), aided
and abetted by first mate
Smee (Bob Hoskins)
(© Amblin Entertainment)

Left *Amistad*: Spielberg
confers with Morgan
Freeman
(© Dreamworks SKG)

Above *Jurassic Park*: A brachiosaurus grazes, courtesy of state-of-the-art CGI (© Amblin Entertainment)

Below *The Lost World: Jurassic Park*: Spielberg coaches a baby stegosaurus in its motivation (© Amblin Entertainment)

Above *Schindler's List*: 'The list is Life.' (© Universal Pictures)

Left *Schindler's List*: Oskar Schindler (Liam Neeson) cuts an imposing figure in his bid to save lives (©Universal Pictures)

Below *Saving Private Ryan*: 'This time, the mission is a man.' (© Dreamworks SKG)

Decoration, Make-Up, Original Score, Best Song 'Miss Celie's Blues' –
but Spielberg was excluded from Best Director (eventually won by
Sydney Pollack for *Out of Africa*, (1985)). Rumours proliferated as to
the reason for the blatant snub: envy over Spielberg's success, the
attacks from within the black community or perhaps a perception of
the film as a shameless attempt to win an Oscar were all mooted. When
the Director's Guild of America – usually a firm indicator as to who
will win the Best Director Oscar – gave its award to Spielberg and his
team, it echoed many statements of support, including one from
Warner Bros, a rare outburst from a studio against the Academy,
displaying 'shock and dismay' at Spielberg's omission. At the time,
Spielberg brushed off any idea of a Hollywood vendetta against him or
any feelings of personal bitterness but on – ironically enough – Oprah
Winfrey's chat show in 1996, Spielberg admitted he was 'real pissed off'
at the exclusion. Yet the Academy had the final word: at the ceremony
held on 24 March, *The Color Purple* did not win a single Oscar.

At other awards ceremonies, *The Color Purple* won a Golden Globe
for Whoopi Goldberg in the Best Dramatic Performance category. The
film was also nominated for Best Picture, Director, Original Score and
Best Supporting Actress for Oprah Winfrey. The film also won a
Casting Society Award for Reuben Cannon and the BAFTAs saw
Menno Meyjes's screenplay garner the film's only nomination.

THE SIZZLE! Even before filming began, *The Color Purple* came
under attack from black groups by sheer dint of its having been made
by a white director. Before the movie had rolled out to cinemas, a
demonstration had taken place outside Quincy Jones's offices
complaining of *Purple*'s stereotypical slant. The strongest opposition
against the movie came from the Coalition Against Black Exploitation,
who labelled the movie as depicting all blacks as 'in an extremely
negative light. It degrades the black man, it degrades black children, it
degrades the black family.' Such knee-jerk descriptions seem to bare
scant resemblance to Spielberg's movie. Interestingly, the same black
groups who attacked the film for its racism – in particular the
National Association for the Advancement of Colored Peoples –
sprang to its defence when the Academy failed to recognise the film
with any Oscars.

JOIN THE DOTS: Kids – *The Sugarland Express, Jaws, Close
Encounters of the Third Kind, 1941, E.T. The Extra-Terrestrial,
Twilight Zone: The Movie, Indiana Jones and the Temple of Doom,
The Color Purple, Empire of the Sun, Hook, Jurassic Park, Schindler's
List, The Lost World: Jurassic Park, Amistad.* **Kidnapped kids** – *The
Sugarland Express, Close Encounters of the Third Kind, Indiana Jones*

and the Temple of Doom, Empire of the Sun, Hook, Schindler's List, Amistad. **Historical setting** – *1941, Raiders of the Lost Ark, Indiana Jones and the Temple of Doom, Empire of the Sun, Schindler's List, Amistad, Saving Private Ryan.* **Based on a book** – *Jaws, Empire of the Sun, Hook, Jurassic Park, Schindler's List, The Lost World: Jurassic Park, Amistad.* **Absent fathers** – *The Sugarland Express, Close Encounters of the Third Kind, E.T. The Extra-Terrestrial, The Color Purple, Empire of the Sun, Indiana Jones and the Last Crusade, Hook.*

FINAL ANALYSIS: *The Color Purple* entered the cinema weighed down by baggage and loaded perception as Steven Spielberg's first grown-up film (Critics conveniently forgot *Duel* and *The Sugarland Express*). Viewed, at best, as a defiant statement of movie-making maturity and, at worst, a blatant attempt to tackle Academy-friendly themes in order to win an Oscar, the film did not establish Spielberg in the top echelons of Important Directors Who Should Be Taken Seriously – such critical kudos would have to wait until *Schindler's List* – even adding to his reputation as a sultan of schmaltz who could reduce a hard-hitting novel to an optimistic childlike view of the world. More than any other Spielberg film, *The Color Purple* is the movie that highlights the divide between how the audiences and critics approach the director (and movies in general): the popular success of the film suggests audiences reacted (and still react) positively to his bold emotionalism, whereas critics are quick to dismiss his romantic, traditional style of storytelling as overt manipulation.

Some fifteen years on, it is clearer to see that *The Color Purple* falls somewhere between the searing drama that aficionados of the book hoped for and the gooey schmaltz its detractors often describe it as. Allowing more space to show off his underrated ability with actors, the movie is a curious hybrid of film-making bravura – no other director could turn the mailbox waiting for Nettie's letters into a character through sheer camera movement – and sanitised soap opera. For every moment that stuns with its brutal power – Mister's forceful separation of Celie and Nettie, the indelible image of Celie's blood-red handprint on a stone after Mister's son throws a rock at her, Celie standing up to Mister for the first time – the movie offers equal dollops of syrupy sentiment that soft peddles the drama. Where Walker's world is intimate and confessional, Spielberg's film's is accessible and broad; where the book is naked and honest, the film is removed and elegiac.

On its own terms, *The Color Purple* remains an entertaining, highly polished family drama. Within Spielberg's career, it is perhaps best viewed as an interesting, if not entirely successful, exercise in his flexing a different set of muscles.

SPIELBERG ON SPIELBERG: 'I've always been a grown-up. I've been playing in the sandbox for years – as a grown-up. But there was always something I was holding back. Something in me would say, "Go for the easy challenge and not the hard task." So what I went for was the fast-paced, energetic entertainments. And I won't stop doing them! But I thought that I could satisfy my own curiosity – about my adult side. It's as if I've been swimming in water up to my waist all my life – and I'm great at it – but now I'm going into the deeper section of the pool.'

Empire of the Sun (1987)

(Colour, 152 mins)

Studio Warner Bros
Produced by Steven Spielberg, Kathleen Kennedy, Frank Marshall
Executive Producer Robert Shapiro
Screenplay by Tom Stoppard
Based on the novel by JG Ballard
Director of Photography Allen Daviau ASC
Production Designer Norman Reynolds
Edited by Michael Kahn ACE
Music John Williams
Costume Designer Bob Ringwood
Casting Maggie Cartier
Second Unit Director Frank Marshall
Assistant Director David Tomblin
Production Manager Ted Morley
Art Director Frederick Hole
Casting–USA Mike Fenton, Jane Feinberg, Judy Taylor
Production Co-ordinators Margaret Adams, Jennie Raglan
Script Supervisor Nikki Clapp
Camera Operators Mike Roberts, Barry Brown
Sound Mixers Colin Charles, Tony Dawe
Supervising Art Director Charles Bishop
Supervising Construction Manager Bill Welch
Special Effects Supervisor Kit West
Senior Effects Supervisor David Watkins
Visual Effects by Industrial Light and Magic
Model Aeroplanes Supervisor Peter Aston
Stunt Co-ordinator Vic Armstrong
Transport Co-ordinator Brian Hathaway
Wardrobe Supervisor Patrick Wheatley
Chief Make-up Artist Paul Engelen
Supervising Hairdresser Vera Mitchell
Post-Production Supervisor Arthur Repola

Associate Editors Colin Wilson, Martin Cohen, Craig Bassett
Supervising Sound Editors Charles L Campbell, Lou Edemann
Aerial Co-ordinators Jeff Hawke, James Good
Chief Zero Pilot Tom Danaher
Chief Mustang Pilot Ray Hanna
Mustang Pilots Hoof Proudfoot, Mark Hanna
Additional Optical Effects by Industrial Light and Magic, Dennis Muren, Michael
Pangrazio, John Ellis

CAST: Christian Bale (*Jim Graham*), John Malkovich (*Basie*), Miranda
Richardson (*Mrs Victor*), Nigel Havers (*Dr Rawlins*), Joe Pantoliano
(*Frank Demerest*), Leslie Phillips (*Maxton*), Masato Ibu (*Sgt Nagata*),
Emily Richard (*Jim's Mother*), Rupert Frazer (*Jim's Father*), Peter Gale
(*Mr Victor*), Takatoria Kataoka (*Kamikaze Boy Pilot*), Ben Stiller
(*Dainty*), David Neidorf (*Tiptree*), Ralph Seymour (*Cohen*), Robert
Stephens (*Mr Lockwood*), Zhai Naj She (*Yang*), Guts Ishimatsu (*Sgt
Uchida*), Emma Piper (*Amy Matthews*), James Walker (*Mr Radik*),
Jack Dearlove (*Singing Prisoner*), Anna Turner (*Mrs Gilmour*), Ann
Castle (*Mrs Phillips*), Yvonne Gilan (*Mrs Lockwood*), Ralph Michael
(*Mr Partridge*), Sybil Maas (*Mrs Hug*), Burt Kwouk (*Mr Chen*), Tom
Danaher (*Colonel Marshall*), Kong-Guo Jun (*Chinese Youth*), Takao
Yamada (*Japanese Truck Driver*), Hiro Arai (*Japanese
Sergeant/Airfield*), Paul McGann (*Lieutenant Price*), Marc De Jonge
(*Frenchman*), Susan Leong (*Amah*), Nicholas Dastor (*Paul*), Edith
Platten (*Paul's Sister*), Shirley Chantrell (*Chinese Cook at Detention
Centre*), John Moore (*Mr Pym*), Ann Queensberry (*Mrs Pym*), Sylvia
Marriott (*Mrs Partridge*), Frank Duncan (*Mr Hug's Father*), Ronald
Eng (*Mr Chen's Aide*), Za Chuan Ce, Shi Rui Ching (*Shopkeepers*), Lu
Ye, Guo Xue Lian, Ge Yan Zhao (*Merchants*).

BUDGET: $38 million

MPAA: PG

BBFC: PG

TITLE SEQUENCE: In white lettering over a black background, the
following opening crawl begins, also read aloud in a clipped English
accent.
   'In 1941 China and Japan had been in a state of undeclared war for
four years. A Japanese army of occupation was in control of much of
the countryside and many towns and cities.
   'In Shanghai thousands of Westerners, protected by the diplomatic
security of the international settlement, continued to live as they had
lived since the British came here in the 19th century and built in the

image of their own country . . . built banking houses, hotels, offices, churches and homes that might have been uprooted from Liverpool or Surrey.

'Now their time was running out. Outside Shanghai the Japanese dug in and waited for . . . Pearl Harbor.'

PLOT SUMMARY: It's December 1941. Growing in the British enclave of the international settlement of Shanghai, eleven-year-old Jim Graham lives a luxurious life with his well-to-do parents, attending choir practice, going to fancy-dress parties and dreaming of joining the Japanese air force. The utopia is spoiled as the mounting tensions between the Chinese and the Japanese force the Grahams to move into a hotel. The situation grows worse and, as Japanese troops launch an attack on Shanghai, Jim is separated from his parents in the panic-stricken mêlée.

Completely alone, Jim returns to his empty home, quickly runs out of supplies and fails miserably in his attempts to surrender to the Japanese army. After a run-in with a street ruffian, Jim is saved by two American merchant seamen, Basie and Frank, who give the boy food and shelter. In return, Jim leads them back to his old neighbourhood, with promises of rich pickings for their black-market dealings. However, arriving back at Jim's house, Basie is caught and beaten by the Japanese and the trio end up prisoners in a detention centre. Basie teaches Jim the fundamentals of survival, yet attempts to abandon the kid as the healthier prisoners are selected to go to a prison camp. Using his new-found resourcefulness, Jim cajoles the guards into joining the journey to the camp at Soochow.

Flashforward to 1945. Basie is the camp's Mr Big, while Jim is his right-hand man, running errands and wheeling and dealing in useful commodities – chiefly sweet potatoes and soap. Although housed in the English contingent, sharing a cubicle with a begrudging couple, Mr and Mrs Victor, and taking scripture lessons from Dr Rawlins, Jim feels that his heart belongs to other nations: in particular the Japanese, as he watches the air force go through their operations – he strikes up a distant empathy with a rookie kamikaze pilot – and the Americans, whose vitality he admires in direct contrast to the Brit lethargy. After successfully setting a pheasant trap for Basie on the outskirts of the camp, Jim earns the right to live in the American barracks.

His joy is short-lived, however, as Basie is badly beaten by a camp guard, Sergeant Nagata, and Jim is forced to return to the Victors. As Jim salutes a Japanese Zero as it ascends into the sky, his world is further upturned as the fighter explodes, heralding the arrival of the American air force, who begin bombing the camp. With Basie breaking his promise and leaving without Jim, the youngster joins the mass exodus to a stadium filled with the flotsam and jetsam of Western life. While others move on, Jim nurses Mrs Victor, who refuses to go on any further. Her death the following morning coincides with the burst of the Nagasaki A-bomb – Jim mistakes the bomb's cataclysmic white light for her soul departing to heaven – which sees Jim return to the Soochow camp, surviving on supplies dropped from the skies. He is reunited with the young Japanese flyer he has befriended, the latter shot by one of Basie's scavengers, who have returned to the camp. Jim refuses to set off with Basie and is discovered by American soldiers cycling around the camp in a state of jubilant delirium. Eventually, Jim is reunited with his parents, whom he barely recognises.

BACKSTORY: Published in 1984, JG Ballard's *Empire of the Sun* chronicled the author's own experiences as a child interned in a Japanese prison camp at Lunghua near Shanghai. Best known for cerebral (often science-fiction) works such as *Crash*, Ballard took forty years to pen his wartime experiences – 'it took 20 years to forget and 20 years to remember these horrendous events' – the result earning numerous literary awards and translation into eighteen languages.

Originally, Spielberg acquired *Empire of the Sun* at the behest of his hero David Lean. Lean had initially wanted to direct the picture with Spielberg producing but, as Lean got further into adapting the novel, he found it was impossible to forge into a viable movie script. 'I worked on it for about a year and in the end I gave it up because I thought, this is like a diary. It's bloody well written and very interesting but I don't think it's a movie for me because it hasn't got a dramatic shape.' Lean turned to an adaptation of Joseph Conrad's *Nostromo* and, with his mentor's blessing, Spielberg took over the reigns on *Empire*.

Before Spielberg came on board the project, Harold Becker was lined up to direct with Robert Shapiro producing from a screenplay penned by Tom Stoppard. When Spielberg took over he hired Menno Meyjes to rewrite Stoppard's work, yet retained Stoppard to do the final draft, shaping subsequent drafts with the playwright.

Spielberg and Stoppard seemed a bizarre meeting of minds: the world's most populist film-maker collaborating with the creator of erudite riffs on Shakespeare (*Rosencrantz and Guildenstern Are Dead*). Pairing down the sprawl of Ballard's quasi-autobiography, Spielberg, through Stoppard, zeroed in on the relationship between Jim and Basie, although the novel's hint of sexual ambiguity in the relationship between Basie and Frank and their predatory interest in Jim is eschewed. Spielberg also toned down the catalogue of Japanese atrocities – the public stranglings, the piles of maggot-ridden corpses –

as described in the book and the sense of a poverty-stricken Shanghai. In the film, Jim's chauffeur-driven Packard passes a solitary beggar in the street. In the novel, the vagabond is just one in streets teeming with vagrants – Jim's car even casually crushes his foot. A further omission is the sense of Jenny Victor as Jim's first obvious object of lust – a whiff of the idea remains in the scene where Jim is caught watching Mr and Mrs Victor making love through the net curtain.

As for scenes embellished in the transition from script to screen, Jim setting pheasant traps for Basie on the outskirts of the camp was a mere paragraph in Ballard, whereas, in the movie, the action is embellished into a taut, tense, cinematic set-piece that is typically Spielberg. Other Spielberg–Stoppard inventions include the elaborate flurry of salutes that welcome Jim into the American quarters – in the book, they can hardly stand him.

The collaboration between Spielberg and Stoppard was by both accounts a harmonious, fruitful one – Spielberg taught the playwright how to tell the story visually; Stoppard taught the film director how to use oblique dialogue to make subtle points – with the only disagreement coming with the end of the picture. Stoppard's notion was that, even after being reunited with his parents, the experiences of Jim's odyssey meant that his life would never be pleasant again. The notion was completely antithetical to Spielberg's worldview – the film now concludes on a more ambiguous note.

ORIGINS: Even though he decided not to direct the film, the biggest influence on *Empire of the Sun* remained David Lean. While the correlations are reflected in the appropriations of Lean's sense of scope, sweep and camera stylings – in particular, Leans's signature crane shot moving from a lone figure to reveal a mass of swarming people – there are particular references to the Lean filmography: Jim's life as street urchin, the Jim–Basie/Oliver–Fagin parallels, the foggy look of Shanghai and Jim being slapped after asking for more food at the detention centre echo Lean's version of *Oliver Twist*; the corpses of Chinese rebels strewn across rooftops above the main streets recall *Zhivago*; from *Lawrence of Arabia*, the little cough of that film's Turkish Bey has obviously been caught by *Empire*'s Sergeant Nagata, and Lawrence striding across the train tops is mirrored in Jim's jubilant reaction on the camp roofs at the arrival of the US planes. Yet the most pervasive point of reference is *The Bridge on the River Kwai*, not only because of the Japanese camp setting, but more pertinently in the skewered view of war shared by both protagonists: like *Kwai*'s Captain Nicholson (Alec Guinness), Jim loses sight of which side he's supposed to be on, identifying more with the Japanese than the Brits – as Nicholson refers to 'my bridge' so Jim talks blissfully of 'our runway'.

Keeping with the epic tradition, Victor Fleming's *Gone With the Wind* is a further touchstone. At one point, in an image borrowed from the book, Jim walks past a massive poster for the film, the poster image filling the entire frame as if Jim had stepped into the movie. With the poster depicting the burning of Atlanta that echoes the chaos of Shanghai that surrounds Jim, Spielberg uses the Hollywood fantasy version of conflict to contrast with his more realistic version. *Empire* also owes a debt to another Victor Fleming film, *Captains Courageous* (1937). This is the yarn of a spoiled rich kid (Freddie Bartholomew) who falls off an ocean liner only to be rescued by a Portuguese sailor (an Oscar-winning Spencer Tracy), and *Empire* shares the story strand of a privileged boy out of his element and the sense of a child coming under influence and tutelage of a group of hardened men.

Basie and his cohorts planning their escape echoes a scene in Billy Wilder's *Stalag 17* (1953). Indeed, Basie's cynical scheming seems to be cut from the same cloth as William Holden's Sefton.

The hardened, unsentimental education Jim receives growing up on the streets is undoubtedly informed by François Truffaut's *Les Quatres Cents Coups* (1959), in which Truffaut's alter ego, Antoine Doinel (Jean Pierre Leaud), learns to survive on his wits in Paris. Other more scattershot precedents include such Movie Brats favourites as *Citizen Kane* (the stadium full of bric-a-brac is reminiscent of *Kane*'s final-scene storage house), *The Ten Commandments* (the prisoners' exodus from the camp recalls the framing of the fleeing Hebrews) and *The Searchers* (Jim's reunion with his parents is as similarly awkward as the moment Natalie Wood returns to her homestead).

CASTING: Sifting through 4,000 kids over a nine-month period, Spielberg chose thirteen-year-old Christian Bale to play Jim. Prior to *Empire*, Bale's primary acting experience had been on stage with Rowan Atkinson in *The Nerd*, in the BBC's *Heart of the Country* and in a TV miniseries, *Anastasia*, playing the Czar's haemophilliac son opposite Amy Irving. As with the young cast of *E.T.*, Spielberg earned Bale's respect by first becoming a peer – the pair often raced remote-control cars on set – then coaxing and moulding his portrayal, always taking time to sketch out the emotional resonances of each scene.

Although making a splash in his film debut, garnering an Oscar nomination for *Places in the Heart* (1984), John Malkovich was primarily lauded for his work with his Steppenwolf Theater Company by the time he was cast in *Empire of the Sun*. Malkovich gives an unusual, detached performance that doesn't really reveal the complexity of Basie as described in Ballard.

Spielberg would have probably spotted Nigel Havers in David Lean's *A Passage To India* (1984) before he cast him as Dr Rawlings

(Dr Ransome in the book). Havers also caught the eye as an aristocratic athlete in *Chariots of Fire* (1981). To play the long-suffering Mrs Victor (Vincent on the page) Spielberg hired Miranda Richardson, whose previous biggest film role was *Dance With a Stranger* (1985). Spielberg also gave a rare serious role to the British comedy institution Leslie Phillips, essaying the role of Maxton (another name change: from Maxted in the book), the friend of the Graham family who looks out for Jim in the concentration camp.

PRODUCTION: *Empire of the Sun* started shooting in Shanghai on 2 March 1987. After initially being told that filming in the People's Republic of China would take at least four years' wrangling, the producers Frank Marshall and Kathleen Kennedy looked at Buenos Aires, Vienna, Stockholm, Hong Kong, Lisbon and even Liverpool as possible alternatives. Yet, sticking to their guns, Marshall and Kennedy bartered with the Shanghai Film Studios and the China Film Co-Production Corporation and short-circuited the negotiating process down to a year.

Shooting in Shanghai took only 21 days, but the scale of *Empire* was such that the first day of filming encompassed 5,000 extras gathered on the Bund, Shanghai's main waterfront highway, with a further 5,000 being drafted in to re-create the widespread panic of the Japanese invasion. It was the first major Hollywood movie to extensively lens in China, and the authorities allowed Spielberg to change road signs, cover the streets in dense fog and even shut off seven blocks of the main thoroughfares – the first time a film unit had done that since 1959. Although filming of the exteriors of Jim's house took place in Shanghai, where the streets of the international settlement had remained relatively unchanged, the interiors were captured in England to avoid the problem of relocating the fifteen or so Chinese families who were living in each Shanghai house. Other interiors – such as the detention centre – were captured in and around the *Raiders* stamping ground of Elstree.

The 900-square-metre set construction of the prison camp was erected on the banks of the Gualalquivir River, near Jerez in Spain. For five weeks the torrential rain delayed the location's construction. After the rain came a squadron of mosquitoes.

For the flying, three US P-51 Mustangs were employed, piloted by a former Red Arrows ace, Ray Hanna, valued at $500,000 apiece.

TICS OF THE TRADE: 'Ever since *Duel*,' Spielberg noted on *Empire*'s release, 'I've been looking for a visual narrative – a motion-picture story – that could be told exclusively through visual metaphors and nonpretentious symbolism. And nothing came along until *Empire*.'

Ironically, considering it came from a literary source, plot points and meaning in *Empire* are propelled by pure imagery, Ballard's words translated into haunting, slightly surreal pictures to render Jim's mindset manifest. Jim touching a Zero with sparks flying off just before he salutes the Japanese pilots perfectly replicates his idealised view of his enemy and the world – see also the jaw-dropping shot of a Mustang pilot waving to Jim as the US air force demolishes the camp. Remaining among the most stunning images in the Spielberg portfolio, these shots typify the way Allen Daviau's cinematography blurs Jim's differentiation between fantasy and reality.

Time and again, Spielberg makes his points visually rather than through reams of exposition: when Jim attempts to resuscitate his kamikaze pal, for a split second he is trying to bring back to life his childhood self. The point is made again after Jim throws his suitcase (the literal baggage of his childhood) into the river. The floating case echoes the bobbing coffins glimpsed in the film's opening shot – a blatant signifier of the death of innocence.

Some of the movie's strongest images are ripped straight from Ballard and heightened with Spielbergian touches. Jim signals to HMS *Petrel* on the night of the Japanese invasion; a blast sends him flying across the room. As he lands, the camera whip-pans to three mirrors, Jim's image fractured into a troika of reflections – Spielberg suggesting that, as his life is shattered by war, his personality has become similarly distorted. Moreover, after being separated from his parents, Jim returns to his family home and enters his mother's bedroom, noticing a footprint in talcum powder. Yet the prints multiply (and include handprints), as Spielberg etches a subtle, terrifying evocation of a struggle. The scene ends with Jim opening a window to blow away traces of the fight, the dust (and his mother?) now gone for good.

CLASSIC LINES:
Jim: 'If the Americans land, the Japanese will fight.'
Dr Rawlins: 'You admire the Japanese?'
Jim: 'Well, they're brave, aren't they?'
Dr Rawlins: 'That's important, is it, Jim?'
Jim: 'It's a good thing if you want to win a war.'
Dr Rawlins: 'But we don't want them to win, do we? Remember, we're British.'

Basie: 'Jim, didn't I teach you anything?'
Jim: 'Yes! You taught me that people will do anything for a potato.'

Jim: 'Learned a new word today. Atom bomb. It was like God taking a photograph.'

VISUAL EFFECTS: Because the aircraft were required to undertake complicated aerial manoeuvres that would have been very difficult to accomplish in a studio setting against a blue screen, *Empire of the Sun* saw the model work unfold in the harsh reality of the Jerez location. Powered by motorcycle engines, a squadron of radio-controlled 1:3 scale models, including Japanese Zeros, American Mustangs and the single B-29 bomber, were among the largest models ever assembled for a movie, with wing spans running from seven to eighteen feet and speeds ranging from thirty to ninety miles an hour. The advantage of using such large-scale models was that the miniatures could share the frame with the actors and still look like actual aircraft. The illusion was aided by pyrotechnic charges buried into the ground that would be detonated to correspond to the remote-control bomb drops of the models. The scant roster of effects to be created at ILM included a computer-generated squadron of aircraft flying over Shanghai, a wide aerial view of a stadium and the blinding light and shock waves of the Nagasaki bomb, created through animation processes.

SOUND EFFECTS: Despite the impressively noisy aural re-creation of street riots and the aircraft raids on the concentration camp, the most telling use of sound in *Empire* is a moment of quiet simplicity: after being separated from his parents, Jim returns home and goes about his normal life, setting the table and eating dinner. Significantly, the antiquated clock ticking in the dining room stops halfway through the scene – an easy-to-grasp yet potent metaphor for the end of an era.

WHAT'S THE SCORE: Many of the strongest moments in the *Empire of the Sun* score come from existing music: the lively rendition of the march 'The British Grenadiers' offers a brazen counterpoint to Jim striding through the camp, puffing (and coughing) on a cigar, to take his place in the American barracks. The movie also makes good use of Chopin's Mazurka, Opus 17, No. 4, a nostalgic piano composition that represents Jim's cosseted home life of toy planes and glowing fireplaces. Yet the most expressive piece of source music is the Welsh lullaby 'Suo Gan' ('humming song') that appears three times in the movie: over the opening imagery of the watery coffins leading to Jim singing it solo in the choir; during the sequence where Jim performs the song as a hymn to the kamikaze pilots; and during the final moments where Jim rediscovers his parents. While a translation of the lyric reveals apposite themes of a desire for maternal love and angelic imagery, the atmosphere of 'Suo Gan' is even more appropriate – haunting, melancholic and bizarrely beautiful.

Sporadically, John Williams's fusion of ethereal choirs and soaring strings adds overkill to Spielberg's already heightened visuals but occasionally the balance is sublime as in the solo voice that scores the slow-motion shot of the Mustang pilot waving at Jim. Also successful is the upbeat 'Exsultate Justi', a rousing, voice-driven anthem that celebrates Jim's liberation and jubilation at the end of the war. In the purely orchestral section of the score, Williams gives us a spirited theme for Jim's ducking and diving as the camp's fix-it guy, some experimental percussion to follow Jim setting the pheasant traps and a main theme for Jim that can break the heart when played in a sentimental style yet sets spirits soaring when replayed in full-blown, epic-sweep mode.

CUT SCENES: Remembering his work as Wu Han in *Temple of Doom*, Spielberg cast David Yip in *Empire* to play a character known only as the Eurasian, a mixed-race opportunist who is given looted furniture, cars and valuables in return for helping to interrogate the aircrews of downed US aircraft. After flying the English-based actor to Spain, Spielberg cut the character out of the movie completely.

A further cut came within the scene Maxton shares with Jim as they first arrive at the concentration camp. The scene was lost due to a continuity blunder. 'What happened was that an extra had been chosen by mistake who was eighteen stone – he had a very big gut on him – and we were supposed to be starving' recalled Leslie Phillips. 'Wherever I went there was me looking drawn and haggard, Christian looking pretty awful for a kid and this bloody great fat man. So we couldn't use any of it.'

GEDDIT! The 'JG' of JG Ballard stands for Jim Graham, the character played by Christian Bale.

The title of the novel *Empire of the Sun* can also be read as a pun on Empire of the Son – an allusion to Jim's pre-eminent status in the camp.

Originally Spielberg wanted Ballard to read the opening narration. Although Ballard recorded it, another voice was used.

JG Ballard has a small role in the film dressed in a John Bull outfit at the Lockwoods' fancy dress party. Spielberg originally offered Ballard a Roman-armour costume to wear.

As Jim throws his suitcase into the water, the image of a character in silhouette against light playing off water is reminiscent of *The Sugarland Express*.

FACTOID FRENZY: The Chinese Army were played by real members of the Chinese Army.

Look out for a young Ben Stiller as Dainty, one of Basie's right-hand men in the concentration camp.

Because the Chinese government had outlawed rickshaws, the *Empire* unit constructed fifty brand-new ones and taught men how to use them.

The cast and crew bought so many souvenirs that the 747 couldn't get off the ground because of the added weight. A second plane had to be chartered.

THE CRITICAL FACULTY: 'Mr Spielberg gives *Empire of the Sun* a visual splendor [sic], a heroic adventurousness and an immense scope that make it unforgettable.' (Janet Maslin, *New York Times*.) Light spectacle in the sense of light opera (or lite beer), *Empire of the Sun* packs the wallop of a fading shadow boxer . . . *The Sorrow And The Pity* remade as *Oliver!*' (J Hoberman, *Village Voice*.) '*Empire of the Sun* is a visually seamless fusion of kinesthetic energy and literary sensibility, pulse-pounding adventure with exquisitely delicate sensitivity . . . I was stirred and moved on a level I forgot existed.' (Andrew Sarris, *Village Voice*.) 'Spielberg . . . once again proves he is our top picturemaker. He has energised each frame with allusive legerdemain and an intelligent density of images and emotions. He has met the demands of the epic form with a mature spirit and wizardly technique. Spielberg has dreamed of flying before and this time he has earnt his wings. (Richard Corliss, *Time*.) 'This is the stuff of illustrious literature but cold cinema. This is Spielberg's most mature film to date. His visual mastery is everywhere evident.' (Iain Johnstone, *Sunday Times*.) 'The film's admirable first hour is stunning in its recreation of the confused Shanghai . . . The picture jumps forward from 1942 to 1945 and thereafter it loses its clarity, dramatic grip and simple coherence.' (Philip French, *Observer*.)

BOX OFFICE: Opening in the US on 9 December 1987, *Empire of the Sun* eventually grossed a disappointing $66.7 million worldwide – even less than *1941*. Considering the movie cost $38 million, it is probably Spielberg's commercially least successful movie to date. Although the film was too serious to generate big business, it is surprising that it failed to find an audience at all. Perhaps this has something to do with Spielberg being stereotyped as a director in the minds of the audience as well as the critics.

AWARDS: *Empire of the Sun* was nominated for six Academy Awards – Best Art Direction/Set Decoration, Cinematography, Best Costume Design, Film Editing, Original Score and Sound – but failed to take home any awards from the 1988 ceremony. Most likely to be aggrieved over the situation would be the cinematographer Allen Daviau, whose work on *Empire* had brought home the American

Society of Cinematographers award, and Spielberg, who, while nominated for the Director's Guild of America award (usually a strong indicator of the Academy voting), did not even make the Oscar shortlist. The film faired rather better at the BAFTAs, winning Best Cinematography, Sound and Score but also earning nominations in the Best Adapted Screenplay, Costume Design and Production Design categories. At the Golden Globes, the film was nominated for Best Motion Picture – Drama and Best Original Score, but lost out on both counts. The National Board of Review awarded the film Best Picture, Director and Juvenile Performance for Christian Bale. Bale also won a Young Artist Award as Best Young Actor In a Motion Picture, where the movie also picked up Best Family Motion Picture – Drama.

JOIN THE DOTS: Kids – *The Sugarland Express, Jaws, Close Encounters of the Third Kind, 1941, E.T. The Extra Terrestrial, Twilight Zone: The Movie, Indiana Jones and the Temple of Doom, The Color Purple, Hook, Jurassic Park, Schindler's List, The Lost World: Jurassic Park, Amistad.* **Kidnapped Kids** – *The Sugarland Express, Close Encounters of the Third Kind, Indiana Jones and the Temple of Doom, Hook, Schindler's List, Amistad.* **World War Two** – *1941, Raiders of the Lost Ark, Empire of the Sun, Indiana Jones and the Last Crusade, Schindler's List, Saving Private Ryan.* **Aircraft** – *Close Encounters of the Third Kind, 1941, Raiders of the Lost Ark, Indiana Jones and the Temple of Doom, Indiana Jones and the Last Crusade, Always, Hook, Saving Private Ryan.* **Suburbia** – *Close Encounters Of The Third Kind, E.T. The Extra-Terrestrial.* **Historical Setting** – *1941, Raiders of the Lost Ark, Indiana Jones and the Temple of Doom, The Color Purple, Schindler's List, Amistad, Saving Private Ryan.* **Based on a book** – *Jaws, The Color Purple, Hook, Jurassic Park, Schindler's List, The Lost World: Jurassic Park, Amistad.* **Based on real-life events** – *The Sugarland Express, 1941, Schindler's List, Amistad, Saving Private Ryan.* **Absent fathers** – *The Sugarland Express, Close Encounters of the Third Kind, E.T. The Extra-Terrestrial, The Color Purple, Indiana Jones and the Last Crusade, Hook.*

SEND IN THE CLONES!: Also released in 1987, John Boorman's *Hope and Glory* made an interesting companion piece to *Empire*. Based on Boorman's experiences of growing up in Blitz-ridden Blighty, the film suggests how the childish imagination can transform a warzone into a playground and, like *Empire*, explores the resilience of children and their ability to adapt to any environment. Smaller in scale but warmer in tone than *Empire, Hope and Glory* was generally better received than Spielberg's epic.

FINAL ANALYSIS: The mixed critical reception and audience rejection of *Empire* stunted Spielberg's desire to attempt a diversity of material and the subsequent four movies – *Last Crusade, Always, Hook* and *Jurassic Park* – saw Spielberg, in some senses, regressing until he was ready for *Schindler*. In this respect, *Empire* is significant as it looks like an enormous stepping stone towards the complexity of *Schindler* to the extent that the latter is unthinkable without *Empire*. Both films share multifaceted protagonists (the wheeler-dealer Jim is a pint-sized version of the wheeler-dealer Schindler) and consistent themes (loss, incarceration and survival), yet *Schindler*, without the need to filter everything through a young boy's perception, has a veracity and immediacy that *Empire*'s astonishing visuals never quite attain. Yet, in other respects, *Empire* is still the darker, tougher film. Rather than finding hope in 1,100 survivors, it trades in a brittle morality: in war, good people die and innocence is casually slaughtered – in detailing the end of childhood, Spielberg has rarely been more grown up.

However, despite all its dark messaging, it is a near catastrophe that the public ignored *Empire of the Sun* because for about an hour it is Spielberg at his masterful best: helped by a fantastic performance from Christian Bale, Spielberg mixes an unsurpassed epic grandeur with telling snapshots into a tottering youthful psyche. It all makes for vivid, unforgettable cinema. Yet, as David Lean was correct to identify, Jim's quest loses story structure and dramatic momentum as he reaches the camp and – with the possible exception of the destruction of the camp – never scales the heights of the opening. But, despite its second-half flaws, *Empire of the Sun* remains one of the director's most intensely beautiful and endlessly fascinating films.

SPIELBERG ON SPIELBERG: 'I'm closer to the 40s personally than I am to the 80s. I love that period. My father filled my head with war stories – he was a radio man on a B-25 fighting the Japanese in Burma. I have identified with that period of innocence and tremendous jeopardy all my life. I collect documentaries and I think I have every one made from that period. It was the end of an era, the end of innocence, and I have been clinging to it most of my adult life. But hitting forty, I really had to come to terms with what I've been tenaciously clinging to, which was a kind of celebration of a kind of naïveté, that has been reconfirmed countless times in the amount of people who have gone to see *E.T., Back to the Future* and *Goonies*. But I just reached a saturation point and I thought *Empire* was a great way of performing an exorcism on that period.'

Indiana Jones and the Last Crusade (1989)

(Colour, 127 mins)

Studio Paramount/Lucasfilm
Produced by Robert Watts
Executive Producers George Lucas, Frank Marshall
Screenplay by Jeffrey Boam
Story by George Lucas and Menno Meyjes
Music John Williams
Edited by Michael Kahn ACE
Director of Photography Douglas Slocombe BSC
Production Designer Elliott Scott
Costumes Designed by Anthony Powell with Joanna Johnston
Casting by Maggie Cartier, Mike Fenton CSA (Casting Society of America), Judy Taylor CSA, Valerie Massalas
Second Unit Directors Michael Moore, Frank Marshall
Associate Producer Arthur Repola
First Assistant Director David Tomblin
Production Supervisor Patricia Carr
Production Manager Roy Button
Second Assistant Directors Lee Cleary, Patrick Kenney
Sound Design Ben Burtt
Mechanical Effects Supervisor George Gibbs
Visual Effects Supervisor Michael McAlister
Visual Effects by Industrial Light and Magic
Stunt Co-ordinator Vic Armstrong
Make-up Supervisor Peter Robb-King
Chief Make-up Artist – Prosthetics Nick Dudman
Supervising Sound Editor Richard Hymns
Animal Consultant Mike Culling
Special Visual Effects by Industrial Light and Magic

CAST: Harrison Ford (*Indiana Jones*), Sean Connery (*Professor Henry Jones*), Denholm Elliott (*Marcus Brody*), Alison Doody (*Dr Elsa Schneider*), John Rhys-Davies (*Sallah*), Julian Glover (*Walter Donovan*), River Phoenix (*Young Indy*), Michael Byrne (*Vogel*), Kevork Malikyan (*Kazim*), Robert Eddison (*Grail Knight*), Richard Young (*Fedora*), Alexei Sayle (*Sultan*), Alex Hyde-White (*Young Henry*), Paul Maxwell (*Panama Hat*), Mrs Glover (*Mrs Donovan*), Vernon Dobtcheff (*Butler*), JJ Hardy (*Herman*), Bradley Gregg (*Roscoe*), Jeff O'Haco (*Half-Breed*), Vince Deadrick (*Rough Rider*), Marc Miles (*Sherriff*), Ted Grossman (*Deputy Sheriff*), Tim Hiser (*Young Panama Hat*), Larry Sanders (*Scout Master*), Will Miles (*Scout No. 1*), David Murray (*Scout No. 2*), Frederick Jaeger (*World War One Ace*), Jerry Harte (*Professor Stanton*), Billy J Mitchell (*Dr*

Mulbray), Martin Gordon (*Man at Hitler Rally*), Paul Humpoletz (*German Officer at Hitler Rally*), Tom Branch (*Hatay Soldier in Temple*), Graeme Crowther (*Zeppelin Crewman*), Luke Hanson (*Principal SS Officer at Castle*), Chris Jenkinson (*Officer at Castle*), Nicola Scott (*Female Officer at Castle*), Louis Sheldon (*Young Officer at Castle*), Stefan Kalipha (*Hatay Tank Gunner*), Peter Pacey (*Hatay Tank Driver*), Pat Roach (*Gestapo*), Suzanne Roquette (*Film Director*), Eugene Lipinski (*G-Man*), George Malpas (*Man on Zeppelin*), Julie Eccles (*Irene*), Nina Almond (*Flower Girl*).

BUDGET: $44m

MPAA: PG-13

BBFC: PG

TITLE SEQUENCE: Playing another variation on *Raiders'* opening gag, *Last Crusade* begins with the Paramount mountain logo, which dissolves through to a similar-shaped rock. As John Williams's score mixes a soaring spacious feel with an air of mystery, the credits play over a scene of a mounted Boy Scout troop trekking through the desert landscape. The scoutmaster brings the troop to a halt – a fat kid falls off his horse – and the youngsters dismount their steeds. Some of their number break away from the pack and begin to explore some caves. Spielberg's name appears as the Scouts discover an Indiana Jones-type figure, decked out in khaki and a fedora, supervising what looks like nefarious activity. Incidentally, *Last Crusade* returns to the same font as *Raiders*, perhaps comforting the audience that this adventure will be a return to the spirit of the first movie after the darkness of *Doom*.

PLOT SUMMARY: Once again keeping in line with the tradition established by the first two flicks, *Last Crusade* kicks off with an exciting action set piece that most films would be proud to have as their climax. It's Utah, 1912. Discovering a gang stealing the Cross of Coranado, young Indiana Jones pinches the priceless artefact and bolts off on his steed, before switching modes of transport to a circus train. Running over and through various train carts, the subsequent action establishes the origins of the Indy mythos: the fear of snakes (young Indy falls into a snake trough), the bullwhip (young Indy uses it to keep a lion at bay), the scar on his chin (Indy lashes himself with said bullwhip) and the fedora, given to him by the leader of the gang, who reclaims the cross for a private owner.

Years later, adult Indy regains the cross in a fight aboard a storm-tossed vessel. Back teaching archaeology at university, Indy is recruited by an art collector, Walter Donovan, to find the whereabouts of the Holy Grail, which had been established by Indy's now missing father Henry. Armed with his father's notebook, Jones and a museum curator, Marcus Brody, hook up in Venice with Jones Sr's assistant, Dr Elsa Schneider, who leads them to a Crusader's tomb. As they make their way through catacombs, past an abundance of rats, Jones discovers the final clue to the Grail's location.

Indy's efforts are being tracked by the Brother of the Cruciform Sword, a group dedicated to keeping the Grail secret, and, after a high-speed boat chase, their leader Kazim informs Indy that his father is being held captive in a German castle. As he bluffs his way into the sanctum by posing as a Scottish lord, Indy learns that not only is his father being held captive but the Nazis are behind the whole operation. Although stunned when both Elsa and Donovan reveal themselves as Nazi sympathisers, Indy liberates his father in a thrilling motorcycle chase and heads to Berlin to recapture the stolen diary, which contains vital clues to three tests that must be overcome before the Grail can be recovered.

Reclaiming the diary at a Nazi book-burning rally – Indy gets it signed by Hitler – Indy and Henry renew their icy relationship (both have bedded Elsa) aboard an airship heading out of Germany, yet they are discovered and escape on a biplane after engaging German fighters in battle. Meeting up with Brody and Indy's sidekick Sallah, the heroes take on a Nazi tank before arriving at the Grail temple. Captured by the Nazis, Indy is forced to undertake the three tests, his mission given extra urgency by Donovan mortally wounding Henry, meaning that only the rehabilitating powers of the Grail can save him. Indy achieves all three tasks and is joined by Donovan and Elsa in front of the last surviving Crusader, who invites them to pick the Grail from a number of options. Elsa purposely picks the wrong one and Donovan dies a hideous death after drinking from the gaudy goblet. Indy 'chooses wisely' and uses the healing powers of the Grail to resuscitate his father. Elsa ignores the knight's warning and attempts to take the Grail beyond the temple's seal, leading herself and the other Nazis to perish as the Temple implodes. Indy, Henry, Sallah and Brody remain safe and ride off into a blazing sunset.

BACKSTORY: The five-year gap between *Temple of Doom* and *Last Crusade* was partly due to the problems developing a viable script. Lucas's early idea for *Indy III* was as a kind of haunted-house movie – he had even gone so far as to commission a screenplay from the writer of *Romancing the Stone*, Diane Thomas – yet Spielberg felt he had covered that terrain with *Poltergeist* (1982) and had no wish to return to it. The notion of a quest for the Holy Grail featured very early in script discussions, yet the film-makers had reservations.

'I did not like the concept of the Holy Grail at first because I had always associated it with Monty Python and I could not really relate it to any present-day myth,' ran the Spielberg argument. 'The Grail legend was interesting to me symbolically because it represented the search for one's self – but making a movie about that seemed too esoteric for this genre.'

After he had put the idea back on the shelf, the next idea involved the Chinese legend of the Monkey King (half man, half monkey), set in lower Africa, with Chris Columbus working through several drafts of the screenplay. All agreed that Columbus's writing captured the spirit of the first film, yet was perhaps too outlandish for the Indy ethos – at one point Indy rode a rhinoceros in a multivehicular chase – and, considering the African setting, perhaps the accusations of racism levelled against the first film had some baring. Still, some elements of Columbus's script made the cut: an elaborate tank chase and the young Jones tackling a rhino, this time with the animal ramming its horn through a railway carriage as the youngster battles on board a speeding train.

With Columbus's elaborate ideas rejected, Lucas continued to have further thoughts about how the Holy Grail could be used as a story device. In particular, he added the idea that drinking from the actual Grail would guarantee immortality, whereas sipping from a false one would signal instant death. Various drafts of the Grail idea were worked on, first by *Color Purple*'s Menno Meyjes – his draft featured final incarnations of the three tests Indy faces – and then by *Innerspace*'s Jeffrey Boam.

By now, Spielberg had warmed further to the Grail idea, but he still felt the yarn lacked an extra dimension. It was about this time that the figure of Indy's father entered discussions, although there is some debate as to who actually dreamed up the idea.

'I did not want Indy on a headlong pursuit without a subplot that was almost stronger than the actual Grail itself,' said Spielberg. 'So I came up with the father–son story because the Grail is symbolic in finding the truth in one's life – the truth we are always looking for, consciously or unconsciously. For me that was represented by Indy and Henry meeting. In this context the Grail made sense to me. They actually go after the Holy Grail but their quest is also symbolic of their search for each other.' Yet Boam, who worked closely with Lucas as Spielberg was making *Empire of the Sun*, attributed Jones Sr's introduction to the producer.

Whoever created Henry, the character went through a number of revisions. In Meyjes's early drafts, Indy doesn't discover Henry until the very end of the movie. Boam's screenplay pulled Jones Sr into the action much earlier, an expansion that saw the screen time of the Grail cultists the Brother of the Cruciform Sword drastically reduced. The character changed even more after Sean Connery was cast. Originally conceived as more of a bookish professor lost in the world of his son's adventures, Henry was envisaged by Connery as a more forthright character, part Victorian patriarch, part quixotic academic, part action man.

'When I met them and discussed what I thought it was all about,' Connery remembered, 'they sort of flinched a little because I wanted to base my character on a Sir Richard Burton idea, someone who would have been indifferent to his son growing up and would have gone off and not been heard of for six months and think nothing of it and not feel guilty at all. That's quite un-American of course and I think it shocked them in a way.'

The opening was another aspect of the movie that changed radically from script to screen. In Jeff Boam's original screenplay, the movie kick-started with a Western pastiche. The story opens with Indy as an adult searching for an Inca artefact in the Southwest. He moves into a bar, which turns out to be a bandit's hideaway, filled with booty including the antiquity he is looking for. Indy obviously attempts to steal the relic and naturally a big bar-room brawl takes centre stage. While all liked the idea in principle, everybody agreed it just wasn't enough. So, after much further discussion, the idea of returning to Indiana's childhood arose. Again, considering his affinity with kids in general and his nostalgia for his Boy Scout days in particular, it would seem likely that making Indy a resourceful Boy Scout would be a Spielberg idea. But it was actually a Lucas idea – in fact, suspecting that Spielberg might feel he had overdosed on movies about kids, Lucas feared that Spielberg might reject the notion.

ORIGINS: Setting the opening scene of *Last Crusade* in Monument Valley, the setting for many John Ford Westerns, is the first indication that *Indy III* is once again going to be a journey through movie history. The appearance of a circus train most likely springs from Spielberg's childhood memory of the first film he ever saw, Cecil B De Mille's *The Greatest Show on Earth* (1952) and its spectacular train-crash climax. The train set piece also features Indy evading his enemy by hiding in a magician's disappearing cabinet – a trick pulled by the title character in Hitchcock's *The Lady Vanishes* (1938). Connery's presence is not the only element to invoke memories of James Bond: *From Russia With Love* (1963), *Live And Let Die* (1973) and *Moonraker* (1979) all feature boat chases similar to that of *Last Crusade*, with *Moonraker* (1979) even taking in the Venice locale.

As before, Republic Serials provided a litany of motifs, story strands and set pieces which Lucas, Spielberg et al purloined: like *Last Crusade*, *Darkest Africa* (1936) saw the search for a diary – in *Africa*'s case Joba's Holy Book of Laws – become central to the plot and featured exotic animals as a means of threat. In *Undersea Kingdom* (1936), Ray 'Crash' Corrigan fought on board a tanklike vehicle, as did Ralph Byrd in *Dick Tracy Returns* (1938), a film that also featured a train as a backdrop for action. More *Last Crusade*-alikes appeared the following year in *Dick Tracy's G-Men*, including a big set piece depicting biplane skirmishes. *King of the Texas Rangers* (1941) was one of the many Republic serials to set their action on an airship, whereas the American agent played by Kane Richmond in *Spy Smasher* (1942) undergoes an interrogation very similar to the one conducted by Vogel on Indy and Henry. *G-Men Vs The Black Dragon* (1943) saw the hero Rex Bennett (Rod Cameron) engulfed in a burning building and escape by means of a secret exit, as do Indy and Henry, beaten back by flames in the German castle. A similar scene also adorns *King of the Forest Rangers* (1946), which also boasts a high-speed (well, low-speed, actually) boat chase in the vein of *Last Crusade*'s. Finally, *Secret Service In Darkest Africa* (1943) features the archetypal evil Nazi, Luger, played by Sigurd Tor, who is more than a match for *Last Crusade*'s Colonel Vogel.

CASTING: As, to some extent, the James Bond movies sired the *Indiana Jones* series, the idea of Sean Connery playing Indiana Jones's father is a total masterstroke. When the character was conceived as an ineffectual old man, Lucas was thinking of a John Houseman type, maybe a character actor from the RSC. It was Spielberg's notion to bring in Connery, who was gaining autumnal kudos for a range of character parts. The sticking point seemed to be that Connery was only twelve years senior to Ford. To blur the age gap, Jeff Boam came up with the idea that both father and son would be rivals in their affections for Elsa, something Lucas and Spielberg were initially reluctant to run with. The twilight machismo of Connery eventually swung them.

River Phoenix had previously played Harrison Ford's son in Peter Weir's *The Mosquito Coast* (1986). The actor, best known at that point for *Stand By Me* (1986) and *Running On Empty* (1988), shared some of Ford's looks and demeanour, and seemed an ideal candidate to play Indy as an adolescent. Having featured in *A View To a Kill* (1985) and *A Prayer for the Dying* (1987), Alison Doody was cast as the scheming love interest Elsa Schneider, lending the role an icy sexuality new to Indy movies. To play the distinctly Belloq-esque Walter Donovan, the producer Robert Watts suggested his next-door neighbour, Julian Glover. *Last Crusade* also welcomed back Denholm Elliott as Brody and John Rhys-Davies into the Indy fold, again reinforcing the return to the values of the first film.

PRODUCTION: Continuing the convention of scouring the world for locations, *Indiana Jones and the Last Crusade* started filming in Almeira, Spain, on 16 May 1988. The team returned to Indy's spiritual home at Elstree studios for ten weeks, shooting scenes inside Donovan's swanky apartment, the inner sanctums of the Grail temple, the German castle and Zeppelin and the Venetian catacombs filled with rats: the company bred their own rodents for wide shots; for fire scenes, mechanical critters were employed for the comfort of the actors and the safety of the rats. After a few days in Venice capturing exteriors, *Last Crusade* moved on to Jordan to shoot in the ancient city of Petra, doubling as the Canyon of the Crescent Moon – the home of the Grail temple.

TICS OF THE TRADE: Without the exaggerated comic-book framings of *Raiders* and the dark expressionistic feel of *Temple of Doom*, *Last Crusade* is the visually least intriguing of the three Indy pictures. While utilising the revealing camera arcs and dolly moves that charge the smallest moment, Spielberg, once again working with the cinematographer Douglas Slocombe, captures the action in a bright, low-contrast look that owes much to the adventure films of the 30s – witness the lighting in Donovan's apartment as he draws Indy into his plan – but seems a little flat compared with the atmosphere of the previous films.

Although Spielberg seems more interested in his actors this time round – there are far more close-ups – there are still lovely Spielbergian touches and camera conceits: to indicate that the airship is heading back to Germany, rather than show a miniature craft change direction, Spielberg lingers on the shift in shadows moving across a dining room table; the link between the young Indy and adult Indy storylines, seamlessly achieved by a simple piece of editing – as young River Phoenix bows his head wearing the famous fedora, we cut to Harrison Ford lifting his head, ready to take a punch in the face.

Spielberg also finds a home for his beloved simultaneous zoom and dolly technique. Just before Indy is to take the leap of faith that is the final test to acquire the Ark, the camera moves in and zooms out on a dying Henry's face, accentuating the peril in the situation and the desperation in his dialogue: 'You must believe, boy, you must believe.'

CLASSIC LINES:
Elsa *(exploring the catacombs)*: 'What's this?'
Indy: 'Ark of the Covenant.'
Elsa: 'Are you sure?'
Indy: 'Pretty sure.'

Indy: 'Nazis. I hate these guys.'

Walter Donovan: 'Germany has declared war on the Jones boys.'

Indy: 'It's disgraceful. You're old enough to be her grandfather.'
Henry Jones: 'I'm as human as the next man.'
Indy: 'Dad, I was the next man!'

Sallah: 'Please, what does it always mean, this . . . this "Junior"?'
Henry Jones: 'That's his name. [points to himself] Henry Jones . . .
    [points to Indy] . . . Junior.'
Indy: 'I like Indiana.'
Henry Jones: 'We named the dog Indiana.'

COMIC RELIEF: The heart of *Last Crusade*'s comedy comes from the sparring of Ford and Connery, full of warm comic interplay new to the Indy movies. Occasionally the humour is too obvious or broad to hit the spot: young Indy jumping from a rock to a horse only for the horse to move away at the last minute; the sound of Indy bashing down on the big X on the floor is greeted with the bemused look of the librarian as it coincides exactly with the sound of books being stamped; the comedy roll of Ford's eyes and his (almost to camera) 'Ah, Venice' as he passionately kisses Elsa. However, *Last Crusade* does contain comedic treasure: with the Nazis desperate to find the whereabouts of Marcus Brody, Indy launches into an elaborate description of Brody as a master of disguise whose knowledge of foreign culture and customs allows him to 'blend in, disappear' with any environment – cut to Marcus bumbling along a crowded train station, sticking out like a sore thumb; the exchange of glances between Indy and Henry and the Nazi fighter pilot as the burning plane overtakes the car in the tunnel. And best of all, Henry, Sallah and Brody peering over the cliff looking for what they think is Indy's grave while Indy has climbed up behind them and tries to see what they are looking at. An old joke, flawlessly played.

VISUAL EFFECTS: As usual with the other Indy pictures, ILM's visual effects for *Last Crusade* are scene setters and embellishments rather than elements that swamp a story. Centred on an eight-foot Zeppelin airship model carved out of foam, the Joneses-versus-Luftwaffe dogfight was created through a mixture of full-sized mock-ups (shot against blue screen) and aircraft miniatures: as the burning plane chases the car down a tunnel, a model car and plane were pulled along on cables at speeds of thirty miles an hour down an ignited miniature tunnel created in eight-foot sections. Close-ups of Ford and Connery in the car were shot against blue screen but without the dirty windscreen, which was inserted optically later, as it would have interfered with the transmission of blue. The moment where, at the sight of Henry brandishing his umbrella, a flock of seagulls are sent flying into the path of another fighter causing it to crash was created by a mixture of cross-shaped feather balls and wire-mounted toy birds flown into a miniature model – actually the model from the fire tunnel reassembled!

As well as creating the *Last Crusade*'s travelogue feel through a series of matte paintings – the German castle, the Berlin airport, the (fictional) Republic of Hatay skyline were all painted on glass – ILM also rolled a quarter-scale model tank off a cliff and created the three challenges that Indy has to overcome at the end, the most difficult being the leap of faith that entails crossing a bridge that is invisible to the human eye because the surface and texture precisely matches the cliff face opposite. The effect was created by a nine-by-thirteen-foot miniature chasm, made out of green polystyrene and painted by the film's model maker Paul Huston. Shots of Ford stepping out on to a blue screen were then interpolated into the model, with a finger puppet creating a shadow that would double for Ford's shadow.

The most elaborate effect in *Last Crusade* detailed the demise of Donovan, rapidly ageing into decomposition, then death, after swigging water from the wrong Grail. Rather than keep cutting away to an actor in various states of old-age make-up, Spielberg specified that the moment should be captured in a single take. Three separate, articulate, full-size puppets of Julian Glover were created in various states of deterioration and photographed, the shots blended into a single take by digital manipulation. To finish the shot off, a skeleton created out of brittle polymer was suspended on wires, then exploded against a wall using small pyrotechnic charges.

SOUND EFFECTS: As with the previous Indy movies, the sound is up front and vital, embellishing the cartoon feel, yet also helping to sell the drama when required: listen to the gunshot from Donovan's handgun that slays Henry – a big booming sound designed to reflect the emotional intensity of the moment rather than slavishly re-create any kind of weaponry authenticity.

WHAT'S THE SCORE? Marking a departure from the first two pictures in that it relies less on the familiar *Indiana Jones* march for heroic effect, John Williams's score for the *Last Crusade* covers around 110 minutes of a 127-minute film, creating a wealth of original material without straying too far from the *Raiders* formula. This time round we get the frantic orchestral flurries of young Indy's quest; the noble, elegant, very English theme that signifies the Holy Grail; the driving scherzo that constitutes a kind of pursuit theme, be it during the motorcycle chase or the plane-versus-car showdown. As before, Williams uses a slightly parodic martial motif to identify the Nazis, unsettling strings to represent the creepy animal bits and a relentless rhythmic pounding to heighten fistfights in the face of an impending doom such as Indy's punch-up before the whirring propeller of a huge tanker or trading blows atop a tank heading towards a precipice.

There are also some blatant nods to Indy's musical past: his recognition of the Ark in the ancient markings of the catacombs is graced with a reprise of the Ark's mysterious theme, and *Raiders'* signature brass does get an airing at the most triumphant moments – Indy bursting out of a crate riding a motorbike with Henry in the sidecar and, after narrowly missing being crushed to death hanging off the gun turret of a tank, rallying to kick more Nazi butt with a little help from that uplifting march.

CUT SCENES: One scene omitted featured a woman film director documenting the Nazi rally. The moment was intended as a reference to the film-maker Leni Riefenstahl and her propaganda documentary, *Triumph of the Will* (1934).

In the original cinema release when Donovan is trying to aquire help from the Sultan, he points to a chest of gold items and says, 'Donated by the finest Jewish families in Germany.' In the later releases for TV and video the word 'Jewish' was edited out.

GEDDIT! As young Indy sprints along the speeding train, he hides out in a carriage named 'Dr Fantasy's Magic Caboose' – a reference to the co-executive producer Frank Marshall, who performs magic under the Dr Fantasy pseudonym.

The dog barking when young Indy passes with the cross in his hand is an Alaskan malamute, the same type as Lucas's dog, which provided the character Indiana with his Christian name.

Donovan's wife was played by Julian Glover's wife Isla Blair, actually credited as 'Mrs Glover'.

The actor Pat Roach appears as a thug in all three *Indiana Jones* movies. He's both the giant Sherpa and a mechanic in *Raiders*, he's the chief guard (who gets crushed by the rock crusher) in *Temple of Doom* (1984), and he's a Gestapo officer in *Last Crusade*.

Once again, the *Jaws* stuntman Ted Grossman appears in a Spielberg film – here he plays Deputy Sheriff.

FACTOID FRENZY: To keep cool in the Spanish sun, Sean Connery and Harrison Ford would often perform shots from the waist up without any trousers on.

Last Crusade is the second film in which Michael Byrne portrays a Nazi opposite Harrison Ford. The first was *Force 10 from Navarone* (1978).

Last Crusade is the second film in which Michael Sheard, who appears uncredited as Hitler, has played the bad guy in a film starring Harrison Ford – he was Admiral Ozzel in *The Empire Strikes Back*. He even played the epitome of unspeakable evil as Mr Bronson in TV's *Grange Hill*.

THE CRITICAL FACULTY: '*Indy 3* is the same, different and better. It infuses vitality into action-adventure, a movie staple whose ravenous popularity and endless predictable permutations have nearly exhausted it.' (Richard Corliss, *Time*.) 'The director can now handle action sequences standing on his head, but there are signs of tiredness in the pow-zap formula . . . He now appears to be running on the spot in Boy's Own territory.' (Anne Billson, *Sight and Sound*.) 'The Connery–Ford clowning distracts us from the doldrums of punches and chases and plot explication. The movie isn't bad; most of it is enjoyable. But it's familiar and repetitive – it's a rehash.' (Pauline Kael, *New Yorker*.)

BOX OFFICE: Opening in the US on 24 May 1989 on 2,327 screens, *Indiana Jones and the Last Crusade* grossed $46.9 million in its first week of release. Despite the huge popularity of *Batman* that summer, *Last Crusade* became Spielberg's most profitable movie since *E.T.*, earning $494.7 million around the world.

AWARDS: Best Sound Effects Editing was the only Oscar picked up by *Last Crusade* at the 1990 Academy Awards ceremony, its other two nominations coming for Best Sound and Best Original Score. In addition to nominations for Best Sound and Special Effects, Sean Connery picked up a Best Supporting Actor nomination at the BAFTAs, as he did in the Golden Globes.

JOIN THE DOTS: Roller-coaster plotting – *Jaws, 1941, Raiders of the Lost Ark, Indiana Jones and the Temple of Doom, Jurassic Park, The Lost World: Jurassic Park*. **World War Two** – *1941, Raiders of the Lost Ark, Empire of the Sun, Schindler's List, Saving Private Ryan*.

Aircraft – *Close Encounters of the Third Kind, 1941, Raiders of the Lost Ark, Indiana Jones and the Temple of Doom, Empire of the Sun, Always, Hook, Saving Private Ryan.* **Dolly zoom** – *The Sugarland Express, Jaws, E.T. The Extra-Terrestrial.* **Historical setting** – *1941, Raiders of the Lost Ark, Indiana Jones and the Temple of Doom, The Color Purple, Empire of the Sun, Schindler's List, Amistad, Saving Private Ryan.* **Absent fathers** – *The Sugarland Express, Close Encounters of the Third Kind, E.T. The Extra-Terrestrial, The Color Purple, Empire of the Sun, Hook.*

SEND IN THE CLONES: *The Mask of Zorro* (1998) played similar antics to *Last Crusade*'s Ford–Connery partnership as Antonio Banderas is instructed in the ways of the Z by a father figure played by Anthony Hopkins – the film is one of the few *Indy*-modelled blockbusters to capture its spirit of adventure. Among the many *Indiana* licks borrowed by *The Mummy* (1999) was a fistfight set aboard a rainswept boat that mirrors Indy's fight to regain the Cross of Coranado.

However, the most discernible influence of *Last Crusade* was the creation of *The Young Indiana Jones Chronicles* (1992) by Lucas (without Spielberg's involvement) for ABC Television. Designed with a remit to educate as well as entertain, the show followed the youthful Indy's globetrotting adventures as he came into contact with historical figures such as Picasso, Lawrence of Arabia, Winston Churchill and Mata Hari. Sean Patrick Flanery took over the role from River Phoenix and Harrison Ford was persuaded to return for one episode, 'The Mystery of the Blues', as an aged Indy reminiscing about his adventures with his college roommate Elliot Ness in Prohibition Era Chicago. *Young Indiana Jones* was pivotal to Lucas in developing production techniques and key crew personnel – the writer-director of *The Green Mile* (1999), Frank Darabont, came up through the *Young Indy* ranks – yet it lacked the excitement factor of the movies and ultimately failed to find an audience.

FINAL ANALYSIS: After the mixed critical reception of *The Color Purple* and *Empire of the Sun*, returning to the familiarity, ease and box-office certainty of the *Indiana Jones* series must have been incredibly attractive to Spielberg. As threequels go, *Last Crusade* ranks as one of the best, pulling off that difficult follow-up trick of providing the same experience but different. As such, the movie retains much of what was great about *Raiders*, such as the soaring zest for adventure, the reinvention of pulpy material and the hoaky appropriation of actual mythology and religion – as well as the trilogy for a single character, it is also possible to view the films as a troika starring the world's most popular three faiths: Judaism (*Raiders*), Hinduism (*Temple of Doom*) and, with *Last Crusade*, Christianity. But, happily, it also finds some new spins on the old format – the Ford–Connery repartee, the treacherous heroine and a vaguely emotional core that never descends into syrup make for one hugely enjoyable summer blockbuster.

Yet the harsh treatment dished out to *Temple of Doom* seems to have undermined Spielberg's nerve, both in terms of storytelling intensity and visual style, and (with the exception of the failing-father story strand) it is difficult to detect his interests and personality in the mix. Although his hand is clearly on the exuberance of the train opening and the relentless thrills of the tank chase, the action scenes generally lack the craft and panache of Spielberg's best – the boat set piece and motorcycle sequence look particularly 'second unit' – and the tone is often too light and campy to make the various perils and threats riveting, even on its own comic-strip terms. At the time, *Last Crusade* was considered the definite end of the series – can you get a stronger sense of closure than the heroes riding off into the sunset? – and was easily good enough not to leave a bad taste in the mouth. But, while remaining cracking fun, it feels a little bland compared with the richness of *Raiders* and the kineticism of *Doom*.

SPIELBERG ON SPIELBERG: 'I've learned more about movie craft from making the *Indiana Jones* films than I did from *E.T.* or *Jaws*. And now I feel I have graduated from the college of Cliff-Hanger U. I ought to have paid tuition.'

Always (1989)

(Colour, 123 mins)

Studio Universal/United Artists
Producers Steven Spielberg, Kathleen Kennedy, Frank Marshall
Co-producer Richard Vane
Screenplay by Jerry Belson
Based on *A Guy Named Joe* screenplay by Dalton Trumbo, from a story by Chandler Vague and David Boehm, adapted by Frederick Hazlitt Brennan
Director of Photography Mikael Salomon
Edited by Michael Kahn ACE
Music John Williams
Production Design by James D Bissell
Costume Design Ellen Mirojnick
Casting by Lora Kennedy
Unit Production Manager Gary Dangler
First Assistant Director Pat Kehoe

Aerial Sequence Design Joe Johnston
Sound Design Ben Burtt
Supervisor of Visual Effects Bruce Nicholson
Supervising Sound Editor Richard Hymns
Art Director Chris Burian-Mohr
Stunt Co-ordinator Steve Lambert
Special Effects Supervisor Mike Wood
Special Visual Effects by Industrial Light and Magic

CAST: Richard Dreyfuss (*Pete Sandich*), Holly Hunter (*Dorinda Durston*), Brad Johnson (*Ted Baker*), John Goodman (*Al Yackey*), Audrey Hepburn (*Hap*), Roberts Blossom (*Dave*), Keith David (*Powerhouse*), Ed Van Nuys (*Nails*), Marg Helgenberger (*Rachel*), Dale Dye (*Fire Boss*), Brian Haley (*Alex*), James Lashly (*Charlie*), Michael Steve Jones (*Grey*), Kim Robillard (*Air Traffic Controller*), Jim Spaceman (*Dispatcher*), Doug McGrath (*Bus Driver*), Sherriel L Bowens, Acencion Fuentes, Todd Jacobson (*Children on Bus*), JD Souther (*Singer*), David Jackson, David Kitay, Gene Strimling (*The Band*), Roy Harrison (*Fisherman No.1*), Ted Grossman (*Fisherman No. 2*), Gerry Rothschild (*Carl the Barkeep*), Loren Smothers (*Bartender*), Talena Ottwell (*Bar Girl*).

BUDGET: $29.5 million

MPAA: PG

BBFC: PG

TITLE SEQUENCE: Over the Universal logo, the sound of crickets chirping builds on the soundtrack. 'Universal And United Artists Presents' and 'Always' pop up in white lettering against a black screen, the title font in a more grandiloquent style, as the cricket sounds are enriched by eerie bird calls.

PLOT SUMMARY: *Always* opens with the kind of simply staged but bravura introduction you get only in Spielberg films. Two fishermen (the Elmer Thud type of hunters Spielberg had previously satirised in *Sugarland* and *Jaws*) drift in a boat on the middle of a huge lake. A huge aircraft descends silently on the water behind them and begins speeding towards their boat. With the aircraft noise growing ever louder, the fishermen finally wake up to the aircraft bearing down on them and try to start their outboard engine. The power stalls, the men look doomed – until the aircraft lifts off the water, barely missing the two bozos' heads.

The daredevil flying is the handiwork of a firefighting pilot, Pete

Sandich, who along with his pal Al Yackey is dousing a rampant forest fire with chemical retardant in the American Northwest. After he barely makes it back to his base owing to engine failure, Pete's risk-taking subsequently becomes the subject of much tension with the unit dispatcher, and also his girlfriend, Dorinda Durston. As it is Dorinda's birthday, the tension is temporarily forgotten – wearing a white dress that Pete bought for her, she reduces the male-dominated mess tent to horny coyotes, particularly catching the eye of a courier pilot, Ted Baker, who delivered Pete's present to her. However, the subject of Pete's risk-taking resurfaces that evening when Dorinda makes him a deal: if he gives up the fancy flying and takes a safe instructor's job in Colorado, she will leave behind her own flying aspirations and become his gal on the ground. He agrees but is immediately called out on another job. During the hazardous flight, the propeller of Al's plane catches fire and, although Pete puts out the flames in a dangerous midair dive, his own engine ignites in a spectacular fireball, his plane exploding into smithereens as Al looks on in horror.

Wandering through a burned-out forest, Pete meets a guardian angel, Hap, who tells him that he is dead and has a new job to do: lend spiritual sustenance and guidance to an upcoming pilot – Ted Baker. With Pete acting as a conscience at the rookie's shoulder, Baker (still pining for Dorinda) enrols at the training school in Colorado, now run by Al. Al quickly banishes Ted for incompetence, then finds Dorinda, a shadow of her former self since Pete's death, working at an air-traffic control in San Diego. Al persuades her to come back to Colorado, a move that coincides with Baker (and Pete) returning to the flight school, Pete convincing Ted that he should not give up on his dream girl without ever knowing it is Dorinda.

The inevitable happens when Ted and Pete literally run into Dorinda's house during a wayward spot of aircraft taxiing. As Ted's piloting skills improve through Pete's telepathic encouragement, the couple get to know each other, first as Ted resuscitates a school bus driver suffering from a heart attack and then over an intimate dinner. This stokes Pete's jealousy, and he begins to interfere with the budding romance. This disruption of Dorinda's life is put into perspective by Hap, who informs Pete that anything he does for himself is a waste of spirit and he must learn to let his earthbound love go.

Back on terra firma, Ted is called out to help save a group of ground-based fighters trapped in the midst of a raging forest inferno. Not wanting to lose another man at the hands of a fire, Dorinda takes the plane herself and, with Pete by her side, creates a path for the stranded firefighters to the safety of a river. Forced to crash-land in a lake, Dorinda is saved from death by Pete. In saving her life, he has given up on the chance for her to be reunited with him – and happily watches her walk away from him into a new life with Ted.

BACKSTORY: *Always* represents the one (and only) remake in Spielberg's career to date. Aged twelve, Spielberg had been fascinated with Victor Fleming's 1944 wartime fantasy *A Guy Named Joe*, in which Spencer Tracy played a World War Two flying ace (Pete Sandidge) who loses his life (and his love, Dorinda, played by Irene Dunne) dive-bombing a Nazi ship. Pete subsequently joins a spectral squadron of deceased pilots imbued with a mission to instruct a new generation of live ones. Pete's charge, Ted Randall (Van Johnson), falls for Dorinda and the spirit instructs Randall in both aerial combat and the romancing of his former love. Despite some good effects work by Arnold Gillespie and nifty dialogue by Dalton Trumbo, the passage of time has not been kind to *Joe*: a heavy-handed fantasy marred by a leaden tone and browbeating war propaganda. For the record, the film does not contain any character called Joe – the title refers to the US Air Force practice of calling a regular guy a 'Joe'.

Still in his adolescence, the young Spielberg was probably attracted to the World War Two milieu and the film's more emotional aspects – it was apparently only the second film to make him cry after *Bambi*. The adult Spielberg admired Fleming's diversity as a cinematic craftsman – Fleming was the architect behind *Captains Courageous* (1937), and *The Wizard of Oz* and *Gone With the Wind*, both in 1939 – and was drawn to the film's conception of the spirit as an invisible conscience rather than a visible ghost.

While the idea had been percolating in the Spielberg subconscious since 1974, it was first announced as a project in 1980, placed at MGM. Deciding that the story should replace *Joe*'s war-torn setting with a more contemporary context, Spielberg first commissioned Diane Thomas to update the project. Thomas had proved adept at updating moribund genres (as well as snappy male–female sparring) in Robert Zemeckis's *Romancing the Stone* (1984) yet her work on *Always* was tragically cut short by a fatal car accident. Subsequently, Spielberg brought in numerous writers – Jerry Belson, Tom Stoppard, Ron Bass – with Belson working over the final draft and receiving sole screen credit.

Yet it wasn't the difficulty in finding a suitable screenplay that delayed *Always* for almost a decade. It was Spielberg's diffidence about directing such overtly emotional material: 'In a lot of the earlier drafts, Richard [Dreyfuss] walked through walls. He put his hands through things. He glowed. It was riddled with gimmicks and tricks and the kind of stuff I do really well. I guess that's why I didn't want to do it . . . Every special effect we had was written out of the movie . . . I had a lot of false starts, but I think it came down to the fact that I wasn't ready to make it . . . If I had of made it in 1980, I think it would have been more of a comedy. I'd have hidden all of the deep feelings.'

As an adaptation of *A Guy Named Joe*, *Always* kept certain scenes verbatim: the moment in which Pete gives Dorinda a dress for her birthday – see **Classic lines** – is an exact replay of the corresponding scene in *Joe*. Elsewhere, the changes are to make the story more palatable to a more modern audience: in *Joe*, it is difficult to swallow that Irene Dunne's Dorinda can steal an aircraft and dive-bomb a prized Japanese ammunitions factory; in *Always*, Hunter's Dorinda stealing a plane to rescue a band of firefighters ensnared by forest fires feels much more credible – interestingly, Spielberg keeps Pete's speech extolling Dorinda's future almost word for word. Only occasionally does *Joe* improve on *Always*: in Fleming's film, Dunne's Dorinda is a much more sophisticated, complex image of womanhood than Hunter's. Moreover, her appearance in Pete's dress is watched by a single pilot. In Spielberg's take, the whole canteen gather to watch Dorinda's parading – she causes a stampede to the sinks when she tells them only pilots with clean hands can dance with her. Spielberg's showmanship may be funnier but it lacks the beguiling gentility of the original.

ORIGINS: As well as *A Guy Named Joe*, a number of films have dealt with the consequences of life and love after death. The most famous example is Michael Powell and Emeric Pressburger's *A Matter of Life and Death* (1946), which features Peter Carter (David Niven), a pilot who falls for the voice of an American WAC (Kim Hunter) just as his plane is going down in flames. He seemingly survives the crash but only after a clerical error in Heaven. As he was supposed to die in the air crash, a debate begins to see whether he should live or die. *Here Comes Mr Jordan* (1941) saw Robert Montgomery as a boxing champ die in another plane crash, yet, due to live another fifty years, returns to Earth with a celestial emissary, Mr Jordan (Claude Reins), to find another body in which to finish his life. It was remade by Warren Beatty in 1978 as *Heaven Can Wait*. This notion of celestial intervention is hugely pertinent to both *Joe* and *Always*.

The Pete–Dorinda sparring owes a huge debt to the emotional battle of wits played out by Spencer Tracy and Katharine Hepburn over nine films, most famously *Adam's Rib* (1949) and *Pat and Mike* (1952). The notion of romance featured in *Always* (1989) may have been influenced by the work of David Lean. Both Lean's *Brief Encounter* (1945) and *Summer Madness* (1955) feature characters (in the latter's case Katharine Hepburn) renouncing love in favour of loneliness, an idea that permeates Pete's letting Dorinda go in *Always*'s final scene. Lean's *Blithe Spirit* (1945) has the ghost of a novelist's first wife disrupt her former husband's current marriage, which may have also had some bearing on the comedic possibilities inherent in a lover returning from the dead.

Always's fliers' canteen could easily have come from Howard Hawks's *Only Angels Have Wings* (1939), another movie that throws a sassy broad (Jean Arthur) into the mix with a group of pilots. The fast-talking banter of Hawks's screwball comedies also influenced the early scenes of Pete and Dorinda's verbiage. Later on, Dorinda's descent down the stairs to the rapture of the awed airmen echoes a moment in John Ford's *They Were Expendable* (1945), featuring Donna Reed. Starring Fred MacMurray and Paulette Goddard, *The Forest Rangers* (1942) played romantic shenanigans against the backdrop of raging forest fires, while *Hellfighters* (1968) saw oil fields burn on a similar scale to *Always*, once again the macho firemen (John Wayne, Jim Hutton) battling women as well as fire.

CASTING: *Always* marked the return of Richard Dreyfuss to a Spielberg movie for the first time in twelve years. The pair had discovered their shared admiration for *A Guy Named Joe* on location in Martha's Vineyard for *Jaws*, with Dreyfuss pleading with Spielberg to let him play the Spencer Tracy role if ever a remake came to fruition. However, when the director began rethinking the project in the early 80s, he sought more conventional male leads such as Paul Newman to play Pete and Robert Redford to play Ted – an idea dropped when both actors wanted to play Pete. Spielberg initially believed that Dreyfuss was perhaps too idiosyncratic to be a romantic lead, but what changed the director's mind was Dreyfuss's performance in *Stakeout* (1988): 'That was the first time I really found Richard to be a really attractive leading man.'

In the early incarnation of *Always*, Debra Winger was Spielberg's idea for Dorinda. Holly Hunter entered the equation after the director saw her in the off-Broadway production of *The Miss Firecracker Contest* and, following her Oscar-nominated turn in another love-triangle comedy, *Broadcast News* (1987), the role was hers. Hunter gives *Always* an energy that often keeps the sentimentality at bay. At five foot six, she is also one of the few actresses who can make Richard Dreyfuss look tall.

A past master at playing blue-collar best-friend types – he played second string to Dennis Quaid in *The Big Easy* (1987) and Al Pacino in *Sea of Love* (1989) – John Goodman filled *Joe*'s Ward Bond role of Al Yackey. Having previously worked with Hunter on the Coen Brothers' *Raising Arizona* (1987), Goodman invests Al with his likable, always watchable presence. A competing rodeo cowboy, Brad Johnson, had just one beer commercial on his thesping CV when Spielberg cast him as Ted Baker. A bundle of nerves at his audition, he called the producer Kathleen Kennedy by the wrong name and spilled a Dr Pepper over his clothes, but the mixture of this klutziness and all-American good looks won the day. Occasionally working for him, his general balsawood quality looks out of place against the lively talents of the rest of the cast.

Just coming off *Last Crusade*, Spielberg originally wanted Sean Connery to act as Pete's guardian angel, Hap. When the actor proved unavailable, Spielberg switched sexes and cast a sixty-year-old Audrey Hepburn to represent the more maternal side of nature. A genuine Hollywood legend – *Roman Holiday* (1953), *Breakfast At Tiffany's* (1961), *Charade* (1963), *My Fair Lady* (1964) – Hepburn was wooed out of retirement, partly to work with Spielberg and partly because the small role would not interfere with her work as a UNICEF ambassador. Sadly, *Always* proved to be the last film she completed before her death in 1993.

PRODUCTION: Nearly two years before *Always* was a go project, Spielberg sent film crews out to capture the fires that devastated Yellowstone National Park. With the permission of the Forest Service, the film crews flew in their planes as the blazes raged, and much of the material that was later back-projected behind Pete and Al during the flying sequences was footage from the Yellowstone catastrophe.

Principal photography on *Always* began with the mountain greenery of Libby, Montana, serving as the firefighting air-attack base that opens the film. For the Colorado flying school, the unit discovered an old World War Two base in Ephrata, Washington, the desert-like terrain providing a strong contrast to the picturesque Montana locale. Studio work was finished up on the soundstages at Universal and Lorimar studios.

TICS OF THE TRADE: On James Cameron's personal recommendation, Spielberg hooked up with the Danish cinematographer Mikael Salomon after seeing his work in Cameron's *The Abyss* (1989). From the stunning simplicity of the opening shot the result is a collaboration – pun intended – made in heaven. The cold blue light that emanates from Dorinda's fridge, casting Pete with a deathly pall while Dorinda is bathed in the warm glow of her fire, is a visual encapsulation of the whole movie but still stunningly naturalistic. As Pete talks to Dorinda for the first time after his death, Spielberg and Salomon have the guts to have her in silhouette, keeping all the emphasis on Dreyfuss's words but forcing us to fill in the emotion on Dorinda's face. Time and again,

Salomon adds nuance to Spielberg's trademark 'God light': the poignant moment where Dorinda dances to 'Smoke Gets In Your Eyes' is given an extra emotional level by the nostalgic but never overblown autumnal light streaming in the windows. The risk-taking and subtlety of Salomon's cinematography does much to undercut the mawkishness that threatens to pervade the whole film.

CLASSIC LINES:

Dorinda (*reacting to Pete's birthday gift of a dress*): 'Oh Pete. Girl clothes. (*to men approaching the present*) Get back! Don't you touch it! (*back to Pete*) Why didn't you tell me before I lost my temper?'

Pete: 'So you do like dresses?'

Dorinda: 'It's not the dress, it's the way you see me.'

Pete (*final line*): 'That's my girl . . . and that's my boy.'

VISUAL EFFECTS: Under the guidance of the Spielberg regulars Industrial Light and Magic – in particular the aerial sequence supervisor Joe Johnston – *Always*'s aircraft were originally going to be created through a mixture of radio-controlled miniatures and models suspended from wires. However, tests ultimately saw the radio-control option scrapped, partly because the smoke and wind effects made the planes difficult to control and partly because, flying at speeds up to seventy miles an hour, the miniatures were moving too fast for the camera operators to follow.

Instead, planes were flown dangling from a crane mounted on a truck. Six A-26 Invaders and two PBY Super Catalinas were constructed (helped by reference footage of their real-life counterparts) as fifth-scale models, the large size dictated by flames, which notoriously give away scale when seen against smaller models. Created at an abandoned airstrip near Tracy, the woodlands depicted in daytime shots were a miniature, 500 feet long by 300 feet wide, with hundreds of Christmas trees set on fire doubling as the Montana location.

For Dorinda's night-time excursion, the forest sections were re-created in an empty steel plant in Bethlehem (San Francisco, not near Jerusalem), meaning optimum control of light and safety could be maintained.

For one of the most exciting shots of the sequence – the Invader flying straight at the camera – the crew shot the scene in a mirror, as a straight-on, high-speed approach would have endangered the camera crew. Canny dogs that they are, ILM also remembered to reverse the aircraft lettering and numerical designation so it read correctly in the reflection.

SOUND EFFECTS: As much as *Always* is a love letter to the beauty of planes in flight, it is also a rhapsody to the sound of aircraft engines. Assembled with tender care by the sound designer Ben Burtt and his team, the various engine burrs and propeller whirrs give the flight scenes an incredible air of danger and excitement, an effect heightened by the dynamic *whoosh* sounds that are meticulously placed every time a plane moves through a blast of cloud.

WHAT'S THE SCORE? Filled with lots of airy musical wash, *Always* is probably the most forgettable score John Williams has ever created for a Spielberg movie. There are some strong moments – the powerful string motif heard as Pete and Al drive to the aircraft on Pete's last mission, the boisterous slice of Americana that underscores Ted's plane chasing the truck into Dorinda's house and the stirring main theme that exults Dorinda's solo flight – but the majority of it is just twinkly, synth-dominated wallpaper that fails either to enhance the film or lodge in the memory.

CUT SCENES: As was his usual practice, Spielberg reshaped *Always* after assessing the reaction of preview audiences. The major changes concerned the climax of the movie. In the original version, Dorinda's final flight was intended to be much more stylised, with her descent into the forest resembling a plunge into hell. Then, her subsequent ascent into the clouds would be a journey into heaven, very serene and quiet. Spielberg subsequently decided to adopt a more naturalistic approach, perhaps feeling the expressionism lifted the audience out of the moment. The film's final moments were also due to be much more fanciful. In the early cuts, Pete was due to walk away from Dorinda and Ted and then rise into the night sky as if climbing a stairway to heaven – very *A Matter of Life and Death*. Yet the notion was dropped after it tested badly, which left Spielberg without a closing shot for the movie. ILM subsequently took the shot of Dreyfuss walking away and composited it into a background of the runway under the starry sky.

GEDDIT! Playing Fisherman No. 2 in the opening scene is Ted Grossman which has an extra resonance if you know that Grossman appeared in *Jaws* as the guy in the rowing boat who gets his leg chomped off.

A *Guy Named Joe* plays on the television in *Poltergeist* (1982), which was co-written by Spielberg.

The moment where Dorinda and Ted stop to help a school bus careering out of control recalls a similar scene in *Duel*.

Dale Dye, who plays the fire boss, would later go on to put the actors through boot camp in *Saving Private Ryan*.

FACTOID FRENZY: Following the scene where Pete and Al speak in cartoon voices after sucking in helium, the end credits feature the bizarre caution: 'Inhaling of helium from balloons is dangerous, and can cause serious injury or death.'

After filming had finished, Spielberg presented Dreyfuss, Hunter and Goodman with new $25,000 Mazda Miatas with personalised number plates suggesting their characters' names.

Audrey Hepburn's contract stipulated that her $1 million fee would be paid directly to UNICEF.

Spielberg originally contacted Irving Berlin to see if he could use his song 'Always' as the film's main theme. When Berlin, then 94, said he had future plans for the song, Spielberg tried the song 'I'll Be Seeing You', but it tested badly in previews. Ultimately, the director made witty use of the Jerome Kern ballad 'Smoke Gets In Your Eyes'.

THE CRITICAL FACULTY: 'Was there no-one among Spielberg's associates with the intellectual stature to convince him that his having cried at *A Guy Named Joe* when he was twelve was not a good reason for him to remake it?' (David Denby, *New York*.) 'Spielberg's miscalculation was to forget *A Guy Named Joe* responded to a most particular need. Coming in WWII, when young lives were so palpably precarious and the need for comforting illusion so great, it had a ready audience. These were Americans who, if not more naive than we, were at least more willing to suspend their cynicism.' (Ralph Novak, *People*.) 'A better title for *Always* might be *Forever* which is roughly its running time.' (Sheila Benson, *Los Angeles Times*.) 'Now that Spielberg is no longer twelve hasn't he realised there is a queasiness in the idea of playing Cupid to the girl you loved and lost, and fixing her up with the next guy.' (Pauline Kael, *New Yorker*.) '*Always* is filled with big sentimental moments [but] it lacks the intimacy to make any of this very moving. Though the story calls out for simplicity, it unfolds in an atmosphere of forced laughter and forced tears. Gentle and moving as it means to be, *Always* is overloaded. There is barely a scene that wouldn't have worked better with less fanfare.' (Janet Maslin, *New York Times*.)

BOX OFFICE: Opening in the US on 22 December 1989 – the same year as *Indiana Jones and the Last Crusade*, resulting in the first time Spielberg pulled off his now customary coup of releasing two features in the same calendar year – *Always* grossed $43 million on its stateside theatrical run, winding up with a worldwide gross of $77.1 million.

AWARDS: Despite being released in a late December slot, generally considered the optimum time to garner Oscar consideration, *Always* received no nominations at the Academy Awards or the BAFTAs. While nods for direction, acting or writing were unlikely, Mikael Salamon's cinematography and ILM's breathtaking visual-effects work should surely have gained nominations.

JOIN THE DOTS: Aircraft – *Close Encounters of the Third Kind, 1941, Raiders of the Lost Ark, Indiana Jones and the Temple of Doom, Empire of the Sun, Indiana Jones and the Last Crusade, Hook, Saving Private Ryan.* **Contemporary setting** – *The Sugarland Express, Jaws, Close Encounters of the Third Kind, E.T. The Extra-Terrestrial, Twilight Zone: The Movie, Hook, Jurassic Park, The Lost World: Jurassic Park.*

SEND IN THE CLONES! Starring Demi Moore, Patrick Swayze and (an Oscar-winning) Whoopi Goldberg, Jerry Zucker's *Ghost* (1990 – a mere year after *Always*) took the notion of an afterlife romance and, by injecting a more contemporary sensibility and bigger emotional punch, fashioned the kind of box-office gold that was expected of *Always*. Anthony Minghella's *Truly, Madly, Deeply* (1991) took a more cerebral take on the lovers-separated-by-bereavement motif, with Juliet Stevenson being haunted and hindered by her deceased lover Alan Rickman while trying to forge a new love with Michael Maloney. Ron Bass, who worked on drafts of the *Always* screenplay, followed a similar path in his screenplay for *What Dreams May Come* (1998), based on a story by *Duel*'s Richard Matheson, in which a dead Robin Williams tries to rescue his widow from hell after she has committed suicide. Like *Always*, it is a decidedly sentimental take on the pain of separation. Ron Howard's hymn to firefighters, *Backdraft* (1991), benefited much from *Always*, purloining Spielberg's cinematographer Mikael Salomon with all his knowledge of filming fire to create unforgettable inferno imagery. Finally, Richard Dreyfuss and Holly Hunter reunited for Lasse Halstrom's *Once Around* (1991), written by *Hook*'s Malia Scotch Marmo, with Hunter playing a thirtysomething pressured into romance by her family, only to find they disapprove of her choice, Dreyfuss's brash, vulgar salesman. The film caused fewer ripples than *Always* and Spielberg's claim that the couple would develop into a kind of Tracy–Hepburn partnership proved completely unfounded.

FINAL ANALYSIS: The forgotten film of Spielberg's career – even *The Sugarland Express* is occasionally remembered because it was his debut – if *Always* did little to enhance Spielberg's career, it did little to detract from it either. Although it was neither the showcase for Spielberg as an actor's director (many Spielberg films feature far better performances) nor the personal 'relationships' movie it was once mooted as, it actually does continue to document some of Spielberg's favourite preoccupations, despite outward appearances: a fascination with World War Two iconography, the power of flight as a means of exhilaration and escape, a group of men overcoming nature to beat the odds and a definition of love that transcends normal boundaries.

Failing to capture the sparkle of the golden-age romantic comedies or the insight of Woody Allen, the film is a strange mixture of contemporary relationship neuroses and old-school Hollywood love story. The most powerful, affecting scene in the movie sees Dorinda and Al shouting at each other, both feeling the pain at losing Pete. For probably the only time in the movie, Spielberg captures the way that people actually talk to each other rather than the way they talk in the movies and, graced with great performances from Hunter and Goodman, the argument is all the more moving for that. That the film eschews even a nod towards reality in favour of movie patois and emotions may have accounted for its failure to find a really big audience.

But, taken on its own terms, it is nonetheless far more entertaining than its critics give it credit for. Improving on *A Guy Named Joe* no end, *Always* is a highly enjoyable confection of unabashed sentiment, quiet poignancy, knockabout comedy and brilliantly realised action all enveloped in consummate film-making artistry. Taking a baseball bat to the notion that romantic comedies cannot be entirely cinematic, the film contains some of the most lucid, spellbinding images in Spielberg's career. Yet it falls down because the sophistication of the technique far surpasses the maturity and emotional resonance of the relationship dissected – we are still waiting for the grown-up love story Spielberg has long been threatening to make. A minor work, then, but with some major flourishes.

SPIELBERG ON SPIELBERG: 'A lot of people said *Always* was the one movie where you have to cast movie stars. If you'd had Kevin Costner and Michelle Pfeiffer and made it exactly the same way it would have gone through the roof. That might have been true but you have to understand Kevin Costner is not my alter ego: Richard Dreyfuss is. Some movies don't take off and there's a thousand reasons why. But I would still have cast Richard and Holly Hunter. It was a good experience for me to make that movie because it was all about human emotions. I have no regret at all.'

Hook (1991)

(Colour, 142 mins)

Studio: Tristar
Producers Kathleen Kennedy, Frank Marshall, Gerald R Molen
Co-producers Gary Adelson, Craig Baumgarten
Associate Producers Bruce Cohen, Malia Scotch Marmo
Screenplay Jim V Hart, Malia Scotch Marmo
Screen Story Jim V Hart, Nick Castle. Adapted from the original stage play and books by Sir James M Barrie
Director of Photography Dean Cundey ASC
Production Designer Norman Garwood
Editing Michael Kahn ACE
Music John Williams
Costume Design Anthony Powell
Executive Producers Dodi Fayed, Jim V Hart
Casting Janet Hirshenson CSA, Jane Jenkins CSA, Michael Hirshenson
Unit Production Manager Gerald R Molen
Visual Consultant John Napier
Visual Effects Supervisor Eric Brevig
Special Effects Supervisor Michael Lantieri
Choreographer Vince Paterson
Art Directors Andrew Precht, Thomas E Saunders
Stunt Co-ordinator/Action Choreographer Gary Hymes
Sound Mixer Ron Judkins
Make-up Supervisor Christina Smith
Special Make-up Greg Cannom
Hair Supervisor Judith A Cory
Supervising Sound Editors Charles L Campbell, Rick Franklin
Special Visual Effects by Industrial Light and Magic

CAST: Dustin Hoffman (*Captain Hook*), Robin Williams (*Peter Banning/Peter Pan*), Julia Roberts (*Tinkerbell*), Bob Hoskins (*Smee*), Maggie Smith (*Granny Wendy*), Caroline Goodall (*Moira*), Charlie Korsmo (*Jack*), Amber Scott (*Maggie*), Laurel Cronin (*Liza*), Phil Collins (*Inspector Good*), Arthur Malet (*Tootles*), Isaiah Robinson (*Pockets*), Jasen Fisher (*Ace*), Dante Basco (*Rufio*), Raushan Hammond (*Thud Butt*), James Madio (*Don't Ask*), Thomas Tulak (*Too Small*), Alex Zuckerman (*Latchboy*), Ahmad Stoner (*No Nap*), Bogdan Georghe, Adam NcNatt (*Lost Boys*), Rene Gonzalez Jr, Brian Willis, Brett Willis (*Additional Lost Boys*), Ryan Francis (*Young Peter*).

TITLE SEQUENCE: Against a black screen, 'TriStar Pictures Presents' appears in simple yellow lettering followed by 'An Amblin Entertainment', both played out in silence. The arrival of the title

'Hook' in a more ornate, theatrical font signals the start of a homespun piano tune that will lead us into the opening scene of a school production of *Peter Pan*. Not the most exciting entry in the Spielberg opening-gambit canon.

PLOT SUMMARY: A high-flying lawyer, Peter Banning, is closing a high-powered deal, meaning he is oblivious to the love and affection of his two children. Ignoring Maggie's performance in the school production of *Peter Pan* and missing Jack's crucial end-of-season baseball game, Peter accompanies his family to London to speak in tribute of Granny Wendy for her work with orphans, yet always has one ear pressed to the mobile phone. As Peter speaks at the dinner thrown by Great Ormond Street Hospital, an unseen Captain James Hook invades Wendy's house and kidnaps the children, challenging Peter to return to Neverland to rescue them.

Granny Wendy tries to convince Peter that he is Peter Pan grown up but her argument falls on deaf ears. However, it begins to gain credence after Peter is flown to Neverland by the fairy Tinkerbell, and dropped in the middle of Piratetown. After a grand entrance led by his first mate, Smee, Hook fails to believe the bloated, unable-to-fly middle-ager before him is his nemesis Pan, so Tinkerbell bargains for three days to get Peter into match fitness. The action intercuts Peter's training sessions and uneasy reassimilation into his former gang, the Lost Boys – the leader, Rufio makes him particularly unwelcome – with Hook trying to gain Jack's and Maggie's affections in order to further undermine Pan. While Maggie is resolute in her love for her father, Jack falls under the influence of the wily pirate.

After licking Rufio in a battle of words and subsequent food fight, Peter has now reignited his childish tendencies and is accepted as the Pan. The rescue mission of the children from a baseball game organised by Hook – an emotional Peter watches Jack hit the ball out of the park, something that has always eluded him – is aborted as Peter becomes dismayed at how far Jack has entered into Hook's thrall. Returning to the Lost Boys' settlement, Peter is hit on the head by the baseball from Jack's home run and he begins to recount his forgotten early years to Tinkerbell: being rescued as an infant by Tinkerbell; his adventures with Wendy and her brothers; his falling in love with Wendy's granddaughter Moira.

During this reminiscing session Peter recalls that the reason he abandoned eternal childhood was to become a father – Jack is his happy thought, which enables him to soar through the sky, a reborn Pan. Marshalling his troops, Pan leads the Lost Boys into war against Hook's galleon. Although Maggie and Jack are rescued, Hook runs through Rufio and Peter realises that Neverland will never be safe if his adversary is allowed to live. A final duel commences with Peter outwitting a plethora of dirty tricks to overcome Hook, who is seen off by the stuffed crocodile that took his hand many years before. Bidding a sad farewell to the Lost Boys, Peter returns to London, his family and a new, improved brand of fatherdom.

BACKSTORY: During the 80s Spielberg flirted with various attempts to get *Peter Pan* to the screen. His conceptualisation was to do a live action version of Barrie's play, employing the fantasy of the Disney cartoon version yet taking fewer liberties with the events and tone of Barrie's original. At this point, the project was conceived as a potential musical – John Williams and the lyricist Leslie Bricusse were hired to create songs – with Michael Jackson mooted as the star. Jackson, who had entered Spielberg's circle after recording the *E.T. Storybook* album, is a lifelong *Pan* fan, even calling his Disneyland-esque estate Neverland. However, in September 1984, the trade paper *Variety* announced that Spielberg would make a nonmusical version of *Peter Pan* with Spielberg outlining that Jackson was never in the running for the title role.

Although Tom Stoppard took a crack at the screenplay and a production designer, Elliott Scott, had been commissioned to visualise sets, the project wasn't heard of until March 1988, when Spielberg confirmed that it was permanently shelved, his appetite for it diminished by the birth of his son Max.

Yet the notion of allying Spielberg with *Peter Pan* proved too mouthwatering for Hollywood to resist. The opportunity presented itself with a script placed at Columbia by a first-time writer, James Hart. Hart was looking for a way to put a new spin on Barrie's premise, and serendipity landed in his lap in the form of his young son Jake, who asked, 'Daddy, did Peter Pan ever grow up?' While reassuring the kid that Pan stayed eternally young, Hart seized on the idea of Pan as an ageing corporate raider battling Wall Street pirates, ignoring his family and leaving the realm of imagination behind.

Despite his constant monicker in the popular press as 'the kid who won't grow up', Spielberg found numerous identification points with Hart's respinning of the *Pan* mythos. 'He's very representative of a lot of people today who race headlong into the future, nodding hello and goodbye to their families. I'm part of a generation that is extremely motivated by career and I've caught myself in the unenviable position of being Peter Banning from time to time. I've seen myself overworked, and not spending enough time at home, and I've got a couple of good lessons from making the movie.'

Interestingly, although the Disney and other versions of *Peter Pan* were ingrained in his memory, Hart didn't come to read Barrie's novel until he was 33 years old. His adaptation stuck close to the spirit of the original. 'Tiger Lily and the Indians were in all my drafts,' he remembered, 'and were cut out for political reasons: they were not even shot.' Other elements of Hart's work were redrafted by other writers: the writer of *Once Around*, Malia Scotch Marmo, was brought in at the request of Dustin Hoffman to beef up the role of Hook – she shares a screen credit with Hart. Carrie Fisher was hired to punch up Tinkerbell with some spirited one-liners, much to Hart's chagrin: 'I wrote a very specific voice for Tinkerbell . . . I made her a sniping, feisty, tough task driver for Peter, who was madly in love with her. But it was very poorly rewritten in my opinion. It took all the edge off her . . . And the flying sequence turns into a joke instead of a celebration of youth and what it would be like for an adult to fly.'

ORIGINS: Written in 1904, JM Barrie's play *Peter Pan* has a forgotten strain of darkness that has been obscured by years of 'look-behind-you' pantomime stagings. Adapted into a novel in 1911 and constantly evolving until Barrie's death in 1937, his story of the boy who wouldn't grow up is full of sadness and cruelty – babies forgotten by their nannies, Peter's bloodthirst for pirates – that underpin the magic.

Subsequent film versions of the yarn have forsaken Barrie's darkness. The first cinematic adaptation was a silent version made by Herbert Brenon in 1924. Barrie had agreed to a movie but only if he could pick the actress: stars such as Mary Pickford, Gloria Swanson and Lillian Gish were all rejected in favour of a New Jersey teenager, Betty Bronson. More a filmed play than anything else, the film opened in Christmas week, then disappeared without a trace. In his formative years, Spielberg would have probably seen the Broadway musical televised live in 1955 with the entire original cast. But the biggest influence would come from the 1953 Disney animated version. It was directed by Wilfred Jackson, Clyde Geronimi and Hamilton Luske, and the very broad slapstick and over-the-top sentimentality is very akin to *Hook*, if the quite magical flying sequences are not.

Hook also owes a huge debt to the swash and buckle of the pirate genre. The final battle between the Lost Boys and Hook's crew tries to emulate the stirring swordplay of Errol Flynn in classics such as *Captain Blood* (1935) and *The Sea Hawk* (1940). Perhaps a more resonant influence is Vincente Minnelli's *The Pirate* (1948) – Gene Kelly woos Judy Garland by posing as a Caribbean cutthroat – both in terms of its overproduced spectacle and garish look. Indeed, the colour-saturated look and artificial feel of many of Minnelli's musicals – especially the exteriors done as interiors such as in *An American In Paris* (1951) – loom large over the Neverland look.

The plot line of a kid under pressure to hit a home run and be good at baseball forms a major part of Ron Howard's *Parenthood* (1989), and scenes with the Lost Boys in the tree house resemble the Disney version of *Swiss Family Robinson* (1960).

CASTING: Spielberg had made no secret of the fact he was desperate to work with Dustin Hoffman. Impressed with Hoffman since his career-making turn in *The Graduate* (1967), Spielberg had chased the actor to play David Mann in his TV movie *Duel* – he refused on the grounds he was a movie star, not a TV actor – and, during 1987, spent five months collaborating with Hoffman on *Rain Man* with an eye to directing it – his commitment to *Last Crusade* meant he had to jump ship. Spielberg finally got the chance to direct Hoffman in his straight-to-camera links on a documentary about the life of the abstract expressionist artist Willem de Kooning and the two constantly looked for a project together. In retrospect, *Hook* was probably not the best choice of material for their big-screen collaboration. Modelling his pirate on the right-wing commentator William F Buckley, Hoffman gives Hook a strange, somewhat muted presence.

Robin Williams was the only choice to play Peter Banning. He's renowned for his wild improvisations and manic kineticism, but Spielberg squats on all that energy in the film's early scenes and you can feel Williams wanting to cut loose – perfect for Banning's repression of his youthful self. Yet, as he relocates his childhood self, WIlliams slips into mawkish man-child mode that is irritating rather than exuberant. If he had the chance again, Spielberg would play Williams differently. 'I feel I made a mistake. I should have released Robin and let him go in wildly funny directions. I contained Robin. I feel the audience would have enjoyed the film a lot more if Robin had been allowed to be funnier earlier. But Peter Pan isn't exactly a funny character and JM Barrie would have been spinning in his grave if we ever played Peter as a stand-up comic.'

Hot after *Pretty Woman* (1990), Julia Roberts arrived on the *Hook* set an emotional minefield. Having been signed for the role for a $2.5 million fee, she admitted herself into hospital (claiming exhaustion) before filming began, called off her forthcoming nuptials to Kiefer Sutherland, then flew to Ireland to join her new boyfriend Jason Patric. With rumours rife that she was about to be replaced by Michelle Pfeiffer or Kim Basinger, Roberts did show up for work, her scenes mostly laborious technical work against a blue screen.

Spielberg's alter ego Richard Dreyfuss wanted to play Hook's
right-hook man Smee. But Spielberg, perhaps fearing ego overload
with Hoffman, opted for Bob Hoskins, who had first encountered
Spielberg as executive producer on *Who Framed Roger Rabbit?*
(1988). Richard Attenborough was first choice to play Tootles but
was too busy directing *Chaplin*. Instead, Spielberg cast the British
character actor Arthur Malet and kept Attenborough's CV on file
for *Jurassic Park*. For Granny Wendy, Spielberg originally cast a
David Lean favourite, Peggy Ashcroft. After she pulled out with back
trouble, the costume designer, Anthony Powell, suggested Maggie
Smith, who, ironically enough, had played Pan in a London
Pantomime in 1973.

PRODUCTION: With the Christmas 1991 release date set in stone,
Hook started principal photography on 19 February that year. On that
very first day, filming was interrupted by a marching band sent by the
director of *Lethal Weapon* (1987), Richard Donner, playing the
Raiders march and other themes from Spielberg movies. Such
ostentatious gestures of showbiz were almost a daily occurrence on the
Hook set. The cream of Hollywood stopped by to watch Spielberg at
play: Warren Beatty, Jeff Bridges, Sean Connery, Tom Cruise, Kevin
Costner, Francis Coppola, Robert De Niro, Danny DeVito, Richard
Dreyfuss, Richard Gere, Whoopi Goldberg, Liza Minnelli, Gary
Oldman, Michelle Pfeiffer, Prince, Tim Robbins, Susan Sarandon,
Steven Seagal and Bruce Willis (see **Factoid frenzy**) all paid visits to the
Hook soundstages partly to witness the frequent good-natured 'battle
of wits' between Williams and Hoffman.

Perhaps because he had so many gargantuan toys to play with, or
the on-set frivolity proved counterproductive, Spielberg went 40 days
over his 76-day shooting schedule. Although working with huge
logistics, a large cast of inexperienced kids, a pernickity Dustin
Hoffman, a frazzled Julia Roberts and complicated special effects, the
director shouldered the responsibilty for the runaway movie himself. 'I
began to work at a slower pace than I usually do . . . For some reason
the film was such a dinosaur coming out of the gate. It dragged me
along behind it . . . Every day I came on to the set, I thought, is this
flying out of control?'

TICS OF THE TRADE: Shot in an anamorphic (wide-screen) ratio
used in numerous Hollywood extravaganzas, *Hook* has a strange feel
of being simultaneously expansive and theatrical in its staging. To
achieve some shots to introduce the scale of Piratetown or establish the
ball game inside the studio, the cinematographer Dean Cundey
modified a camera rig designed for photographing Olympic skiing

events. Dubbed the Cable Cam, the carriage approximated a ski chair lift and enabled Cundey to capture shots following Robin WIlliams through the air, even through the trees.

In terms of its lighting design, *Hook* has a progression from the naturalistic delicacy of light in Wendy's house to the full-blown Technicolor opiate of Neverland, where the early-morning light is pink and the late-afternoon shadows are lavender. The fantastic shot featuring the shadow from a toy dinosaur marauding behind Banning or the flashes of dramatic lighting as Hook steals Peter's kids (reminiscent of *Close Encounters*) offer arresting moments of flash and thunder. But, ultimately, *Hook* remains one of Spielberg's less interesting films visually.

CLASSIC LINES:
Lost Boys: Kill the pirate!
Peter: I am not a pirate! It so happens that I am a lawyer!
Lost Boys: Kill the lawyer!

Captain Hook: I hate, I hate, I hate Peter Pan!

Captain Hook: What would the world be like without Captain Hook?

COMIC RELIEF: For anyone over the age of six, there isn't a lot to laugh at in *Hook*.

VISUAL EFFECTS: Initially, Industrial Light and Magic were hired to do only 44 shots for *Hook*. But, as Spielberg's ideas grew more grandiose, so the effects load grew larger, ballooning to 243 shots without the schedule ever elongating. The chief reason for the change was Tinkerbell. For scenes with Tink on her own – such as in the nursery Wendy house – Julia Roberts often acted with outsized props and sets wearing a 2½ foot long set of wings that lay on her back. For flying sequences, Roberts was shot against a blue screen and combined with separately shot wings and surrounding glowball elements.

Created by two sheets of plastic and a thinner slither of clear cellophane, Tink's wings were nine inches long and attached to a computer-controlled flapping rig designed to replicate the movements of Roberts's body. At one point Spielberg decided that to suggest Tink's sadness, her wings should droop. This was accomplished with the nine-inch wings, and Spielberg was so delighted with the effect that he wanted all of the pixie's wing shots to include even the slightest flutter. It was this decision that sent the number of effects shots soaring.

To create Peter's flight over Neverland, Robin Williams, like Roberts, dangled in front of a blue screen. For shots of Peter flying around the Nevertree and over Hook's galleon, Williams was suspended from cables on a variety of flying rigs mounted on a gridwork of overhead tracks. The cables were very thick and very safe and were removed with recently developed digital technology that blends the colour to the left and right of the visible wires.

WHAT'S THE SCORE? In 1985, when Spielberg was considering making *Peter Pan* as a musical, John Williams and the lyricist Leslie Bricusse were commissioned to write songs for the project. By the time the project was scrapped, they had completed around ten ditties for the movie, three of which subsequently found a home in *Hook*. 'We Don't Wanna Grow Up', an ode to staying young and carefree in the *Pan* mode, is a lively little ditty sung in the opening play. 'Pick 'Em Up' is a dreadful number sung as the Lost Boys whip Peter back into shape. 'When You're Alone' is a syrupy ballad sung by Maggie to comfort herself while she's in Hook's claws – captured with all the souped-up artificiality of a Technicolor musical, Amber Scott's rendition has a bizarre poignancy.

Other motifs and phrases from the progenitor of *Hook* found their way into the 1991 version and, because Williams was working on the project over such a long period of time, this may explain why the film has such a rich, varied, imaginative score. *Hook* overflows with fantastic themes covering an astonishing array of moods: playful lightness (the flurry of flute work that accompanies the arrival of Tinkerbell), full-on terror (Jack and Maggie's kidnap is played out to full-blown orchestral swirls), piratical playfulness (Smee's shifty theme, the rousing motif that accompanies the journey of Hook's hook to its owner), joyous spirit (the ebullient food fight march), overtures flooded with melancholy (Peter remembering his past), soaring adventure music (Peter in flight), bellicose brilliance (the lengthy cue detailing the final battle). Usually the quality of the John Williams score is a good barometer to the quality of the Spielberg movie. Here, perhaps for the only time, Williams provides music that far outstrips the calibre of the movie it accompanies.

CUT SCENES: Much to the writer James Hart's chagrin, a whole sequence depicting how Wendy became a mother to the Lost Boys was discarded after shooting. For Hart, it added a whole new slant on the tale, making *Hook* a story about mothers as well as fathers.

Additional footage of Jack coming under Hook's wing was shot but never used: these include Jack discovering a chest of baseball cards, a mock horse race – Jack rides Smee – and an imaginary ride in a lifeboat caught in a thunderstorm.

A further excision happens just before Maggie sings 'When You're

Alone'. As Maggie cries for her mommy, a captive Lost Boy asks her
what a mommy is. Her reply is a litany of saccharine – 'They play
with you when you're lonely . . .' – that ends with the recollection
from the Lost Boy that mommies sing lullabies. Maggie agrees and
launches into the tune.

Finally, for some unfathomable reason, Spielberg seems to have cut a
nifty piece of swordplay that sounds better than anything that ended
up on the screen. During improvisations of the final Pan–Hook duel,
Spielberg had the idea that the swish of a sword ignited some unlit
candles. The candles were rigged and the shot captured. Why it doesn't
feature in the finished film is a complete mystery.

GEDDIT! The pirate Gutless, shut in the wooden chest with the
scorpion, was played by Glenn Close.

One of the pirates who attempt to steal Peter's shoes when he first
arrives in Neverland is played by the singer Jimmy Buffett. The music
impresario and *Color Purple* producer Quincy Jones and the rocker
David Crosby also appear as cutthroats.

The five-year-old Peter Pan is played by Dustin Hoffman's son,
Maxwell. Hoffman's other son, Jacob, takes the role of a little-league
baseball player in an early scene.

In the flashback depicting young Peter's story, Wendy is played by a
young Gwyneth Paltrow. A long-time Paltrow family friend, Spielberg
gave her the role – no auditions, no screen tests – while they were
waiting in line to see *The Silence of the Lambs*.

In Piratetown look out for vendors such as Dick Moby's Whale
Burgers and Molen's Kitchen, named after the producer Gerald R
Molen – it is the shop where Tinkerbell takes on the pirates.

When Tootles floats out of the window at the end, he says, 'Seize the
day', which has significance for Robin Williams, who starred in *Seize
the Day* (1986), and *Dead Poets Society* (1989) (in which this was a
catchphrase).

Smee says 'Goooooooood morning, Neverland!', a reference to
Robin Williams in *Good Morning, Vietnam* (1987).

FACTOID FRENZY: Because Tinkerbell was often in the air and her
feet were in shot, Julia Roberts had an assistant whose sole
responsibility was cleaning them. He was paid the equivalent of
£2,000 for the pleasure.

To play adult pirate extras, 150 surly Hell's Angels were press-
ganged from biker hangouts in LA. They were forbidden to mingle
with A-list stars, and there was a near mutiny when the extras realised
they were being fed pretzels and water while the stars munched on
chilli and soup.

Days after blaming the current high cost of movies on the unreasonable demands of film crews, Bruce Willis visited the *Hook* set and found himself spat on from the rafters by hacked-off workers.

THE CRITICAL FACULTY: '*Hook* is a huge party cake of a movie with too much frosting. After the first delicious bite, sugar shock sets in . . . By the time this overstuffed epic comes to its conclusion you feel like you've been watching the dance of an eight hundred pound elf.' (David Ansen, *Newsweek*.) 'A turgid, bombastic mess' (James Vernicre, *Boston Herald*.) 'The film has been engineered for merchandising potential and the widest possible appeal. What's missing is the one thing that really counts: charm.' (Peter Travers, *Rolling Stone*.) 'It's tricks feel strained: we're constantly aware of the heartbreaking effort it's taking to produce them, and there's no kind of magic at all.' (Pauline Kael, *New Yorker*.) 'Gets the prize for the most lavish, extravagant, opulent ode to simple joys and basic values ever made.' (Georgia Brown, *Village Voice*.)

BOX OFFICE: Opening in the US on 10 December 1991, *Hook* grossed $20 million in its first week (in 2,197 theatres), eventually grossing around $119 million in its American run. A sizeable hit in anyone's books but, perhaps due to the trio of Hoffman, Williams and Roberts, the promise of Spielberg's returning to childlike fantasy after his forays into adult drama and the exorbitant budget, the film was perceived as a bomb. Doing much better abroad, *Hook* ended up with a total worldwide gross of $288 million.

AWARDS: Nominated for four Academy Awards – Best Art Direction/Set Decoration, Visual Effects, Make-up and Best Song for 'When You're Alone' – *Hook* remained unrewarded. Elsewhere, Dustin Hoffman was nominated for a Golden Globe in the Best Actor (Comedy/Musical) category and Julia Roberts had the embarrassment of being nominated as the worst supporting actress at the Razzies, the annual celebration of the dregs of cinematic achievement held the night before the Oscars.

THE SIZZLE! Originally James V Hart's screenplay had been developed with Nick Castle in mind to direct. A long-time collaborator with John Carpenter – he had even played the Shape in *Halloween* (1978) – and, aptly enough, writer-director of *The Boy Who Could Fly* (1986), Castle took the project to TriStar, where Mike Medavoy, Spielberg's first agent, was now in charge. Believing it was ideal material for his former client, Medavoy sent the script to Spielberg, who rapidly committed himself to directing it. Subsequently, Castle was removed from the picture, gaining a $500,000 pay-off, a story credit and an offer to make a movie with TriStar in the future. Gaining pejorative publicity by seemingly using his status to muscle in on another director's project, Spielberg maintained that he would not have approached the material if he knew another director was attached.

JOIN THE DOTS: Kids – *The Sugarland Express, Jaws, Close Encounters of the Third Kind, 1941, E.T. The Extra-Terrestrial, Twilight Zone: The Movie, Indiana Jones and the Temple of Doom, The Color Purple, Empire of the Sun, Jurassic Park, Schindler's List, The Lost World: Jurassic Park, Amistad.* **Kidnapped Kids** – *The Sugarland Express, Close Encounters of the Third Kind, Indiana Jones and the Temple of Doom, Empire of the Sun, Schindler's List, Amistad.* **Aircraft** – *Close Encounters of the Third Kind, 1941, Raiders of the Lost Ark, Indiana Jones and the Temple Of Doom, Empire of the Sun, Indiana Jones and the Last Crusade, Always, Saving Private Ryan.* **Contemporary setting** – *The Sugarland Express, Jaws, Close Encounters of the Third Kind, E.T. The Extra-Terrestrial, Twilight Zone: The Movie, Always, Jurassic Park, The Lost World.* **Based on a book** – *Jaws, The Color Purple, Empire of the Sun, Jurassic Park, Schindler's List, The Lost World, Amistad.* **Absent fathers:** – *The Sugarland Express, Close Encounters of the Third Kind, E.T. The Extra-Terrestrial, The Color Purple, Empire of the Sun, Indiana Jones and the Last Crusade.*

SEND IN THE CLONES! Obviously few would choose to emulate the excess of *Hook*. But the film did find itself part of a cycle of movies in the early 90s that tried to reimagine the selfish 80s corporate ethos in the caring, sharing 90s. The most prominent example would be Mike Nichols's *Regarding Henry* (1991).

FINAL ANALYSIS: The themes of *Peter Pan* are so pertinent to Spielberg's universe – the preservation of innocence, the importance of play, the thrill of adventure in far-off lands, the pure joy of flight, to name a few – that audiences and critics expected *Hook* to be his magnum opus. That there is a tired feeling to the movie may well be because Spielberg has connected with these notions on so many previous occasions – particularly in *E.T.* – and so ran out of ways to make them live. That said, it is tempting to read *Hook* as a $70 million autobiography: the story of a highly successful businessman caught between the grown-up (*The Color Purple, Empire of the Sun*) and the childish (*Indiana Jones*), between professional obsession and familial love and responsibility. In previous Spielberg films (*The Sugarland Express*, *Close Encounters*, the Spielberg-scripted *Poltergeist*), the mother was portrayed as rescuer of the children, whereas the father had been reduced to a bystander (or nonexistent). With *Hook* (and subsequently *Jurassic Park* and *Schindler*), it is the father figure who turns saviour, a shift perhaps represented by Spielberg himself becoming a parent.

The opening moments of *Hook* are beautifully naturalistic shots of kids watching a homespun version of *Peter Pan*: that Spielberg's film never comes close to inducing such genuine childlike delight is its biggest and most surprising disappointment. But you do get the impression that buried somewhere in *Hook* is a great movie trying to get out. The bookends of the film are vividly created: Peter's initial self-absorption, Jack's growing resentment and the magic of a (distinctly Victorian) London are neatly, economically sketched, whereas the resolution within Wendy's nursery has a beautiful airy sense to it. But the puerile mishmash of juvenile farce – where exactly in Barrie is the skateboarding? – and ersatz pantomime of the Neverland section is so poorly misjudged, so bereft of wonder, that it is difficult to equate it with the same gentle genius that made *E.T.*

At times, the movie looks as if Spielberg never jettisoned his idea to turn *Pan* into a musical, creating a gaudy detached spectacle but rarely capturing the exhilaration of childhood regained. What is particularly heartbreaking is that the re-creation of Peter's early life is so splendidly realised that it really leaves you hankering to see what Spielberg might have made if he had adopted a more classical approach to Barrie.

SPIELBERG ON SPIELBERG: 'I was not entirely happy with *Hook*. I hadn't seen it for eighteen months after its initial release but when I did I realised what I had done: I had made a wonderful movie about Kensington. From the beginning of the picture to when Peter flies out of the window in Kensington, is I think, some of my best work. For some reason, the moment he gets to Neverland it sort of becomes children's theatre. There's nothing wrong with that but it becomes a kids' movie and I'm talking about kids of twelve, not seventeen. The movie seems to have a great deal of appeal for under-twelve-year-olds, or at least for adults like myself who have the hearts of twelve-year-olds. But many of us have hearts that have grown and aged along with ourselves. A lot of people didn't think there was enough grown-up appeal.'

Jurassic Park (1993)

(Colour, 127 mins)

Studio Universal
Produced by Kathleen Kennedy, Gerald R Molen
Screenplay by Michael Crichton, David Koepp
Based on the novel by Michael Crichton
Director of Photography Dean Cundey ASC
Production Designer Rick Carter
Edited by Michael Kahn ACE
Music John Williams
Unit Production Manager Paul Deason
First Assistant Director John T Kretchmer
Full-Motion Dinosaurs Dennis Muren ASC
Live-Action Dinosaurs Stan Winston
Dinosaur Supervisor Phil Tippett
Special Dinosaur Effects Michael Lantieri
Casting by Janet Hirshenson CSA, Jane Jenkins CSA
Art Directors Jim Teegarden, John Bell
Stunt Co-ordinator Gary Hymes
Paleontologist Consultant Jack Horner
Make-up Supervisor Christina Smith
Re-recording Mixers Gary Summers, Gary Rydstrom, Shawn Murphy
Sound Design Gary Rydstrom
Supervising Sound Editor Richard Hymns
Full-Motion Dinosaurs and Special Visual Effects by Industrial Light and Magic
Co-visual Effects Supervisor Mark AZ Dippe

CAST: Sam Neill (*Dr Alan Grant*), Laura Dern (*Dr Ellie Sattler*), Jeff Goldblum (*Ian Malcolm*), Richard Attenborough (*Hammond*), Bob Peck (*Muldoon*), Martin Ferrero (*Gennaro*), BD Wong (*Dr Wu*), Joseph Mazzello (*Tim Murphy*), Ariana Richards (*Lex Murphy*), Samuel L Jackson (*Jack Arnold*), Wayne Knight (*Denis Nedry*), Jerry Molen (*Harding*), Miguel Sandoval (*Rostagno*), Cameron Thor (*Dodgson*), Christopher John Fields (*Volunteer No. 1*), Whit Hertfield (*Volunteer Boy*), Dean Cundey (*Mate*), Jophery Brown (*Worker in Raptor Pen*), Tom Mishler (*Helicopter Pilot*), Greg Burson ('*Mr DNA*' *voice*), Adrian Escober (*Worker at Amber Mine*), Richard Kiley (*Jurassic Park Tour Voice*).

BUDGET: $90 million

MPAA: PG

BBFC: PG

TITLE SEQUENCE: Spielberg's original concept for the opening of *Jurassic Park* envisaged the sphere of the Universal globe dissolving into an inhuman eye, the camera moving out to reveal that the eye belongs to a raptor. But that idea was scrapped, probably because it reveals too much of the dinosaurs too soon. Instead, the appearance of the Universal globe is accompanied by tropical jungle sound effects cutting to titles in an exotic font played out against black – the sound effects continue, enriched by a menacing tribal drums-and-choir orchestration. The sequence is brief, leading us straight into the action with minimum fuss but setting up an air of expectancy and danger.

PLOT SUMMARY: On Isla Nublar, an island off the coast of Costa Rica, a group of workers, supervised by a game warden, Robert Muldoon, attempt to get a beast – it will turn out to be a velociraptor – into a holding pen. However, before it can be safely stored in captivity, the dinosaur mauls and kills one of the workers.

The dinosaur is an attraction at Jurassic Park, a theme park-cum-prehistoric zoo where the animals are genetically engineered dinosaurs and the brainchild of a millionaire leisure impresario, John Hammond. The upshot of the worker's death is that Hammond is advised by his lawyer, Donald Gennaro, to obtain some endorsements concerning the safety of the whole enterprise to quell the fears of the investors. So Hammond enlists the help a of renowned paleontologist, Alan Grant, and a paleobotanist, Ellie Sattler. Gennaro brings on board a chaos theoretician, Ian Malcolm, and the group travel to Isla Nublar to conduct a tour of the park.

On arrival at Nublar, the ride to the command centre takes in a grazing brachiosaurus (Spielberg breaking his *Jaws* rule of delaying the revelation of the creature), which fills the party with wonderment. Although stunned by the creature and the processes surrounding the dinosaurs' return from extinction – they're re-created from the DNA of a prehistoric mosquito trapped in amber – Grant, Sattler and Malcolm still have grave doubts about the manipulation of nature. Still, the party agree to take the automated tour, joined by Hammond's grandchildren, Tim and Lex, much to the annoyance of the child-hating Grant.

As the tour begins with a distinct lack of dinosaurs we simultaneously follow the story of the park's computer wizard, Dennis Nedry, who is secretly closing down security systems to enable himself to steal dino embryos to sell on to a rival project. The park vehicles have stalled in front of a pen and, with the electric fences down, the worst happens: a tyrannosaurus (T rex) goes on the rampage, killing Gennaro and terrorising the kids in the car, who are saved by Grant and Malcolm, who is injured in action.

After the relatively slow start, the storylines now build up at a fiendish lick: Nedry is killed off by a spitting dilophosaurus; Grant and the kids hole up for the night amid singing brachiosauruses; Hammond retraces Nedry's tracks to reinstall security; Muldoon and Ellie rescue the injured Malcolm but only after a quick getaway from a marauding tyrannosaurus. With Grant and the kids slowly bonding, Hammond decides the only way to restore safety to the park is to reboot the whole computer system. Ellie and Muldoon journey out of the bunker to reactivate the power from the generator, the latter providing a distraction from the now escaping velociraptors. We jump back and forth between Tim struggling to climb a dead perimeter fence and Ellie's attempts to turn the power on, thus making the fence live, resulting in Grant rescuing the frazzled youngster as he is jolted off by the electric shock.

Grant and the kids finally meet up with Ellie and they seek refuge in the command centre. Seeing off Muldoon in a vicious attack, a brace of raptors stalk the children into a kitchen, then into the control room. Eventually they are cornered by the raptors in the visitor centre rotunda, but the day is saved by the tyrannosaurus which kills the predatory raptors, facilitating a human escape. Hooking up with Malcolm and Hammond, the survivors leave the island behind in a helicopter.

BACKSTORY: A doctor turned novelist turned film-maker, Michael Crichton had first married dinosaurs and their re-creation through DNA tampering in a screenplay that revolved around a singular scientist who was secretly experimenting on the cloning of prehistoric life. The idea languished unformed until 1989, when Crichton, realising that the public clamour for dinosaurs was not a passing fad, decided to turn the idea into a novel, fearing that a movie version would be both impractical and expensive.

Steven Spielberg first entered the *Jurassic Park* equation after collaborating with Crichton on the TV series *ER*. Spielberg quizzed Crichton about his future projects and, learning that he was putting the finishing touches to a dinosaur novel, immediately expressed an interest. Although Crichton sent Spielberg the galley proofs and had committed to Spielberg directing the movie version privately, the novel still became the subject of a serious bidding war with the rights going on sale at a non-negotiable $1.5 million. Three days after the novel was offered for sale, it was announced that Steven Spielberg would be directing *Jurassic Park*.

Although he'd decided against a film version first time round, Crichton agreed to do early drafts, with the understanding that other writers would be brought in to punch up the characters. After

Crichton had finished his two drafts firmly establishing the story structure, *Jurassic*'s co-producer, Kathy Kennedy, asked the *Hook* writer Malia Scotch Marmo to give the project a spin. One of Marmo's radical early changes was to eliminate the Ian Malcolm character altogether and transfer most of his dialogue to Grant, beefing up Grant's character into a crusader against the commercialism of science. Other Marmo initiatives were making Ellie and the kids much stronger (with Malcolm gone, the foursome made more like a nuclear family) and adding a visual motif of plant life encroaching into the control room to mirror how nature overpowers the man-made world.

Ultimately Spielberg hired the writer of *Death Becomes Her* (1992), David Koepp, to do some eleventh-hour rewrites. With only two sequences locked in – the tyrannosaurus attack on the vehicles and the raptors stalking the kids in the kitchen – Koepp opted not to plunder the Crichton or Marmo screenplay and returned to the book. With the draft finished in under ten weeks, the fresh approach saw the excision of two sequences from the novel that had made it into both Crichton and Marmo drafts – a set piece where Grant and the kids flee the tyrannosaurus on a raft and later Muldoon hunting and tranquillising the huge beast – and Malcolm reinstated with added wisecracks.

Additionally, Koepp created shading and verbal sparring to Grant and Ellie by adding an ongoing feud about the issue of children. By giving Grant a deep-rooted hostility to children, Koepp generated a human tension and subsequent character arc that was not present in Crichton. The idea also helped alleviate another problem suggested by the novel, that the children seemed slightly superfluous to the action: now they would have the function of teaching the socially inept Grant that there is more to life than fossils.

A further deviation from Crichton came in the characterisation of John Hammond. On the page, Hammond read like a much more unsympathetic, ruthless character. The movie softens that, giving him a nurturing sensibility – watch him encourage the baby raptor out of its shell – and the flair of a showman while recasting his fatal flaw as a desire to play God.

A final change in *Jurassic*'s storyline was created by emerging technology. Originally, the climax of the action saw Grant kill the raptors with a bazooka and also crushing one in the jaws of the skeletal tyrannosaurus. Yet Spielberg was so impressed with the computer-generated tyrannosaurus that was emerging from ILM that he felt the audience would want the crown prince of dinosaurs to return. Hence, the tyrannosaurus was given the job of killing the predators, again reaffirming the notion that man is redundant in the face of the natural world.

ORIGINS: Perhaps the biggest influence on *Jurassic Park* can be detected in Michael Crichton's own back catalogue: *Westworld* (1973), written and directed by Crichton, similarly concerned a multimillion-dollar holiday resort dedicated to re-creating the past – this time the old west – that was undone after the attractions started to run amok, chiefly Yul Brynner as a murderous gunslinger who attacks the visitors. The film also spawned a sequel, *Futureworld* (1976). *Jurassic* also touched base with a key element in other Crichton-scripted movies *The Andromeda Strain* (1971), *Coma* (1978), *Runaway* (1984) – scientific and technological endeavours become destructive when twisted by human motives.

Dinosaur movies are nearly as old as the cinema itself. Winsor McCay's *Gertie the Dinosaur* (1914) combined a sketch cartoon of a lovable brontosaurus with live-action footage of McCay himself. *Jurassic Park* references this film not only by featuring an animated dinosaur in Hammond's tour film but also in Hammond's interaction with himself to explain the wonder of DNA cloning, similar to McCay's interaction with Gertie.

Sir Arthur Conan Doyle's *The Lost World*, filmed in 1925 by Harry O Hoyt and in 1960 by Irwin Allen, features a South American plateau bursting with dinosaurs, yet within a modern time frame. As in *Jurassic*, Doyle plays fast and loose with geological time frames. Other dino-related flicks that Spielberg probably lapped up in his youth may have been *Beast of Hollow Mountain* (1956), *Journey to the Centre of the Earth* (1959), *Mysterious Island* (1961), *One Million Years BC* (1966) – not to mention the *Rite of Spring* animated section from *Fantasia* (1940). *Dinosaurus* (1960) sees a sixty-ton brontosaurus tamed by a young boy and that may have had some bearing on *Jurassic*'s playful scene with the brachiosaurus in the trees. Further scenes of playful dinos can be found in *Baby: Secret of the Lost Legend* (1983) and Amblin's own *The Land Before Time* (1988). Like *Jurassic*, *When Dinosaurs Ruled the Earth* (1971) also made the distinction between carnivorous dinosaurs and the more gentle veggiesaurus – the film's title also pops up on the banner in the visitor centre that is brought down by the tyrannosaurus's roar.

Yet if Spielberg drew parallels with any monster movie from his youth, it would be *King Kong* (1933). The director hoped to emulate the Merian C Cooper classic not only in its realistic depiction of a secluded island inhabited by creatures but also in the level of credibility invested in the story by the state-of-the-art special effects (by the stop-motion animation pioneer, Willis O'Brien). The influence is made explicit as, approaching the Kong Island-type gates that guard Jurassic Park, Ian Malcolm quips, 'What have they got in there? King Kong?'

Away from overt dinosaur movies, Jack Cardiff's horror flick *The Mutations* (1974) is perhaps the first film to moot the cloning of dinosaurs from fossilised DNA in a scene where a geneticist, played by Donald Pleasance, lectures his students. Howard Hawks's *Hatari* (1962), which follows a group of international game hunters, tapped into the man-versus-nature dynamic that is very much a part of *Jurassic*. The finale of a very different Hawks film, *Bringing Up Baby* (1938), also echoes the conclusion of *Jurassic*: Cary Grant and Katharine Hepburn dangle precariously from a dinosaur skeleton in a similar vein to Sam Neill and Laura Dern.

CASTING: To keep the budget down and not to outshine the dinosaurs, Spielberg filled *Jurassic Park's* dramatis personae with talent, not stars. With some early contenders, Harrison Ford, Kurt Russell and Richard Dreyfuss, all falling into the latter category and William Hurt turning the project down flat, Spielberg opted for Sam Neill to play the paleontologist Alan Grant. Distinguishing himself in homegrown films such as *My Brilliant Career* (1979), Neill had caught the eye as a slightly edgy leading-man presence in *The Final Conflict* (1981), *A Cry in the Dark* (1988), *Dead Calm* (1989) and *The Hunt For Red October* (1990).

Laura Dern became Grant's partner Dr Ellie Sattler, but only after Robin Wright Penn and Juliette Binoche had turned down the role. Dern is best known for her work in indie flicks such as David Lynch's *Blue Velvet* (1986) and *Wild At Heart* (1990), plus her Oscar nomination for *Rambling Rose* (1991), and *Jurassic Park* marked her first foray into big-budget action adventure.

As the brash mathematician and chaos theorist, Ian Malcolm, Jeff Goldblum was the one and only choice, already a past master at delivering offbeat geeks in *The Big Chill* (1983) and *The Fly* (1986). Also top of Spielberg's wish list was Sir Richard (now Lord) Attenborough as John Hammond. Although Attenborough had not been in front of the camera for fifteen years, Spielberg had wanted the writer-director to play the part of Tootles in *Hook*, a move foiled by Attenborough's directing duties on *Chaplin* (1992). Although the director was still completing the biopic as *Jurassic* began shooting, Spielberg shifted the schedule to accommodate.

Spielberg had seen Joseph Mazello when casting around for Robin William's son in *Hook*. Mazello was too young to play Jack but he kept him in mind when auditioning for *Jurassic's* dino-obsessed kid Tim – Mazello had appeared on TV in *Unspeakable Urges* aged five and, with roles in *Presumed Innocent* (1990) and *Radio Flyers* (1992) under his belt, was considered a veteran aged nine. For Lex, Spielberg spotted Ariana Richards in a TV movie, *Separated At Birth,* although she had already appeared in features such as *Prancer* (1989) and *Tremors* (1990).

PRODUCTION: After locations in Costa Rica and Mexico were rejected, *Jurassic Park* started filming on the Hawaiian island of Kauai on 24 August 1992. As most of the movie was going to be shot in the confines of a studio, the Kauai shoot was really designed to open the action out, rooting the story in its exotic locale. Excluding a brief excursion to the Mojave Desert (doubling for Montana) to shoot Grant uncovering the remains of raptors, the rest of the first-unit schedule was spent on the soundstages of Universal and Warner Bros.

Perhaps because the technical and logistical problems seemed insurmountable, the preproduction time was so extensive that making the actual movie was plain sailing.

'From the beginning, I was afraid that a movie like *Jurassic Park* could get away from me,' Spielberg noted. 'There had been other pictures – *Jaws*, *1941*, *Hook* – where the production schedule simply got away from me and I was dragged behind the schedule. I was determined not to let it happen this time. So I walked away from a lot of takes where, on my last picture, I might have stayed for four or five more . . . I probably drove everyone to the brink of insanity in order to complete this movie on budget and on schedule.'

Ironically, for a film whose theme is the ability of forces of nature to play havoc with man's attempts to contain them, the only setback suffered by the crew on the location was the devastating arrival of Hurricane Iniki on 11 September: with the unit preparing to shoot backgrounds for the galimimus stampede, winds of 130 miles an hour and 160 mile-an-hour gusts savaged the island, creating waves of over twenty feet, forcing the crew to seek refuge in the ballroom of the Western Kauai Hotel.

TICS OF THE TRADE: Knowing the audience need to digest a lot of technical gobbledegook surrounding DNA extraction and cloning to make the whole scenario believable, the *Jurassic Park* writers had to find a way to deliver the data in an accessible, entertaining manner. It was Spielberg's idea to create a theme-park-style instructional animation film – hosted by Mr DNA – that was fun to watch, reinforced the amusement-park milieu and could distil the information into manageable chunks without resorting to a hoary and dull tour-of-the-lab sequence.

Visually *Jurassic Park* follows the Spielbergian tenet of locating the fantastical in a believable setting. The look is crisp, realistic and colour-saturated, with only the visitor centre's bunker really coming in for the dramatic-shafts-of-light-and-smoke approach. The camera is often highly mobile, almost becoming a character in the story, perhaps best emphasised as it gets swept along by the herd of fleeing galimimuses.

When dealing with the mechanical dinos, the cinematographer Dean Cundey placed the creatures in sketchy cross-lighting patterns and kept the frame moving to breathe life into them: a raptor's head in the control room covered in reflections from VDU displays is a scary, dazzling mixture of the hi-tech and the primal that lies at the heart of the story.

Once again, Spielberg beautifully masterminds the surprises – the shock of Ellie discovering Arnold's severed arm immediately topped by the emergence of a raptor – and the suspense: as Tim and Lex seek shelter in the visitor centre dining room, they begin tucking into a table full of a desserts. After shots of happy-go-lucky eating, we cut to Lex's face, a study in abject terror (perfectly captured by Ariana Richards) as she spots an offscreen velociraptor. Yet what really sells the shot is the quivering jelly sitting on her spoon, a fantastic visual representation of her growing fear.

However, Spielberg's genius is best summed up in *Jurassic Park's* signature shot: small ripples in a glass of water sitting on the jeep dashboard, caused by the mighty foot stomps of the tyrannosaurus. The inspiration for the shot came to Spielberg while he was stuck in traffic, listening to the riproaring funk of Earth, Wind and Fire on the car stereo, the thumping base causing the rear-view mirror, and everything else in the car, to vibrate. Yet the seemingly simple effect proved to be the effects supervisor Michael Lantieri's biggest headache. Contacting sound engineers and physics experts, Lantieri was scrabbling around for a solution until the night before the shot was going before the camera. Simply by placing a guitar string under the glass and plucking it, perfect concentric circles began to appear in the water. A genius method of suggesting size and scale, the shot is a perfect way to prime an audience that scares are on the way.

CLASSIC LINES:

John Hammond: 'Dr Grant, my dear Dr Sattler . . . Welcome to Jurassic Park.'

John Hammond: 'All major theme parks have delays. When they opened Disneyland in 1956, nothing worked.'

Ian Malcolm: 'Yeah, but John, if the Pirates of the Caribbean breaks down, the pirates don't eat the tourists.'

Ian Malcolm: 'God creates dinosaurs. God destroys dinosaurs. God creates man. Man destroys God. Man creates dinosaurs . . .'

Dr Ellie Sattler: 'Dinosaurs eat man. Woman inherits the Earth.'

COMIC RELIEF: A lot of *Jurassic Park's* comedy stems from character traits, particularly the sly one-liners of Ian Malcolm. Spielberg also gets laughs from his kids: a brachiosaurus sneezing saurian snot all over Lex ('Bless you!' shouts Tim to the dino, to add insult to injury); Grant's pretence at being electrocuted as they reach the perimeter fence and Tim's hair standing up on end as he does receive a shock.

However, the biggest laugh in the movie comes as, walking around the sick triceratops, Malcolm comes across a steaming heap of dino dung, uttering, 'This is one big piece of shit.' The camera pulls back to show Ellie elbow deep in another triceratops turd, perfectly timed to get maximum 'Urghs' from the audience.

VISUAL EFFECTS: Ruling out the traditional ways dinosaurs had been created on celluloid – stop-motion animation, men in suits, reptiles with prehistoric-type adornments stuck on – Spielberg sought a new level of veracity for the creatures populating Jurassic Park. His initial plan was to create the creatures in only large-scale mechanical versions, contacting Bob Gurr, the designer of Universal Studios' *King Kong* attraction, to discuss the feasibility. Yet it was deemed that the capabilities for movement would be limited, so Spielberg went another route: the dinosaur menagerie would be mostly created by Stan Winston, the puppetry genius behind *The Terminator* (1984) and *Aliens* (1986), with full-length body shots of the animals captured by an update of the stop motion process pioneered by ILM called Go-Motion: a computerised take on the old one-frame-at-a-time method, Go-Motion not only allowed movements to be stored and repeated but also added a blur factor, making it much more realistic than the old process.

Having spent a full year in paleontological research, Winston and his team created the beasts in a skeletal frame of fibreglass and clay, covering the complicated internal hydraulics with latex skin. The dilophosaurus, or spitter (the creature's spitting facility is actually a Crichton fabrication), and raptors were, for the most part, full-scale mechanical puppets with interchangeable heads to accommodate different actions and inserted legs to show movement. The tails were controlled by concealed rods.

Yet the star of Winston's show was the twenty-foot-high, 13,000-pound tyrannosaurus, performed beautifully on set, but the biggest problem surrounding the creature was not its hydraulic or computer systems but the copious amounts of water it retained from the rain machines simulating the torrential downpour. The water damaged the skin and added extra weight that threw the mechanics off kilter, so the crew employed industrial-strength dryers to save the creature after every shot.

As Winston was creating his mechanical marvels, a breakthrough happened at ILM that changed the entire face of *Jurassic Park*. During the early stages of visual-effects conceptualisation, Spielberg had asked ILM's Denis Muren to mull over how a scene involving a herd of running galimimuses might be achieved. As Spielberg put *Jurassic* on the back burner to concentrate on *Hook*, ILM took great steps forward with computer-generated imagery in James Cameron's *Terminator 2: Judgement Day* (1991), and Muren thought that this approach may be the way to tackle the stampeding dinos. Test footage of skeletal galimimuses convinced Spielberg that CG could handle the herd, but Muren's team went one better: scanning Stan Winston's tyrannosaurus model into a computer, the animators Mark Dippe and Steve Williams created a sequence of the creature running in broad daylight in a forest background, a photo-realistic breathing entity.

The results were so spectacular that Spielberg decided to eschew the Go-Motion technique and do most of the dinosaur shots through mouse-pad magicking, even cutting into Stan Winston's shot load. ILM were now commissioned to do 52 shots, including the introduction of the brachiosaurus, long shots of dinosaur herds, the tyrannosaurus running alongside the jeep (including the famous shot of the creature looming large in the rear-view mirror), various shots of raptors (including the fantastic moment in the kitchen where the raptor leaps on to the work surface), and the entire rewritten end sequence where the heroes are saved from raptors by the returning tyrannosaurus.

Spielberg placed extra demands on the animators, requiring that the dinosaurs be inserted into moving camera shots and be held for up to twenty seconds at a time. For placing the creatures under such scrutiny, new software packages were invented for creating muscle movements and skin textures. Lots of little touches really sell the illusion of the dinosaurs interfacing with their environment: on location, the mechanical-effects supervisor Michael Lantieri added little touches such as rigging a log to shed bark as if hit by the hoof of a galimimus, which would be inserted digitally later. Moreover, look out for the digitally inserted tiny splashes of water that jump up as the tyrannosaurus stomps after Malcolm.

SOUND EFFECTS: Although there is much reference material on the way dinosaurs looked, there is practically no evidence to suggest how they sounded. Unusually, *Jurassic*'s sound-effects process actually started before filming began: Gary Rydstrom and his crew created dinosaur sounds first so the puppeteers could gauge the mouth movements of the creatures on set.

In an attempt to convey a sense of intelligence, many raptor screams were taken from dolphins recorded underwater at Marine World. The dolphin noises would be used in conjunction with a throaty clicking sound slowed down to become more guttural, the call of an African crane, a goose scream and the sounds of horses breathing employed to double for raptor respiratory systems.

The call of the brachiosaurus came from both whale songs and donkey brays slowed down with added echo. The dilophosaurus had its sound broken into two types: for the early, playful spitter, Rydstrom employed a variety of swan calls; yet as it turns nasty, an egret sound is mixed with Rydstrom's own voice (to add a sense of weight) to suggest venom. The rattling noise produced by an exotic insect doubled for the sound of the spitter's vibrating cowl.

Yet the most complex-sounding character was the mighty tyrannosaurus. The vocal effects came from a diversity of sources – elephant, alligator, penguin, tiger and dog sounds – all mixed together to create a rich, naturalistic dinosaur vocabulary. Whale blowholes repeated into a regular rhythm created tyrannosaurus breathing patterns. For his world-shattering roar, a blast from a baby elephant created the high end of the frequency, while the low end was provided by alligator growls and tiger shrieks.

WHAT'S THE SCORE? Not really considered a classic within the Spielberg–WIlliams canon, *Jurassic Park* nonetheless contains a varied, exciting listening experience. Consciously trying to avoid the incessant menace of the *Jaws* motif, Williams characterises the dinosaurs with a noble, stirring, moving theme that – as heard on the first appearance of the brachiosaurus – invests the creatures with a sense of timeless grace and scale. A secondary, soaring *Jurassic Park* theme sees brass take flight, highlighting the more adventurous aspects of the story.

Williams once again covers a lot of musical ground in the incidental scoring: urgent, building strings highlight the growing sense of panic as Tim climbs the electric fence; haunting choral sounds greet the baby raptor's emergence into the world; a sympathetic, ennobling theme accompanies the discovery of the sick triceratops; a shifty rhythm underscores Nedry stealing the embryos. However, for all Spielberg's much-stated dependence on John Williams for effect, the most memorable set piece does not contain a single note of his music: the tyrannosaurus attack is played out with a carefully orchestrated symphony of dino clomps, gargantuan roars and hard rain. Sometimes great film scoring constitutes knowing where *not* to insert music just as much as knowing where to place it to the fore.

CUT SCENES: A couple of scenes from *Jurassic Park*'s shooting script were jettisoned just before reaching the camera. In its original conception, the sequence in the hatchery was to have included a hatching triceratops and an older, baby raptor that would playfully run up Tim's arm. The scene was subsequently scaled down to a hatching raptor. Another effects-heavy scene to be eliminated just prior to filming saw Lex enjoy a bareback ride on a baby triceratops. Stan Winston and his crew spent months developing a five-foot infant, yet the idyllic scene was deleted at the eleventh hour due to its superfluous position within the story.

A trimming that occurred once filming was under way is revealed in the trailer: during the drive from the helipad to the visitor centre, Ellie leans from the jeep and pulls off a leaf from an exotic but extinct plant. In the completed cut the action is missing but Ellie is holding the frond as Grant swivels her head to see the brachiosaurus.

UNSUNG HERO: The dinosaur supervisor Phil Tippett, whose animation expertise and intuitive understanding of creature movement took Jurassic Park's realism to another level. A stop-motion veteran of the *Star Wars* trilogy and *Dragonslayer* (1981), Tippett was commissioned by Spielberg to create the Go-Motion dinosaur shots that supplement the mechanical creatures.

When Spielberg switched from Go-Motion to CGI, Tippett was initially devastated. Yet his talents were sensibly retained: initially this took the form of a month-long programme of mime classes to help the computer animators master the nuances of movement and expression. But the development of the Dinosaur Input Device (DID) meant Tippett had a much more hands-on effect on *Jurassic Park*. The DID allowed Tippett and his team to animate sequences in a traditional stop-motion way by employing armatured model dinosaurs equipped with encoders at pivot points, which would register movements in the computer. In short, the DID allowed Tippett to retain the finesse of his art without going anywhere near a keyboard.

GEDDIT! The role of Harding – the park vet who is looking after the sick triceratops – is played by *Jurassic Park*'s co-producer Gerald R Molen, billed here as Jerry Molen.

The mate – Nedry's contact on the boat – is played by the film's cinematographer Dean Cundey.

For the heart-stopping moment where Lex falls through the vent into the jaws of a raptor, Ariana Richards's face was digitally pasted on to to the body of a stuntwoman.

In Michael Crichton's novel, John Hammond proudly says that the narrator on the prerecorded park tour is Richard Kiley. Later, Kiley was hired to play himself in that role for the movie – possibly the only instance of a celebrity 'appearing' in a book, and then later cast as him- or herself in the film version.

FACTOID FRENZY: Despite all the advanced technology on display in *Jurassic Park*, the film does boast at least two shots where the dinosaurs are men in suits. The raptor that ambushes Muldoon is inhabited by a Stan Winston employee, John Rosengrant. For certain shots, the raptors in the kitchen scene are played by Rosengrant and the conceptual artist, Mark 'Crash' McCreery.

For the scene where the park vehicle chases Grant and Tim down the tree, the vehicle was dropped down three different sides of the same fifty-foot artificial tree creating the illusion of a never-ending drop.

Fred Sorenson was the pilot who flew the crew off Kauai when the hurricane hit during production. He played Jock, the pilot who flew Indiana Jones away in the opening sequence of *Raiders*.

A poster campaign for London Buses that appropriated the *Jurassic Park* logo and typeface raised the ire of Spielberg, who threatened legal action if the advert was not dropped. Ultimately Spielberg let the poster – entitled 'Jurassic Parker' – run its course.

In December 1995, *Jurassic Park* became the first mainstream film in the UK to be dubbed into Hindi.

THE CRITICAL FACULTY: 'No film could be more personal to Spielberg than this one . . . a movie whose subject is its process, a movie about all the complexities of fabricating entertainment in the microchip age. It's a movie in love with technology [as Spielberg is] yet afraid of being carried away by it.' (Richard Corliss, *Time*.) '*Jurassic Park* packs the thrills of a great entertainment but it doesn't resonate like a great movie.' (Julie Salamon, *Wall Street Journal*.) 'Doesn't have the imagination – or the courage – to take us any place we haven't been a thousand times before. It's a creature feature on amphetamines.' (Terence Rafferty, *New Yorker*.) 'The movie delivers where it counts – in excitement, suspense and the stupendous recreation of giant reptiles.' (*Variety*.) '*Jurassic Park* isn't as sorry a mess as Spielberg's last movie, the unspeakable *Hook*. It's the same kind of mess, though . . . Remarkably tedious and toothless.' (Andrew Sarris, *Observer*.)

BOX OFFICE: Opening in the US on 10 June 1993, *Jurassic Park* took less than four months to break the previous worldwide box-office record of $701 million set by *E.T.* Breaking the record set by *Batman Returns* (1992) for the biggest opening weekend in movie history by ending the two days with $50.1 million, the film notched up $100 million in nine days, then $200 million in 23 days. *Jurassic* completed its theatrical run with a worldwide gross of $913 million. *E.T.* fought off the raptors stateside, though, earning $399.9 million to Jurassic's $357.1 million. In addition, consumer products – stamped with the motto 'If it's not *Jurassic Park*, it's extinct' – topped $1 billion.

AWARDS: *Jurassic Park* became the first Spielberg film to have a one hundred per cent success rate at the Academy Awards, winning in all three categories – Best Visual Effects, Sound and Sound Effects Editing – for which it received nominations. *Jurassic* also won the People's Choice Awards nod for Favourite All-Round Motion Picture of 1994. Similarly, *Jurassic Park* won the Lloyd's Bank Audience Award, voted for by the public at the BAFTA, where it once again picked up the award for Best Visual Effects. Finally, *Jurassic Park* was nominated in three categories at the MTV Movie Awards: Best Movie, Best Action Sequence, Best Villain for the tyrannosaurus.

THE SIZZLE! In the UK, *Jurassic Park* found itself the centre of a ratings controversy after the film was granted a PG certificate from the British Board of Film Classification. Although the BBFC tested the film on 200 primary-school children and all publicity materials carried a disclaimer – 'the film contains sequences which may be particularly disturbing to younger children or children of a sensitive disposition' – parents groups, buoyed by screaming tabloid editorials, argued that the certification was too lenient. In retrospect, the BBFC's decision seems sensible, displaying a tacit understanding of what kids really want to see and are able to stomach.

JOIN THE DOTS: Kids – *The Sugarland Express, Jaws, Close Encounters of the Third Kind, 1941, E.T. The Extra-Terrestrial, Twilight Zone: The Movie, Indiana Jones and the Temple of Doom, The Color Purple, Empire of the Sun, Hook, Jurassic Park, Schindler's List, The Lost World: Jurassic Park, Amistad.* **Roller-coaster plotting** – *Jaws, 1941, Raiders of the Lost Ark, Indiana Jones and the Temple of Doom, Indiana Jones and the Last Crusade, Jurassic Park, The Lost World: Jurassic Park.* **Contemporary setting** – *The Sugarland Express, Jaws, Close Encounters of the Third Kind, E.T. The Extra-Terrestrial, Twilight Zone: The Movie, Always, Hook, Jurassic Park, The Lost World: Jurassic Park.* **Based on a book** – *Jaws, The Color Purple, Empire of the Sun, Hook, Schindler's List, The Lost World: Jurassic Park, Amistad.*

SEND IN THE CLONES! In true Roger Corman style, *Carnosaur* (1993) beat Spielberg's epic into cinemas by one month. Based on the book by the British sci-fi author John Brosnan, the movie concerns a mad scientist who creates genetically engineered dinosaurs that run amok. The film managed enough business to spawn two sequels. Perhaps taking an even more Spielberg approach to dinosaurs than *Jurassic Park*, *Prehysteria* (1993), directed by the low-budget gurus Albert and Charles Band, was a straight-to-video effort that featured the whimsical adventures of five miniature dinosaurs that have hatched from ancient eggs and inveigled themselves into a suburban American home. Also in 1993, *Super Mario Bros* saw mad Dennis Hopper lead a band of dinosaur mutants bent on world domination. Other films to tap into the post-*Jurassic* dinosaur ballyhoo included Amblin's own *The Flintstones* (1994) and the animated *We're Back!* (1996), a sequel to *The Land Before Time* (1988), *Pterodactyl Woman from Beverly Hills* (1994) and *Theodore Rex* (1995), a dire comedy in which a cop played by Whoopi Goldberg teams up with a dinosaur to solve a crime. Moreover, a film such as *Dragonheart* (1996), starring a CG dragon voiced by Sean Connery, would be unthinkable without the advances in technology forged by *Jurassic*.

Movies that have spun action and adventure out of the messing with genetic codes include *Mimic* (1997), *The Relic*, (1997) and *Deep Blue Sea* (1999), earning itself the nickname 'Jurassic Shark'.

JURASSIC PARK GOES POP: *Toy Story 2* (2000) makes playful reference to *Jurassic*: as Rex The Dinosaur chases his pals down the toy-store aisle, he grows big in the rear-view mirror in a direct parody of a classic *Jurassic* shot.

The opening titles of *The Naked Gun 33 ⅓: The Final Insult* (1994) have a police car (represented only by a siren) enter Jurassic Park and encounter a tyrannosaurus, which instead of giving out a mighty roar, lets loose a cackling laugh. The *Jurassic* jibes continue as the film moves to a staging of the Academy Awards: Spielberg is nominated for *Geriatric Park*, where genetics have gone haywire in a retirement home.

Nielsen's *Spy Hard* (1996) also features gags at *Jurassic*'s expense: in particular a moment where a bad guy is eaten by a raptor and the dinosaur burps. In *Wayne's World 2* (1993), Wayne (Mike Myers) and Garth (Dana Carvey) pull off into a forest on a rainy night to hear stomping footsteps, see water shaking and come face to face with tyrannosaurus. In contrast, a porn spin off can be found in *Jurassic Poke* (1993).

TV 'toon *Animaniacs* featured a skit where two film critics were lured to the premiere of *Jurassic Park* and the tyrannosaurus stepped out of the scene and crushed them. More animated references come in *The Simpsons* episode 'Bart Gets An Elephant' as Stampy The African Elephant peers into the window outside chez Simpson in the mode of the tyrannosaurus placing his beady eye against the jeep. In 'Itchy & Scratchy Land', Professor Frink speaks about chaos theory and the theme park chopper bares an insignia that mimics *Jurassic*'s. Also in the episode 'Sweet Seymour's Baadasssss Song', Apu informs the hapless principal that his novel is a dead spit for Crichton's plot. Further references also appear in 'Treehouse Of Horror V'.

The Spielberg epic also found its way into the rap world through the group Jurassic 3. Video games to have taken *Jurassic* licks include the *Turok* franchise and *Dino Crisis*. There is also a *Jurassic Park* Theme Ride at Universal Studios-although Spielberg always gets out before the final drop!

FINAL ANALYSIS: A triumphant return to something approaching top form after the indulgent excess of *Hook*, *Jurassic Park* crucially re-established Spielberg's golden touch at the box office – something that, with the exception of the *Indiana Jones* movies, had been wayward since *E.T.* A consolidation rather than a growth of Spielberg's interests, *Jurassic*'s influence is most visible in transforming digital effects from a supporting role into a major player. The irony that a film so fervently anti-technology in theme could be made possible only by the most cutting-edge technology available was lost on no one. Similarly, as the camera lovingly pans around the fictional *Jurassic Park* gift shop filled to the rafters with (the now useless) merchandise bearing the park (and film) logo (a strangely self-reflexive moment for Spielberg), it was evident that *Jurassic* was about to usher in a new, heightened level of blockbuster merchandising.

Jurassic Park falls just below the benchmark of 'classic' Spielberg: the director's tendency to race through the shooting schedule may have undermined the trademark nuances – particularly in performance – that differentiate his work from the blockbuster norm. While the technical challenge of realising believable dinosaurs on the big screen for the first time may have engaged him, it seems that Spielberg already had one eye on the challenge of *Schindler's List* all the way through the kind of movie he knew he could do upside down in his sleep.

However, the movie is still streets ahead of most summer movies. By combining the relentless ride of *Duel*, the menace of *Jaws*, the wonderment of *Close Encounters*, the close calls of *Raiders*, the childlike viewpoint of *E.T.* (and very little from *1941*), it could be the most Steven Spielbergy Steven Spielberg film ever made. The perfect marriage between story and storyteller.

SPIELBERG ON SPIELBERG: 'I'm sick of hearing about *Jurassic Park*, although I'm thankful for everything that has happened. I'm not *really* sick of hearing about it because *Jurassic Park* was some of the most fun I've ever had. I didn't make it to change the way people saw the world. I made the movie because it was entertaining, and because it was the kind of movie I wanted to see, which is my motivation for making a lot of my movies. I've often said, "Gee I wish I could see a picture like that," and then turned it around and made it, if I want to see it that bad. I'd always wanted to do a dinosaur movie. So this in a sense was my hobby movie.'

Schindler's List (1993)

(Black & white and colour, 197 mins)

Studio Universal, Amblin Entertainment
Produced by Steven Spielberg, Gerald R Molen, Branko Lustig
Co-producer Lew Rywin
Executive Producer Kathleen Kennedy
Screenplay Steven Zaillian, based on the novel by Thomas Keneally.
Director of Photography Janusz Kaminski
Production Design Allan Starski
Edited by Michael Kahn ACE
Music by John Williams
Violin Solos Itzhak Perlman
Costume Designer Anna Biedrzycka-Sheppard
Casting by Lucky Englander, Fritz Fleischhacker, Magdalene Szwarcbart, Tova Cypin, Liar Meiron, Juliet Taylor
Unit Production Manager Branko Lustig
First Assistant Director Sergio Mimica-Gezzan
Art Directors Elva Skoczkowska, Maciej Walczak
Make-up Supervisor Christina Smith
Camera Operator Raymond Stella ASC
Production Sound Mixers Ronald Judkins CAS, Robert Jackson
Supervising Sound Editors Charles L Campbell, Louis E Edemann
Re-recording Mixers: Andy Nelson, Steve Pedersen, Scott Millan
Consultant Leopold Page
Stunt Co-ordinator Krzsyztof Kotowski
Special Visual Effects by Industrial Light and Magic

CAST: Liam Neeson (*Oskar Schindler*), Ben Kingsley (*Itzhak Stern*), Ralph Fiennes (*Amon Goeth*), Caroline Goodall (*Emilie Schindler*), Jonathan Sagalle (*Poldek Pfefferberg*), Embeth Davidtz (*Helen Hirsch*), Malgoscha Gebel (*Victoria Klonowska*), Shmulik Levy (*Wilek Chilowicz*), Mark Ivanir (*Marcel Goldberg*), Beatrice Macola (*Ingrid*), Andrzej Seweryn (Julian Scherner), Friedrich Von Thun (*Rolf Czurda*),

Krzysztof Luft (*Herman Toffel*), Harry Nehring (*Leo John*), Norbert
Weisser (*Albert Hujar*), Adi Nitzan (*Mila Pfefferberg*), Michael
Schneider (*Juda Dresner*), Miri Fabian (*Chaja Dresner*), Anna Muchar
(*Danka Dresner*), Albert Misak (*Mordecai Wulkan*), Michael Gordon
(*Mr Nussbaum*), Aldona Grochal (*Mrs Nussbaum*), Jacek Wojcicki
(*Henry Rosner*), Beata Paluch (*Manci Rosner*), Piotr Polk (*Leo
Rosner*), Ezra Dagan (*Rabbi Menasha Levartov*), Beata Nowak
(*Rebecca Tannenbaum*), Rami Hauberger (*Josef Bau*), Uri Avrahami
(*Chaim Nowak*), Adam Siemion (*OD/Chicken Boy*), Magdalena
Dandourian (*Nuisa Horowitz*), Pawel Delag (*Dolek Horowitz*),
Shabtai Konorti (*Garage Mechanic*), Oliwia Dabrowska (*Red Genia*),
Henryk Bista (*Mr Lowenstein*), Tadeusz Bradecki (*DEF Foreman*),
Wojciech Klata (*Lisiek*), Elina Lowensohn (*Diana Reiter*), Ewa
Kolasinka (*Irrational Woman*), Bettina Kupfer (*Regina Perlman*),
Grzegorz Kwas (*Mietek Pemper*), Viti Matula (*Investigator*).

BUDGET: $22 million

MPAA: R

BBFC: 15

TITLE SEQUENCE: After the Universal logo – played out in
respectful silence – the first image sees a match being struck and a
candle being lit. We are in an antique European house as a Jewish
family ignite candles and recite the prayers that precede the Sabbath. A
series of dissolves sees the candles burn down – the title 'Schindler's
List' appears perfectly positioned between two candles – until we are
left with a single candle: as it slowly dies, the smoke leads us into a
match cut to the (now black-and-white) emissions of a steam train in
Poland, 1939. As well as placing the survival of Jewish ritual within a
contemporary setting (something Schindler helped facilitate), the
opening framing device also foreshadows a scene towards the end of
the film as Schindler reminds the freshly liberated rabbi that he should
be preparing for the Sabbath. Interestingly, only three credits appear,
the usual lengthy roll call forsaken to quickly draw us into the
verisimilitude of the piece.

PLOT SUMMARY: Krakow 1939. As Polish Jews are rounded up by
the occupying German forces, an Austrian entrepreneur and *bon
vivant*, Oskar Schindler, carouses with Nazi officials. With powerful
friends intact, Schindler takes over a confiscated enamelware factory
with the intent of supplying pots and pans to the German army. He
enlists the services of a Jewish accountant, Itzhak Stern, who not only

provides Schindler with clandestine investors but also fills the factory with unpaid workers, turning it into a safe haven for the increasingly threatened Jewish community. In March 1941, as the district of Podgorze is transformed into a Jewish ghetto, Schindler's fortunes are on the up: his business is raking in the profits, his trust and friendship with Stern is gradually emerging, the Nazis are in his pocket, even the reappearance of his wife Emilie cannot dampen his spirits (or his infidelity).

Seeds of darkness, however, are sown as the Nazis' grip on Krakow grows tighter. Schindler's troubles increase as Stern is placed on a train heading for a concentration camp, saved only by last-minute on-the-platform bargaining by Schindler. This sense of foreboding is fully realised with the arrival in Krakow of an SS *Untersturmführer*, Amon Goeth, supervisor of a forced-labour camp being erected in Plaszow. Goeth receives orders to vanquish the Jewish ghetto and herd the survivors into the camp, wiping out centuries of Jewish culture and history over one day and night. From a safe distance, Schindler watches the brutal *Aktion*, drawn particularly to the fate of a girl in a red coat walking blithely through the horror.

With his workforce now incarcerated, the industrialist befriends Goeth, persuading him to create a sub-camp at his factory so work can resume. We follow multiple stories at Plaszow – Schindler installs Stern to manage Goeth's business affairs, 'buying' various Jews to work at his factory; Goeth starts a rash of impromptu killing sprees and displays a (forbidden) fascination with his Jewish housekeeper, Helen Hirsch – as Schindler continually tries to curb Goeth's erratic behaviour with psychological mind games: this results in Goeth's allowing Schindler to hose down a trainload of death-sentenced prisoners and intervening in Schindler's imprisonment, brought about by kissing a Jewish girl at his birthday party.

On Schindler's release (it's now 1944), the Nazis' strategies have gone from bad to unthinkably worse – the exhumation and burning of 10,000 Jewish corpses (their ashes drift down on Schindler like snow) is followed by orders that the Plaszow Jews are to be shipped off to the larger death camp at Auschwitz. As the sick are separated from the healthy in a humiliating ordeal, Schindler decides to act. With Stern's help, he draws up a list of essential workers and bargains with Goeth for their lives, offering up suitcases full of cash in exchange for the liberation of 1,100 Jews to work in his newly founded munitions factory in Bruunlitz – he even wins the safety of Helen Hirsch in a game of cards.

While the men on Schindler's list arrive at the sanctity of Bruunlitz, an administrative error sees the women put on a train bound for Auschwitz. Schindler negotiates their safe release (with diamonds), but

only after the women have gone through the nightmare of being forced
into communal showers. Over the next seven months, Schindler's
factory never produces a single shell and the Jews slowly begin to
recontact their culture. As the war ends, the workforce present
Schindler with a token of gratitude – a ring inscribed with the
Talmudic message 'Whoever saves one life, saves the world entire' – a
gesture that causes Schindler to break down, crying that if he had only
worked harder he could have saved more lives.

Now a hunted war criminal, Schindler, reunited with his wife, flees
to the West, leaving the Jews to take the first steps into their liberated
future.

As they begin their journey to freedom, Spielberg cuts to a coda in
colour with the real-life *Schindlerjuden* (Schindler's Jews) walking arm
in arm, then, accompanied by their families and the actors who played
them, laying stones on Schindler's graveside in the Catholic cemetery
on Mount Zion in Jerusalem.

BACKSTORY: In October 1980, the writer Thomas Keneally arrived
in Beverly Hills to publicise his new novel *Confederates*. Ducking into
an air-conditioned leather-goods store to cool down, Keneally struck
up a conversation with the store owner, Leopold Page, who, learning
his customer was an author, announced he had the 'best story of the
century'. Page informed him that his real name was Poldek Pfefferberg,
a concentration camp survivor who owed his life to the benevolent
actions of Oskar Schindler, a one-time Nazi turned saviour of Jews.
His interest piqued by Schindler's story, Keneally cancelled his flight
home and moved into Pfefferberg's house, wading through documents
and building up reminiscences. The ensuing two years saw Keneally
interview around fifty *Schindlerjuden* and fashion a fictionalised
account of factual events – on publication in 1982, the book, entitled
Schindler's Ark, won the prestigious Booker Prize, a literary award
given only to novels.

Yet, before Spielberg (or even Keneally) had heard of Schindler's
heroics, Pfefferberg had tried to get the industrialist's story on to the
big screen. Making it his life's work to spread the Schindler story,
Pfefferberg had set up a deal with MGM in 1963 to make a movie,
even getting as far as a finished script by Howard Koch with Sean
Connery lined up to play Schindler. Although the project fell through
after Connery's departure, Pfefferberg still made a very welcome
$37,500 for the (by then) impoverished Schindler.

Schindler's List entered Spielberg's life after Sid Sheinberg sent him a
copy of the *New York Times* book-review section featuring a glowing
appraisal of Keneally's novel. Although Spielberg did not commit to
direct, he displayed enough interest in the project for Universal to

purchase the rights. For just under ten years, Spielberg procrastinated, constantly trying to hand off the project to other directors. Top of his list was Roman Polanski, who, as a child, had escaped from the Krakow ghetto on the day the Nazis began the *Aktion* – not only was his mother gassed at Auschwitz but Polanski even had two uncles who were actually on Schindler's list. Perhaps too close to such painful subject matter, Polanski refused Spielberg's constant overtures. Spielberg also courted Sydney Pollack and offered to produce *Schindler* for Martin Scorsese – the latter felt only a Jewish director could do the story justice.

Billy Wilder was another renowned director who expressed a strong interest in *Schindler's List*. Wilder, an Austrian Jew, fled to Berlin during Hitler's rise to power, and most of his family perished in concentration camps. He perhaps saw the film as a fitting end to his career. The Australian director Fred Schepisi, a Keneally veteran after filming the author's *The Chant of Jimmie Blacksmith* (1978), also pestered to make *Schindler*, teasing Spielberg that he would overegg it with huge camera moves.

If procuring a director was problematic, so was finding a writer who could lick Keneally's 400-page tome into a manageable screenplay. First, Keneally's two drafts, then a version by the *Out of Africa* screenwriter Karl Luedtke failed to pass muster. Martin Scorsese's involvement brought another new writer into the fray: Steven Zaillian whittled down the screenplay to a swift 130 pages. Spielberg commented, 'I liked Steve's screenplay but I wanted the story to be less vertical – less a character study of Oskar Schindler, and more of a horizontal approach, taking in the Holocaust as the *raison d'être* of the whole project. What I really wanted to see was the relationship between Oskar Schindler – the German point of view – and Itzhak Stern – the Jewish point of view. And I wanted to invoke more of the actual stories of the victims – the Dresners, the Nussbaums, the Rosners.'

So, when Spielberg came on board, the screenplay swelled to 350 scenes over 195 pages. Initially two or three pages in the original script, the massacre in the ghetto sequence was finally played out over thirty. Fleshing out Zallian's narrative skeleton, Spielberg layered the story with testament from both Keneally's novel and the oral remembrances of survivors: a family stuffing their jewels into pieces of bread and swallowing them (based on a story told to Spielberg by Niusia Karakulska, the real-life girl kissed by Schindler at his birthday party); the stamping on a light bulb rather than a glass during the wedding ceremony held at the Plaszow; the concentration camp women pricking their fingers and rubbing the blood on their faces to add colour to their cheeks.

As is usually the case with adapting history for movies, Zaillian combined characters and speeded up events to enhance dramatic clarity. Itzhak Stern is a composite of three real people: the actual Stern, a plant manager named Abraham Bankier and Amon Goeth's stenographer Mietek Pember, who coaxed Schindler into his benevolent direction. The list itself was not finished by Schindler and Stern but by Schindler and a fellow humanitarian, German Raimund Titsch. By transferring the action to Stern, it reinforces the idea that the accountant is in some way Schindler's conscience, battling Goeth for possession of the Schindler soul. Moreover, in reality, it took Schindler three weeks to negotiate the release of the Auschwitz-bound women – rumours suggest that, to speed up proceedings, Schindler sent Nazi officials hookers – whereas in the movie he wangles their release in just a night. Equally, as laid out in Keneally, the fact that Schindler loathed Goeth from the start is also blurred in the film.

Some of the actions contained in the book yet omitted from the film are equally instructive in revealing Spielberg's dramatic structure: in Keneally, Schindler gets involved with the Jews' plight before the extermination of the Krakow ghetto, travelling to Budapest in a boxcar in order to be informed by Zionist agents, warning Stern in advance about the Nazi *Aktion* in Krakow and kissing the Jewish girl at his birthday. Spielberg delays Schindler's transformation until after the Nazi *Aktion*, presenting the audience with a more dramatic way of experiencing Schindler's change of heart.

Other telling excisions include Schindler purchasing weapons from the SS and distributing them to the *Schindlerjuden* at Bruunlitz, Schindler frolicking with an SS blonde in a water tank at Bruunlitz while his wife nursed sick prisoners below (makes the character too unsympathetic) and Stern, on his very first meeting with Schindler, relating the Talmudic dictum 'Whoever saves one life, saves the world entire', that appears on the ring in the film's final scenes (the seed for Schindler's rehabilitation would have been planted too early). Indeed, ignoring historical fact, neither Keneally nor Spielberg mentions the fact that Schindler later sold the ring to buy schnapps!

ORIGINS: With relatively few films daring to tackle the monumental subject of the Holocaust – *The Diary of Anne Frank* (1959), *Judgment At Nuremburg* (1961), *The Pawnbroker* (1965), *Sophie's Choice* (1982) – there was little for Spielberg to draw on in terms of cinematic reference. If Spielberg adopted anything from another representation of the Holocaust, it would have to be Claude Lanzmann's *Shoah* (1985), a 9-hour-43-minute exploration of the Holocaust. *Schindler's List* shares a similar sense of collating anecdotes and remembrances. (See **The sizzle!**)

Despite *Schindler*'s un-Hollywood feel, it is possible to find some influence from other film-makers in *Schindler's List*, particularly David Lean. Like the best of Robert Bolt's screenwriting for Lean, in particular *Lawrence of Arabia* (1962), *Schindler*'s screenplay serves up multidimensional historical figures with often ambiguous motivations. Moreover, there is at least one specific reference point with a Lean movie: as Schindler looks down on the invasion of the Krakow ghetto from his horse on a hillside, it recalls the moment in *Dr Zhivago* (1965) where Zhivago (Omar Sharif) watches the Tsarist cavalry wade into the demonstration – both scenes playing out moments of carnage on a human face.

Visually, Spielberg has acknowledged the debt *Schindler's List* owes to the handheld camerawork during the shoot-out at the Burpelson Air Force Base in Stanley Kubrick's *Dr Strangelove* (1964). Before setting out for Poland, the cinematographer Janusz Kaminski screened the Polish film *The Passenger* (1966), which includes scenes set in the concentration camp, and *In Cold Blood* (1967) and, in particular, studied Gregg Toland's photography on John Ford's *The Grapes of Wrath* to demonstrate how style could create mood. Of *Grapes* Kaminski says, 'It was beautiful, but it wasn't overstylised. That was my approach to shooting *Schindler's List*.'

Yet the biggest visual influence on Kaminski did not come from cinema at all. A photographer working in East European Jewish settlements between 1920 and 1939, Roman Vishniac recorded the nuances of Jewish life with a delicate lucidity and under incredible personal risk. 'A Vanished World', a collection of Vishniak photographs, became Kaminski's reference bible. 'I found inspiration in that book because this man, Roman Vishniac, had nothing – inferior equipment, inferior film stock and only available light – yet he managed to create beautiful pictures with a real timeless quality.' Although Kaminski appropriated precise details from Vishniak – the window displaying the skull-measuring device employed by Nazis to distinguish Jew from Aryan – it was more in the overall feel that the influence is ever present. 'I tried to follow his style in working with light,' Kaminski expounded. 'His pictures feel real: they're not silhouetted or heavily contrasted as in other photos of the period and not art-directed or organised . . . I liked the softness and fading around the edges and what he was doing with faces – always half light, half dark.'

CASTING: Although Kevin Costner, Mel Gibson, Robert Duvall, Harrison Ford, the Australian actor Jack Thompson and Daniel Day-Lewis had all expressed an interest in portraying the multifaceted Schindler, Spielberg was resolute in his conviction that he did not want an established name in the role. The Polish actors Piotr Fronczewski and Andrzej Seweryn were also considered, the latter even flying to the US for a screen test.

The director first encountered Liam Neeson after the Irish actor had provided a foil for the procession of wannabe Jims during the casting sessions of *Empire of the Sun*. After promising turns in *Excalibur* (1981) and *The Bounty* (1984), Neeson's career had lost momentum and he was earning a living as a house painter. As Schindler began to creep into his consciousness, Spielberg took his wife Kate Capshaw and her mother to a Broadway production of Eugene O'Neil's *Anna Christie*, starring Neeson. As the group chatted backstage afterwards, the elder Capshaw informed Neeson how moved she was by his performance, to which Neeson responded by instinctively hugging the woman. As they left the after-show revelry, Kate suggested to her husband that Schindler would have done precisely the same thing. A screen test was set up before Spielberg left to shoot *Jurassic Park* and Neeson got the nod.

Ben Kingsley was the one and only choice to play the accountant Itzhak Stern. Renowned for his Oscar-winning eponymous role in *Gandhi* (1982), Kingsley was well versed in Nazi history after playing Simon Wiesthenal, a head hunter of Nazi criminals, in the TV movie *Murderers Among Us – The Simon Wiesthenal Story* (1989).

For the role of Amon Goeth, Spielberg hooked up with Tim Roth, who refused to undergo Spielberg's practice of videotaping. Spielberg spotted Ralph Fiennes playing TE Lawrence in the TV movie *A Dangerous Man* and playing a demented Heathcliff in *Wuthering Heights* (1992). Fiennes did agree to a video test and the results shocked Spielberg to his very core. 'Ralph did three takes and I still, to this day, haven't seen takes and two and three. He was absolutely brilliant. I saw sexual evil. It's all about subtlety. There were moments of kindness that would move across his eyes. Then, they'd instantly turn cold.'

Giving him the part, Spielberg made one request of Fiennes: he must bulk up his bodyweight before shooting began. Following a diet of weight-gain products consisting of vegetable fats and a few pints of Guinness after every meal, the actor arrived in Poland some 25 pounds heavier.

PRODUCTION: *Schindler's List* started filming on 1 March 1993 in Poland, with scenes depicting the Jews shovelling snow outside Schindler's factory. While the production designer Allan Starski created 148 sets in 35 locations, many of the scenes in the movie were shot on the actual locations – Schindler's factory and apartment building, the SS headquarters and prison, the gate and railway track leading to Auschwitz – with the Plaszow concentration camp created in a quarry adjacent to the real-life locale. The Krakow ghetto was re-created in

Kazmierz, which was deemed more striking than the now decrepit Podgorze.

The film was scheduled for a 75-day, six-days-a-week shoot over winter and spring, and Spielberg kept his preplanning to a minimum, plunging himself into the experience with a controlled emotional intensity. Rarely, by all accounts, did Spielberg sit in his director's chair, and shots were captured in two or three takes, adding a greater sense of urgency and immediacy. Occasionally, Spielberg would rehearse a street scene full of extras, then send his actors, with instructions to improvise dialogue and actions, into the fray.

Yet before he could give *Schindler* his undivided attention, Spielberg had to finish off *Jurassic Park*. Hiring two satellite channels – one visual, one audio – at $1.5 million per week, Spielberg spent three nights a week checking ILM footage and listening to John Williams's score, both scrambled to avoid piracy. After finishing up on *Jurassic Park*, its editor, Michael Kahn, would insist that Spielberg spend a couple of hours watching *Schindler* footage to keep his head in the new film.

What he was forging by day could not have been further from what he was viewing by night. 'The worse days came any time I had to have people take their clothes off and be humiliated and reduce themselves down to livestock,' Spielberg told *Time* magazine, particularly in reference to the Auschwitz shower scene. 'That's what tore me up the most. It was the worst experience in my life.'

While re-creating such deep despair was tough enough, the production also provoked strong feelings from the local populace: graffiti in the Old Square in Krakow depicted a Star of David hanging from a gallows; an old woman, catching sight of Ralph Fiennes in uniform, thanked the actor for killing so many Jews in the past, hoping he would see off the rest of them this time. In a bar one night, Ben Kingsley looked on as a middle-aged German businessman asked one of the Israeli actors, 'Are you a Jew?' When the answer came back yes, the German drew a finger across his throat, then jerked an imaginary noose tight: 'Hitler should have finished the job.' So angered was Kingsley (a Gentile) that he had to be physically restrained from attacking the man. The quiet sense of rage that suffuses *Schindler* was reinforced by moments like that.

A minimal crew travelled to Jerusalem to film the 128 *Schindlerjuden* paying their respects at the Catholic cemetery for the film's coda, an idea that had been conceived in Krakow. *Schindler's List* officially wrapped on 23 May 1993.

TICS OF THE TRADE: Despite strong entreaties from Universal to shoot the film in colour, Steven Spielberg had always planned to shoot

Schindler's List in black and white. While conscious that, for modern audiences, their primal experiences and memories of the Shoah came from the monochrome imagery of newsreels and documentary – Spielberg's own initial exposure to the horrors of the Holocaust came in the form of a documentary called *The Twisted Cross* shown during high school – shooting in black and white may have also been a way of safeguarding that the film did not become overly Hollywoodised.

Jettisoning his usual controlled approach – no storyboards, no shot lists, sometimes not even a firm idea about which scenes were going to be shot – Spielberg attacked *Schindler* through instinct. Initially, Spielberg was going to rely more heavily on the Steadicam, yet during a scene captured early in the shooting schedule, depicting mothers being separated from their children at a concentration camp, the cinematographer Janusz Kaminski put the camera on his shoulder and followed the action intuitively. With the footage looking as if it had been stolen from some archive, subsequently around 40 per cent of the movie was shot hand-held, the whiplash pans and jerky movements infusing the film with a raw documentary feel that expressed the ever-present feel of danger and disorientation.

As well as the shaky, constantly moving camera work – even shots that employed a dolly track were hand-held by the operator, Raymond Stella – Spielberg and Kaminski opted to keep in many of the 'imperfections' that would normally be edited out: overexposure, flare into the lens, even shots that are not completely in focus are present to add a sense of grabbed moments rather than of meticulous set-ups. Behind the seemingly ad-hoc approach, there is also a great deal of craftsmanship: colour filters were employed to give the faces a ghostly white cast as opposed to grey.

However, the appropriation of verité describes only half the visual appeal of *Schindler's List*. As with *E.T. The Extra-Terrestrial*, Spielberg adopted a thematic approach to the look of the picture: therefore, if the lighting and camera motif for the Jews is the raw raggedness of documentary, the Nazis are characterised by the high style of German Expressionism. That Kaminski is equally proficient in both styles speaks volumes for his protean mastery of the medium.

Schindler is often bigger in the frame than the other characters – witness how he dwarfs Stern walking down the platform after he has liberated the accountant from the train bound for the concentration camps – emerging as a safe presence, literally larger than the life that surrounds him. Moreover, he is often invested with the lighting of a movie star: as we first see him, he has the rim lighting, catching his cigarette smoke, that makes him look every inch the matinée idol. Carefully crafting his protagonist's look, Kaminski cut a tiny slit in a cardboard sheet and constantly directed a light source toward's Neeson's face to literally put a gleam in his eye.

CLASSIC LINES:

Stern: 'Let me understand. They put up all the money. I do all the work. What, if you don't mind my asking, would you do?'

Schindler: 'I'd make sure it was known the company's in business. I'd see that it had a certain panache. That's what I'm good at. Not the work, not the work . . . the presentation.'

Schindler: 'Finish the page and leave one space at the bottom.'

Stern: 'You . . . The list is an absolute good. The list is life. All around its margins lies the gulf.'

COMIC RELIEF: Without ever detracting from the seriousness of the piece, Spielberg does manage to inject some moments of lightness into *Schindler*'s dark recesses. The montage of Schindler interviewing secretaries is a masterpiece of comic editing: in a series of quick cuts, he gazes longingly at a number of beautiful, if ineffectual, typists, struggling over a slow words-per-minute rate – the pattern is upturned in the final shot with Schindler totally uninterested in an efficient yet bulbous battleaxe who makes light work of his typing test. The film also mines effective laughs from witty scene transitions. Stern is loaded on to a train bound for a concentration camp. Schindler searches the length of the platform, informing two Nazi lackeys that, if his right-hand man isn't released, they'll be 'in southern Russia by the end of the month'. We cut to a purposeful tracking shot with the two men working harder than Schindler to locate the carriage that incarcerates Stern. Moreover, the implacable bonhomie inherent in Schindler's character (and Neeson's performance) gives the film a much-needed shot of vitality and energy.

VISUAL EFFECTS: *Schindler's List* offered Industrial Light and Magic a rare opportunity to work on a movie that wasn't a toothless summer fantasy for popcorn-munching kids. The biggest challenge was to create Genia's red coat within the black-and-white footage that surrounded it. This was achieved by Spielberg filming the shots in colour, then ILM desaturating (or draining) all the colour out to match the black-and-white footage. For the coat to remain red, a process called digital rotoscoping was employed: a technique where the colour image of the coat is retained on a frame-by-frame basis. The same process was used in a scene near the end as the candle flicker glows with warm colour. Other ILM tasks included enhancing the smoke that comes from the candle in the title sequence and

creating digital matte shots to help create overviews of Krakow and
Plaszow.

SOUND EFFECTS: From the opening sound of a match being struck
and the candles igniting into fire, it is evident that sound will play a
big role in conveying the drama of *Schindler's List*, employing an
approach that could be described as artfully constructed disorder.
Much of the terror informing the destruction of the ghetto is built
around a collage of nightmarish sounds – boots stomping on
woodwork, dogs barking unseen in thoroughfares, gunfire echoing in
sewers – reaching a surreal moment as a German soldier plays a
frenetic piece of Mozart on an abandoned piano. From the gasping for
air by the Jewry incarcerated in train wagons to the leather creak of
Schindler's coat designed to emphasise his luxurious lifestyle as he
talks about 'the presentation' (see **Classic lines**) there are sound effects
in *Schindler's List* that are doing just as much work as the images to
unravel and deepen the drama.

WHAT'S THE SCORE? In a tactic designed to maximise the
naturalistic, unmediated feel of the action, *Schindler's List* eschews
original score for much of its 197-minute running time. Yet, in the
sparing moments it is deployed, John Williams creates music that
reinforces the imagery without ever feeling overreaching or
manipulative: the powerful choral work that accompanies the
exhumation and burning of 10,000 corpses is a moving, eloquent elegy
for the dead; the violin swirls and jabs that accompany the women
into the showers at Auschwitz are violent and terrifying. Yet the score
is not all themes of foreboding. Elsewhere, the music is tender and
nostalgic for a sense of Hebraic history; the longest cue in the film,
following the creation of Schindler's workforce, brilliantly builds a
sense of optimism and growing community, tapping into Jewish
musical traditions without ever descending into overt *Fiddler on the
Roof*-isms. Although it is never overstressed in the framework of the
film, Williams also provides a haunting main theme that is a perfect
summation of the compassion that marks out Spielberg's whole
approach.

CUT SCENES: Typical of Spielberg's conscious efforts to keep
Schindler un-Hollywood, a dramatic card game of 21 in which
Schindler and Goeth play for Helen Hirsch was lost. This was one of
Neeson's favourite scenes, which Spielberg deemed felt too much like
'a *Cincinnati Kid*' moment, so it was subsequently sacrificed.
    A further scene in which Goeth, stripped of his uniform, arrives at
Schindler's factory only to discover that Schindler was the one who

condemned Goeth at a military tribunal was also excised, as it allowed too much sympathy to creep into the depiction of the camp commandant.

UNSUNG HERO: The screenwriter Steven Zaillian for turning an unwieldy novel into a literate, dense, emotionally charged screenplay, at once completely accessible yet pandering to no one. Although *Awakenings* suggested his skill at adaptation of dark subject matter into something entertaining and uplifting, *Schindler* reveals an intelligence and lack of sentimentality rare in a Hollywood screenplay. Initially producing a 130-page screenplay, Zaillian found that the heart of the story lay in the tussle between Stern and Goeth for Schindler's goodness, making comparisons between the business Schindler was running and the business of murder run by Goeth. Moreover, what Zaillian managed to solve that no other writer on the project had previously managed was to address why Schindler turned from opportunist to benefactor. During the liquidation of the ghetto, Schindler spotted a little girl in a red coat walking through the theatre of cruelty impervious to the violence that surrounded her. Although some view the splash of colour in the black-and-white world as an expressionistic blip that jars with the rest of the movie – Spielberg also plays fast and loose with the point of view by depicting the girl in shots that Schindler could not see – the image subtly suggested all sorts of thoughts and feelings going on inside Schindler without ever articulating or insisting on any.

GEDDIT! It is the *Schindler's List* co-producer Branko Lustig who plays the maître d' as Schindler enters the nightclub. An actual Auschwitz survivor, Lustig has produced films such as *Fiddler on the Roof* (1971) and *Sophie's Choice* (1982) and *Holocaust* on TV.

Caroline Goodall, who plays Oskar Schindler's wife Emilie, played Peter Banning's wife Moira in *Hook*.

Apart from being dedicated to the 'six million Jews who . . .', the film also includes a dedication 'For Steve Ross'. Ross was the Time Warner CEO who became a mentor for Spielberg before he died in 1992.

FACTOID FRENZY: In the US, many cinemas showing *Schindler's List* issued a code of conduct suggesting, among other things, that eating popcorn would not be appropriate in this film.

So as not to conflict with the monochrome verisimilitude of the movie, Spielberg insisted that all behind-the-scenes footage and set publicity shots be done in black and white.

When *Schindler's List* premiered on American television on 23

February 1997, NBC broadcast it in its entirety without any commercial breaks. With eight minutes of ads preceding the film, it was the longest broadcast without interruptions for breaks since the assassination of President Kennedy. Sixty-five million American households watched the film that night.

To alleviate the harshness of the *Schindler* shoot, Spielberg would often call Robin Williams to get light relief.

While filming in Poland, Spielberg was awarded the Order of the Smile, an award bestowed by children in honour of *E.T.* To reinforce an oath of bringing joy to the world's children, the ceremony consisted of drinking a whole glass of lemon juice without sugar and then managing a smile afterwards. Apparently Spielberg mastered the test with ease.

Schindler's List brought an upsurge in tourism to Krakow. Kazimierz's Jewish bookshop invites tourists to 'Visit Places In *Schindler's List*'.

CRITICAL FACULTY: 'It is by far the finest, fullest dramatic film ever made about the Holocaust. And few American movies since the silent era have had anything approaching this picture's narrative boldness, visual audacity and emotional directness.' (Terrence Rafferty, *New Yorker.*) 'Spielberg's very nature as a filmmaker has been transformed; he's reached within himself for a new language and without losing any of his innate fluency or his natural-born storytelling gift, he's found a style and a depth of feeling that will astonish both his fans and his detractors who believed he was doomed to permanent adolescence.' (David Ansen, *Newsweek.*) 'Mr Spielberg has made sure that neither he nor the Holocaust will ever be thought of in the same way again.' (Janet Maslin, *New York Times.*) 'It's as if he understood for the first time why God gave him such extraordinary skills . . . I didn't think I could be affected this way anymore.' (David Denby, *New York.*) 'A feel-good entertainment about the ultimate feel-bad experience of the 20th Century.' (J Hoberman, *Village Voice.*) 'Spielberg leads us down false paths. We see smoke and it's not a crematorium, it's a train. We see the showers and they spout not gas but water. All the cadavers we see we don't know and all the people we identify with are saved. And that's not how history goes.' (Danielle Heymann, *Le Monde.*)

BOX OFFICE: Opening on 15 December 1993 (just in time for Oscar nominations), by March the film had grossed $45.9 million in the US. *Schindler's List* grossed $321.2 million worldwide, $225.1 million coming from outside the US. This is all the more remarkable when you consider that the three-hour-plus running time curtailed the amount of screenings a cinema could put on in one day. Yet perhaps the most interesting box office reaction came from Germany, with cinemagoers racking up an astonishing 5,854,809 in admissions, the film sparking off a national re-examination of that period in the country's history. Such an aura grew up around *Schindler's List* that, when ten parents refused to let their children watch the film in school, the German authorities threatened to fine the families £17.

AWARDS: After three nominations (*Close Encounters of the Third Kind*, *Raiders of the Lost Ark*, *E.T. The Extra-Terrestrial*) and one very public snubbing (*The Color Purple*), Steven Spielberg finally won his first Best Director statuette at the 63rd Academy Awards ceremony on 31 March 1994. Nominated for twelve Academy Awards in total, *Schindler's List* also won Oscars for Best Picture, Screenplay Based on Material From Another Medium, Cinematography, Film Editing, Music, Art Direction/Set Decoration. It was also nominated for Best Actor (Liam Neeson), Supporting Actor (Ralph Fiennes), Costume Design, Make-up and Sound.

At the British Academy Awards, *Schindler* took home Best Film, the David Lean Award for Direction, Supporting Actor (Ralph Fiennes), Cinematography, Editing and Score. The film was also cited in the categories of Best Actor (Liam Neeson), Supporting Actor (Ben Kingsley), Costume Design, Make-up, Production Design and Sound. *Schindler* also nabbed Golden Globes for Best Motion Picture (Drama), Director and Best Screenplay. John Williams picked up a Grammy for the score.

THE SIZZLE! In January 1993, Spielberg's request to film inside the killing grounds of Auschwitz was denied by the World Jewish Congress: 'Our concern is the preservation of dignity of a place which is the largest Jewish burial ground in the world,' the World Jewish Congress Vice President Kalman Sultanik stated at the time. 'We do not want it turned into a Hollywood back lot.' Although nine other films had previously been granted permission to film inside the camp, Spielberg conceded, shooting outside the main grounds and reconstructing the Plaszow labour camp in a quarry near Krakow.

In many countries around the world, *Schindler* became the subject of much censorship controversy. The film was banned in Malaysia, Dubai and Jordan on religious grounds and in the Phillipines for being too sexually explicit – the ban was later overturned by President Ramos. On a different note, the Russian premiere of the film, planned for June 1994, was delayed after the security forces discovered that a neo-Nazi group, the Werewolves, intended to assassinate Spielberg. The film finally screened in September.

Despite appearing in the film's closing moments, Schindler's widow Emilie made several outbursts in the German press, claiming that the film's canonisation of Schindler was phony and undermined her actual participation in saving Jewish lives.

Schindler's List became the focus of a heated debate among intellectuals and the Jewish community not only over its serving up the Holocaust as an 'entertainment' but also filtering Jewish history through the story of a Nazi opportunist. Most vociferous in the argument was Claude Lanzmann, the director of *Shoah*, who criticised *Schindler's List* for shifting the emphasis to the 1,100 Jews who survived and away from the six million who died: 'The project of telling Schindler's story confuses history . . . It's a way to make it not a crime of humanity but a crime against humanity.' In a rare public response, Spielberg retorted, accusing Lanzmann of trying to be 'the only voice in the definitive document of the Holocaust.'

JOIN THE DOTS: Kids – *The Sugarland Express, Jaws, Close Encounters of the Third Kind, 1941, E.T. The Extra-Terrestrial, Twilight Zone: The Movie, Indiana Jones and the Temple of Doom, The Color Purple, Empire of the Sun, Hook, Jurassic Park, The Lost World: Jurassic Park, Amistad.* **Kidnapped kids** – *The Sugarland Express, Close Encounters of the Third Kind, Indiana Jones and the Temple of Doom, Empire of the Sun, Hook, Amistad.* **World War Two** – *1941, Raiders of the Lost Ark, Empire of the Sun, Indiana Jones and the Last Crusade, Saving Private Ryan.* **Historical setting** – *1941, Raiders of the Lost Ark, Indiana Jones and the Temple of Doom, The Color Purple, Empire of the Sun, Amistad, Saving Private Ryan.* **Based on a book** – *Jaws, The Color Purple, Empire of the Sun, Hook, Jurassic Park, The Lost World: Jurassic Park, Amistad.* **Based on real-life events** – *The Sugarland Express, 1941, Empire of the Sun, Amistad, Saving Private Ryan.* **Absent fathers** – *The Sugarland Express, Close Encounters of the Third Kind, E.T. The Extra-Terrestrial, The Color Purple, Empire of the Sun, Indiana Jones and the Last Crusade, Hook.*

SEND IN THE CLONES! The most important legacy left by *Schindler's List* was the creation by Spielberg in 1994 of the Survivors of the Shoah Visual History Foundation, an international programme established to videotape the testimonies and oral histories of Holocaust eyewitnesses. Spielberg subsequently put his name and money behind various Holocaust-related documentaries: the Emmy-award-winning *Survivors of the Holocaust* (1996), *The Lost Children of Berlin* (1996), Jon Blair's Oscar-winning *Anne Frank Remembered* (1995) and *The Last Days* (1998), James Moll's powerful account of the Final Solution in Hungary.

After *Schindler's List*, a number of films centring on the Holocaust appeared but unusually from a comedic perspective, including *Life Is Beautiful* (1998) (a huge hit internationally, the film also bagged Benigni a surprise Best Actor Oscar), *Train of Life* (1998) and Peter Kassovitz's *Jakob The Liar* (1999).

FINAL ANALYSIS: Like *E.T.*, *Schindler's List* was a film that preempted a radical change in the perception of Spielberg. After the mixed reactions to his previous attempts at maturity, *The Color Purple* and *Empire of the Sun* (many critics conveniently forgot *Duel* and *The Sugarland Express*), the film proved to most of the world that he could make a serious, adult film dealing with 'dark' issues, bereft of sentimentality. Coming out from his mantle as the cinema's greatest dream weaver, Spielberg accompanied the film around the world, turning into a kind of statesman meeting world leaders, reiterating what he saw as the film's significance: that the need to preserve Holocaust testament and Jewish heritage is a race against time and that the lessons of the past should be warnings for the future.

Contrary to what many critics argued at the time, *Schindler* is not the departure for Spielberg the film is often painted as. Stylistically, it contains many moments of camera blocking and razor-sharp editing that are pure Spielberg: the snaking Steadicam shot that follows Schindler into the nightclub (reminiscent of Indy's introduction in *Temple of Doom*), the intercutting of the Jewish wedding celebrations, Schindler's birthday party and Goeth's brutal beating of Helen are redolent of Spielbergian storytelling economy. Also, thematically, the film has roots in other Spielberg films – in general the sense of familial separation that marks many Spielberg films and in particular the loss and fight for survival at the heart of *Empire of the Sun*.

Yet what is different about *Schindler's List* is Spielberg's unyielding commitment to his subject matter. Although it is possible to find analogies between the director and his protagonist (both are marked by the push and pull between commercial success and social awareness), the sense of passionate involvement comes from Spielberg's memories of growing up Jewish in a seemingly Gentile America – seeing the concentration camp numbers etched on a relative's arm, being a member of the only family in his neighbourhood not to have Christmas lights and, as he grew older, beaten up for his religion – and his rediscovery of his Jewish faith in later life.

A cynic might argue that the world's most commercially successful film director 'doing' the Holocaust in black and white and over three hours is a marketing department's dream or the ultimate flexing of a film-maker's muscle, but the rich texture, biting intelligence and simmering anger that pervade the whole film confirm there is more going on here than studio spin or directorial hubris. Spielberg knows and feels this subject matter inside out and that level of intellectual and emotional comprehension is present in every frame.

The film is not perfect – Schindler's breakdown at the end feels forced and false – but such minor quibbles are dwarfed by the scale and scope of the ambition and the monumental extent to which Spielberg pulls it off. From the sweep of history (the liquidation of the ghetto is as powerful as anything ever to flicker on a screen) to the most evocative detail (the Nazis using stethoscopes to seek out people hiding in walls, children hiding from their captors by wallowing in faeces), Spielberg's eye, heart and mind have never been so forcibly engaged.

Beyond any cinematic achievement, the real importance of *Schindler's List* lies in its instructiveness. As Saddam Hussein terrorised the Kurds and ethnic cleansing rattled through Bosnia, Spielberg's emphatic reassertion of the systematic slaughter of European Jewry under Nazism was both timely and telling, forcing the subject (and its far-reaching implications) back into the public consciousness in ways that a nine-hour documentary could never do. In 1993, prior to its release, a public-opinion poll revealed that nearly 25 per cent of young Americans had never heard of the Holocaust or were unsure of what the term meant. The real success of *Schindler's List* is that future generations will know and understand. And probably never forget.

SPIELBERG ON SPIELBERG: 'Most of my movies aren't real life. There were moments in *Purple* and *Empire* that had real life to them, but they're not start-to-finish real life. All this time on *Schindler's List*, I knew I had to look. Then, when I started looking, I couldn't stop.'

The Lost World: Jurassic Park (1997)

(Colour, 134 mins)

Studio Universal
Producers Gerald R Molen, Colin Wilson
Screenplay by David Koepp
Based on the novel *The Lost World* by Michael Crichton

Director of Photography Janusz Kaminski
Editor Michael Kahn ACE
Production Designer Rick Carter
Music by John Williams
Executive Producer Kathleen Kennedy
Full-Motion Dinosaurs Dennis Muren
Live-Action Dinosaurs Stan Winston
Special Dinosaur Effects Michael Lantieri
Unit Production Manager D Scott Easton
First Assistant Director Sergio Mimica-Gezzan
Casting by Janet Hirschenson CSA and Jane Jenkins CSA
Art Director Jim Teegarden
Set Designers Pamela Klamer, Linda King
Set Decorator Gary Fettis
Conceptual Artist John Bell
Illustrators Stefan Dechant, Warren Manser, James Oxford
Costume Supervisor Sue Moore
Key Hairstylist Judy Alexander-Cory
Supervising Key Make-up Artist Christina Smith
Sound Design Gary Rydstrom
Production Sound Ron Judkins, Robert Jackson
Re-recording Mixers Gary Summers, Gary Rydstrom, Shawn Murphy
Supervising Sound Editor Richard Hymns
Second Unit Director David Koepp
Full-Motion Dinosaurs and Special Visual Effects by Industrial Light and Magic

CAST: Jeff Goldblum (*Dr Ian Malcolm*), Julianne Moore (*Dr Sarah Harding*), Pete Postlethwaite (*Roland Tembo*), Arliss Howard (*Peter Ludlow*), Richard Attenborough (*John Hammond*), Vince Vaughn (*Nick Van Owen*), Vanessa Lee Chester (*Kelly Curtis*), Peter Stormare (*Dieter Stark*), Harvey Jason (*Ajay Sidhu*), Richard Schiff (*Eddie Carr*), Thomas F Duffy (*Dr Robert Burke*), Joseph Mazzello (*Tim*), Ariana Richards (*Lex*), Thomas Rosales (*Carter*), Camilla Belle (*Cathy Bowman*), Cyd Strittmatter (*Mrs Bowman*), Robin Sachs (*Mr Bowman*), Elliott Goldwag (*Senior Board Member*), J Patrick McCormack (*Board Member*), Ross Partridge (*Curious Man*), Ian Abercrombie (*Butler*), David Sawyer (*Workman*), Geno Silva (*Barge Captain*), Alex Miranda (*Barge Captain's Son*), Robert 'Bobby Z' Zajonc (*InGen Helicopter Pilot*), Jim Harley (*Harbour Master*), Colton James (*Benjamin*), Carey Eidel (*Benjamin's Dad*), Katy Boyer (*Benjamin's Mom*), David Koepp (*Unlucky Bastard*), Eugene Bass Jr (*Attorney*), Bari Buckner (*Screaming Woman*).

BUDGET: $73 million

MPAA: PG-13

BBFC: PG

TITLE SEQUENCE: Following the full fanfare of the Universal logo, sounds of howling winds and crashing waves build over a black screen. The first images see the camera flying over a tumultuous sea – ominous music begins on the soundtrack – the camera tilting up to a tropical island, accompanied by subtitle 'Isla Sorna, 87 Miles southwest of Isla Nublar' (the site of Jurassic Park). The brief credits appear over a complicated camera movement as we go from waves smashing against rocks, panning on to a boat being buffeted by the swirling water, before a champagne bottle, carried by a waiter, enters the foreground and moves along to a civilised beach picnic in progress.

PLOT SUMMARY: *The Lost World* starts with a scene that mirrors the beach-frivolity-turning-to-terror axis of *Jaws*: straying from the sanctity of her family, a girl explores Isla Sorna, discovering a seemingly friendly small dinosaur, a compsognathus. However, as more 'compies' dance around the girl's feet, their playfulness turns to menace and they launch a swift attack, leaving their victim wounded.

In New York, chaos theorist Ian Malcolm, a survivor of the first Jurassic Park disaster, is summoned by the InGen dynamo and Park creator John Hammond. Hammond explains that Isla Sorna is home to Site B, the breeding ground for the creatures showcased at Jurassic Park, where a thriving dinosaur ecosystem has developed. To gain protection from the InGen board – Hammond's nephew Peter Ludlow has ousted his uncle as head of the company – Hammond recruits Malcolm to join a team documenting the dinosaurs. Malcolm displays an understandable reluctance to face off against further saurians. Hammond coerces him with the information that Malcolm's paleontologist girlfriend Sarah Harding is already heading up the expedition on Sorna.

Malcolm arrives on Sorna accompanied by a documentarian, Nick Van Owen, and an equipment specialist, Eddie Carr. Bowled over by the sight of a roaming stegosaurus, the group meet Sarah, who is in her element. Malcolm's tension about the mission is further increased when he discovers his daughter Kelly has surreptitiously joined him. The recriminations are abandoned, however, as helicopters from InGen – led by Ludlow and a legendary big-game hunter, Roland Tembo – arrive and the hi-tech hunters begin rounding up the dinos, looking to take them back to the US for a new Park in San Diego. Looking on in horror Van Owen (a clandestine eco-warrior) releases the captured triceratops that stampedes the InGen base camp. With Malcolm, Kelly and Carr taking refuge in a high hide, Van Owen and Harding rescue a wounded baby tyrannosaurus and bring it back to their trailer for treatment. However, the creature's parents follow them and, despite the safe return of the offspring, push the trailer over a cliff. Eddie is killed in the rescue of Malcolm, Sarah and Van Owen.

The team is now joined by Ludlow's hunters amid much animosity and begin a trek to the deserted InGen encampment to find a radio. En route, Tembo's partner Dieter is killed by compies, the tyrannosaurus takes more lives and the party is finally attacked by velociraptors. Van Owen manages to call in the helicopters and the survivors are lifted out, but only after Malcolm, Sarah and Kelly do battle with more velociraptors. From the air, the team are horrified to see an ensnared tyrannosaurus ready for shipment.

In San Diego, Ludlow invites the media to await the ship carrying the tyrannosaurus and baby to the mainland. His smugness is scuppered as the boat careers into the dock, the crew are revealed as dead and the tyrannosaurus escapes to maraud San Diego. Malcolm and Sarah lure the creature back to the harbour using the baby as bait. The tyrannosaurus is manoeuvred safely back into the cargo hold, the parent looking proudly on as the infant devours Ludlow to death. As the dinosaurs are returned to Sorna under military supervision, Hammond goes on TV and announces that the island will become a man-free dinosaur sanctuary. Graced by a pteranodon – a type of pterodactyl – majestically coming in to land, the final image shows a multiplicity of dinosaurs living in harmony.

BACKSTORY: When *Jurassic Park* became the biggest money spinner in movie history, it was inevitable that the film would spawn a sequel. What was less certain would be the extent of Spielberg's involvement. That Spielberg decided to direct *The Lost World* sprang from a number of interests: he wanted to ensure the quality of the franchise in the wake of the *Jaws* sequels, needed to ease himself back into directing after the rigours of *Schindler's List* with a lighter adventure story, and, not inconsequentially, he had enjoyed making the first movie so much.

In the end Michael Crichton's *Lost World* novel ended up being a strange hybrid of sequel to his original book and sequel to elements of the film–most notably the return of Ian Malcolm, who had been killed off on the page yet survived on the screen. Spielberg and *The Lost World* screenwriter David Koepp developed the story as Crichton was crafting his novel, but, in the end, little of Crichton's vision reached the screen. What remained was Crichton's plausible set-up involving the greedy exploits of InGen and the book's central set-piece involving two tyrannosaurus pushing a trailer off a cliff. Many of the book's subsidiary characters, such as the eleven-year-old genius Arby Benton and the corporate thief Lewis Dodgson, were jettisoned. Hammond's nephew Ludlow and hunter Roland Tembo were entirely Koepp creations.

Like Crichton's novel, the movie also added new species (not in *Jurassic Park*) of dinosaur, including the chicken-like compsognathus, stegosaurus (adult and baby), pachycephalosaurus, ptcranodon, mamenchisaurus and a parasaurolophus. An idea that was resisted involved the creation of a super-raptor, which Spielberg deemed stretched too far into the realms of a horror movie. Elements of Crichton's first *Jurassic Park* novel that found a home in the second movie include the opening compy attack (like Crichton, Spielberg didn't have the heart to kill the girl to underline the menace) and the scene where the tyrannosaurus lunges through the waterfall. It was Jeff Goldblum who came up with the idea that the only plausible way to get Malcolm back to Jurassic Park was to have his girlfriend paleontologist already stationed there. Moreover, Kelly was originally scripted as Malcolm's student but, after Spielberg decided that he wanted Vanessa Lee Chester for the role, she was transformed into Malcolm's daughter.

As with *Jurassic Park*, Spielberg also changed the ending once the production was under way. Originally, the hunters escaped the raptors in the long grass by taking to the sky in hang-gliders contained in their backpacks. Once in midair, however, the team were picked off by pteranodons. After a battle with raptors in an abandoned village – a scaled-down version of this idea remains in the film – the pteranodons attacked the InGen helicopter flying the heroes to safety. Perhaps with one eye on gazumping *Godzilla* (1998), which was simultaneously in production, Spielberg added a new final act in which the tyrannosaurus would stomp all over San Diego.

ORIGINS: As well as the two other movie versions of *The Lost World* (1925 and 1960, see **Origins** in the *Jurassic Park* entry), there have been numerous movies that have recycled aspects of Sir Arthur Conan Doyle, in particular the notion of a hidden haven of prehistoric life: *Unknown Island* (1948) pitted men in suits against the actor Richard Denning; *Lost Continent* (1951) starred Cesar Romero (the Joker on TV's *Batman*), John Hoyt, Whit Bissell and Hugh Beaumont battling dinosaurs created by an atomic rocket that lands on a South Seas Island; Spielberg has cited his own enjoyment of *The Land Unknown* (1957), a little-seen B movie starring the erstwhile action hero Jock Mahoney, who lands in an Antarctic valley where dinosaurs still roam; *The Valley of Gwangi* (1968) sees a bunch of cowboys tackling tyrannosaurs in a hidden Mexican valley; *The Land That Time Forgot* (1974) and *The People That Time Forgot* (1977), based on stories by Edgar Rice Burroughs, starred Doug McClure as a ship captain who discovers a dinosaur hideaway. The concept was even taken into outer space by the producer Bert I Gordon in *King Dinosaur* (1955), as astronauts discover the saurians on the planet Nova. *King Kong* (1933 version), *Dinosaurus!* (1960) and *When Dinosaurs Ruled the Earth* (1970) would have also influenced the depiction of a secret universe of dinosaurs.

There are also a number of antecedents for *The Lost World*'s San Diego sequence in which a mainland environment comes under attack from a giant beast. While the granddaddy of all these movies is still *King Kong*, other frames of reference may have been provided by the movies of the legendary stop-motion animator Ray Harryhausen – in particular *The Beast From 20,000 Fathoms* (1953), which sees a rhedosaurus rampage on Coney Island, and *It Came From Beneath the Sea* (1955), in which a giant octopus levels San Francisco. While *The Lost World* was obviously influenced by Toho Studios' *Godzilla* cycle of movies, perhaps a more pertinent antecedent would be the British movie *Gorgo* (1960), in which a baby dinosaur is caught in Irish waters and placed in a circus, only to be rescued by its mother – the theme of a parent rescuing a child forms the heart of *The Lost World*. This idea also has a strong place in another Spielberg favourite, Disney's *Bambi* (1942).

CASTING: Although Sam Neill and Laura Dern were contractually obligated to return for a sequel, Spielberg and David Koepp opted not to reprise Alan Grant and Ellie Sattler. Now even a bigger name since the success of *Independence Day* (1996), Jeff Goldblum held centre stage this time round, his plot function shifting from the first movie: in *Jurassic Park*, Malcolm was the harbinger of doom and occasional comic relief; in *Lost World*, he is much more active in initiating action and driving the story forward. Also returning from the first movie was Richard Attenborough as John Hammond in brief bookends shot over two days at the Mayfield Senior School, doubling as Hammond's mansion. The beginning of the scene also features cameos from Ariana Richards (Lex) and Joseph Mazzello (Tim), who have no discernible reason for appearing except to provide a believable continuity between the two films.

Julianne Moore was selected to play the paleontologist Sarah Harding. With her gentle features and American indie credentials, Moore was an unlikely candidate to head up a summer blockbuster. Spielberg spotted Moore in her brief appearance as a doctor in *The Fugitive* (1993) and arranged to meet her without any particular project in mind. When *The Lost World* arrived on his slate, Spielberg made good on his promise that the pair would work together. She had previously acted opposite Jeff Goldblum in *Nine Months* (1995).

For the role of the wildlife photographer Nick Van Owen, Vince Vaughn came into Spielberg's thinking after the director was asked to approve the use of the *Jaws* theme during a party scene in Doug Liman's *Swingers* (1996) – the Vegas-set comedy that made Vaughn hot. Vaughn later worked with Moore on Gus Van Saint's *Psycho* (1999) remake. Pete Postlethwaite was cast as the game hunter Roland Tempo after Spielberg saw his performance in *In the Name of the Father* (1993), declaring Postlethwaite 'one of the greatest actors in the world today'. He collaborated again with Spielberg on *Amistad*.

PRODUCTION: *The Lost World* started shooting on 4 September 1996, in Eureka, California, with the first scene shot being that of Dieter under attack from compies – in actuality a dozen puppets were attached to the actor Peter Stormare, either stuck to his Velcro suit or by magnets. The film was shot in various locations around California with Burbank streets doubling for San Diego.

Reuniting much of the *Jurassic* crew, the shoot progressed smoothly, coming in six days under its 72-day schedule. Part of the reason for the swiftness of production was the improved performance of Stan Winston's mechanical creations, which had been retooled and updated, performing with more expression and fluidity this time round. For the scenes involving two tyrannosaurus, the brace of behemoths, weighing in at nine tons each, were erected at Stage 24 on the Universal lot and the various props and scenery moved around them, be it the trailer vehicle or the InGen encampment and nearby waterfall (shot towards the end in case the water damaged the creature's mechanisms). Being the ultimate movie stars, the monsters didn't go to the set: the set came to the T-rexes.

Perhaps an indicator of the level of his emotional involvement in the project, Spielberg turned over the shooting of two sequences – Malcolm on the subway and Malcolm's boat arriving at Isla Sorna – to the screenwriter David Koepp. Yet, rather than leave Koepp to his own devices, Spielberg set up a fibre-optic telephone link between the set and his New York apartment. The link-up came with monitors – one showing the view through the camera, the other Spielberg's face – to enable a clear line of communication.

With plans to shoot the Isla Nublar beach attack in New Zealand scrapped, principal photography was completed on the island of Kauai – where the first movie was shot – on 20 December.

TICS OF THE TRADE: If *Jurassic Park* takes its visual cue from its theme-park milieu – bright, comforting, almost bland – *The Lost World* has a much more raw, primordial look. With the *Jurassic* cinematographer Dean Cundey unavailable, Spielberg turned to

Schindler's lensman, Janusz Kaminski, and the pair created a bold lighting schema that relies on high contrast to suggest the threat and danger of a jungle without fences or rules.

As with *Jurassic*, Spielberg comes up with imaginative ways to hint at unseen menace and violence. Best of all, in this respect is the aerial shot of a velociraptor attack represented only as dark swathes being cut through a field of high grass, pulling helpless victims out of view. The almost neon-green light cast across the field adds a surreal sense to the scene.

A further mark of Spielberg's innate understanding of how to terrify the audience comes when the tyrannosaurus pushes the research trailer over the cliff. Sarah falls on to the window of the upended vehicle and, as she lies flat and helpless, the glass – ever so slowly – begins to fissure, the sense of tension practically unbearable. Much more memorable than anything involving the dinosaurs, the moment ranks high in the Spielberg canon of spine-tingling moments.

CLASSIC LINES:
John Hammond: 'Thank God for Site B.'

John Hammond: 'Don't worry, I'm not making the same mistakes again.'
Ian Malcolm: 'No, you're making all new ones.'

Ian Malcolm: 'Oooh! Ahhh! That's how it always starts. Then later there's running and screaming.'

Dr Sarah Harding: 'I'll be back in five or six days.'
Ian Malcolm: 'No, you'll be back in five or six PIECES!'

VISUAL EFFECTS: Stan Winston and ILM had their work cut out on *The Lost World*. While *Jurassic Park* had improved on years of sub-standard dinosaur re-creations, the sequel had only a three-year gap to create a new level of amazement. If the high point of the mechanical creations is the Winston created baby tyrannosaurus – a 50 lb mock-up boasting 45 points of movement and operated by completely self-contained mechanisms – the digital roster was now up to 80 different dinosaurs, including the stegosaurus herd, the stampeding dinosaurs chased by the hunters (horses stood in for dinos on location to produce actual puffs of dust that would be matched by computer generated creations), the twin tyrannosaurus attack, the raptors and the tyrannosaurus on the mainland.

If never capturing the wow factor of *Jurassic Park*, the effects work on *The Lost World* raises the ante on its progenitor in numerous ways. Visualised by digital storyboards created from the actual background footage, the dinosaurs hold up under much closer scrutiny this time round – the skin, bone structure and muscle are rendered in even more detail – and are captured in much more imaginative, elaborately designed camera shots: following a motorcyclist through the legs of a stampeding brachiosaurus would have been impossible first time round.

WHAT'S THE SCORE? A much more vivid, darker-edged score than the first movie, John Williams's music sounds like it could come from any jungle adventure movie during Hollywood's golden age. Big and bold, the main theme is exotic excitement exemplified and the whole score is given an on-safari feel through the widespread use of ethnic percussion. This time round, there is little pause for breath or wonder. Instead, the score alternates between scary dissonance – particularly in relation to the compies – and a driving full-on force for the action sequences. The orchestra gets a real work-out during the dinosaur hunt, the trailer-over-the-cliff set piece and the tyrannosaurus chasing its prey into the waterfall. Unlike many sequels, *The Lost World* rarely returns to the music of the original – when it does occur at the end, even the main theme seems speeded up as if caught up in the sweep of the story.

CUT SCENES: Fitting in between the attack on Isla Sorna and Malcolm at the subway, Spielberg excised a strong scene in which Ludlow addresses the InGen board. Ludlow warns of a lawsuit brought about by the compies' attack on Cathy Bowman and the death settlements arising from the first Jurassic Park tragedy and makes a motion to have John Hammond removed as the CEO of the company. The motion is carried. Much more adult than the rest of the movie, much of the same information is disseminated throughout the movie and the scene does ruin the neat transition to Malcolm.

A further deleted scene involves Roland Tembo, who meets Ajay in a Kenyan bar, and Ajay tries to tempt him on to the prehistoric safari. Tembo breaks off their conversation to come to the aid of a waitress being mauled by a group of loud-mouthed American tourists. When the ringleader suggests he can take on Tembo with one hand tied behind his back, Tembo ties up and dispatches the American with a severe beating. Tembo returns to Ajay, reiterating that there is little left to hunt that can challenge him.

Also absent is the scene of two tyrannosaurus attacking the high hide after Kelly is left all alone by Eddie, and a brief scene in which the raptors fight the tyrannosaurus – a grudge match after the first film – in the latter's nest.

Finally axed from the San Diego sequence was a groansome David Koepp joke – the doghouse clearly read 'Rex' (tyrannosaurus).

GEDDIT! The ship that brings the tyrannosaurus to San Diego is the SS *Venture*, also the name of the ship that brought the star of *King Kong* (1933) to New York.

In the San Diego video store, there is a poster advertising a movie with Arnold Schwarzenegger as King Lear. This is a nod to Schwarzenegger's performance as Hamlet in *The Last Action Hero* – the movie that was royally trounced by *Jurassic Park* in the 1993 summer blockbuster stakes. Also displayed in the video shop are fake posters for *Tsunami Sunrise*, starring Tom Hanks, and a sequel to Robin Williams's flop *Jack*.

When fleeing the tyrannosaurus on the streets of San Diego, one of the Japanese businessmen says in Japanese, 'I came to America to get away from all this' – a reference to the *Godzilla* and *Gojira* cycle of films.

In the same scene, the executive producer Kathleen Kennedy, the director of photography Janusz Kaminski and Spielberg's assistant Marc Fusco are among the crew running from the tyrannosaurus.

The screenwriter David Koepp is the unlucky bastard who is killed by the tyrannosaurus running for the door. He appears in the credits as 'Unlucky Bastard'.

FACTOID FRENZY: As a teen prankster, Spielberg once filled a bag with white bread, milk, Parmesan cheese, creamed corn and peas, took the solution to a local movie house and, making over-the-top vomiting noises, squeezed the gooey mixture from the balcony on the people below. The movie was stopped immediately and the ushers sought out the jokers, who fled for their lives. The film they were watching was Irwin Allen's 1960 version of *The Lost World*.

The official *Lost World* website underwent a humorous makeover as a hacker sabotaged the homepage logo with their own image: *The Lost World: Jurassic Park* became *Duck World: Jurassic Pond*, with the skeletal tyrannosaurus replaced by a cute little duckie. The image remained live for twelve hours before it was removed.

The baby triceratops, created for *Jurassic Park* but dropped, finally found a home in *The Lost World*.

THE CRITICAL FACULTY: 'The good news is that this time around, Spielberg has sharpened his claws and really let rip . . . If *The Lost World* marks a return, for Spielberg, of the sort of high-spirited brinkmanship that we haven't seen in his filmmaking since the first two Indiana Jones pictures, it is because he has remembered that entertaining an audience and tormenting them are not necessarily all that different.' (Tom Shone, *Sunday Times*.) 'More inchoate energy, if less shape than *Jurassic Park* . . . a free association riff on the first film's plot.' (Nigel Andrew, *Financial Times*.) 'Compared to *Jurassic Park* . . . *The Lost World* is better crafted but less fun.' (J Hoberman, *Village Voice*.) 'Delivers everything that its predecessor didn't, plus some fashionable new themes: parental guilt, yaa-boo-sucks to bloodsports and – an old Hollywood favourite – nature good, big business bad!' (Anne Billson, *Sunday Telegraph Review*.) 'It looks like a director on autopilot . . . Profoundly slick . . . The special effects brook no argument. That is all. The rest is amazing dross.' (Derek Malcolm, *The Guardian*.)

BOX OFFICE: Opening in the US on 23 May 1997, *The Lost World* grossed $97 million in its opening weekend before making $229 million on its American run. The film finished second to the Spielberg-produced *Men In Black* (1997), which took $244 million. Outside the US, the dino sequel earned $382 million (including $25 million in the UK), making a worldwide gross of $590 million, the biggest global hit of the year.

AWARDS: *The Lost World* was nominated for only one Academy Award – Best Visual Effects – but was beaten by the all-conquering *Titanic*. At the Blockbuster Entertainment Awards, Jeff Goldblum and Julianne Moore received Best Sci-fi Actor/Actress nominations and the tyrannosaur attacking San Diego was cited at the MTV movie awards for Best Action Sequence. John Williams's score was once again nominated for a Grammy. Embarrassingly, the awards ceremony that featured The *Lost World* most prominently was the Razzies, the celebration of cinematic dross staged the night before the Oscars. The film was nominated (but didn't win) in the categories of Worst Remake or Sequel, Worst Screenplay and Worst Reckless Disregard For Human Life and Public Property.

THE SIZZLE! Jack Horner, the dinosaur adviser on both the *Jurassic* movies, came out against *The Lost World* in the press, claiming that it was not in keeping with the current thinking about dinosaurs. While the first movie was praised for its credible depiction of dinosaurs as animals, the sequel was lambasted for leaning too heavily on movie clichés and situations. Chief among these were the notion of the tyrannosaurus as a voracious predator – all indications suggest it fed off dying or dead prey – the shifting size of the dinosaurs and the ability of the stegosaurus to use its tail as a spiked weapon, which was not possible due to its anatomy. But what upset Horner most of all was the idea that tyrannosaurs don't get mad, they get even. 'The underlying fictional theme of the movie is that animals get revenge, which of course they don't do in real life. If you take a baby from a tyrannosaurus rex mother, she is not going to come and kick your car off a cliff.'

JOIN THE DOTS: Kids – *The Sugarland Express, Jaws, Close Encounters of the Third Kind, 1941, E.T. The Extra-Terrestrial, Twilight Zone: The Movie, Indiana Jones and the Temple of Doom, The Color Purple, Empire of the Sun, Hook, Jurassic Park, Schindler's List, Amistad*. **Roller-coaster plotting** – *Jaws, 1941, Raiders of the Lost Ark, Indiana Jones and the Temple of Doom, Indiana Jones and the Last Crusade, Jurassic Park*. **Contemporary setting** – *The Sugarland Express, Jaws, Close Encounters of the Third Kind, E.T. The Extra-Terrestrial, Twilight Zone: The Movie, Always, Hook, Jurassic Park*. **Based on a book** – *Jaws, The Color Purple, Empire of the Sun, Hook, Jurassic Park, Schindler's List, Amistad*.

SEND IN THE CLONES! Perhaps the biggest-budget imitator of *Jurassic*-style thrills to follow *The Lost World* was the resurrection of Toho Studios' *Godzilla* (1998) by the *Independence Day* film-makers Roland Emmerich and Dean Devlin. To the tune of $120 million and an unparalleled marketing blitzkrieg, the update was a flat retread of other movies, in particular a pack of *Godzilla* offspring that looked remarkably like *Jurassic*'s velociraptors. *Mighty Joe Young* (1998) also featured nasty hunters, eco-warnings and a creature on the loose in a modern city in an update of the 1949 *Kong* rip-off. Disney's *Dinosaur* (2000) once again used CGI to re-create prehistoric life forms in a cute tale of dinosaurs trekking across wastelands to find a new nesting home. Technically impressive but emotionally underwhelming. Directed by Brad Silberling, *T-Rex Back To The Cretaceous* (1998) was a *Jurassic* rerun made specially for the large screen I-Max format. BBC's *Walking With Dinosaurs* (1999) attempted to re-create an observational nature documentary employing similar technology to that utilised by ILM. Narrated by Kenneth Branagh, the result produced some of the most amazing effects ever achieved for the small screen. Finally, *Barney's Great Adventure* (1998) starred the popular, if frankly unrealistic, singing purple tyrannosaurus.

Jurassic Park 3 finally went into production in the autumn of 2000 with Spielberg as executive producer and Joe Johnston (*Honey,*

I Shrunk The Kids, *The Rocketeer*, *Jumanji*) directing. Reputedly set in between the previous movies, the threequel was written by the *Election* (1999) pairing of Jim Taylor and Alexander Payne from a story idea by Spielberg, and sees Sam Neill return as Alan Grant. The rest of the cast is fleshed out by Tea Leoni, Alessandra Nivola and William H Macy. The movie will hit cinemas in summer 2001.

FINAL ANALYSIS: After the glow of critical kudos that graced *Schindler's List*, Spielberg's return to the blockbuster arena in general and the familiarity of *Jurassic Park* in particular seemed a strange, regressive move. While creating popcorn-pounding entertainment may have been necessary light relief between the horrors of the Holocaust and the slavery of *Amistad*, his spell as a serious artist didn't lead to a creative rejuvenation of Spielberg as showman. The biggest feeling you get watching *The Lost World* is of a film-maker treading water.

In certain regards, however, *The Lost World* surpasses its predecessor, creating a much more interesting visual experience and some brilliantly crafted moments of suspense – the glass and the grass in particular. But there is little in the story that has appeared to engage Spielberg. Some of his core themes are skirted around – the rescue of children (albeit dinosaur children), estranged parent–sibling relationships – and there is a certain amount of glee in the film's nastier elements, but Spielberg fails to find a compelling quality to link the action. All the care in characterisation, construction of story and marshalling of story suspense and emotional resonance that Spielberg brought to the action genre is prevalent by its absence. It lacks the sense of fun and wonder of the original – which in itself failed to live up to the is-it-as-good-as-*Jaws*? acid test – and the fact that Spielberg has decided not to direct the third movie is perhaps the strongest indicator that the novelty and commitment went a.w.o.l. in *The Lost World*.

SPIELBERG ON SPIELBERG: 'I read reviews where they compared *The Lost World* to *Schindler's List*. I did, I read reviews where they said, "Oh, *The Lost World* is a much darker film than *Jurassic Park*. Obviously Spielberg was influenced by the subject matter of the Holocaust and brought his new, dark personality into what was supposed to have been entertainment." At that point, I threw up my hands and said, "Fine, anybody can compare anything to anything they want.'

Amistad (1997)

(Colour, 154 mins)

Studio DreamWorks in association with HBO Pictures
Producers Steven Spielberg, Debbie Allen, Colin Wilson
Screenplay David Franzoni
Director of Photography Janusz Kaminski
Editor Michael Kahn ACE
Production Designer Rick Carter
Music John Williams
Executive Producers Walter Parkes, Laurie McDonald
Co-executive Producer Robert Cooper
Co-producer Tim Shriver
Associate Producers Bonnie Curtis, Paul Deason
Production Supervisor Angela Heald
First Assistant Director Sergio Mimica-Gezzan
Unit Production Manager Paul Deason
Casting Victoria Thomas
UK/Africa Casting Priscilla John
Puerto Rico Additional Casting Tere Lopez
Script Supervisor Janina Stern
Camera Operator Mitch Dubin (underwater: Pete Romano)
Art Directors Chris Burian-Mohr, Jim Teegarden, Tony Fanning
Conceptual Artist Kadir Nelson
Illustrator James Oxford
Costume Designer Ruth E Carter
Costume Supervisor Sue Moore
Make-up Department Head Ve Neil
Prosthetic Effects Creation Steve Johnson's XFX Inc.
Music Editor Ken Wannberg
Production Sound Mixers Ronald Judkins, Robert Jackson
Re-recording Mixers Andy Nelson, Anna Behlmer, Shawn Murphy
Supervising Sound Editors Charles L Campbell, Louis Edemann
ADR Supervisor Larry Singer
African Language/Cultural Adviser Dr Arthur Abraham
Stunt Co-ordinator M James Arnett
Special Effects Supervisor Tom Ryba
Visual Effects Supervisor Scott Farrar
Special Visual Effects by Industrial Light and Magic

CAST: Morgan Freeman (*Theodore Joadson*), Nigel Hawthorne (*Martin Van Buren*), Anthony Hopkins (*John Quincy Adams*), Djimon Hounsou (*Cinque*), Matthew McConaughey (*Roger Baldwin*), David Paymer (*Secretary Forsyth*), Pete Postlethwaite (*Holabird*), Stellan Skarsgard (*Tappan*), Razaaq Adoti (*Yamba*), Abu Bakaar Fofanah (*Fala*), Anna Paquin (*Queen Isabella*), Tomas Millian (*Calderon*), Chiwetel Ejiofor (*Ensign Covey*), Derrick N Ashong (*Buakei*), Geno Silva (*Ruiz*), John Ortiz (*Montes*), Ralph Brown (*Lieutenant Gedney*),

Darren Burrows (*Lieutenant Meade*), Alan Rich (*Judge Juttson*), Paul Guillfoyle (*Attorney*), Peter Firth (*Captain Fitzgerald*), Xander Berkeley (*Hammond*), Jeremy Northam (*Judge Coglin*), Arliss Howard (*John C Calhoun*).

BUDGET: $40m

MPAA: R

BBFC: 15

TITLE SEQUENCE: The first film to be directed by Spielberg to lead off with the DreamWorks SKG logo – a cherub fishes off a half-moon that transforms into the 'D' of DreamWorks – the movie once again uses white lettering on black, this time a formal font to mirror the gravitas of the subject matter. We hear a haunting solitary African vocal. Before the movie begins, the chant fades down and the sounds of waves and thunder creep up. Sombre but potent.

PLOT SUMMARY: Off the coast of Cuba, 1839, in the midst of a tumultuous thunderstorm, a group of 53 African slaves held captive in the hold of a Spanish slave ship, *La Amistad*, break free and begin an insurrection, killing most of the ship's crew. Led by Sengbe Pieh, dubbed Cinque by the Spanish, they force their captors Jose Ruiz and Pedro Montes to navigate back to Africa. Surreptitiously, however, the Spaniards steer the vessel towards the United States, where *La Amistad* is intercepted by a US naval patrol. The mutineers are soon imprisoned in New Haven and stand trial for murder with various parties – Ruiz and Montes, the Spanish Court, the Americans who salvaged the ship – claiming the right to own the slaves.

The plight of the slaves is taken up by two anti-slavery campaigners, Theodore Joadson (himself once a slave) and Lewis Tappan. After failing to engage the service of ex-President (and abolition sympathiser) John Quincy Adams to argue their corner, Joadson and Tappan enlist the assistance of a property rights lawyer, Roger Baldwin. While all the time attempting to bond with Cinque, Baldwin establishes the journey of the slaves, who were shipped to Havana in the notorious slave ship *Tecora*. As the case becomes a national issue, President Van Buren fears that an abolitionist victory would prejudice his chances of re-election among the pro-slavery Southern states and has the more malleable Judge Coglin appointed to the case.

Returning to seek extra advice, Joadson goes back to Adams, who suggests the secret to winning the trial is to discover who the Africans are. Learning the language and employing the services of a translator,

Joadson and Baldwin set Cinque up in court to tell his heartrending story: sold into slavery by fellow Africans collaborating with Iberian slave traders, he was herded aboard the *Tecora* bound for Cuba. Cramped in subhuman conditions – because there was not enough food to survive the whole trip, fifty-odd slaves were thrown overboard – Cinque wound up aboard *La Amistad* at the mercy of Ruiz and Montez. With his story corroborated by a British naval officer, Coglin sets the Africans free, to much jubilation.

However the celebrations are curtailed as Van Buren orders a retrial in the Supreme Court. With Cinque not talking to Baldwin and resigned to his death, Baldwin implores Adams to represent the slaves' cause. Adams agrees and delivers a powerful address that sees the Africans released for good. As the Lombuko slave fortress is destroyed by the British, Cinque and the *Amistad* slaves set out on the voyage home.

BACKSTORY: Originally, Spielberg was going to segue from the fantasy of *The Lost World* to the history of *Saving Private Ryan*. Yet the decision to sandwich *Amistad* in between saw the realisation of a long-gestating project. Around the same time she was finished with the leg warmers of Lydia Grant in the TV version of *Fame*, the actress-producer Debbie Allen discovered two volumes of writings entitled *Amistad I* and *II* by African-American writers, historians and philosophers. Piqued by the slave-ship story, she optioned the rights to *Black Mutiny*, William Owens's historical account of the incident (in the closing credits of *Amistad*, this book is acknowledged as a major source of reference material). The project languished for just under a decade until she saw *Schindler's List* and took the project to Spielberg. After he had set up a half-hour meeting with Allen, Spielberg's inquisitiveness saw the discussion run to an hour and a half. He was hooked, partly because of conversations that were already taking place in the Spielberg family home.

'We were really talking to Theo [Spielberg's adopted black son] about slavery and where he came from and who his great grandparents might have been. So when I heard the story I immediately thought that this was something that I would be proud to make, simply to say to my son, "This is about you."'

Once Spielberg was on board *Amistad*, the job of fleshing history out into a 120-page screenplay fell to David Franzoni, best known as the writer of the HBO film *Citizen Cohn* (1992). Franzoni's drafts were subsequently polished by the *Schindler's List* adaptor Steve Zaillian before the film went before the camera.

Like *Schindler's List*, *Amistad* does not strictly conform to historical accuracy. The character of Theodore Joadson is a fictionalisation, a character designed to represent the influence of black abolitionists such as David Walker, James Pennington and Henry Highland Garnat. Moreover, one of the film's liberties with the truth involves the meeting between Adams and Cinque – they never actually met. But perhaps the most startling omission of historical fact that marks *Amistad* concerns Cinque's fate after he is released back to Africa. In the movie, a subtitle informs us that he returns to find his homeland in a state of civil war. In reality he became a slave trader. Surely such information would have added complexity to rather than diluted the drama.

ORIGINS: Unsurprisingly, very few American film-makers have tackled the spectre of slavery. DW Griffith's *Birth of a Nation* (1915) and various versions of *Uncle Tom's Cabin* (1910, 1914, 1927) presented slaves in a pernicious piece of stereotyping. Richard Flesicher's *Mandingo* (1975) depicted life on an 1840 Louisiana slave plantation in an equally risible manner – also see (or don't see) Peter Hunt's musical *1776* (1972). On TV, the eight-part dramatisation of Alex Haley's novel *Roots* (1977) did much to propel the issue of black servitude back into the national consciousness. Perhaps the film most pertinent to *Amistad* is Tay Garnett's *Slave Ship* (1937), an action adventure film that stars Wallace Beery as a ship's captain who has a slave mutiny on his hands. One of the only films to depict the Middle Passage, it shares with *Amistad* scenes of slaves being thrown overboard.

Yet *Amistad* probably owes more to the courtroom-drama genre than to any slavery film, in particular Stanley Kramer's *Inherit the Wind* (1960) – a re-enactment of the real-life events of a teacher tried for expounding Darwin's theories of evolution in a public school in a fundamentalist state – which influenced Spielberg in its use of structure. Elsewhere, Adams showing Cinque his African violet is perhaps a sly nod to the hothouse scene in *In the Heat of the Night* (1967), and the court where Adams makes his final oration recalls the pristine quality of John Ford's *The Sun Still Shines* (1953).

Visually, *Amistad* stems from a multiplicity of sources. Both Spielberg and his cinematographer, Janusz Kaminski, were drawn to the work of the Spanish artist Goya, particularly in relation to the film's foreboding prison scenes. Spielberg admits, 'That might be a little sacrilegious considering what the Africans went through at the hands of the Spanish in this film, but I thought Goya had a look – especially in his later work – that was darker and more brooding and I really liked his use of light.' A further inspiration came from another artistic style of the period, in particular a trend in painting known as *genre* painting, which offered iconographic images of American life of that time. Much of the colour and framing of *Amistad*, chiefly a kind of still-life tableau, related directly to these paintings.

CASTING: Travelling from the West African republic of Benin to France, Djimon Hounsou (pronounced 'Jye-mon Oon-soo') was homeless and destitute on the Paris streets until he was spotted by a fashion snapper – subsequent pictures led Hounsou to the superstar photographers Thierry Mugler and Herb Ritts and to catwalk stardom. Before *Amistad*, Hounsou had previously appeared before a moving camera only in pop videos (for Madonna, Paula Abdul, Steve Winwood) and in small parts in *Unlawful Entry* (1992) and *Stargate* (1994). His Cinque audition caught the eye of the casting director Victoria Lewis, who immediately forwarded the tape to Spielberg, who had already seen upward of 150 actors for the role. 'He was just my mind's eye of Cinque,' Spielberg stated. 'A man who was courageous, sympathetic, angry, yet vulnerable and dignified. Without that casting I would have had to postpone the film for at least a year.'

Perhaps indicative of the reverence Spielberg (and America in general) reserve for their leaders, both the American presidents are played by revered British character actors: Nigel Hawthorne brings a little of his absent-minded leadership from *The Madness of King George* (1994) to bare on Martin Van Buren while Anthony Hopkins, fresh from playing a shadier president in Oliver Stone's *Nixon* (1995), fully inhabits the role of John Quincy Adams. Initially playing Adams as an irascible old codger, Hopkins's delivery of the final address owes less to theatrical grandstanding and more to revealing a gentle, humbled eloquence – his delivery is almost musical.

Matthew McConaughey first heard of the *Amistad* story at lunch at Spielberg's house in the Hamptons. He believed he was there to talk about *Ryan*, but the conversation quickly turned to *Amistad* and McConaughey was immediately hooked. This was the second time McConaughey had played an enthusiastic lawyer fighting for the rights of a black defendant, the first being in *A Time To Kill* (1996).

The first actor to be brought on board *Amistad* was Morgan Freeman. Imbuing Theodore Joadson with the Zen-like presence displayed in *The Shawshank Redemption* (1994) and *Se7en* (1995), Freeman unfortunately has little dramatic meat to sink his teeth into.

PRODUCTION: With a stripped-down crew from the *The Lost World*, *Amistad* went before the cameras on 18 February 1997. Much of the film was shot on various locations around Newport, Rhode Island. Washington Square served for the setting of several of the courtroom scenes, whereas Newport mansions doubled for the palaces of Queen Isabella II and the chambers of President Van Buren.

Boston's State House became the House of Representatives circa 1839 and Mystic Seaport provided New Haven's harbour and waterfront area.

To capture actual footage at sea, the production moved to a 'floating city' off the San Pedro coastline for five days of filming. Only daytime exteriors were shot on the ocean: the completely realistic night-time boat footage saw an 85 per cent scale model constructed in a Van Nuys hangar while a hull section was constructed on Universal's Stage 12 – the location where the prison scenes had earlier been re-created. El Morro, a sixteenth-century Spanish fort, served as the slave factory of Lomboko and the Cuban slave market where the *Amistad* slaves were shot.

Due to the minuscule 48-day shooting schedule, Spielberg created a fast shooting pace that may well have been dictated by the abominable realities the production was creating. Most disturbing among these were the cold water poured over the African actors and the shackles that cast members were forced to wear during filming. 'They weren't fake movie chains,' noted Spielberg, 'they were the real thing. They hung heavy on the neck and created chafing, and you could understand how chains worn for months could create scarring for life. They had to carry this poundage with them and I think, more than anything else, that became the "time machine" that placed them at a time in 1997 that was no different from 1839.'

TICS OF THE TRADE: In many respects, *Amistad* represents a broader departure from Spielberg's visual style than *Schindler's List*. The biggest break from the regular Spielberg look was to radically restrict the number of elaborate camera moves. In fact there are only three dolly moves in the whole movie – two moves towards Adams, one into Cinque – the film-makers placing the action in a more proscenium style of framing.

'We wanted to keep things realistic and big camera moves can sometimes detract from the realism,' explained Kaminski. 'Steven wanted to challenge himself and I think it's much harder to create movement for a scene through the use of panning and tilting and blocking. When you're in a courtroom, you're watching and not moving. People move toward you and away from you, and it's very dramatic. We wanted the audience to feel as if they were observers in the courtroom.'

Although he may have denied himself his usual camera kineticism, Spielberg conjures up some indelible images, particularly in the opening slave insurrection. Spielberg plays out Cinque's escape from his shackles in extreme close-up – his eyes illuminated by lightning, rain dripping from his nose and lips – and finds a breathtaking low angle as Cinque pulls the sword out of his white-shirted victim. Spielberg echoes the composition at the end as Cinque examines his wrists, his chains now removed.

In visualising the story, Kaminski strove for an unromanticised realism but through completely different techniques from the handheld veracity of *Schindler*. Chief among these was a photographic process called ENR, used extensively by Darius Khondji, the lensman behind *Se7en*, *Evita* (1996) and *Alien Resurrection* (1997). ENR enhances the shadow areas and desaturates the colour. Compounding this colour-reduction process by adding smoke to many scenes and working hard in the printing process to reduce the warmth of the images – the glow given by candles in the film is white, not stereotypical Hollywood orange – *Amistad* has a cold muted look that subtly mirrors the despair of the story without resorting to cliché. Keen to avoid the chocolate-box pictorialism of most period films, Kaminski surrenders only once to obvious visual opulence: the splendour of the Spanish court is bathed in warm, beautiful tones, the romantic imagery contrasting sharply with the harsh look given to the *Amistad* defendants.

CLASSIC LINES:
Cinque: 'Give us free. Give us free. Give us free. Give us free. Give us free.'

Tappan: 'They may be of more value to our cause in death than in life.'

Cinque: 'What kind of a land is this where you almost mean what you say? Where laws almost work?'

John Quincy Adams: 'Do you understand what the Supreme Court is?'
Cinque: 'The place where they finally kill us.'

WHAT'S THE SCORE? With much of *Amistad* concerned with the dynamics of dialogue, John Williams must have struggled to make his music count. But, used sparingly, the score finds some latitude to delineate the drama. Williams utilises regional African vocal and instrumental elements with taste and intelligence, particularly in the haunting vocal that opens and closes the film, the combination of choral arrangement and percussion that drives the slave mutiny and the life-affirming anthem 'Dry Your Tears, Afrika'. Williams also creates a separate theme to represent John Quincy Adams, a trumpet-dominated ode to American values. Dividing the score into a USA-versus-Africa dynamic may seem a simplistic approach but it is highly effective in evoking geographical and cultural contrasts.

UNSUNG HERO: The production designer Rick Carter, who created a rich array of differing worlds – from the belly of a slave ship to the American seats of power via the court of Queen Isabella to a New England prison – with a limited budget (by Hollywood standards) to vivid effect. Obviously a big part of Carter's work was to get rid of any traces of the twentieth century from contemporary Newport – to dress the Washington Square exterior, storefronts were camouflaged, street lamps and parking meters were removed and 10,000 cubic feet of dirt covered the roads. Other technical challenges saw Carter simulate the rocking of the *Amistad*'s deck in the studio by a series of airbags that inflated and deflated, augmented by massive wave-generating dump tanks. Yet, working closely with the cinematographer Janusz Kaminski, Carter gave the story a real living, breathing texture, be it the foreboding of the prison interiors or the government buildings in Washington that have never looked so white. Perhaps the greatest compliment you can pay Carter's work is that, unlike those of most historical dramas, the sets of *Amistad* never call attention to themselves yet still contribute to the drama subliminally.

GEDDIT! Harry A Blackmun, who plays the US Supreme Court Justice Joseph Story, served as a US Supreme Court Justice from 1970 to 1994.

Credited as Jerry Molen, a frequent Spielberg producer, Gerald R Molen, plays the part of a magistrate.

The moment where Cinque moves off into the mist of the prison courtyard to show Baldwin how far he has travelled offers a visual reminder of Elliott approaching the barn in *E.T. The Extra-Terrestrial*.

FACTOID FRENZY: Spielberg was denied permission to shoot in the actual Supreme Court for Adams's final address, so the film-makers re-created an exact replica on a soundstage in Connecticut.

Ironically enough, 'Amistad' is the Spanish word for friendship.

Djimon Hounsou had originally learned all his dialogue in his native dialect, Goun. At the last minute, Spielberg asked him to relearn all the lines in Cinque's dialect Mende – just twelve days before the shoot.

For scenes set aboard *La Amistad*, the unit used two different historic schooners: Maryland's state ship, the *Pride of Baltimore II*, on the East Coast, and Californian's state ship, the *Californian*, off the coast of – surprise – California.

The lyric for the anthem 'Dry Your Tears, Afrika' come from a poem by Bernard Dadie, which accompanies the closing credits.

THE CRITICAL FACULTY: 'Of the great movies disrespected in their time, *Amistad* is among the most entertaining and the most conscientious . . . It's an insult to regard this new form of drama as a civics lesson (besides, what country could need it more?).' (Armond White, *Film Comment*.) 'The intent is admirable, the execution spotty . . . Although Morgan Freeman has a unique capacity for giving the illusion of depth to whatever role he takes, his part here is so ephemeral that a DreamWorks lawyer would have no trouble arguing it doesn't exist.' (J Hoberman, *Village Voice*.) 'Artistically solid if not always dramatically exciting.' (Todd McCarthy, *Variety*.)

BOX OFFICE: Receiving its world premiere in Washington, DC, on 4 December 1997, the film was not released to the public until the following week, 10 December. Released at the height of the awards season – the only time of the year serious movies may do well – *Amistad* earned $4 million in its first week with the total American gross reaching $44 million by 5 April. The film also earned an additional $16.2 million outside the US. Considering the difficult subject matter and lengthy running time, not a disastrous take but for a Spielberg film it was considered a flop. And the reason the film didn't find an audience according to its director? 'I kind of dried it out and it became too much of a history lesson.'

AWARDS: A prime contender for Oscars before the nominations were announced, *Amistad* was eventually nominated for four Academy Awards at the 1998 ceremony – Best Supporting Actor (Anthony Hopkins), Cinematography, Costume Design and the seemingly mandatory Music nomination for John Williams – yet didn't win anything. It did, however, win the Broadcast Film Critics Association Award for Hopkins's Best Supporting Actor turn, the BFCA also nominating the film for Best Picture. Stellan Skarsgaard won an Outstanding European Achievement in World Cinema award at the 1998 European Film Awards, but the citation was probably more for his work in Hollywood in general than *Amistad* in particular. At the Golden Globes, *Amistad* was nominated for Best Motion Picture (Drama), Best Director, Best Performance in a Motion Picture (Djimon Hounsou) and Best Performance by an Actor in a Supporting Role for Anthony Hopkins. It won zilch. John Williams's score was once again nominated for a Grammy.

THE SIZZLE! In November 1997, the renowned African-American author Barbara Chase-Riboud claimed that *Amistad* had stolen its treatment of history from her 1989 novel *Echo of Lions* and filed a $10 million lawsuit alleging infringement of copyright against DreamWorks. Unlike most lawsuits Spielberg faced, this was from a reputable source: author of the acclaimed novel *Sally Hemings* (which sold 3.5 million copies), Chase-Riboud, through her editor Jacqueline Kennedy Onassis, sent *Echo of Lions* to Amblin in 1988 as a potential movie but the yarn was rejected, deemed more suitable for a TV miniseries. Then her lawyers argued that *Amistad* pilfered the interpretation of events laid out in *Echo*, particularly the portrayal of Cinque as a proud, fierce defender of freedom and the character of Joadson, who, they argued, was based on a character from *Echo* called Braithwaite and named after a character called Judson. The thread of the contention suggested that the text cited as the film's inspiration, *Black Mutiny* by William Owens, was a reactionary account of the events that bore little resemblance to what eventually appeared on the screen. While the dispute threatened to delay the release of the film, Judge Audrey Collins failed to grant the injunction banning the film, DreamWorks lawyers accusing Chase-Riboud of plagiarism by citing 88 points of similarities between *Echo of Lions* and *Black Mutiny*. The injunction was lifted just two days before the film was to open.

JOIN THE DOTS: Kids – *The Sugarland Express, Jaws, Close Encounters of the Third Kind, 1941, E.T. The Extra-Terrestrial, Twilight Zone: The Movie, Indiana Jones and the Temple of Doom, The Color Purple, Empire of the Sun, Hook, Jurassic Park, Schindler's List, The Lost World: Jurassic Park*. **Kidnapped kids** – *The Sugarland Express, Close Encounters of the Third Kind, Indiana Jones and the Temple of Doom, Empire of the Sun, Hook, Schindler's List, Saving Private Ryan*. **Historical setting** – *1941, Raiders of the Lost Ark, Indiana Jones and the Temple of Doom, The Color Purple, Empire of the Sun, Schindler's List*. **Based on a book** – *Jaws, The Color Purple, Empire of the Sun, Hook, Jurassic Park, Schindler's List, The Lost World*. **Based on real-life events** – *The Sugarland Express, 1941, Empire of the Sun, Schindler's List*.

FINAL ANALYSIS: On its release, *Amistad* was manacled with *Schindler's List* analogies that were understandable, if invidious. From this vantage point, the further we get away from the earlier movie the more impressive *Amistad* looks. It seems an oddment in Spielberg's career, but the more you return to it, the more layers there are to peel away. Ignoring the suspense factor that is vital to most courtroom dramas, *Amistad* is alive to the political and cultural complexities of the case, rejecting glib notions of brotherhood in favour of an empathetic view of the outsider.

The biggest downfalls of the picture are that it occasionally feels dramatically inert – Spielberg's decision to relate the story through a series of tableaux does little to excite the interest – and that it relies too much on telling, not showing. However, when it does show, it is fantastic: the opening slave insurrection is charged and ferocious and the images of the Middle Passage – the scrabbling for food, the mother–baby drop overboard and the sight of slaves being dragged into the ocean tied to nets filled with rocks – are captured with a breathtaking brutality. There is also a cinematic intelligence coursing through the film that its critics rarely give it credit for: the President's recruitment of a new judge to the case is shown upside down through the lens of a camera recording the moment, a simple metaphor for the topsy-turvy principles that Van Buren embodies. It is a small moment but *Amistad* is rich in such detail. Perhaps the only thing lacking to make it truly memorable was some more passion.

SPIELBERG ON SPIELBERG: 'Listen, I got calls from relatives consoling me on the *Amistad* grosses on the second weekend. I got really nice calls the first weekend saying, "Gee, it did really good in so few theatres" and the second weekend it was "Gee, it did so poorly in so many more theatres." I said, "Hey, have you seen the movie yet?" "Uh, no."'

Saving Private Ryan (1998)

(Colour, 169 mins)

Studio DreamWorks, Paramount Amblin Entertainment Mutual Film
Producers Steven Spielberg, Ian Bryce, Mark Gordon, Gary Levinsohn
Co-producers Bonnie Curtis, Allison Lyon Segan
Written by Robert Rodat
Director of Photography Janusz Kaminski ASC
Production Design Tom Sanders
Film Editor Michael Kahn ACE
Music John Williams
Costume Design Joanna Johnston
Casting Denise Chamian
Associate Producer/Production Manager Mark Huffam
First Assistant Director Sergio Mimica-Gezzan
Second Assistant Director Adam Goodman
Art Directors Ricky Eyes, Tom Brown, Chris Seagers, Alan Tomkins
Sound Designer Gary Rydstrom
Special Effects Supervisor Neil Courbould
Sound Mixer Ronald Judkins
Stunt Co-ordinator Simon Crane
Supervising Art Director Daniel T Dorrance
Senior Military Supervisor Capt. Dale Dye USMC (ret.)
UK Casting Priscilla John

Supervising Sound Editor Richard Hymns
Camera Operators Mitch Dubin, Chris Haarhoff, Seamus Corcoran
Corpse and Animal Effects Supervisors Neil Gorton, Steve Painter
Prosthetics Supervisor Conor O'Sullivan
Key Make-up Artist Lois Burwell
Visual Effects Supervisor Stefen Fangmeier
Visual Effects Co-Supervisor Roger Guyett
Special Visual Effects by Industrial Light and Magic

CAST: Tom Hanks (*Captain Miller*), Tom Sizemore (*Sergeant Horvath*), Edward Burns (*Private Reiben*), Barry Pepper (*Private Jackson*), Adam Goldberg (*Private Mellish*), Vin Deisel (*Private Carparzo*), Giovanni Ribisi (*T/4 Medic Wade*), Jeremy Davies (*Corporal Upham*), Matt Damon (*Private Ryan*), Ted Danson (*Captain Hamill*), Paul Giamatti (*Sergeant Hill*), Dennis Farina (*Lieutenant Colonel Anderson*), Joerg Stadler (*Steamboat Willie*), Maximilian Martini (*Corporal Henderson*), Dylan Bruno (*Toynbe*), Daniel Cerqueira (*Weller*), Demetri Goritsas (*Parker*), Ian Porter (*Trask*), Gary Sefton (*Rice*), Julian Spencer (*Garrity*), Steve Griffin (*Wilson*), William Marsh (*Lyle*), Marc Cass (*Fallon*), Markus Napier (*Major Hoess*), Harve Presnell (*General Marshall*), Dale Dye, Bryan Cranston (*War Department Colonels*), Amanda Boxer (*Mrs Margaret Ryan*), Harrison Young (*Ryan as Old Man*), Kathleen Byron (*Old Mrs Ryan*), Rob Freeman (*Ryan's Son*), Thomas Gizbert (*Ryan's Grandson*).

BUDGET: $90 million

MPAA: R

BBFC: 15

TITLE SEQUENCE: The DreamWorks logo, its wistful, whimsical theme tune deemed inappropriate, leads us into white-on-black credits – the words 'Saving Private Ryan' are underlined for added dramatic emphasis – scored with military drumming and a solitary trumpet. Underneath the music, the sound of a flag blowing in the wind becomes more prominent, keying us into the opening image of the Stars and Stripes flapping in extreme close-up.

PLOT SUMMARY: Following a brief opening sequence in which an old man, accompanied by his family, breaks down in front of a grave in a war veterans' cemetery, Spielberg throws the audience head first into the most vividly realised, harrowing sequence of World War Two combat ever committed to celluloid. It's D-Day, 6 June 1944. Captain John Miller rides with his men into battle on the shores of Omaha

261

Beach. Disembarking on the beach, Miller watches his soldiers shot to pieces: gut-wrenching fragments of violence – a soldier looking for his severed arm, Miller dragging a body only to find the torso has been ripped from the legs – organised by frenzied, frenetic editing into a convulsing collage of conflict.

Yet, somehow, Miller and battle-hardened Sergeant Horvath move the unit up the beach inch by inch, and, with the sharpshooting skills of the God-fearing rifleman Private Jackson, take control of the foxholes and bunkers that have rained bullets down on them. As the battle subsides, the men take stock and souvenirs – Horvath collects sand in a tin marked France – while the camera surveys the bloodstained beach, picking out the corpse of one S Ryan.

Out of the carnage and confusion, a simple plotline emerges. At the behest of General George C Marshall, Miller and his outfit – Horvath, Jackson, the cynical wise guy Reiben, the sensitive medic Wade, the sentimental Carparzo, the defiantly Jewish Melish and the newly seconded interpreter Upham – are ordered to undertake an exercise of military PR: to locate and bring home a Private James Ryan, whose brothers Sean, Peter and Daniel have been killed in action and who is missing deep in enemy territory.

The unit's dubious feelings about the merits of the mission – why risk the lives of eight men just to save one? – are sharpened as Carparzo is killed trying to save the lives of some French children in a derelict village. After spending the night in a church, where the talk turns to Captain Miller's unknown background, the company strike lucky the following morning, finding a soldier who informs them that Ryan has joined a squad of soldiers holding a bridge at (the fictional village of) Remelle. En route Miller decides to ambush a machine-gun post – going against the unit's wishes – resulting in the death of Wade and the capture of a German soldier. Reiben threatens to desert after Upham persuades the captain to let the prisoner go, yet the mutiny is quelled by Miller's revelations of his life before the war: his personal view of the brutalising effects of combat and the mission as merely a ticket home strikes a chord with the rest of his troops, who agree to continue.

Approaching Remelle, Miller's unit get ready to open fire on a German half-track when their strike is pre-empted by a bazooka attack by a trio of US soldiers. One of them, it transpires, is Ryan, but, learning of this rescue mission, he decides to stay with his unit and defend the bridge. Initially flabbergasted and angry, Miller and his men decide to stay and help the beleaguered bridge babysitters.

German Panzer tanks arrive in the village and a feral battle begins. Jackson is blown from his belltower sniping position by a tank. Upham, paralysed by fear, is unable to save Melish from a brutal stabbing. The Americans are driven back across the bridge – Horvath is slain while crossing – yet are saved by a couple of P–51 Mustang fighters. As the tanks continue their advance, a wounded Miller blows up the bridge and dies by Ryan's side. As he looks at the man who saved his life, the image of the young Ryan morphs into the face of the old man at the veterans' cemetery at Miller's grave side, hoping his life has justified the tragic losses that made it possible.

BACKSTORY: Perhaps fondly recalling his homespun war flicks *Escape To Nowhere* and *Fighter Squadron*, Spielberg originally conceived *Saving Private Ryan* as a broader-based action-adventure movie. But, after he had heard the experiences of war veterans, the film became a much harder, realistic depiction of combat with a teasing moral quandary at its centre.

Ryan started life as a spec screenplay by Robert Rodat, best known as the writer behind the well-received children's film *Fly Away Home* (1996). Rodat's script was inspired in general by the reinterest in D-Day surrounding the fiftieth anniversary and in particular by a monument in his New Hampshire village that listed everybody from the hamlet who has been lost in war. Looking at the monument, Rodat noticed that every war contained repeated surnames of family members who had died in the same war.

Shifting his subsequent research from straight history books to first-person accounts of battle, Rodat fashioned a story that eschewed the big picture of military tactics to concentrate on the day-to-day dangers and scrabble for survival facing the regular soldier. The story ultimately drew heavy parallels with the true story of the Niland brothers documented in the historian Stephen Ambrose's book *Band of Brothers*. Later serving as adviser on *Ryan*, Ambrose documents the fate of three brothers who went missing in combat – two were killed on D-Day, a third was reported killed that same week in Burma but later turned up alive. After their mother received all three death-notification telegrams on the same day, a rescue mission (led by an army chaplain rather than a squad of soldiers) was set up to pull the fourth son, Frederick, out of the front line.

Rodat's screenwriting tour of duty encompassed eleven drafts for the producer Mark Gordon, who placed the script at Paramount. The interest of Hanks in the script in turn lured Spielberg (and DreamWorks) on board, and *Ryan* quickly became a happening project. Almost immediately, Spielberg's and Hanks's involvement saw revisions in the screenplay, as it was taken apart bit by bit. 'We talked about Ryan being dead,' Hanks recalled. 'We talked about Ryan being wounded and not being able to be moved. We talked about Ryan being an oaf, a boor, a guy we all hated. We talked about Ryan being the greatest, neatest, coolest guy we ever knew. We talked about getting Ryan and the adventure being about every conceivable thing.'

In Rodat's original conceptualisation of the story, Miller had died at the end but Paramount brass had felt uncomfortable with the idea, so Rodat produced a version where Miller survived. Early on in his collaboration with Rodat, Spielberg asked to see the writer's discarded ideas and scenes and immediately reinstated Miller's doomed fate to create an added poignancy. From this session, Spielberg also put back the notion of a bookend depicting the elderly Ryan visiting Miller's grave: the finished scene was in part informed by Spielberg's memory of a visit to the veterans' cemetery at Normandy during the promotional tour of *Duel* and witnessing a man collapsing in front of all the crosses and the Stars of David and being helped to his feet by his family.

Prior to shooting, Spielberg brought in two other writers to help pin down the script. Frank Darabont, the writer-director of *The Shawshank Redemption* (1994) and *The Green Mile* (1999), contributed two drafts, including the (not inconsiderable) addition of the Omaha beach assault to the start of the movie. The writer of *Out of Sight* (1998), Scott Frank, cleaned up the story while Rodat returned once the movie was shooting to incorporate Spielberg's improvisations. These included moments during the aborted rescue of the French children in the rain-sodden village, and Upham stricken by fear on a staircase as a German soldier straddles Melish and sinks a knife into his chest. Interestingly, the killer whispers something in German to Melish that is actually words of comfort, roughly translated as 'Don't struggle, I don't want this to hurt. Relax and let me kill you.' The words of compassion were infinitely more chilling than any sadistic *bon mots*.

ORIGINS: As much as it is a comment on war, *Saving Private Ryan* is also a comment on war movies, taking on the stock characters and plot conventions of the classic combat movie and imbuing them with much more ambiguity. Perhaps the closest to *Ryan* is Lewis Milestone's *A Walk in the Sun* (1945), in which a platoon of infantrymen are assigned to head inland from the beach and secure a farmhouse defended by the Germans. Milestone's evocation of the landing at Salerno echoes around *Ryan's* embarkation at Omaha, and the soldiers in both films display the same sense of desperate camaraderie.

A precursor of *Ryan's* story core, Lloyd Bacon's *The Fighting Sullivans* (1944), followed the lives of five brothers who were eventually killed serving on a cruiser, the *Juneau*. With the scenes of combat kept to a minimum, the film concentrates more on sunny childhoods and celebration of homespun values, really ending where *Ryan* picks up – the true story of the Sullivans is alluded to in *Ryan* as it is explained to General Marshall that the Ryan brothers were all split up because of the death of the Sullivans.

If perhaps somewhat dated now, a number of films prefigure Spielberg's depiction of the common foot soldier's view and a raw honesty in depicting the visceral impact of war. King Vidor's *The Big Parade* (1925), Lewis Milestone's *All Quiet on the Western Front* (1930) and Robert Aldrich's *Attack!* (1956) – Jack Palance getting his arm crushed by a tank would fit very comfortably in Spielberg's war – could all lay claim to be the *Private Ryan*s of their day. The portrait of a small band of soldiers forced to cohere into a fighting unit is central to Howard Hawks's *Air Force* (1943), John Ford's *They Were Expendable* (1945) and the films of Samuel Fuller such as *The Steel Helmet*, *Fixed Bayonets* (1951) and *The Big Red One* (1980). Two William Wellman pictures, *The Story of G.I. Joe* (1945) and *Battleground* (1949), have also been cited by Spielberg as huge influences: the latter's depiction of wounded men crying out for their mothers infused the harsh reality of *Ryan*. A further influence is Sydney Pollack's little-seen *Castle Keep* (1969), which sees Yank soldiers defend a tenth-century mansion filled with treasure. This impressed Spielberg with its mixture of black humour within the brutality.

From the final showdown at Remelle, Miller's desperate attempts to prime a detonator recalls a number of images from *The Bridge on the River Kwai* (1957), and the derelict locale suggests *A Bridge Too Far* (1977), but the biggest influence may come from Bernhard Wicki's *Die Brucke* (1959), which sees a group of young leaderless Germans wait in fear as the ominous rumbling of tanks grows increasingly near.

Visually, the biggest influence on *Private Ryan* was the eight black-and-white images shot by the war photojournalist Robert Capa, who accompanied the soldiers on D-Day and captured their every move as they diced with death on the beaches of Normandy. An error in the lab meant that only a handful of images survived but they remain a surreal, bleached-out testament to the bravery and brutality that marked 6 June 1944. This astonishing piece of reportage became the frame of reference for Spielberg and his cinematographer Janusz Kaminksi in shaping the savage sheen of *Ryan*. The camera work in the battle scenes was heavily influenced by the imagery in John Huston's documentary *The Battle of San Pietro* (1944): afraid of getting their heads blown off, Huston and his camera crew stuck very close to the ground, hence the images are dominated by grass and foliage in the foreground – a trick appropriated by Spielberg to connote combat conditions. Spielberg also borrowed the whip pans and the sense of always arriving late for an action to suggest that the action was unfolding before the lens rather than being preplanned.

CASTING: Although he appeared in the Amblin-produced *The Money Pit* (1986), *Big* (1988) and *Joe Versus the Volcano* (1990), scripted by Spielberg's sister Anne, it is perhaps surprising it took so long for Steven Spielberg to direct Tom Hanks. Establishing himself in broad comedy – see the above plus *Bachelor Party* (1984) and *Dragnet* (1987) – Hanks evolved during the 90s into a kind of Everyman, perhaps best typified by his performance as Jim Lovell in *Apollo 13* (1995) – like Captain Miller, a regular Joe leading a small group of men under extraordinary duress.

Giving a far more restrained performance that either of his Oscar turns in *Philadelphia* (1993) and *Forrest Gump* (1994), Hanks delineates a man trying to preserve his humanity while events surrounding him do their best to quash it, and this lends *Ryan* an unsentimental but moving centre.

Miller's right-hand man, Sergeant Horvath, was inhabited by the brutish presence of Tom Sizemore – Spielberg had probably spotted his no-nonsense machismo and mad-eyed stare in *Natural Born Killers* (1994) and *Heat* (1995). Matt Damon was uppermost in Spielberg's mind when the director was thinking of the small but pivotal role of Private Ryan after catching the actor in *Courage Under Fire* (1996), yet Spielberg was concerned that Damon was too skinny. Spielberg's doubts were put to rest after Robin Williams introduced (a more rounded) Damon on the set of *Good Will Hunting* (1997), and, two weeks later, Damon got the nod. In a note of serendipity that graces most Spielberg productions, *Good Will Hunting* subsequently projected Damon to stardom, adding a privileged golden-boy aura around his persona that was perfect for the character of Ryan. For the rest of the platoon, Spielberg found his grunts – Edward Burns, Adam Goldberg, Giovanni Ribisi, Barry Pepper, Vin Deisel, Jeremy Davies – in the ranks of American indie actors.

Foregoing a traditional rehearsal period, Spielberg put his actors through a six-day spell in boot camp to give a sense of the deprivations of combat. Their task master, Captain Dale Dye, a 22-year marine veteran who served in Vietnam and Beirut and started training actors for movies with *Platoon* (1986), put the actors through their paces with five-mile runs, weapons training, a unique brand of callisthenics entitled 'caterpillar push-ups' and 'atomic sit-ups' and sleep interruption. Dye dubbed the thespian platoon Turds, with Hanks earning the special privilege of Turd No. 1. (In the publicity blurbs surrounding *Ryan*, much was made of the group staging a mutiny, wanting to leave, but Hanks talking them into staying on.) In a clever ploy, Spielberg kept Damon away from boot camp as a method of engendering a resentment between the core platoon and the object of their mission.

PRODUCTION: *Saving Private Ryan* started shooting on 27 June 1997 on an eight-mile stretch of holiday beach at Curracloe in Wexford on the east coast of Ireland. Originally planning to stage the D-Day landings in England, the production switched locations to Ireland encouraged by favourable tax incentives, the likelihood of inclement weather – the conditions were overcast on 6 June 1944 – and by the refusal of the British Army to spare enough troops to act as extras. For three and a half weeks, Spielberg marshalled his principals, crew, 750 members of the Irish reserve forces – many of them had previously seen action as extras on *Braveheart* (1995) – in a re-creation of the Omaha beach slaughter. Subsequently, the production decamped to the abandoned aerospace facility at Hatfield to stage the search for Ryan in bombed-out villages, the French countryside and the rear-guard action at Remelle for a further ten weeks.

'A war is fought fast, and I really wanted to keep all the actors off balance,' said Spielberg, outlining his reasons for the fast pace of the shoot. 'I wanted to work fast enough so they always felt that they were in combat, they always felt as if they were under fire, they always felt as if they were in jeopardy.

TICS OF THE TRADE: Attempting to capture the chaos of combat in all its messy horror, Spielberg once again threw away the storyboards for *Private Ryan*. Instead, he took the unusual step (for any movie) of shooting the film in a rigid chronology. The continuity was particularly vital in building the terror and detail of the Omaha beach attack: going completely hand-held – usually with two cameras, occasionally as many as five – Spielberg (who operated a camera himself) averaged around three takes per shot, not letting the sequence fall into a formulaic set piece.

'We were attempting to put fear and chaos on film. If the lens got splattered with blood, I didn't say, "Oh, my God, the shot's ruined, we have to do it again." We just used it in the picture. Our camera was affected in the same way a combat cameraman's would be when an explosion or bullet hit happened.'

Shooting the film in a more lifelike 1:85 format rather than in the spectacle mode of widescreen, Spielberg and Kaminski used a diversity of strategies to render the feel of documentary footage shot in wartime. First, Kaminski had the protective strip removed from some of the lenses to make them function and react like lenses from the 40s, resulting in a foggy, hazy image that remained sharp. The next trick was to set the camera shutter at a 45- or 90-degree angle rather than the normal 180-degree. The effect meant that there was less blurring, more sharpness within the frame, creating a greater sense of urgency and reality: the technique was particularly effective in capturing flying sand particles blown into the air by explosions. Borrowing a technique used by the cameraman Doug Milsome in *Full Metal Jacket*, Kaminski also threw the camera shutter out of sync to create a streaking effect to run from the top to the bottom of the frame. The ploy was risky, for, if the effect didn't work, the footage would be unsalvageable, but it created some of *Ryan*'s most powerful, ghostly images.

To further increase the nausea, Kaminski also employed a device called an Image Shaker, which can be mounted on a hand-held camera to create a vibration effect that approximates to the impact of explosions on the camera. Initially used only sparingly in moments with explosions or tank movement, the Image Shaker material looked so great in the dailies (or rushes) that it became an effective tool in rendering the grunt's-eye view. Indeed, after the Americans have gained control of the beach, Spielberg returns to his more traditional dolly move into Captain Miller swigging from a canteen to signify that a form of equilibrium has returned.

It was Spielberg's idea to desaturate the colour some 60 per cent – although the red of blood is kept potent – enhanced by the ENR process that Kaminski first employed on *Amistad*. Compared with the bleached-out look of combat, the scenes set on the home front – in the War Department and at Mrs Ryan's home – have a warm, bright quality to further define what the soldiers are missing out on.

CLASSIC LINES:

Private Reiben: 'You want to explain the math of this to me? I mean, where's the sense in risking the lives of the eight of us to save one guy?'

Captain Miller: 'Anyone wanna answer that?'

Medic Wade: 'Hey, think about the poor bastard's mother.'

Private Reiben: 'Hey, Wade, I got a mother, you got a mother, the sarge has got a mother. I'm willing to bet that even the captain's got a mother. Well, maybe not the captain, but the rest of us have got mothers.'

Captain Miller: 'He better be worth it. He better go home and cure a disease, or invent a longer-lasting lightbulb.'

Captain Miller: 'Sometimes I wonder if I've changed so much, my wife is even gonna recognise me whenever it is I get back to her . . . and how I'll ever be able to . . . tell about days like today.

COMIC RELIEF: *Saving Private Ryan*'s smattering of humour is characterised by a streak of the absurd: chiefly the very funny vignette early on in which the group discover the wrong Private Ryan – this one's brothers are still in school – and Miller's grilling of a soldier whose hearing has been damage by a grenade going off by his head, so he just repeats Miller's questions about Ryan in a very loud voice.

Taking their cue from the *Willie and Joe* comic strips created by the cartoonist Bill Maudlin (the characters are referenced in *1941*), often the gags arise when the characters use dry observation to express the anger and disillusionment that comes with duty. This stunned worldview is most prevalent in the word 'FUBAR', the meaning of which is kept from Upham throughout the whole movie. If you don't want to know look away now – 'FUBAR' is an acronym for 'Fucked Up Beyond All Recognition'.

VISUAL EFFECTS: In realising Spielberg's vision of the chaos and confusion on Omaha beach, the special effects supervisor, Neil Courbould, and his forty-strong crew utilised a record number of over 17,000 squibs to represent the blitzkrieg of bullet hits. For large volleys of bullet hits, a network of pipes were laid under the sand (or water) pulsing out compressed air to disrupt the terrain. To capture graphic shots of soldiers losing limbs, twenty amputee stunt men were brought in and fitted with prosthetic limbs. The limbs would be separated from the performer by a breakaway joint section that was connected to a squib. The images of soldiers being blown through the air were achieved with the help of a fifty-ton crane, which hoisted the amputees into the air. They were able to release themselves from the wire and land on the beach, minus a limb.

To enhance the practical effects of explosions and bullets, Industrial Light and Magic were drafted in to tackle forty shots with challenges ranging from seemingly simplistic blood sprays to expansive scenes of the aftermath of the Normandy beach. For the opening Omaha beach assault numerous digital wounds were added to intensify the graphic nature of the scene without ever putting the actors at risk from explosive squibs.

ILM also added an afterthought dreamed up in the cutting room by Spielberg that is one of the film's most memorable images: the bullets travelling underwater that hit the soldiers flailing under the weight of their heavy equipment. Recalling *Jaws*' climactic moments in which Roy Scheider's bullets fizz past the shark – in actuality wax projectiles filled with Alka Seltzer to create added bubbles – *Ryan*'s digital bullets actually decelerate during their trajectory and are given extra verisimilitude by trails of bubbles.

SOUND EFFECTS: If the colours of *Private Ryan* are desaturated, the opposite approach is taken by the sound, which is as large and in the ear as possible, throwing the audience completely into the ferocity of D-Day: the hard waves crashing against the Higgins landing craft, the bluntness of explosions aeons away from the overegged fireballs of Bond movies and the cacophony of bullets and ricochets that rain down on the whole sequence. Particularly effective are the fizzing sounds that follow the bullets underwater. In search of perfection, the *Ryan* sound crew ensured they found the right German ammo for the sequence and recorded the bullets impacting into different surfaces: sand, dirt, mortar, a mess kit and, most bizarrely, half a slaughterhouse cow draped in a uniform to get exactly the right sound of bullets ripping through clothes into flesh.

On top of spot effects, the sound design of individual sequences also goes into overtime to key into subjective views of the white heat of combat: when Miller surveys the carnage that surrounds him, twice on Omaha beach, once at Remelle, the sound is sucked down to a muted din – a soldier screaming while looking for his severed arm sounds miles away, flames are denied their ferocious roar – creating the aural equivalent of shellshock. Each time, it takes the whistling and explosion of a shell to snap the sound (and Miller) back to the here and now.

WHAT'S THE SCORE? Not wanting to hype or sentimentalise the drama, *Saving Private Ryan* probably contains the least music of any Spielberg movie. Rather than score the (already kinetic) action set pieces, Williams fills in the emotional gaps during the reflective beats – the aftermath of Omaha beach, secretaries noticing the deaths of the Ryan boys, Miller's revelations about his world back home – creating a mournful trumpet and string backdrop to enrich moments of contemplation.The big theme comes in the form of 'Hymn to the Fallen', a dignified, powerful mixture of orchestra and choir that plays over the end credits.

CUT SCENES: Miller's speech revealing details about his life back home was much longer in the original script, yet Spielberg felt the character would not be so forthcoming in the situation, so slashed much of the dialogue.

UNSUNG HERO(ES): The camera operators Mitch Dubin, Chris Haarhoff and Seamus Corcoran, whose breathtaking work is a major reason *Ryan*'s battle scenes are so dynamic and terrifying. Wisely, Spielberg rejects the use of crane shots and overhead views, keeping the camera directly in the line of fire at all times. Unlike most hand-held camerawork that takes place at shoulder height, most of *Ryan*'s action was captured at ground level, following soldiers running very low to avoid getting hit by gunfire. 'We had three separate cameras rolling,' recalls Dubin of Miller's move up Omaha beach. 'I was following Tom Hanks as he ran. When we rolled, Steven called action, all hell broke loose. I just remember running for my life and following Tom. When we hit the shingle, we both looked at each other, astonished that we had actually run through this whole event. We did it in one take and moved on. The shot really set the tone for the rest of the film.' The camera is virtually a character in all of Spielberg's films but the perfectly accomplished hand-held work in *Ryan* goes one stage further: it is the leading player.

GEDDIT! The Edith Piaf song that the soldiers question the meaning of before the final battle is the one that the commandos of *The Dirty Dozen* (1967) question in their tents.

The tagline from *Schindler's List* – 'He who saves one life saves the world entire' – is equally applicable to *Saving Private Ryan*. Equally, Miller's description of P–51 Mustangs as 'angels on our shoulders' could have easily come from *Empire of the Sun*.

Dale Dye has a brief cameo as the War Department colonel who expresses doubts to Colonel Marshall that Ryan is still alive.

Ryan shares numerous connections to the sitcom *Friends*: Adam Goldberg and Giovanni Ribisi both played recurring characters on the show; Goldberg played Chandler's loony flatmate Eddie and Ribisi featured as Phoebe's half-brother Frank. Moreover, Edward Burns directed Jennifer Aniston in his second film, *She's the One* (1996).

The German soldier who is released by Miller is named Steamboat Willie in the credits due to his constant referencing of the Walt Disney cartoon. *Steamboat Willie* (1928) was the third cartoon to star Mickey Mouse and the first to feature sound.

FACTOID FRENZY: To gauge what the war veterans really thought of *Ryan*, Spielberg joined in various veterans' Internet discussions, hiding behind the anonymous alias of a curious teenager.

A point of clarification: the soldier who kills Melish is not Steamboat Willie, the German let go by Miller and co. Once liberated, Steamboat Willie is the soldier who later shoots Miller at Remelle and is subsequently killed by Upham. Spielberg cast two actors who looked alike, hoping to intensify the strain of confusion.

Saving Private Ryan started shooting on exactly the same day as *Star Wars: Episode I – The Phantom Menace* (1999).

When the historian Stephen Ambrose first saw the movie, he asked the projectionist to stop the screening during the Omaha beach scene so he could walk outside and compose himself.

The letter by Abraham Lincoln that General Marshall quotes is in fact wrong. Of Mrs Bixby's five sons, only two were dead.

THE CRITICAL FACULTY: '*Saving Private Ryan* is a brilliant commentary on a certain kind of war movie – those depicting a small unit with a job to do . . . a war film that, entirely aware of its genre's conventions, transcends them as it transcends the simplistic moralities that inform its predecessors to take the morally haunting high ground.' (Richard Schickel, *Time*.) 'Cast away the opening and climactic battles and you get two hours of war movie cliché as old as the crust on Audie Murphy's first pair of jockey shorts . . . If [Spielberg] wasn't so busy getting us to obey his directorial commands, he might realise that with realism comes yucky stuff like death and lots of it.' (Michael Anderson, *The Guide*.) '*Saving Private Ryan* is uncertain whether to be an endangered-patrol action movie or a futility of war action movie . . . The sadness is that so much misdirection exists in a film with so much incidental greatness.' (Nigel Andrews, *Financial Times*.)

BOX OFFICE: Opening on 26 July 1998, *Saving Private Ryan* grossed $30 million on its first weekend, going on to make $216 million domestically by the end of May 1999. The figure is all the more impressive when you consider the lengthy running time, the (unusual for Spielberg) R rating and the release date in the height of summer, when popcorn fluff usually holds sway. Outside America, the movie earned a further $224 million, creating a worldwide gross of $440 million.

AWARDS: Beating off the likes of John Madden, Roberto Benigni, Peter Weir and Terrence Malick, Steven Spielberg picked up his second Best Director Oscar for *Saving Private Ryan* at the Academy Awards ceremony held on 21 March 1999. Nominated for eleven awards, *Ryan* also picked up awards for Best Cinematography, Film Editing, Sound and Sound Effects Editing. Categories it lost out in were Best Actor (Tom Hanks), Art Direction/Set Decoration, Make-up, Original Dramatic Score and Screenplay Written Directly for the Screen. Yet the biggest upset of the night came when *Ryan* was pipped to the Best Picture award by *Shakespeare In Love* – as if to add insult to injury, the Academy enlisted Spielberg's compadre Harrison Ford to read out the results. Refusing to attend after-awards press conferences, Spielberg has never publicly commented on the defeat.

At the BAFTAs *Ryan* earned Best Sound and Special Effects awards, losing out in the categories of Best Picture, Director, Actor in a Leading Role (Hanks), Cinematography, Editing, Production Design, Music and Make-up/Hair. At the Golden Globes, the movie won Best

Picture and Best Director, with nominations for Original Score, Best Actor (Hanks) and Best Screenplay. John Williams won his compulsory Best Instrumental Composition Grammy. In awards decided on by the public, Spielberg won Best Director at the *Empire* Movie Magazine awards, Tom Hanks won Best Actor at the Blockbuster Entertainment Awards and, at the MTV Movie Awards, the film was nominated for Best Movie, Best Male Performer (Hanks again) and Best Action Sequence for the Omaha beach landing.

THE SIZZLE! On its release, *Ryan* became the subject of much criticism from veterans' groups in the UK for belittling the involvement of the British in D-Day, portraying the operation (and the war in general) as an American-only conflict. 'I think every country should tell stories about their own history,' was Spielberg's response. 'The British have certainly made some of the great stories about World War Two. I think that we are responsible for telling as much of what we know and who we are as possible. And we expect that of everyone else who has a story to tell.'

JOIN THE DOTS: Kids – *The Sugarland Express, Jaws, Close Encounters of the Third Kind, 1941, E.T. The Extra-Terrestrial, Twilight Zone: The Movie, Indiana Jones and the Temple of Doom, The Color Purple, Empire of the Sun, Hook, Jurassic Park, Schindler's List, The Lost World: Jurassic Park, Amistad.* **World War Two** – *1941, Raiders of the Lost Ark, Empire of the Sun, Indiana Jones and the Last Crusade, Schindler's List.* **Aircraft** – *Close Encounters of the Third Kind, 1941, Raiders of the Lost Ark, Indiana Jones and the Temple of Doom, Empire of the Sun, Indiana Jones and the Last Crusade, Always, Hook.* **Historical setting** – *1941, Raiders of the Lost Ark, Indiana Jones and the Temple of Doom, The Color Purple, Empire of the Sun, Schindler's List, Amistad.* **Based on real-life events** – *The Sugarland Express, 1941, Empire of the Sun, Schindler's List.*

SEND IN THE CLONES! With Spielberg and Tom Hanks serving as executive producers *Band of Brothers* (2001) is a TV miniseries adaptation of Stephen Ambrose's lauded book about the US involvement in the war in Europe, directed by Hanks, *Always'* cinematographer Mikael Salomon and Phil Alden Robinson. Maintaining *Ryan's* connection to *Friends*, David Schwimmer plays one of the soldiers.

As happened with *The Sugarland Express* and *Badlands*, *Saving Private Ryan* saw Spielberg once again go head to head with similar subject matter to Terrence Malick. A much more lyrical, spiritual depiction of the US in combat, *The Thin Red Line* (1998) centred on the conflict in Guadalcanal, juxtaposing the inner tumult of the soldiers with the lush beauty of the tropical paradise. Spielberg's version won the critical and commercial battle.

Stylistically, much of *Ryan*'s camera trickery to render combat more immediate heightened the Gulf War skirmishes of David O Russell's *Three Kings* (2000) and made Ridley Scott's *Gladiator* (2000) epic sword fights more immediate to a multiplex audience.

Craig Moss's *Saving Ryan's Privates* (1998) replays Spielberg's war epic as an eleven-minute porn flick. Played out to the score of *The American President* (1995), it sees a group of soldiers in a sortie to find their buddy's penis. A plethora of genital gags with a moving, er, climax.

FINAL ANALYSIS: Combining the critical respect of *Schindler's List* with box-office figures approaching the numbers of his blockbusters, *Saving Private Ryan* played a vital role in establishing the credibility and kudos of Spielberg's newly founded studio DreamWorks SKG. For his eighteenth feature film as a director, Spielberg found the risk-taking aesthetics and formal experimentation you might find in a first film and employed them to revitalise a genre – the World War Two men-on-a-mission picture – with a power, horror and honesty that renders hymns to gung-ho glory unthinkable in its trail.

Through sheer technical proficiency rather than an overreliance on prosthetic gore, Spielberg pulled off the astonishing trick of putting the audience in the front row of the theatre of war and, in so doing, he makes violence violent again. The movie may begin and end with the Stars and Stripes flapping in a whippy breeze but, far from serving as an icon of American patriotism and supremacy, the flag, desaturated of its primary colours and practically opaque, has never looked so robbed of its iconic fervour. Throughout the whole movie, Spielberg does the same thing to combat, stripping it of its brazen, stirring (cinematic) past and showing it how it truly is: not spectacle, just sickening.

Yet this is not the war-is-hell platitude that has been played across countless, particularly Vietnam, movies. The film is often criticised for being two fantastically realised battle sequences separated by a meandering walk through the country. The film does have faults – the bookends slightly distil the complexity – but the sortie to Remelle is where the heart of the movie lies. What the middle section of *Ryan* movingly demonstrates is that the real heroics of World War Two were not motorcycling out of a POW camp or even holding a bridge under attack but actually keeping your sanity, goodness and humanity intact – not only that acts of decency are possible in combat but that war can also *produce* moments of compassion and tenderness. Evolving from the comic-book depictions of war in *1941* and the *Indiana Jones* movies through the visual splendour of *Empire of the Sun*, Spielberg's version of warfare is sometimes surreal, sometimes unbearable (Melish's death), sometimes poignant (Wade rewriting Carparzo's letters home so they are not stained with blood), but always ambiguous: the plot poses many moral uncertainties but the director never proffers any answers.

SPIELBERG ON SPIELBERG: 'From an historical perspective, the Second World War seems pretty cut and dried, or black and white. But inside a war, and inside combat, it's technically chaotic and personally very chaotic and personally very contradictory. When we look back from the standpoint of history, we can say, "Oh yeah, World War Two clearly set the good and the bad apart from one another." But inside combat, the issue is never that clear. To the soldiers fighting the war, it can be very confusing.'

Work as a Producer

Spielberg's primary goal in becoming a producer was to give young talent a break, a remit that broadened when Amblin became a full production unit in 1984. Not only has the nature of Spielberg's involvement varied from project to project – from practically directing *Poltergeist* to a more *laisser faire* relationship with experienced directors – but so has the type of movie he has chosen to showcase. The early films represent the kind of films he might otherwise have directed, but this approach has widened to encompass diverse, even seemingly anti-Spielberg material. Films between 1984 and 1997 (e.g. *Men In Black*) come under the aegis of Amblin. From *The Peacemaker* (1997) onwards they fall under the DreamWorks SKG banner. Unless otherwise stated, Spielberg served as an executive producer. Directors are indicated in brackets.

I Wanna Hold Your Hand (Robert Zemeckis, 1978)

Spielberg's first outing as a producer came with Robert Zemeckis's ensemble comedy about the Beatles appearance on *The Ed Sullivan Show*. Although charming and exuberant, the film became the lowest-grossing film in the history of Universal.

Used Cars (Robert Zemeckis, 1980)

A black comedy about rival car dealerships. Shares a similar sense of delight in carnage with *1941*. It also bombed.

Continental Divide (Michael Apted, 1981)

A throwback to Tracy-Hepburn comedies, with a hardboiled journo (John Belushi) romantically sparring with a reclusive ornithologist (Blair Brown). The literate script brought *Raiders*' writer Lawrence Kasdan to Spielberg's attention, but Spielberg distanced himself from the uneven finished film.

Poltergeist (Tobe Hooper, 1982)

Released as a counterpoint to *E.T.*, Spielberg's unlikely collaboration with Hooper looks more like another chapter in Spielberg's cinematic autobiography than a horror flick from the director of *The Texas Chain Saw Massacre* (1974). As spectres enter a suburban house built on the sight of an Indian burial ground, and kidnap the daughter, *Poltergeist* follows a supernatural struggle between the parents (played by Craig T Nelson, JoBeth Williams) and the paranormal to win back the child, laced with shocks, scares and a soothing resolution.

Set in a typically suburban milieu full of *Star Wars* bedspreads and Sunday football, the screenplay, written by Spielberg in five days and honed by Michael Grais and Mark Victor, resonated with Spielberg's personal experience – a grinning clown doll, a potentially ominous oak tree, a crack in the bedroom wall were all in Spielberg's childhood. A twisted version of *Close Encounters* – as well as a return to the domesticated horrors of *Something Evil* – *Poltergeist* was subsequently imbued with countless of the director's concerns, including an abducted child at the centre of the plot, a strong mother figure emerging over a weak father, light as a source of mystery, horror, wonder and a relentless momentum in plot and effects. Such was the extent of Spielberg's involvement and his prominence in the film's publicity, that the question surrounding whether Spielberg was actually the director became a source of controversy on release. Feeling his contribution had been belittled, Hooper finally complained to the Director's Guild Of America when Spielberg's name appeared twice as big as his own in a trailer for the film. Spielberg responded by taking out a full page ad in the press thanking Hooper for his 'unique, creative relationship'.

Gremlins (Joe Dante, 1984)

Or 'E.T. with teeth'. Dante's flipside to Spielberg's universe takes much of what Spielberg holds dear – cute creatures, warm domestic environments, a sense of wonder – and twists it into comic subversion.

Fandango (Kevin Reynolds, 1985)

Five buddies undertake a road trip before adulthood and responsibility beckons. Spielberg was unhappy with the finished product, and removed his name from the credits, which is a shame as the film is an underrated gem of a comedy youth picture.

The Goonies (Richard Donner, 1985)

A pre-teen version of *Raiders*, in which a group of underprivileged kids try to save their homes by going in search of hidden treasure.

Back To The Future (Robert Zemeckis, 1985)

Rejected by every major studio in Hollywood, this hugely successful time-travelling comedy, in which a teen (Michael J Fox) returns to the 50s to make sure his parents fall in love, touches base with many distinctly Spielbergian themes and qualities: suburbia; adolescence; a dysfunctional family; the recapturing of a lost innocence – all wrapped up in a beautifully structured fantasy package that uses effects to enhance rather than overwhelm the plot, and culminating with a huge emotional punch. Indeed, considering the impact of Spielberg's parents' divorce, it is surprising that the sense of autobiographical wish fulfilment inherent in the premise did not emanate from him but with director Zemeckis and writing partner Bob Gale. Spielberg's primary input into the project was insisting on changing lead actor Eric Stoltz to Michael J Fox (the original choice) *after* shooting was underway because Stoltz was too intense.

Young Sherlock Holmes (Barry Levinson, 1985)

As per the title. Sections of it involve cult rituals very reminiscent of *Temple Of Doom*.

The Money Pit (Richard Benjamin, 1986)

An 80s take on *Mr Blandings Buys His Dream House*. Lots of elaborate pratfalls that never really come off.

An American Tail (Don Bluth, 1986)

Animated adventures of a Jewish immigrant mouse coming to

America. The lead character, Fievel, is named after Spielberg's grandfather.

* batteries not included (Matthew Robbins, 1987)

A group of aliens rejuvenate a New York tenement. Crossing elements of *Close Encounters*, *E.T.* and 'Kick The Can', this is a pale imitation of Spielbergian interests.

Innerspace (Joe Dante, 1987)

Comedic high tech re-spin of *Fantastic Voyage*. Unpretentious and hugely enjoyable.

Who Framed Roger Rabbit? (Robert Zemeckis, 1988)

A sublime blend of disparate genres (cartoon, murder mystery, movieland comedy) which created 'toon characters that are the equal of the golden age of animation. The perfect vehicle for Spielberg's love of cartoon culture.

The Land Before Time (Don Bluth, 1988)

Cute animated dinosaur fable. Played with familiar Spielberg themes of a youngster searching for his home and family.

Tummy Trouble (Frank Marshall, Rob Minkoff, 1989)

Fun Roger Rabbit short cartoon starring Roger, Jessica Rabbit and Baby Herman in hospital high jinks after Herman swallows his rattle.

Back To The Future Part II (Robert Zemeckis, 1989)

Risk-taking sequel that set up dark alternate realities and revisited the original film. Fast, frenetic but not always fun.

Dad (Gary David Goldberg, 1990)

Mawkish father–son melodrama. Spielberg did it better in *Last Crusade*.

Dreams (Akira Kurosawa, 1990)

Spielberg 'presented' this portmanteau picture for Japan's greatest director. Scorsese starred in one episode as Van Gogh.

Back To The Future III (Robert Zemeckis, 1990)

A Western-set end to the trilogy. Much more exuberant, entertaining and winning than the sequel but not as good as the original.

Gremlins 2: The New Batch (Joe Dante, 1990)

The gremlins hit the big apple in a follow-up that outdoes its predecessor in sight gags, in-jokes and dark subversive comedy.

Arachnophobia (Frank Marshall, 1990)

Giant spiders invade small-town America. A very Spielberg mix of PG scares and laughs but without his finesse or depth.

Roller Coaster Rabbit (Frank Marshall, Rob Minkoff, 1990)

A further short outing for Roger and the gang, this time causing mayhem in an amusement park.

Joe Versus The Volcano (John Patrick Shanley, 1990)

Curio black comedy. Collector's item for boasting the first pairing of America's favourite couple, Tom Hanks and Meg Ryan.

An American Tail: Fievel Goes West (Phil Nibbelink, Simon Wells, 1991)

A bit like *Back To The Future III* with animated mice.

We're Back! A Dinosaur Story (Phil Nibbelink, Simon Wells, Dick Zondag, Ralph Zondag, 1993)

More animated prehistoric adventures aimed at kids too young to see *Jurassic*.

Trail Mix Up (Barry Cook, 1993)

The final Roger Rabbit short – with Roger saving Baby Herman in a saw mill.

I'm Mad (Rich Arons, Audu Paden, Dave Marshall, 1994)

Animaniacs short.

The Flintstones (Brian Levant, 1994)

Poor big-budget live-action reworking of stone-age sitcom. Spielberg credited as Steven Spielrock. Ho ho.

Casper (Brad Siberling, 1995)

Great CGI brings the friendly ghost vividly to life but lacks the Spielberg touch to lift it out of the ordinary. Does touch on the theme of absent parents.

Balto (Simon Wells, 1995)

This story of a heroic half dog-half wolf begins in live action then segues to animation. Bland and sentimental.

Twister (Jan De Bont, 1996)

Effective blockbuster about scientists tracking tornadoes. Fulfils the Spielbergian appetite for destruction, spectacle and clouds that bubble.

Men In Black (Barry Sonnenfeld, 1997)

Massively successful sci-fi comedy which takes a more irreverent look at alien life than is the Spielberg norm.

The Mask Of Zorro (Martin Campbell, 1998)

Lively remake of the serial favourite. Shares much of the same spirit as *Raiders*. Spielberg recommended Zeta-Jones for the female lead and devised much of the action himself.

The Last Days (James Moll, 1998)

Riveting documentary about the last days of the Final Solution in Hungary.

A Holocaust Szemei (Janos Szasz, 2000)

A.k.a. *Eyes Of The Holocaust*, a further documentary remembrance of the Final Solution.

Jurassic Park III (2001)

See **Send In The Clones!** entry for *The Lost World: Jurassic Park*.

Spielberg also acted as uncredited Executive Producer on the following films:
Fandango (Kevin Reynolds, 1985), *Harry And The Hendersons* (William Dear, 1988), *Cape Fear* (Martin Scorsese, 1991), *Noises Off* (Peter Bogdanovich, 1992), *A Far Off Place* (Mikael Salomon, 1993), *A Dangerous Woman* (Stephen Gylenhall, 1993), *Little Giants* (Duwayne Dunham, 1994), *The Little Rascals* (Penelope Spheeris, 1994), *The Bridges Of Madison County* (Clint Eastwood, 1995), *How*

To Make An American Quilt (Jocelyn Moorhouse, 1995), *To Wong Foo, Thanks For Everything, Julie Newmar* (Beeban Kidron, 1995), *The Trigger Effect* (David Koepp, 1996), *The Peacemaker* (Mimi Leder, 1997), *Mouse Hunt* (Gore Verbinski, 1997), *Paulie* (John Roberts, 1998), *Deep Impact* (Mimi Leder, 1998), *Small Soldiers* (Joe Dante, 1998), *Antz* (Eric Darnell, Tim Johnson, 1998), *The Prince Of Egypt* (Brenda Chapman, Steve Hickner, Simon Wells, 1998), *In Dreams* (Neil Jordan, 1998), *Forces Of Nature* (Bronwen Hughes, 1999), *The Love Letter* (Peter Ho-sun Chan, 1999), *The Haunting* (Jan De Bont, 1999), *American Beauty*, (Sam Mendes, 1999), *Galaxy Quest* (Dean Parisot, 2000), *The Road To El Dorado* (Don Paul, Eric Bergeron, 2000), *The Flinstones In Viva Las Vegas* (Brian Levant, 2000), *Gladiator* (Ridley Scott, 2000), *Road Trip* (Todd Phillips, 2000), *Small Time Crooks* (Woody Allen, 2000), *Chicken Run* (Nick Park, Peter Lord, 2000), *What Lies Beneath* (Robert Zemeckis, 2000), *Lucky Numbers* (Nora Ephron, 2000), *Almost Famous* (Cameron Crowe, 2000), *The Contender* (Rod Lurie, 2000), *Meet The Parents* (Jay Roach, 2000), *The Legend Of Bagger Vance* (Robert Redford, 2000), *An Everlasting Piece* (Barry Levinson 2000), *Walk The Talk* (Shirley Barrett, 2000), *Ash* (Katsuhiro Otomo, 2000), *Evolution* (Ivan Reitman, 2001), *Straight Man* (Brad Siberling, 2000).

Spielberg also acted as a sponsor on Brian De Palma's *Home Movies* (1980) and Jon Blair's *Anne Frank Remembered* (1996); the latter won an Academy Award in the Best Feature Length Documentary category.

TV

Despite having his roots in the medium, Spielberg has struggled to cross over his Midas touch with film on to the small screen. Again unless otherwise stated, Spielberg served as an executive producer. U indicates that he was uncredited.
Amazing Stories (1985), *Tiny Toon Adventures* (1990), *Back To The Future: The Animated Series* (1991) U, *A Wish For Wings That Work* (1991), *Fievel's American Tails* (1991) U, *The Water Engine* (1992), *The Habitation Of Dragons* (1993) U, *The Heart Of Justice* (1993) U, *The Plucky Ducky Show* (1993) U, *Class Of '61* (1993), *Animaniacs* (1993), *Family Dog* (1993), *The American Clock* (1993) U, *SeaQuest DSV* (1993), *ER* (1994), *Earth 2* (1994) U, *Freakazoid* (1995), *Tiny Toon Adventures: Night Ghoulery* (1995), *Pinky And The Brain* (1995), *Fudge* (1995) U, *SeaQuest DSV 2032* (1995) U, *Survivors Of The Holocaust* (1996), *Survivors Of The Shoah Visual History Foundation* (1996), *Dear Diary* (1996) U, *High*

Incident (1996) **U**, *Spin City* (1996) **U**, *Ink* (1996) **U**, *Champs* (1996) **U**, *Majority Rules* (1996) **U**, *Toonsylvania* (1998), *Pinky, Elmyra And The Brain* (1998), *Invasion America* (1999) **U**, *It's Like, You Know* (1999) **U**, *Freaks And Geeks* (1999) **U**, *The Others* (2000) **U**, *Battery Park* (2000) **U**, *Anne Frank: The Whole Story* (2001), *Band Of Brothers* (2001).

Work as an Actor

The following is a list of Spielberg's rare forays in front of the camera. Appearances in fictional work only.

Journey To The Unknown (1960)

Spielberg received third billing as 'Spaceship Mechanic Ray Gammar'.

Duel

Spielberg can be briefly glimpsed in the rear-view mirror – big screen version only.

Something Evil

Dubbing mixer: delivers his one line – 'Roll tape!' – adequately.

The Blues Brothers (1980)

The clerk who collects Jake and Elwood's loot. He also delivers the film's last line: 'And here is your receipt.'

Gremlins (1984)

Spielberg can be spotted on a motorised vehicle at the inventor's convention as Rand Pelzer (Hoyt Axton) calls his family on a pay phone.

Indiana Jones And The Temple Of Doom (1984)

A missionary lurking in the background as Indy boards Lao Che's plane.

Fame (1984)

Plays a film-maker who watches the gang put on a show entitled *The Monster That Devoured Las Vegas*.

Citizen Steve (1987)

A short film created by Amy Irving for Spielberg's birthday in 1987.

The Tracey Ullman Show (1989)

Plays himself. Sings 'It's A Small World After All'. Badly.

Hook (1991)

A baseman during the baseball match.

Tiny Toon Adventures (1990)

Voices himself in the episode 'Buster And Babs Go Hawaiian'.

Animaniacs (1993)

Uncredited voices.

Steven Spielberg's Director's Chair (1996)

A film-maker playing himself in his own 'how to make a movie' CD rom.

The Lost World: Jurassic Park (1996)

Reputed to be visible on the TV screen as the dinosaurs are transported back to Isla Sorna.

Men In Black (1997)

Spielberg is glimpsed on a video screen which is depicting aliens on Earth masquerading as humans.

Miscellany

Wagon Train (1957–1965)

Uncredited assistant editor.

Faces (1968)

Uncredited production assistant.

Ace Eli And Rodger Of the Skies (1972)

'Story By' – Spielberg's first professional screen credit. Directed by John Erman, the film shows Spielberg's early interest in distant father-figures and a fascination with flying.

Strokes Of Genius (1984)

Directed the introductory segments to this arts documentary series featuring host Dustin Hoffman.

The Goonies (1985)

Provided the story. Also directed uncredited second unit scenes.

Return To Oz (1985)

Uncredited assistant.

Poltergeist II: The Other Side (1986)

'Based On' story credit.

Poltergeist III (1988)

As above.

Lawrence Of Arabia (1989)

Spielberg co-funded and 'presented' the restoration of Lean's 1962 masterpiece.

Arachnophobia (1990)

Uncredited second unit director.

High Incident (1996)

Uncredited second unit director/camera operator.

The Haunting (1999)

Uncredited second unit director.

The Unfinished Journey (1999)

Spielberg directed this 26-minute documentary film to commemorate the turn of the century – envisaging mankind's past, present and future. Narrated by, among others, President Clinton it had one Gala screening in Washington on 31 December 1999.

Spielberg also receives a 'Special Thanks' credit on *The Locusts* (1997) and Janusz Kaminski's directorial debut *Lost Souls* (2000).

What Lies Beneath (2000)

Uncredited story idea.

Unseen Spielberg

The following is a list of projects that Spielberg was going to make/will make which have yet to see the light of day.

Slipstream

Wishing to break into the industry, Spielberg set out to make a movie on a professional 35mm format about high-speed cycle racers. Bankrolled by Spielberg's father (and various private investors) under the monicker Playmount Productions, *Slipstream* was scripted by Spielberg and buddy Roger Ernest, and was based on the exploits of Spielberg's friends growing up in Saratoga. Despite Spielberg capturing some reputedly great race footage, the film stopped production after funds ran out before the end of shooting.

Snow White

Based on a novella by Donald Barthelme, *Snow White* transplanted the fairy tale into the 60s with 'Snow White' dishing out erotic favours to her septet of house mates. A supposed satire on contemporary mores, it is surprising that Spielberg even considered directing such a risqué project.

Meet Me At The Melba

Spielberg was pursued by producer Allan Carr to direct a version of Bronte Woodward's novel *Meet Me At The Melba* which depicted life in the South during the '30s. Nothing ever came of it.

Dogfight Project

On first arriving in Hollywood, one of Spielberg's initial desires was to direct a WWII dogfight movie, co-authored by *Jaws*' Carl Gottlieb. Spielberg and Gottlieb also hawked around a comedy about life in the Catskills but to no avail.

Flushed With Pride: The Story Of Thomas Crapper

In between *The Sugarland Express* and *Jaws*, Spielberg asked Willard Huyck and Gloria Katz to write a screenplay based on the life of the inventor of the toilet. The mind boggles.

Untitled Pirate Movie

As a follow-up to *Close Encounters*, Spielberg had been developing a sixteenth century adventure yarn about a romantic *ménage à trois* involving a woman and two half-brothers, one an aristocrat, the other a peasant. Spielberg's interest in the project fizzled out.

12 Angry Men

Prior to *1941*, Spielberg considered directing a live TV broadcast of the classic courtroom drama first filmed by Sidney Lumet.

Worlds After

Little is known about this highly clandestine (sci-fi sounding) project announced prior to *Temple Of Doom*.

Reel To Reel

Just before *Raiders* went into production, Spielberg tried to convince Universal to make this backstage Hollywood musical written by Gary David Goldberg. The project died after Universal said no. Spielberg tried to revive it at Columbia with Michael Cimino directing, but to no avail. Other musical projects Spielberg tried to get off the ground include a street musical with Quincy Jones and rumours of big screen adaptations of *Miss Saigon* and *Cats*.

Night Skies

See entry on *E.T. The Extra-Terrestrial*.

After School

Around *E.T.* time, Spielberg was also developing a low-budget comedy with *1941*'s writers Robert Zemeckis and Bob Gale, variously called *After School* or *Growing Up*. The script was intended as a realistic look at LA kids and their rites and rituals between leaving school at three and going home at six, but basically took the form of a nerds versus jocks showdown. Initially drawn to its edgy feel, Spielberg subsequently decided the project was too hard hitting for his sensibilities and withdrew.

The Talisman

Universal bought the rights to the Stephen King/Peter Straub novel. However, as Spielberg dithered over a commitment, the studio lost interest.

Howard Hughes

Spielberg has long been developing a Bo Goldman screenplay about the aviation lover, movie producer and notorious recluse, with Warren Beatty as the oft-mentioned contender to take the title role.

Tintin

Throughout the '80s, a Spielberg version of Hergé's comic strip featuring the teen adventurer was on the cards. It failed to materialise.

Dr Who

Spielberg was said to be planning a feature film version of the BBC sci-fi stalwart with Eric Idle as the Timelord. Nothing ever came of it.

Charles Lindbergh

Spielberg was considering directing the life story of Lindbergh, the first man to fly nonstop from New York to Paris. It may still get made, but it is unlikely Spielberg will direct.

The 1798 Project

A project concerning the 1798 Irish rebellion against the British where 150,000 locals lost their lives. Seems to have been lost for good.

The Time Machine

In 1999, it was intimated that Spielberg would direct a new version of the HG Wells classic. Not yet he hasn't.

Indy IV

On the cards since *Last Crusade* was released, rumours of a fourth Indiana Jones resurface at regular intervals. The sticking points seem to be finding a window in Spielberg, Lucas and Ford's schedule and coming up with a script that everyone can agree on. To this end, M Night Shyamalan, writer-director of *The Sixth Sense* (1999), has been one of many writers linked to generating a new adventure.

Memoirs Of A Geisha

For a long time Spielberg was linked as the director of *Memoirs* based on Arthur Golden's novel. However, as his slate is so heavy, it seems that Columbia are now pressing for another film-maker. The production had already entered the design phase before Spielberg abandoned it to pursue other projects.

A.I. (2000)

Producers Bonnie Curtis, Kathleen Kennedy, Walter F Parkes
Executive Producer Steven Spielberg
Screenplay Steven Spielberg (Based on the short story 'Super-Toys Last All Summer Long')
Cinematography Janusz Kaminski
Editor Michael Kahn
Sound Designer/Sound Re-recording Mixer Gary Rydstrom
Visual Effects Supervisor Dennis Muren
Camera Operator (spacecam) Ron Goodman

CAST: Jude Law (*Gigolo Joe*), Haley Joel Osment (*David Swinton*), Frances O'Connor (*Monica Swinton*), Sam Robards (*Henry Swinton*), Robin WIlliams (*Narrator*).

A.I. started life as a long-cherished Stanley Kubrick project. An adaptation of Brian Aldiss's 1969 short story 'Super-Toys Last All Summer Long', the premise imagines an automated world where the greenhouse effect has melted the polar ice caps, thus submerging coastal cities in water. This automated future places a greater importance on robots, one of whom, a small boy David Swinton, desires to become human. Having met in London during the shooting of *The Shining* and *Raiders*, Kubrick and Spielberg communicated about the project for a number of years, with *Jurassic Park* playing a key role in convincing Kubrick that the character of a completely computer-generated robot was possible.

Following Kubrick's death in March 1999, with A.I. lined up to be the director's next film, Spielberg took over the project drafting a script from Kubrick's 80-page outline. Filming began on 17 August 2000 under watertight security and effects provided by the *Jurassic* combo of Stan Winston and ILM. Although some may bristle at the prospect of the king of commercialism reinventing Kubrick's vision, considering its resemblance to *Pinocchio* in sketch form, Spielberg's bold sense of emotionalism and epic sweep may be better suited to the project than Kubrick's cold, clinical approach.

Minority Report

The most likely contender to be the next Spielberg film after *A.I.* remains in the realm of science fiction. Based on a short story by Phillip K Dick, *Minority Report* is set in Washington DC in 2080 and is centred on the premise that police technology has developed to the point where a crime can be detected before it has been committed. The movie will star Tom Cruise as an officer of the Pre-Crimes Division who must prove his innocence when accused of committing a crime. A more cynical take on sci-fi than *Close Encounters*, *E.T.* and *A.I.*, the movie also marks Spielberg's first foray into a crime picture. Shooting is scheduled to start on 1 April 2001.

I'll Be Home

Written by Spielberg's sister Anne, *I'll Be Home* is a film based directly on his own family. The delay in realising the movie might have something to do with Spielberg working up the courage to be critical about his parents.

Big Fish

In September 2000, Spielberg purchased the rights to Daniel Wallace's novel about a kid who dreams up stories about his dying father. Yet, with such a busy schedule, it's unlikely Spielberg will get round to it until late 2001 at the earliest.

Index of Quotations

Amateur Films

6   'I remember knocking out a script . . .' Spielberg quoted in 'Filming The Fantastic: Steven Spielberg' by Steve Poster in *Starlog*, No. 17, October 17.

8   'One of the five . . .' Spielberg quoted in 'Hard Riders' by Paul D Zinneman, *Newsweek* April 8, 1974.

11   'A 24-minute [sic] short . . .' Atlanta Film Festival programme notes, 1969.

12   'I can't look at it now . . .' Spielberg quoted in 'Close Encounter With Steven Spielberg' by Mitch Tuchman in *Film Comment*, January-February 1978.

TV

14   'That show put me . . .' Spielberg quoted in *Steven Spielberg*, McBride.

23   'That was not intentional . . .' Spielberg quoted in *The Steven Spielberg Story*, Crawley.

24   'Mr Spielberg comes from . . .' Dylis Powell, *Sunday Times*, October 22, 1972.

24   'Film buffs will rightfully be . . .' Tony Scott, *Daily Variety*, November 12, 1971.

25   'Best TV movie of 1971 . . .' Cecil Smith, *Los Angeles Times*, November 8, 1971.

26   '*Duel* is an indictment . . .' Spielberg quoted in *The Steven Spielberg Story*, Crawley.

The Sugarland Express

35   'A high-speed chase . . .' report in 'New Bonnie 'n' Clyde' *Hollywood Citizen News*, May 2, 1969.

37   'I was thinking . . .' Richard Zanuck quoted in *New Yorker*, March 21, 1994.

42   'Spielberg could be that rarity . . .' Pauline Kael, 'Sugarland And Badlands', *New Yorker*, March 18, 1974.

42   'The arrival of an extraordinarily . . .' Paul D Zimmerman, 'Hard Riders', *Newsweek* April 8, 1974.

42   'One is apt to fear . . .' Dilys Powell, 'Westerns On Wheels', *The Times*, June 16, 1974.

42   'A prime example of the new style . . .' Stephen Farber, 'Something Sour', *New York Times*, April 28, 1974.

44   'It's a terrible indictment . . .' Steven Spielberg quoted in 'At Sea With Steven Spielberg' by David Helpern in *Take One*, March/April, 1974.

Jaws

52   'Bruce's eyes crossed . . .' Brian De Palma quoted in 'Summer Of The Shark' by John Charney and Doug Mirrell in *Time* Magazine, June 25, 1975.

53   'Instinctual, relentless, unstoppable . . .' John Williams quoted in *Jaws*, Andrews.

54   'That's when I knew . . .' Spielberg, *ibid*.

55   'A coarsegrained and exploitative work . . .' Charles Champlin, *Los Angeles Times*, *ibid*.

56   'The ads show a gaping shark's mouth . . .' Stanley Kauffman, New Review, quoted in *The Critics Film Guide*, Tookey.

56   'I discerned a tendency to cheer . . .' Dilys Powell, *Sunday Times*, quoted in *Jaws*, Andrews.

56   'A thriller of an exactly . . .' David Robinson, *The Times*, *ibid*

Close Encounters Of The Third Kind

1941

Raiders Of The Lost Ark

E.T. The Extra Terrestrial

120 'Watching this vibrantly comic . . .' Michael Sragow, 'Extra-Terrestrial Perception', *Rolling Stone*, July 8, 1982.

120 'A triumph almost beyond imagining . . .' Kenneth Turan, quoted in *Steven Spielberg: Father Of The Man*, Yule.

120 'A dream of a movie . . .' Pauline Kael, *New Yorker*, June 14, 1982.

120 'The best Disney movie . . .' *Variety*, quoted in *The Critics Film Guide*, Tookey.

120 'E.T. is as contemporary as a laser beam . . .' Vincent Canby, *New York Times*, June 11, 1982.

120 'A fabulous masterpiece . . .' Rex Reed, *New York Daily News*, ibid.

120 'One of the most beautiful fantasy . . .' David Denby, *New York Magazine*, ibid.

120 'A miracle movie . . .' Richard Corliss, 'Steve's Summer Magic', *Time*, May 31, 1982.

124 'When I started E.T . . .' Spielberg quoted in 'A Conversation With Steven Spielberg' by Michael Sragow in *Rolling Stone*, July 12, 1982.

Twilight Zone: The Movie

127 'You're provoked into a lot of thought . . .' George Clayton Johnson quoted in *The Twilight Zone Companion* by Marc Scott Zicree, Bantam, New York, 1989.

130 'Rod's stories were about . . .' Carol Serling, quoted in *Steve Spielberg*, Baxter.

130 'A lump of ironclad whimsy . . .' Pauline Kael, *New Yorker*, quoted in *The Films Of Steven Spielberg*, Brode.

130 '"Kick The Can" is lugubrious self-parody . . .' J Hoberman, 'Zoned Again', *The Village Voice*, July 5, 1983.

130 'The theme is echt-Spielberg . . .' David Ansen, 'Twilight's Last Gleaming', *Newsweek*, June 27, 1983.

132 'A movie is a fantasy . . .' Spielberg quoted in 'Spielberg Philosophical Over E.T. Oscar Defeat' by Dale Pollock in *Los Angeles Times*, April 13, 1983.

Indiana Jones And The Temple Of Doom

138 'In many ways, the visual style of the film . . .' Spielberg quoted in 'Steven Spielberg On Indiana Jones And The Temple Of Doom' by Merry Elkins in *American Cinematographer*, July 1984.

141 'This is brilliance that rides . . .' Richard Corliss, 'Keeping The Customer Satisfied' *Time*, May 26, 1984.

141 'One of the most sheerly . . .' Pauline Kael, *New Yorker*, quoted in *The Critics Film Guide*, Tookey.

141 'Spielberg has gone to such great lengths . . .' Jack Kroll, *Newsweek*, ibid.

141 'That Spielberg should devote himself . . .' David Denby, *New Yorker*, quoted in *The Films Of Steven Spielberg*, Brode.

141 'The most cheerfully exciting, bizarre . . .' Roger Ebert, *Chicago Sun Times*, quoted in The Critics Film Guide, Tookey.

141 'A two hour series of . . .' Derek Malcolm, *Guardian*, ibid.

143 'The picture is not called the Temple of Roses . . .' Spielberg quoted in *Steven Spielberg*, Taylor.

The Color Purple

146 'If she'd presented it to me . . .' Spielberg quoted in 'Spielberg Films The Color Purple', by Glen Collins in *New York Times*, December 15, 1985.

146 'It was an artistic decision . . .' *ibid*.

151 'annoyed at first that brothers wrote it . . .' Alice Walker quoted on the liner notes of *The Color Purple* soundtrack, Warner Bros inc. (925 389–1).

Empire Of The Sun

Indiana Jones And The Last Crusade

Amistad

252 'We were really talking . . .' Steven Spielberg quoted in 'Steven The Good' by Stephen J Dubner in the *New York Times Magazine*, February 14 1999.

253 'That might be a little . . .' Spielberg quoted in the *Amistad* press notes, December 1997.

254 'He was just my mind's eye . . .' Spielberg quoted in 'Incredible Journey' by David Gritten in the *Sunday Telegraph Weekend Magazine*, February 21.

255 'They weren't . . .' Spielberg quoted in the *Amistad* press notes, December 1997.

255 'We wanted to keep . . .' Janusz Kaminski quoted in 'Breaking Slavery's Chains' by Stephen Pizzello in *American Cinematographer*, January 1998.

257 'Of the great movies disrespected . . .' Armond White, 'Against The Hollywood Grain', *Film Comment*, Vol. 34, No. 2, March/April 1998.

258 'The intent is admirable . . .' J Hoberman, 'Sins Of The Fathers', *Village Voice*, December 16, 1997.

258 'Artistically solid . . .' Emmanuel Levy, *Variety*, December 8, 1997.

258 'I kind of dried it out . . .' Spielberg quoted in 'Steven The Good' by Stephen J Dubner in the *New York Times Magazine*, February 14, 1999.

260 'Listen I got calls . . .' Spielberg quoted in 'Crossroads: Steven Spielberg' by Kenneth Turan in the *Los Angeles Times*, December 28, 1998.

Saving Private Ryan

263 'We talked about Ryan . . .' Tom Hanks interviewed in 'Message In A Battle' by Jeff Gordiner in *Entertainment Weekly*, July 24, 1998.

267 'A war is fought fast . . .' Spielberg interviewed in 'Five Star General' by Stephen Pizzello in *American Cinematographer*, August 1998.

267 'We were attempting to . . .' Spielberg, *ibid*.

271 'We had three separate cameras . . .' Mitch Dubin interviewed in 'The Last Great War' by Christopher Probst, *American Cinematographer*, August, 1998

272 '*Saving Private Ryan* is a brilliant commentary . . .' Richard Schickel, 'Reel War,' *Time*, July 27, 1998.

272 'Cast away the opening . . .' Michael Atkinson, *The Guide*, September 11, 1998.

272 '*Saving Private Ryan* . . .' Nigel Andrews, *Financial Times*, September 10, 1998.

273 'I think every country should . . .' interviewed on *War Stories,* by Mark Cousins on September 13, 1998.

275 'From an historical perspective . . .' Spielberg interviewed in 'Five Star General' by Stephen Pizzello in *American Cinematographer*, August 1998.

Bibliography

Andrews, Nigel. *Bloomsbury Movie Guide No. 5: Jaws*, London, Bloomsbury, 1999.

Balaban, Bob. *Close Encounters Of The Third Kind Diary*, New York, Paradise Press, 1978.

Ballard, JG. *Empire Of The Sun*, London, Panther Books, 1985.

Baxter, John. *Steven Spielberg The Unauthorised Biography*, London, HarperCollins, 1996.

Benchley, Peter. *Jaws*, London, Pan Books, 1975.

Biskind, Peter. *Easy Riders, Raging Bulls*. London, Bloomsbury, 1998.

Black, Campbell. *Raiders Of The Lost Ark*, London, Corgi, 1981.

Bouzereau, Laurent. *The Cutting Room Floor*, New York, Citadel Press, 1984.

Brode, Douglas. *The Films Of Steven Spielberg*, New York, Citadel, 1995.

Brooks, Terry. *Hook*, New York, Ballantine Books, 1991.

Crawley, Tony. *The Steven Spielberg Story*, London Zomba Books, 1983.

Crichton, Michael. *Jurassic Park*, London, Arrow, 1991. *The Lost World*, London, Arrow, 1995.

Duncan, Jody. *The Making Of The Lost World*, New York, Ballantine Books, 1997.

Erickson Glenn & Trainor, Mary Ellen. *The Making Of 1941*, New York, Ballantine Books.

Friedman, Lester D & Notbohm, Brent. *Steven Spielberg Interviews*, Mississippi, University Press Of Mississippi, 2000.

Gale, Bob. *1941*, London, Arrow Books, 1979.

Gottlieb, Carl. *The Jaws Log*, London, Tandem Publishing, 1975.

Hughes, David. *The Complete Kubrick*, London, Virgin, 2000.

Jackson, Kevin. *Schrader On Schrader & Other Writings*, London, Faber and Faber, 1991.

Kahn, James. *Indiana Jones And The Temple Of Doom*, London, Sphere Books, 1984.

Kasdan, Lawrence. *Raiders Of The Lost Ark The Illustrated Screenplay*, New York, Ballantine Books, 1981.

Katz, Ephraim. *The Macmillan International Film Encyclopaedia*, London, HarperCollins, 2000.

Keneally, Thomas. *Schindler's Ark*, London, Hodder and Stoughton, 1982.

Kotzwinkle, William. *E.T. The Extra-Terrestrial*, London, Sphere Books, 1982.

McBride, Joseph. *Steven Spielberg*, New York, Simon & Schuster, 1997.

MacGregor, Rob, *Indiana Jones And The Last Crusade*, London, Sphere, 1989.

Martyn, Warren & Wood, Adrian. *I Can't Believe It's A Bigger And Better Updated Unofficial Simpson's Guide*, London, Virgin, 2000.

Monaco, James. *American Film Now*, New York, Oxford University Press, 1979.

Mott, Donald R. & McAllister Saunders, Cheryl. *Steven Spielberg*, Kent, Columbus, 1986.

Palowski, Franciszek. *Witness, The Making Of Schindler's List*, London, Orion Media, 1998.

Phillips, Julia. *Skywalking: The Life and Times of George Lucas*, Elm Tree, 1983.

Pollack, Dale. *Skywalking: The Life and Times of George Lucas*, Elm Tree, 1983.

Pye, Michael & Myles Lynda. *The Movie Brats*, London, Faber and Faber, 1979.

Sellers, Robert. *Harrison Ford A Biography*, London, Robert Hale, 1993.

Shay, Don & Duncan, Jody. *The Making Of Jurassic Park*, New York, Ballantine Books, 1993.

Bibliography

Sinyard, Neil. *The Films Of Steven Spielberg*, London, Hamlyn, 1987.
Slade, Darren & Watson Nigel, *Supernatural Spielberg*, London, Valis Books, 1992.
Spielberg, Steven. *Close Encounters Of The Third Kind*, London, Sphere, 1978.
Taylor, Derek. *The Making Of Raiders Of The Lost Ark*, New York, Ballantine Books, 1981.
Taylor, Phillip M. *Steven Spielberg*, London, Batsford, 1992.
Tookey, Christopher. *The Critics Film Guide*, London, Boxtree, 1994.
Walker, Alice. *The Color Purple*, London, The Woman's Press Ltd.
Yule, Andrew. *Steven Spielberg: Father Of The Man*, London, Little, Brown and Company, 1996.

Picture Credits

All pictures are courtesy of The Ronald Grant Archive, with the following exceptions:

Page 3:   *Raiders of the Lost Ark* – courtesy of The Kobal Collection
Page 4:   *E.T.* (top) – courtesy of the British Film Institute
Page 5:   *Empire of the Sun* – courtesy of The Kobal Collection
Page 8:   *Schindler's List* (both) – author's own

Index

THE MINISTER'S

KT-433-594

THE
MINISTER'S CAT

COMPILED BY
Hamish Whyte
ILLUSTRATED BY
Barbara Robertson

THE MERCAT PRESS
EDINBURGH

First published 1991 by Aberdeen University Press
Reprinted 1992, 1993 and 1997 by Mercat Press

Compilation © Hamish Whyte 1991
Illustrations © Barbara Robertson 1991
Extracts from *Concise Scots Dictionary*
© The Scottish National Dictionary
Association Ltd 1985

A catalogue record for this book is available from
the British Library.

ISBN 1 87 364410 8

Design by Mark Blackadder
Typeset by Hewer Text Composition Services,
Edinburgh
Printed by Martin's The Printers Ltd., Berwick

ACKNOWLEDGEMENTS

Grateful acknowledgement is made to the Scottish National Dictionary Association for permission to include extracts from *The Concise Scots Dictionary* (AUP, 1985) and for allowing the dictionary to be used in this way. I should like to thank all those who helped the game along with information and suggestions: Simon Berry, Anne Escott, Joe Fisher, Janice Galloway, Kevin McCarra, Adam McNaughtan, Graeme and Margaret Whyte. Special thanks to Babs Robertson for her drawings which really make the book. And thanks, as ever, to Winifred for her encouragement and her critical eye.

INTRODUCTION

'The Minister's Cat' is familiar to most Scots. It is an alphabet game, played by any number: in each round each player has to think of an epithet for the cat beginning with the same letter of the alphabet. 'The minister's cat is a . . . cat.' The game works through A to Z and a player who fails to come up with an appropriate adjective is out. It is not really a competitive game in the sense of there being a winner; rather, players try to outdo each other in thinking of extravagant terms for the cat. It's played for fun.

In my experience it is a family game. I associate it with my granny. The Minister's Cat joined other games such as hunt-the-thimble (or Grandpa's half-crown) at the New Year get-together of family and friends.

It is described thus in Alice Bertha Gomme's monumental *The Traditional Games of England, Scotland, and Ireland* (vol. I, 1894): 'The first player begins by saying, "The minister's cat is an ambitious cat," the next player "an artful cat," and so on, until they have all named an adjective beginning with A. The next time of going round the adjectives must begin with B, the next time C, and so on, until the whole of the alphabet has been gone through.'

Interestingly, the informants named by Alice Gomme as supplying her with the details of the game were from the Forest of Dean, Gloucestershire, and Anderby in Lincolnshire. Obviously, the game is, or was, played in England. I have always regarded it as peculiarly Scottish, probably because minister is the usual term applied to Scottish clergymen. However, in England, although not used of Anglican clergymen, minister is, as the *Shorter Oxford English Dictionary* puts it, 'chiefly associated with Low Church views; but still usual in non-episcopal communions.' But then, why a minister (or vicar, parson or priest) in the first place? Why not the doctor's cat, the baker's cat or the candlestick maker's? Perhaps the cat was generally felt to be a fit companion to a man of the cloth: an independent kind of pet fit for a bachelor (as many ministers are), a pet, at least in England, suitably non-conformist? (There is, by the way, a minister's dog: the name of a Tweed salmon fly, made originally from the yellow hairs of the minister of Sprouston's dog in 1915.)

A number of clerical ailurophiles are listed in Christobel Aberconway's *Dictionary of Cat Lovers* (Michael Joseph, 1949): John Jortin D.D., Pope Leo XII, Cardinal Richelieu, Cardinal Wolsey, the Rev. James Woodforde. On this evidence it would seem that Roman Catholic prelates were more potty about pussies than other clergy. Pope Gregory the Great is said to have even made his cat a cardinal! (It is perhaps strange that an animal we tend to link historically with witches should be associated with their traditional persecutors.) But there are even earlier associations with churchmen. The *Book of Lismore* tells the story of three young Irish clerics who went to sea on a pilgrimage with very little provision, but not forgetting their cat which caught fish for them. And the first literary reference in the British Isles to the domestic cat is to be found in a ninth century Irish poem, 'Pangur Ban', about a scholar and his clever cat.

Coming back to Scottish ministers, I have been unable to discover any ministers of the past with cats. There must have been: a mouser would be a must in the manse. I do know that the minister of the church where I grew up had a cat: Mr Towart regularly used Scrap's exploits to point up morals in his children's talks (there was an earlier, more Biblically named cat, Peter, as well). And a Kirkintilloch minister is currently using the game of The Minister's Cat in a similar way.

Whether Scottish or English, the game is certainly a firm favourite in Scotland and what more natural way to play it than by using Scots words. (I am told that the Scots Language Society used to play the game this way at meetings, calling it, predictably, 'The Meenister's Baudrons'.) The words chosen here as examples, illustrated with Barbara Robertson's lovely funny drawings, range from ordinary Scots words like clarty to the more unusual such as veeand. There are old, sometimes obsolete, words, words in contemporary use, words from different parts of the country (the minister's cat is a synthetic cat?). They and their definitions are all taken from *The Concise Scots Dictionary* and a selection of other options (with meanings) is included.

There is also, as is usual, a little cheating.

Scots is such an expressive language for this kind of game (and it often seems, as Barbara Robertson remarked in the course of putting the book together, that all the really fascinating words usually mean 'dirty'). If this compilation has any serious aim it is just to encourage some interest in Scots and not, I hope, to add another tourist bookie to the 'isn't Scots a funny language' pile, though there is always the danger of that. I am no expert on Scots, merely getting to know it – dictionary-trawling for interesting words, remembering words from my childhood and words from reading. Everybody will have their own words and their own style of playing the game. This is only one way of looking at the minister's cat.

The minister's cat is an ALMICHTY cat

---

almichty &c *15-*, **a'michty** *20-* [alˈmɪxtɪ, ɑˈmɪxtɪ] *adj, also* **almichtine &c** *16*; **almichting &c** *16* = almighty *15-*.
n = Almighty *16-*.

ADVOCATE (barrister)
AFLOCHT (agitated)
AJEE (ajar, off the straight)
ALAGRUGOUS
(grim, woebegone)
ALLENARLY (single, only)

The
minister's cat
is a BREENGIN cat.

---

breenge &c *19-*; **brainge &c** [brindʒ; *Fif WC, SW* brendʒ] *v* **1** *vi* rush forward recklessly or carelessly; plunge; make a violent effort *la18-*. **2** *vt* drive with a rush; batter, bang *la19-*, *now Abd Ags*.
n a violent or clumsy rush, a dash, a plunge *la18-*.
breengin &c wilful, pushing, sharp-tongued; bustling *19-*, *now local*.

BOGSHAIVELT
(knocked out of shape)
BONNY (pretty)
BRAID (broad)
BLERIT (debauched-looking)
BUCKSTURDIE (obstinate)

The minister's cat is a CLARTY cat

clart¹ &c; clort &c *la19-*, **klurt** *Sh Ork* [klart,
klort, klert, klɛrt; *Sh Ork* klʌrt] *n* **1** mud, mire
la19-. **2** a lump or clot of something unpleasant
19-. **3** a big, dirty, untidy person *la19-*, *local*.
v **1** *vt* besmear, dirty *19-*. **2** *vi* act in a slovenly,
dirty way; work with dirty or sticky substances
20-, *local*.
~**y 1** dirty, muddy; sticky *la16-*. **2** *of a painting
etc* daubed, smudgy *20-*, *Sh Bnf Abd*. [*cf* eME
biclarten defile]

CADGY (friendly, cheerful)
CAMSTAIRY (quarrelsome)
CANTY (cheerful)
CORRIE-FISTED
(left-handed)
CREESHIE (greasy, fat, dirty)

The minister's cat is a DISJASKIT cat.

disjaskit &c [dıs'dʒaskıt; *Rox also* -'dʒeskıt] *adj*
1 dejected, downcast, depressed *19-, local.* **2**
dilapidated, neglected, untidy *18-, local.* **3**
exhausted, worn out; weary-looking *19-, local.*
[see SND]

DEID (dead)
DOITERED
(confused, as in old age)
DOUR (grim)
DOWIE (dull, weak)
DROUTHY (thirsty)

The minister's cat is an EASY OSY cat.

---

easy &c *la16-*, **esy &c** *15-17*, **aisy &c** *16-e20*
adj **1** = easy *15-*. **2** *followed by the gerund (where
Eng would have infin) 19-*: '*It's easy speakin.*'
easy osy &c *adj, of persons* easy-going, inclined
to be lazy; *of things* involving the minimum of
effort *19-*. *n* an easy-going or lazy person *la19-*,
now Bwk.

EIDENT (diligent)
ELDRITCH (weird, unearthly)
EMBRO (Edinburgh)
ESSART (stubborn)
EVILL-AVISIT
(disposed to wrong-doing)

The
minister's cat is a
FUSHIONLESS cat.

---

fushion &c   *la19-*,   **fusioun &c**   *la15-17*,
foisoun &c   *la14-18*;   **fusoun &c**   *la14-15*,
fusion &c   *la14-e20*,   **fooshion &c**   *e20*
['fuʒən, 'fuʃən, 'fʌʃən; *C, S also* 'føʃən *&c*] *n* **1**
= foison, plenty etc *la14-16*. **2** the nourishing
or sustaining element in food or drink *17-, now
NE Per*. **3** physical strength, energy; bodily
sensation, power of feeling *18-, now NE*. **4**
mental or spiritual force or energy; strength of
character, power *18-, now NE*.
~less 1 *of plants etc* without sap or pith, dried,
withered *19-, now local Sh-Arg*. **2** *of food* lacking
in nourishment, tasteless, insipid *19-, local Sh-C*.
3 *of actions, speech, writing etc* without substance,
dull, uninspired *19-, now Abd C*. **4** *of persons* (1)
physically weak, without energy *18-*; (2) numb,
without feeling *la18-, NE*. **5** *of things* without
strength or durability; weak from decay *19-*. **6**
of persons etc, and their moral or mental qualities spir-
itless, faint-hearted, lacking vigour or ability
19-.

FAUSE (false)
FEART (afraid)
FILSH (weak, faint)
FLISKIE (restless, flighty)
FOOSTY (musty, mouldy)

The minister's cat is a GLEG cat.

gleg &c *adj* **1** *chf of persons* (1) quick, keen in perception, *freq* ~ **of** *or* **in sight, hearing, eye** *etc*, *15-*; (2) quick of movement; nimble, adroit *18-, local*; (3) keen, smart, alert, quick-witted, *freq* ~ **in, of** *or* **at the uptak** *la18-*; (4) lively, sprightly; merry *19-, now Sh NE Per*. **2** *of the senses, esp the sight* sharp, keen *18-, now local Ags-Rox*. **3** *of cutting implements* sharp-pointed, keen-edged *18-, now Per WC Ayr*. **4** *of mechanisms* smooth-working, quick-acting *la18-, now local Ags-Rox*.

GAMPHERD
(bespangled, adorned)
GASH (smartly dressed)
GAWSIE (plump, handsome)
GIRNIE (ill-tempered)
GLAIKIT (stupid, foolish)

The minister's cat is a HEEPOCH-ONDREOCH cat.

---

heepochondreoch [ˈhipɪkonˈdriəx] *adj* listless, melancholy *20-*, *Abd Kinr*. [f Eng *hypochondriac*, w different stress accentuation; see also HYPOCHONDERIES]

HALLACH (crazy, hare-brained)
HAPPITY (lame)
HEICH (tall, high)
HIELAND (Highland)
HYTE (mad, enraged)

The minister's cat is an IN-KNEED cat.

---

in-kneed, in-kne'd *adj* knock-kneed *17-, now Ork N Rox.*

IDLESET (idle)
ILL-HAUDEN (oppressed)
INFAME (infamous)
IVIL (evil)

The minister's cat is a JOCO cat.

joco &c [dʒɔ'ko] *adj* jovial, merry, cheerful, pleased with oneself *la19-, Gen except Sh Ork.* [reduced f Eng *jocose*]

JAFFLED (tired, worn out)
JAGGIE (prickly)
JIMP (small, neat, scanty)
JONICK (genuine, honest)
JOUKING (ducking, dodging)

The
minister's cat
is a KIRKIE cat.

kirk &c *n* **1** = church *la14-, in place-names la12-* (see DOST). **2** (1) *esp* before the Reformation, applied to the Roman Catholic Church, in Scotland and beyond *16-e17*; (2) after the Reformation, applied to the reformed church in Scotland both when episcopalian and when presbyterian in organization; since *la17* largely replaced by CHURCH in most formal contexts, but reappearing in recent years, *usu* as **the K∼**, in all contexts except the official title *Church of Scotland* (CHURCH) *la16-*; see also ∼ *session*, PRESBYTERY, SYNOD, *general assembly* (GENERAL), FREE, *Reformed Presbyterian Church* (REFORM), RELIEF, *seceder* (SECEDE), UNITED. **3** the ruling body or *kirk-session* of a local church *la16-e17*. **4** the *General Assembly* (GENERAL) of the *Church of Scotland* (CHURCH) *la16-e17*.

vt, chf in passive = be churched, *orig chf* of the first church attendance after a birth or marriage, *latterly (la19-)* also after a funeral or *eg* on the appointment of a civic or academic body *15-*.

∼**ie &c** enthusiastically devoted to church affairs *20-, local*.

KELVINSIDE
(Glasgow West End affected)
KENSPECKLE (conspicuous, familiar)
KITTLIE (susceptible to tickling)
KNACKIE (skilful, smart)

The
minister's cat
is a LALLAN cat.

---

lallan *lal8-*; **laland &c** ['lalən] *n* **1** *latterly in pl*
= LAWLAND *n* 2, *lal6-el9*. **2** *now chf in pl* (1)
= SCOTS (*n* 1) *lal8-*; (2) *specif* since about 1940,
the variety of literary SCOTS (*n* 1) used by writers of the Scottish Renaissance movement.
adj **1** = LAWLAND *adj*, *18-*, *now local Kcdn-Ayr*. **2**
using the speech of the *Lowlands* (LAWLAND) of
Scotland, SCOTS-speaking as opposed to GAELIC-
or English-speaking *lal8-*.

LAITHLY (loathsome)
LEAL (faithful)
LEELIKE (lying, fictional)
LOURDIE (heavy, sluggish)
LOWPAN (leaping, bounding)

The
minister's cat
is a MAUKIT cat.

---

mauk &c *18-*, **mauch &c** *e16, 19-* [mɑk; *nEC* mɑx] *n* a maggot *16-, Gen except NE.*
~**ie &c 1** maggoty *la18-, now Fif.* **2** filthy *19-, now Inv Edb.* ~**ie fly** = ~ *flee, 20-, S.* **maukit, maucht** *adj* **1** *esp of sheep* infested with maggots *19-, Cai C, S.* **2** putrid; filthy *la20-, WC.* **3** exhausted, played out *20-, S.*

MAISTERFU
(overbearing, powerful)
MARDLE (clumsy, lazy)
MINGIN (smelly)
MIRACULOUS (very drunk)
MUCKLE (big, great)

The
minister's cat
is a NURRING cat.

nurr; njirr *la19-, Sh-Cai* [n(j)ʌr; *Sh Ork* njɪr] *vi* **1** growl like an angry dog, snarl like a cat *19-, now Sh Cai.* **2** *of a cat* purr *19-, chf Sh.*
n the growl or snarl of an angry dog *19-, now Sh Rox.*
~ing &c growling, snarling; fault-finding *19-, now Sh Cai.* [imit; *cf* NARR and Norw *knurre,* Du *knorren* (*v*) growl, OE *gnyrran* creak]

NAPPY (slightly intoxicated)
NATTERIE (peevish)
NEBBIE (nippy, cheeky)
NESTIE (nasty)
NIRLIE (stunted)

The
minister's
cat is an ORRA cat.

orra *17-*; **ora** *18-e20*, **orray** &c *la16-e19*, **orrow** *la18-19* ['orǝ; *C also* *'orɪ] *adj* **1** (1) *of persons or things* spare, unoccupied; unemployed *la16-*, *now Sh-Per*. (2) *specif of women* unattached (either in marriage or as a servant) *la16-17, C.* (3) *specif of one of a pair* without a partner; unmatched, odd *19-*, *Sh-Ags*. **2** spare, extra, odd, superfluous *18-*, *now NE nEC, WC.* **3** (1) occasional, coming at irregular or infrequent intervals, appearing here and there *la18-*, *local NE-S.* (2) *specif* (a) *of a job* casual, odd, unskilled *19-*; (b) *of a person or animal* doing casual or unskilled work *la19-*. **4** miscellaneous, nondescript *19-*, *now NE Ags Per.* **5** strange, uncommon, abnormal *la19-*, *now EC.* **6** *of persons or things* worthless, shabby, disreputable *19-*, *NE Ags Per.*

OFFEECIOUS (officious)
OGERTFU (fastidious)
ONFOWLLIT (unexhausted)
OORLICH
(miserable with cold etc.)
ORDINAR (ordinary)

The minister's cat is a PERJINK cat.

perjink &c [pər'dʒɪŋk] *adj* **1** trim, neat, smart in appearance *la18-*. **2** prim, strait-laced *la18-*. **3** exact, precise, scrupulously careful, fussy *la18-*.
adv primly, fastidiously, in a precise and careful way *20-*.
n, in pl fussy details, niceties *e19*. [only Sc; *per-* intensifier + prob onomat second element w infl f DINK, JINK[1] etc]

PAWKIE (lively, shrewd)
PERFERVID (ardent)
PERQUEER (expert)
PLACKLESS (penniless)
POOSHINOUS
(poisonous, horrible)

The
minister's cat is
a QUEESITIVE cat.

---

queesitive *adj* = inquisitive *la19-20, local Sh-Per.*

QUENT (quaint)
QUERTY
(vivacious, mischievous)
QUISQUOUS (doubtful)

The
minister's cat
is a RUNKLY cat.

---

runkle &c *vt* **1** wrinkle *la15-*. **2** crease, rumple, crush *18-, now Sh-nEC, WC, SW*. **3** gnarl, twist, distort, curl *18-, now local C*.
n a wrinkle, crease, ridged indentation *16-*.
runkly &c wrinkled *la18-, now NE nEC, WC, S*. [prob OScand *runkla* wrinkle; *cf* Dan *runken* wrinkled, Sw *rynka* wrinkle, Norw dial *rukka* a wrinkle; *cf* WRUNKLE]

RAM-STAM (rash, heedless)
RAUCLE (strong, rough)
REEZIE (tipsy)
ROARIE (drunk, loud)
RUMMLIN (boisterous)

The
minister's cat
is a SCUDDIE cat.

---

scuddie &c *adj* **1** naked, without clothes, or with one garment only *19-*, *now C, S.* **2** mean, scruffy, shabby-looking, in want or straitened circumstances *la19-e20*. **3** stingy, penurious; insufficient, too small *la19-*, *Bnf Abd*.

SAPSY (soppy)
SHOOGLIE (shaky, unsteady)
SLEEKIT (smooth, sly)
SONSIE (plump, attractive)
STOURIE (dusty)

The
minister's cat
is a THRAWN cat.

---

thrawn &c; throwin &c *la16*, **trawn &c**
la20-, Sh Ork Uls [θrɑn; *Abd also* 'θr(j)ɑvən] *adj*
1 twisted, crooked, distorted, misshapen *16-*.
2 *of the mouth, face* wry, twisted with pain, rage
etc, surly *16-*. **3** *of persons, animals, events* perverse, obstinate; intractable; cross, in a DOUR,
sullen mood *la15-*. **4** *of the weather* disagreea-
ble, inclement *la19-, now NE*.

TAPSIE-TEERIE (topsy-turvy)
TAUPIE (foolish)
TENTIE (careful)
TEUCHTER
(disparaging term for Highlander)
TOCHERLESS (without a dowry)

The minister's cat is an UNCO cat.

unco &c *18-*; **uncow &c** *16-e18*, **unca** *19-*, *now Abd*, **uncan &c** *19-*, *Sh*, **unkin &c** *la19-e20*, *Sh Ork* ['ʌŋkə; *Bwk Rox* 'ʌŋkɪ; *Edb also* 'ʌŋkɪ; *'ʌŋku] adj* **1** (1) *of people, animals, things, places* (a) unknown, unfamiliar, strange *16-*, *now NE, C*; (b) so much altered as to be scarcely recognizable *19-*, *now Abd*. (2) *of countries or lands* foreign *19-*, *now Sh, only Sc*; *cf* UNCOUTH 2. **2** *also comparative* ~**er** *la19-*, *superlative* ~**est** *18-* unusual; odd, strange, peculiar *18-*. **3** remarkable, extraordinary, great, awful etc *18-*, *now NE Ags WC, only Sc*: 'ye mak an unco sang about your taxes'. **4** rude, uncouth, unseemly *18-e19*, *only Sc*. **5** reserved, shy, bashful *19-*, *now Sh, only Sc*. *adv* very, exceedingly, extremely *18-*.

UGSOME (repulsive)
UMBERSORROW (fit, robust)
UMQUHILE
(former, late, deceased)
UNBEKENT
(unobserved, unnoticed)
UNDEEMOUS (extraordinary)

The minister's cat is a VEEAND cat.

veeand &c [*'viən(d)] *adj* lacking common sense; in one's dotage *19-e20*, *S*. [see VEED]

VAGRING (vagrant, wandering)
VAUDIE (vain, frisky)
VEECIOUS (vicious)
VOGIE (vain, light-hearted)

The minister's cat is a WULLCAT.

wild; wuld &c *e15, 19-e20,* **wile &c** *la16, la19-, now Arg Wgt,* **will &c** *19-,* **wull &c** *19-* [wəil(d), wɪl, wʌl; *Per also* wʌld] *adj* **1** = wild *la14-.* **2** *of vocal sounds* loud and unrestrained *16-.* **3** strong-tasting, rank *la19-, local Sh-nEC.* **4** nickname for the extreme Evangelical party in the *Church of Scotland* (CHURCH) *la18-19. adv* extremely, very *19-, local.*

wild cat &c *la15-,* **will cat &c** *la16-,* **wullcat &c** *19-* = wild cat. **tummle** *etc* **the, one's** *or* **ower one's wullcat(s), wilkies &c** tumble head over heels, somersault *19-, chf WC;* cf *tummle* or *turn the cat* (TUMMLE, TURN). ~ **coal** poor quality coal *19, WC.* ~**fire 1** = wildfire *18-.* **2** summer lightning, lightning without thunder *la18-, now Ork-Per.* **3** *mining* fire-damp *la19-, now Fif.* **4** name of various wild flowers *19-, now Ags.* ~ **kail** the wild radish; the charlock *19-, SW.* ~ **parrot** an inferior kind of soft coal *20-, Fif sEC, WC.* ~ **rhubarb &c** the common butterbur *la19-, Per-S.*

WABBIT (exhausted)
WAESOME (sorrowful)
WALLY (made of china)
WEE (small)
WERSH
(sickly, depressed, bitter-tasting)

The
minister's cat is
an XTRORNAR cat.

---

extraordinar &c;   **extrornar**   *18-19*
  ['ɛkstrə'ordnər,   ɛk'stror(d)nər,
  ɛkstər'ord(ə)nər] *adj* = extraordinary *la15-.*

XERCIT (experienced)
XTIRPIT (extirpated)
XTRANEARE (foreign)

The
minister's cat
is a YATTERY cat.

---

yatter &c *v* **1** *vi* nag, harp on querulously, scold *19-*, *local.* **2** chatter, ramble on, talk interminably *19-*. **3** *vti, of a person speaking incoherently or in a foreign language* gabble; *of an animal* yelp *19-*. **4** *vi, of teeth* rattle, chatter, *eg* from fear *20-*, *now Ags.*

n **1** (continual) scolding, grumbling *19-*, *now Ork Ags.* **2** continuous chatter, rambling and persistent talk *19-*. **3** the confused noise of many people talking loudly all together, clamour, unintelligible speech *19-*, *local Sh-Per.* **4** an incessant talker; a gossip *19-*.

~**in,** ~**y** fretful, querulous, scolding *19-*, *now Sh.* [only Sc; onomat; *cf* Eng *chatter*, NATTER, Norw dial *jaddre* jabber]

YALLOCHIE (yellowish)
YARE (ready, eager)
YAUPISH (clever, active)
YAWKIN (perplexed)

The
minister's cat
is a ZETLAND cat.

Zetland &c *16-* ['zɛtland; *'jɛtland; *see etymology*] = Shetland, used as the official name of the county until 1975, and as a peerage title. [ON *Hjaltland*, which developed (1) into *Sj- &c* in some Norw dials (> SHETLAND) and *Sh- &c* in Sc and Eng (*lal3-*); (2) into *I-* or *Ih-* [j] in other Norw dials (*el3*), written in Sc as *Yh-* or *3-* [j], the latter having the same form in Sc MSS and prints as *Z-* (see *3 letter*). The spelling-pronunciation [zɛt-] in place of the etymological [jɛt-] was established among the gentry and the professional classes by *e19*, and still survives alongside [ʃɛt-] (SHETLAND)]

ZEILLOUS (zealous)
ZULU (fishing-boat)